Collins Junior Illustrated Dictionary

Collins

Collins Junior Illustrated Dictionary

First published 2000
This edition published 2005
© HarperCollins*Publishers* Ltd 2005

10 9 8 7 6 5 4 3 2 1

ISBN 0 00 720368 3 hardback
ISBN 0 00 720367 5 paperback

Compiler   Evelyn Goldsmith

Literacy consultants   Kay Hiatt, Rosemary Boys
Numeracy consultant   Jan Henley
Science consultant   Rona Wyn Davies

Cover designer   Nicola Croft
Design   Neil Adams, Grasshopper Design Co.
Illustrators   Tim Archbold, Tamsin Cook,
Felicity House, Pat Murray,
Sarah Wimperis, Sue Woollatt
(all of Graham-Cameron Illustration)

Photos
All commissioned photos by Steve Lumb.

The publishers wish to thank the following for permission to use photographs:
Cover photos by NASA (planet) and Bruce Coleman (moth).
Andes Press: p. 61 Diwali; **Art Directors & Trip**: p. 7 acorn, p. 8 aeroplane, p. 12 antelope, p. 29 bridge, p. 31 butterfly, p. 32 cactus, p. 34 carnival, p. 48 coral, p. 62 dragonfly, p. 64 duck, p. 65 Earth, p. 65 eclipse, p. 68 erupt, p. 69 evergreen, p. 86 giraffe, p. 95 harvest, p. 101 horse, p. 102 hurricane, p. 103 illuminations, p. 107 ivy, p. 113 ladybird, p. 115 leaves, p. 128 mill, p. 147 pagoda, p. 172 ray, p. 174 reflection, p. 178 rhinoceros, p. 180 rose, p. 209 statue, p. 223 thatched, p. 230 tractor; **BBC**: p. 213 studio; **Biofotos/Heather Angel**: p. 18 badger, p. 57 desert, p. 81 fox, p. 158 polar bear; **Oxford Scientific Films**: p. 13 ape, p. 14 aquarium, p. 32 camel, p. 38 cheetah, p. 52 crystal, p. 85 gerbil, p. 88 gorilla, p. 103 iceberg, p. 108 jellyfish, p. 148 panda, p. 157 plough, p. 171 rainbow, p. 191 shark, p. 206 springbok, p. 218 swan, p. 226 tiger, p. 253 x-ray; **Papilio**: p. 25 bluebells, p. 56 deer, p. 117 lighthouse.

All other photos and illustrations © HarperCollins*Publishers* Ltd 2005.

Acknowledgements
The publishers would like to thank all the teachers, staff and pupils who contributed to this book:

Models
Lauren Carroll
Stacey Cleary
Tom Crane
Katherine Davis
William Davis
Ruby Feroze
Elizabeth Fison
Jesse Johnson
Ismael Khan
Margaret Omoboade
Zina Patel
Dunia Pavlovic
Petra Pavlovic
Milo Petrie-Foxell
Dexter Sampson
Mauri-Joy Smith
Tom Symonds
Rosie Ward

Schools
Aberhill Primary, Fife; ASDAC, Fife; Canning St Primary, Newcastle upon Tyne; Cowgate Primary, Newcastle upon Tyne; Crombie Primary, Fife; the Literacy Team at Dryden Professional Development Centre, Gateshead; Dunshalt Primary, Fife; Ecton Brook Lower, Northampton; English Martyrs RC Primary, Newcastle upon Tyne; Hotspur Primary, Newcastle upon Tyne; John Betts Primary, London; Lemington First, Newcastle upon Tyne; LMTC Education Development Centre, Northumberland; Melcombe Primary, London; Methilhill Primary, Fife; Newcastle Literacy Centre, Newcastle upon Tyne; Northampton High, Northampton; Pitcoudie Primary, Fife; Pitreavie Primary, Fife; Ravenswood Primary, Newcastle upon Tyne; St Andrew's CE Primary, London; Simon de Senlis Lower, Northampton; Sinclairtown Primary, Fife; Standens Barn Lower, Northampton; Touch Primary, Fife; Towcester Infants, Northampton; Wooton Primary, Northampton.

Printed by Imago Ltd.

Contents

Collins Word Wizard

Using this dictionary

A dictionary tells you what a word means and how to spell it. The words in a dictionary are listed in alphabetical order.

How to find a word

Look up the word **fossil**. What letter does it begin with? Use the alphabet line at the side of the page. The green box tells you that the words on this page start with **f**.

Think about the second letter of the word. You are looking for a word beginning with **fo**. Use the guide word at the top of the page. A guide word at the top left tells you the *first word* on that page. A guide word at the top right tells you the *last word* on that page. The guide word for this page is **frequent** – it starts with **fr**. Does **fo** come before **fr**?

When you think you have the right page, look at the blue words. These are called headwords. The headwords are in alphabetical order. If you run your finger down the headwords on this page, you will see more than one that begins with **fo**. Think about the next letter or letters in your word and look for a headword that begins with **fos**.

Keep looking until you find the word **fossil**.

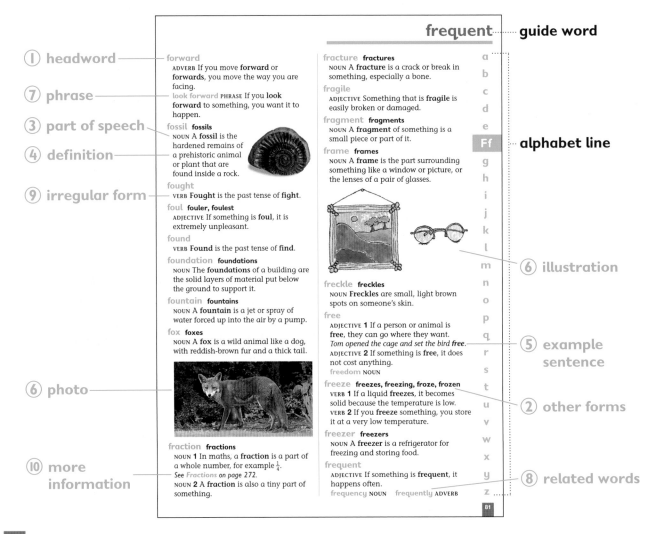

① headword

⑦ phrase

③ part of speech

④ definition

⑨ irregular form

⑥ photo

⑩ more information

frequent ········ guide word

alphabet line

⑥ illustration

⑤ example sentence

② other forms

⑧ related words

forward
ADVERB If you move **forward** or **forwards**, you move the way you are facing.
look forward PHRASE If you **look forward** to something, you want it to happen.

fossil fossils
NOUN A **fossil** is the hardened remains of a prehistoric animal or plant that are found inside a rock.

fought
VERB **Fought** is the past tense of **fight**.

foul fouler, foulest
ADJECTIVE If something is **foul**, it is extremely unpleasant.

found
VERB **Found** is the past tense of **find**.

foundation foundations
NOUN The **foundations** of a building are the solid layers of material put below the ground to support it.

fountain fountains
NOUN A **fountain** is a jet or spray of water forced up into the air by a pump.

fox foxes
NOUN A **fox** is a wild animal like a dog, with reddish-brown fur and a thick tail.

fraction fractions
NOUN **1** In maths, a **fraction** is a part of a whole number, for example $\frac{1}{4}$.
See *Fractions* on page 272.
NOUN **2** A **fraction** is also a tiny part of something.

fracture fractures
NOUN A **fracture** is a crack or break in something, especially a bone.

fragile
ADJECTIVE Something that is **fragile** is easily broken or damaged.

fragment fragments
NOUN A **fragment** of something is a small piece or part of it.

frame frames
NOUN A **frame** is the part surrounding something like a window or picture, or the lenses of a pair of glasses.

freckle freckles
NOUN **Freckles** are small, light brown spots on someone's skin.

free
ADJECTIVE **1** If a person or animal is **free**, they can go where they want.
Tom opened the cage and set the bird free.
ADJECTIVE **2** If something is **free**, it does not cost anything.
freedom NOUN

freeze freezes, freezing, froze, frozen
VERB **1** If a liquid **freezes**, it becomes solid because the temperature is low.
VERB **2** If you **freeze** something, you store it at a very low temperature.

freezer freezers
NOUN A **freezer** is a refrigerator for freezing and storing food.

frequent
ADJECTIVE If something is **frequent**, it happens often.
frequency NOUN   **frequently** ADVERB

a b c d e **Ff** g h i j k l m n o p q r s t u v w x y z

81

Finding out about a word

① The headword is the word you are looking up.

② On the same line as the headword, you will see how to spell other forms of the word, such as plural nouns, verb tenses or other adjective forms, called comparatives and superlatives.

③ Next you will see the part of speech. This tells you what type of word the headword is, such as a noun, verb, adjective, adverb or pronoun.

④ After the part of speech, you will find the definition. The definition tells you what the word means. The definitions are numbered if there is more than one. Each definition has its own part of speech.

⑤ Some words have an example sentence in *italics*. This shows you how the word might be used in speech or writing.

⑥ Some words have a photo or other illustration to help you read the word and understand its meaning.

⑦ A phrase may also be included. For example, under the word **forward**, you will also find the definition of the phrase **look forward**.

⑧ Sometimes, other related words are given at the end, with their parts of speech. These tell you, for example, the noun or adverb form of the word.

⑨ An irregular form of a word is a plural noun or verb tense which does not follow the usual spelling rules. You can find many irregular forms in this dictionary.

⑩ Some definitions tell you where to look for more information, such as another headword, or the pages at the back of the dictionary.

Other features of this dictionary

● Pronunciation is how you say a word. Some words can be spelled the same, but sound different and mean different things – these words are called homographs. This dictionary gives you pronunciation help for some words, including homographs. For example:

tear **tears, tearing, tore, torn**
(*rhymes with* **fear**) NOUN **1** Tears are the drops of liquid that come out of your eyes when you cry.
(*rhymes with* **fair**) VERB **2** If you **tear** something, such as paper or fabric, you pull it apart.

● Some definitions include a label, such as FORMAL, INFORMAL or TRADEMARK. This tells you a little more about the word or how it is used. For example:

Rollerblade **Rollerblades**
NOUN; TRADEMARK **Rollerblades** are roller skates which have the wheels set in one straight line on the bottom of the boot.

Collins Word Wizard

The **Collins Word Wizard** section at the back of the dictionary gives you extra help with grammar, writing and using the Internet.

It has pages to help you understand parts of speech, punctuation and prefixes and suffixes as well as handy hints for learning tricky spellings and cool new words.

Look out for the themed picture pages, web links and games to play with the dictionary.

Aa

abacus **abacuses**
NOUN An **abacus** is a frame with beads that slide along rods. It is used for counting.

abandon **abandons, abandoning, abandoned**
VERB **1** If you **abandon** something, you leave it and do not return. *The cub had been **abandoned** by its mother.*
VERB **2** If you **abandon** a piece of work, you stop doing it before it is finished.

abbreviation **abbreviations**
NOUN An **abbreviation** is a short form of a word or phrase. *The **abbreviation** for compact disc is CD.*
See *Abbreviations* on page 270.

ability **abilities**
NOUN If you have the **ability** to do something, you are able to do it.

able **abler, ablest**
ADJECTIVE If you are **able** to do something, you can do it.

aboard
PREPOSITION If you are **aboard** a ship or plane, you are on or in it.

about
ADVERB **1** You say **about** in front of a number to show it is not exact. *I'll be home at **about** five o'clock.*
PREPOSITION **2** If you talk or write **about** something, you say things to do with that subject. *He is talking **about** boats.*

above
PREPOSITION If something is **above** something else, it is over it, or higher up.

abroad
ADVERB When you go **abroad**, you go to a different country.

absent
ADJECTIVE If someone is **absent**, they are not here.

absolutely
ADVERB You can use **absolutely** to make what you are saying sound stronger. *You must stay **absolutely** still.*

absorb **absorbs, absorbing, absorbed**
VERB If something **absorbs** a liquid, it soaks it up or takes it in.

absurd
ADJECTIVE Something that is **absurd** seems silly, because it is quite different from what you would expect. *It's **absurd** to wear your jumper in this heat.*

abuse
NOUN **Abuse** is cruel treatment of someone.

accelerate **accelerates, accelerating, accelerated**
VERB When someone **accelerates**, they speed up.

accept **accepts, accepting, accepted**
VERB If you **accept** something you have been offered, you say yes to it.

accident **accidents**
NOUN An **accident** is something nasty that happens by chance. *He broke his leg in a climbing **accident**.*
accidentally ADVERB

account accounts

NOUN **1** An **account** is something written or spoken that tells you what has happened.

NOUN **2** An **account** is also money that you keep at a bank.

accurate

ADJECTIVE An **accurate** measurement or description is exactly right.

ache aches

NOUN An **ache** is a dull, lasting pain.

achieve achieves, achieving, achieved

VERB If you **achieve** something, you usually get it by hard work.

achievement NOUN

acid acids

NOUN Some **acids** give food a sharp, sour taste. Lemons and vinegar contain acid. Strong acid can burn your skin.

acid rain

NOUN **Acid rain** is rain that is mixed with dirty gases in the air. It can damage buildings, trees and fish.

acorn acorns

NOUN An **acorn** is a nut. Acorns grow on oak trees.

acrobat acrobats

NOUN An **acrobat** is someone who does difficult and exciting tricks, like balancing on a high wire.

across

PREPOSITION If you go **across** something, you go from one side to the other.

act acts, acting, acted

VERB **1** When you **act**, you do something. *He had to **act** quickly to put out the fire.*

VERB **2** If you **act** in a play or film, you have a part in it.

NOUN **3** An **act** is something that you do.

action actions

NOUN An **action** is a movement of part of your body.

active

ADJECTIVE **1** Someone who is **active** moves about a lot, or is very busy.

ADJECTIVE **2** In grammar, a verb in the **active** voice is one where the subject does the action, rather than having it done to them. See **voice**.

activity activities

NOUN **Activity** is when there are a lot of things happening.

actor actors

NOUN An **actor** is a man or woman whose job is to act in plays or films.

actress actresses

NOUN A female actor is sometimes called an **actress**. See **actor**.

actual

ADJECTIVE You describe something as **actual** when you mean it is real. *The shop said the paint was red, but the **actual** colour was pink.*

actually ADVERB

adapt adapts, adapting, adapted

VERB **1** If you **adapt** to something new, you change in some way that helps you.

VERB **2** If you **adapt** something, you change it to suit your needs. *The book was **adapted** to make a film.*

adaptable

ADJECTIVE Someone who is **adaptable** can change to deal with new situations.

add adds, adding, added

VERB **1** If you **add** something, you put it with whatever you have already. *Put flour in the bowl and **add** an egg.*

VERB **2** If you **add** numbers of things together, you find out how many you have. The sign + means add. *I have two marbles in the bag. If I **add** these three, it makes five altogether.* 2 + 3 = 5

addition

NOUN **Addition** is adding numbers or things together.

address

address **addresses**
NOUN Your **address** is the name or number of your house, and the street and town where you live.

adjective **adjectives**
NOUN An **adjective** is a word that describes someone or something. "Beautiful" and "green" are adjectives.
See *Adjective* on page 263.

admire **admires, admiring, admired**
VERB **1** When you **admire** someone, you think very highly of them.
VERB **2** When you **admire** something, you enjoy looking at it. *They stopped the car to **admire** the view.*

admit **admits, admitting, admitted**
VERB **1** If you **admit** something, you agree that it is true.
VERB **2** If people are **admitted** to a place, they are allowed to go in.

adopt **adopts, adopting, adopted**
VERB If a person **adopts** a child, they make the child their own by law.

adore **adores, adoring, adored**
VERB If you **adore** someone, you love them very much.

adult **adults**
NOUN An **adult** is a grown-up person or animal.

advance **advances, advancing, advanced**
VERB If someone **advances**, they move forward. *The army **advanced** nine miles in one day.*

advantage **advantages**
NOUN An **advantage** is something that helps you do better than other people. *His long legs gave him an **advantage** in the race.*

adventure **adventures**
NOUN If you are having an **adventure**, you are doing something exciting.

adverb **adverbs**
NOUN An **adverb** is a word that answers questions like how, when, where and why. In the sentence "The girl came quietly into the room", the word "quietly" is an adverb telling you how the girl came in.
See *Adverb* on page 263.

advertise **advertises, advertising, advertised**
VERB If you **advertise** something, you tell people about it through newspapers, posters or TV.

advertisement **advertisements**
NOUN An **advertisement** is a notice in the paper, or on a poster or TV, about a job or things for sale.

advice
NOUN If you give someone **advice**, you say what you think they should do.

advise **advises, advising, advised**
VERB When you **advise** someone, you tell them what you think they should do.

aerial **aerials**
NOUN An **aerial** is a wire that sends or receives radio or television signals.

aeroplane **aeroplanes**
NOUN An **aeroplane** is a flying vehicle with wings and one or more engines.

affect affects, affecting, affected

VERB When something **affects** someone or something else, it changes them in some way.

affection

NOUN **Affection** is a feeling of caring for someone.

afford affords, affording, afforded

VERB If you can **afford** something, you have enough money to buy it or do it.

afraid

ADJECTIVE Someone who is **afraid** thinks that something nasty might happen.

after

PREPOSITION If something happens **after** something else, it happens at a later time. *We'll watch television **after** supper.*

afternoon afternoons

NOUN The **afternoon** is the time of day between 12 o'clock (noon) and about six o'clock in the evening.

again

ADVERB If you do something **again**, you do it once more.

against

PREPOSITION **1** If you play **against** someone, you are not on their side.

PREPOSITION **2** If you are **against** something, you are touching it and leaning on it. *She felt tired and leaned **against** the tree.*

age ages

NOUN **1** Your **age** is how old you are.

NOUN **2** An **age** is a special period in history, like the Stone Age.

ago

ADVERB If something happened four days **ago**, it is four days since it happened.

agree agrees, agreeing, agreed

VERB **1** If you **agree** with someone, you think the same about something.

VERB **2** If you **agree** to do something, you say you will do it.

agreement NOUN

ahead

ADVERB Something or someone who is **ahead** of you is in front of you. *She walked fast and went on **ahead** of me.*

aim aims, aiming, aimed

VERB **1** If you **aim** at something, you point a weapon at it.

VERB **2** If you **aim** to do something, you plan to do it.

air

NOUN **Air** is the mixture of gases that we breathe.

aircraft

NOUN An **aircraft** is a vehicle that flies. Helicopters and aeroplanes are aircraft.

air force air forces

NOUN An **air force** is a force that a country uses for fighting in the air.

airport airports

NOUN An **airport** is a place where aircraft land and take off.

alarm alarms

NOUN **1** An **alarm** is something like a bell or flashing light that warns you of something.

NOUN **2** **Alarm** is a feeling of fear. *He looked at the hungry bear in **alarm**.*

album albums

NOUN An **album** is a book that you put things like stamps or photographs in.

alien aliens

NOUN In science fiction, an **alien** is a creature from outer space.

Aa
b
c
d
e
f
g
h
i
j
k
l
m
n
o
p
q
r
s
t
u
v
w
x
y
z

alight

ADJECTIVE If something is **alight**, it is burning.

alike

ADJECTIVE If two or more things are **alike**, they are the same in some way.

alive

ADJECTIVE If a person, animal or plant is **alive**, they are living now.

all

ADJECTIVE You say **all** when you mean the whole of a particular group or thing. *Put **all** your toys away.*

allergy **allergies**

NOUN If you have an **allergy** to something, it makes you ill. *Tom has an **allergy** to nuts, so he must not eat them.*

alley **alleys**

NOUN An **alley** is a narrow path with buildings or walls on both sides.

alligator **alligators**

NOUN An **alligator** is a reptile. It is of the same family as a crocodile, but smaller. *See Reptiles on page 259.*

alliteration

NOUN **Alliteration** is the use of words close together which begin with the same sound, for example "hundreds of huge hairy horses".

allow **allows, allowing, allowed**

VERB If someone **allows** you to do something, they let you do it.

all right

ADJECTIVE **1** If someone is **all right**, they are well or safe. *See if the baby's **all right**.* INTERJECTION **2** You say **all right** if you agree to something.

almost

ADVERB **Almost** means very nearly, but not quite. *He tripped and **almost** fell.*

alone

ADJECTIVE If you are **alone**, there is nobody with you.

along

PREPOSITION If you go **along** something, you move towards the end of it.

aloud

ADVERB If you read something **aloud**, you read it so that people can hear you.

alphabet **alphabets**

NOUN An **alphabet** is all the letters used to write words, written in a special order.

alphabetical

ADJECTIVE **Alphabetical** means arranged in the order of the letters of the alphabet. *She read out the names on the register in **alphabetical** order.*

already

ADVERB If you have done something **already**, you did it earlier.

also

ADVERB You say **also** when you want to add to something you have just said.

alter **alters, altering, altered**

VERB When you **alter** something, you change it in some way.

alternate **alternates, alternating, alternated**

VERB When two things **alternate**, they regularly happen one after the other. *He **alternates** between being friendly and completely ignoring me.*

although

CONJUNCTION You say **although** when you expected something different. ***Although** my dad was cross, he still gave me my pocket money.*

altogether

ADVERB If you say there are a number of things **altogether**, you are counting all of them. *I've picked four apples and you've picked two, so that's six **altogether**.*

aluminium

NOUN **Aluminium** is a light, silver-coloured metal. It is used for making rolls of foil and containers like cans and pie dishes.

always

ADVERB **1** If you **always** do something, you do it every time. *He **always** puts his things away when he has used them.*
ADVERB **2** If something has **always** been so, it has been that way at all times. *They have **always** been good friends.*

a.m.

ADVERB **a.m.** is the time between midnight and noon. *I get up at 7 **a.m.** See **p.m.**

amaze **amazes, amazing, amazed**

VERB If something **amazes** you, it surprises you very much.
amazement NOUN

amazing

ADJECTIVE Something that is **amazing** is very surprising or wonderful.

ambition **ambitions**

NOUN If you have an **ambition** to do something, you want to do it very much.

ambulance **ambulances**

NOUN An **ambulance** is a vehicle that is used to take people to hospital.

among

PREPOSITION **1** If something is **among** a number of things, it is surrounded by them. *He sat **among** piles of books.*
PREPOSITION **2** If something is divided **among** several people, they all have a share.

amount **amounts**

NOUN An **amount** of something is how much there is of it.

amphibian **amphibians**

NOUN An **amphibian** is an animal that is able to live on land and in water.
amphibious ADJECTIVE

See *Amphibians* on page 259.

amuse **amuses, amusing, amused**

VERB If you **amuse** somebody, you make them smile or stop them feeling bored.

analogue

ADJECTIVE An **analogue** watch or clock shows the time with hands that move round a dial. See **digital**.

anchor **anchors**

NOUN An **anchor** is a heavy metal hook on a long chain. It is dropped over the side of a boat to stop it moving.

ancient

ADJECTIVE If something is **ancient**, it is very old.

and

CONJUNCTION You use **and** to join two or more words or phrases together. *I like chocolate, **and** my brother does too.*

angel **angels**

NOUN **Angels** are beings some people believe act as messengers for God.

anger

NOUN **Anger** is the strong feeling you have about something that is unfair.

angle **angles**

NOUN An **angle** is the shape that is made when two lines or surfaces join. The size of an angle is measured in degrees.

60°

angry **angrier, angriest**
ADJECTIVE If you feel **angry**, you are very cross.
angrily ADVERB

animal **animals**
NOUN **Animals** are living things which are not plants. Humans, dogs, birds, fish, reptiles and insects are all animals.

ankle **ankles**
NOUN Your **ankle** is the joint between your foot and your leg.

anniversary **anniversaries**
NOUN An **anniversary** is a day when you remember something special which happened on that date in an earlier year.

announce **announces, announcing, announced**
VERB If you **announce** something important, you tell people about it publicly. *My sister's engagement was **announced** last week.*

annoy **annoys, annoying, annoyed**
VERB If you do something which **annoys** someone, you make them cross.

annual **annuals**
ADJECTIVE **1** Something that is **annual** happens once a year, like a birthday.
NOUN **2** An **annual** is a book that comes out once a year.

another
ADJECTIVE **Another** means one more. *Amy finished her chocolate and took **another** one immediately.*

answer **answers, answering, answered**
VERB **1** When you **answer**, you say or write something to someone who has asked you a question.
NOUN **2** Your **answer** is what you say or write to a question.

ant **ants**
NOUN **Ants** are small insects which live in large groups called colonies.
See *Insects* on page 259.

antelope **antelopes**
NOUN **Antelopes** are animals that look like deer, but their horns are not branch-shaped. They live in Africa and Asia.

antenna **antennae** or **antennas**
NOUN The **antennae** of an insect are the two long, thin parts on its head that it uses to feel with.

anthology **anthologies**
NOUN An **anthology** is a book of writings by different authors.

anti-
PREFIX **Anti-** is put in front of a word to mean against or opposite to that word. See *Prefixes* on page 264.

anticlockwise
ADVERB If something goes **anticlockwise**, it moves in the opposite direction to the hands of a clock.

antique **antiques**
NOUN An **antique** is an old object which is valuable because it is beautiful or rare.

antiseptic **antiseptics**
NOUN An **antiseptic** is a substance that prevents infection by killing germs.

antonym **antonyms**
NOUN An **antonym** is a word that means the opposite of another word.
See *Antonyms* on page 267.

anxious
ADJECTIVE Someone who is **anxious** is nervous or worried about something.

any
ADJECTIVE **1 Any** means one, some, or several. *Do you have **any** milk?*
ADJECTIVE **2 Any** can also mean even the smallest amount. *I mustn't eat **any** nuts.*

anybody

PRONOUN **Anybody** is any person.

anyone

PRONOUN **Anyone** is any person.

anything

PRONOUN **Anything** means any object, event, situation or action.

anywhere

ADVERB **Anywhere** means in, at or to any place. *Just put it down* **anywhere**.

apart

ADJECTIVE If something is **apart** from something else, there is a space between them. *He stood with his feet* **apart**.

ape **apes**

NOUN **Apes** are like monkeys but are larger and have no tails. Chimpanzees and gorillas are apes. The ape in the photo is an orang-utan.

apex **apexes**

NOUN The **apex** is the highest point of something.

apologize **apologizes, apologizing, apologized**; also spelt **apologise**

VERB When you **apologize**, you say you are sorry for something you have done.

apology **apologies**

NOUN An **apology** is something you say or write to tell someone you are sorry.

apostrophe **apostrophes**

NOUN An **apostrophe** is a punctuation mark (') used in contractions and to show belonging.
See *Punctuation* on page 264.

apparatus

NOUN The **apparatus** for a particular task is the equipment you use for it.

appear **appears, appearing, appeared**

VERB **1** When something **appears**, it moves into a place where you can see it.
VERB **2** If something **appears** to be a certain way, that is how it seems.

appearance **appearances**

NOUN **1** Someone's **appearance** in a place is their sudden arrival there.
NOUN **2** Your **appearance** is the way you look to other people.

appetite **appetites**

NOUN If you have an **appetite**, you are looking forward to eating something.

applause

NOUN **Applause** is clapping your hands to show that you liked something.

apple **apples**

NOUN An **apple** is a round crisp fruit which grows on a tree.
See *Fruit* on page 257.

apply **applies, applying, applied**

VERB If you **apply** for something, like a job, you usually ask for it in writing.

appreciate **appreciates, appreciating, appreciated**

VERB If you **appreciate** something, you feel grateful for it.

approach **approaches, approaching, approached**

VERB When someone **approaches** you, they get nearer to you.

approve **approves, approving, approved**

VERB If you **approve** of something, you think it is good.
approval NOUN

approximate

ADJECTIVE An **approximate** answer may not be exactly right. *What is the* **approximate** *distance between those trees?*

b
c
d
e
f
g
h
i
j
k
l
m
n
o
p
q
r
s
t
u
v
w
x
y
z

approximately

ADVERB If you say **approximately**, you mean about. *It is **approximately** 5 metres long.*

apricot   apricots

NOUN An **apricot** is a small, round yellow-orange fruit with a large stone in the centre.

April

NOUN **April** is the fourth month of the year. It has 30 days.

apron   aprons

NOUN An **apron** is a piece of material that you wear to keep your clothes clean when you are cooking.

aquarium   aquaria or aquariums

NOUN An **aquarium** is a glass tank for fish and other underwater animals.

arch   arches

NOUN An **arch** is a curved part of a bridge, wall or building.

archery

NOUN **Archery** is a sport in which people shoot at a target with a bow and arrow.

architect   architects

NOUN An **architect** is a person who designs buildings.

area   areas

NOUN **1** The **area** of something is the size of its surface. To find the area of a rectangle, you multiply the length by the breadth. The area of this rectangle is 12 square centimetres.

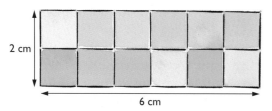

2 cm

6 cm

NOUN **2** You use the word **area** to mean in or around a place. *There are lots of shops in this **area**.*

argue   argues, arguing, argued

VERB If you **argue** with someone, you say that you do not agree with them, and give your reasons.

argument   arguments

NOUN An **argument** is a talk between people who do not agree. In some arguments, people shout angrily.

arithmetic

NOUN **Arithmetic** is about adding, subtracting, multiplying and dividing numbers.

arm   arms

NOUN Your **arm** is the part of your body between the shoulder and the hand.

armchair   armchairs

NOUN An **armchair** is a chair with a support on each side for your arms.

armour

NOUN **Armour** is metal clothing that soldiers used to wear in battle.

army   armies

NOUN An **army** is a large organized group of people who are trained to fight in case of war.

around

PREPOSITION **1** You say **around** when things are in various places. *There are lots of cupboards **around** the house.*

PREPOSITION **2** You can use **around** when something is on all sides of something else. *The Earth's atmosphere is the air **around** it.*

arrange arranges, arranging, arranged
VERB **1** If you **arrange** something like a party, you make plans and organize it.
VERB **2** If you **arrange** things like flowers, you group them in a special way.

array arrays
NOUN **1** An **array** is a group of things set out neatly in columns and rows.
NOUN **2** An **array** is also a large number of things displayed together. *Ben's mouth watered at the array of cakes.*

arrest arrests, arresting, arrested
VERB If the police **arrest** someone, they take them to the police station.

arrive arrives, arriving, arrived
VERB When you **arrive** at a place, you reach it at the end of your journey.
arrival NOUN

arrow arrows
NOUN **1** An **arrow** is a thin stick with a pointed end, which is shot from a bow.
NOUN **2** An **arrow** can also be a sign which shows people which way to go.

art
NOUN **Art** is something like painting or sculpture, which is beautiful or has a special meaning.

artery arteries
NOUN An **artery** is a tube which carries blood from your heart to the rest of your body.

article articles
NOUN **1** An **article** is a piece of writing in a magazine or newspaper.
NOUN **2** An **article** can also be an object. *What is this strange article?*

artificial
ADJECTIVE **Artificial** things are made by people. They do not occur naturally.

artist artists
NOUN An **artist** is a person who does things like painting or sculpture.

ascend ascends, ascending, ascended
VERB When you **ascend**, you move upwards. *He ascended the stairs to his room.*

ascending
ADJECTIVE When things are arranged in **ascending** order, each thing is higher than the one before it. *The numbers 21, 37 and 49 are in ascending order.*

ash ashes
NOUN **1** **Ash** is the dust left after a fire.
NOUN **2** An **ash** is a large tree.

ashamed
ADJECTIVE If you are **ashamed**, you feel sorry about something you have done.

ask asks, asking, asked
VERB **1** If you **ask** someone a question, you are trying to find something out.
VERB **2** If you **ask** someone for something, you want them to give it to you.

asleep
ADJECTIVE If you are **asleep**, your eyes are closed and your body is resting.

aspirin aspirins
NOUN **Aspirin** is a drug which you take to help you if you have a pain, fever or cold. An **aspirin** is a tablet of this drug.

ass asses
NOUN An **ass** is like a horse but smaller and with longer ears.

assemble assembles, assembling, assembled
VERB **1** If you **assemble** something, you fit the parts of it together.
VERB **2** When people **assemble**, they come together in a group.

assembly

assembly assemblies
NOUN **Assembly** is a gathering of all the teachers and pupils in a school.

assistant assistants
NOUN **1** A person's **assistant** is someone whose job is to help them.
NOUN **2** A shop **assistant** is a person who works in a shop selling things.

asthma
NOUN **Asthma** is a disease of the chest. It causes wheezing and makes it difficult for you to breathe properly.

astonish astonishes, astonishing, astonished
VERB If you are **astonished** by something or someone, you are very surprised.

astronaut astronauts
NOUN An **astronaut** is a person who travels in space.

astronomer astronomers
NOUN An **astronomer** is a scientist who studies the stars and planets.

ate
VERB **Ate** is the past tense of **eat**.

atlas atlases
NOUN An **atlas** is a book of maps.

atmosphere atmospheres
NOUN **1** A planet's **atmosphere** is the layer of air or other gas around it.
NOUN **2** You can use **atmosphere** to talk about the general mood of a place. *In the classroom the **atmosphere** was relaxed.*

atom atoms
NOUN An **atom** is the smallest part of any substance.

attach attaches, attaching, attached
VERB When you **attach** something to an object, you join the two things together.

attack attacks, attacking, attacked
VERB If a person **attacks** somebody, they try to hurt them.

attempt attempts, attempting, attempted
VERB If you **attempt** something difficult, you try to do it.

attend attends, attending, attended
VERB If someone **attends** something like a meeting, they are present at it.

attention
NOUN **1** If something attracts your **attention**, you notice it suddenly.
NOUN **2** If you pay **attention** to someone, you listen carefully to them.

attic attics
NOUN An **attic** is a room at the top of a house, just under the roof.

attract attracts, attracting, attracted
VERB **1** If something or somebody **attracts** you, you find them interesting. *Joe was **attracted** to the fair by the lights.*
VERB **2** If something like a magnet **attracts** an object, it makes it move towards it.

attractive
ADJECTIVE If something is **attractive**, it is nice to look at.

audience audiences
NOUN An **audience** is a group of people watching or listening to something like a play, film, talk or piece of music.

August
NOUN **August** is the eighth month of the year. It has 31 days.

aunt aunts
NOUN Your **aunt** is the sister of one of your parents, or the wife of your uncle.

author **authors**

NOUN The **author** of a book is the person who wrote it.

authority **authorities**

NOUN **1** **Authority** is a quality that someone has that makes people take notice of what they say.

NOUN **2** The **authorities** are people like the police who have a lot of power.

autograph **autographs**

NOUN An **autograph** is the signature of a famous person.

automatic

ADJECTIVE An **automatic** machine is one that can do things on its own.

automatically ADVERB

autumn **autumns**

NOUN **Autumn** is the season between summer and winter. The weather cools and many trees lose their leaves.

available

ADJECTIVE If something is **available**, you can get it. *Tickets are available now.*

avalanche **avalanches**

NOUN An **avalanche** is a huge mass of snow and ice that falls down a mountain.

avenue **avenues**

NOUN An **avenue** is a wide road with trees on either side.

avocado **avocados**

NOUN An **avocado** is a fruit with dark green skin and a large stone. See *Fruit* on page 257.

avoid **avoids, avoiding, avoided**

VERB If you **avoid** someone or something, you keep away from them.

awake

ADJECTIVE If you are **awake**, you are not sleeping.

award **awards**

NOUN An **award** is a prize that you are given for doing something well.

aware

ADJECTIVE If you are **aware** of something, you know about it.

away

ADVERB **1** If you move **away** from somewhere, you move so that you are further from that place.

ADVERB **2** If you are **away** from somewhere, you are not in that place. *Katherine is away from school today.*

awful

ADJECTIVE Something **awful** is very unpleasant or bad.

awkward

ADJECTIVE **1** If something is **awkward**, it is difficult to do or use.

ADJECTIVE **2** If people are **awkward**, they move in a clumsy way.

axe **axes**

NOUN An **axe** is a tool with a long handle and a heavy sharp blade at one end. It is used for chopping wood.

axis **axes**

NOUN **1** An **axis** is an imaginary line through the centre of something, around which it moves.

NOUN **2** An **axis** is also one of the two sides of a graph. A graph has a horizontal axis and a vertical axis.

Bb

baby babies
NOUN A **baby** is a very young child.

back backs
NOUN **1** The **back** of something is the part opposite the front.
ADVERB **2** If you go **back** to a place, you go somewhere you have been before.
NOUN **3** Your **back** is the part of your body which is behind you, from your neck to the top of your legs.
NOUN **4** The **back** of an animal is the part on top, between its neck and the beginning of its tail.
back to front PHRASE If you have something on **back to front**, you are wearing it the wrong way round.

background backgrounds
NOUN The **background** of a picture is everything behind the main part.

backwards
ADVERB **1** If you move **backwards**, you move with your back facing in the direction you are going.
ADVERB **2** If you do something **backwards**, you do it in the opposite of the usual way. *Let's try counting **backwards** from one hundred.*

bacon
NOUN **Bacon** is salted meat from a pig.

bacteria
PLURAL NOUN **Bacteria** are very tiny living things which break down waste. They can cause diseases.

bad worse, worst
ADJECTIVE **1** You say somebody is **bad** if they are naughty or wicked.
ADJECTIVE **2** If something is **bad**, it can hurt or upset you in some way.

badge badges
NOUN A **badge** is a sign people wear to show they belong to a school or club.

badger badgers
NOUN A **badger** is a strongly built animal with short legs and neck. It has long grey fur and a striped head.

badminton
NOUN **Badminton** is a game in which players use rackets to hit a small feathered object called a shuttlecock across a net.

bag bags
NOUN A **bag** is a soft container for carrying or holding things.

bait
NOUN **Bait** is food used to trap animals.

bake bakes, baking, baked
VERB When you **bake** food, you cook it in an oven.

baker bakers
NOUN A **baker** makes and sells bread, cakes and pies.

balance balances, balancing, balanced
VERB When you **balance**, you keep steady. *She tried to **balance** on one leg.*

balcony balconies
NOUN A **balcony** is a platform on the outside of a building. Balconies have a railing or wall around them.

bald balder, baldest
ADJECTIVE People who are **bald** have no hair on the top of their head.

ball balls
NOUN Anything round can be called a **ball**. You need a ball for lots of games, like tennis and football.

ballet **ballets**

NOUN A **ballet** is a sort of play where the story is told with dancing and music.

balloon **balloons**

NOUN A **balloon** is a small rubber bag. If you blow hard into it, it gets bigger and makes a very light toy or decoration.

bamboo

NOUN **Bamboo** is a kind of grass with strong hollow stems which are useful as garden canes or for making furniture.

ban **bans, banning, banned**

VERB If someone is **banned** from doing something, they are told by people in charge that they must not do it.

banana **bananas**

NOUN A **banana** is a long yellow fruit which grows on trees in hot countries. See *Fruit* on page 257.

band **bands**

NOUN **1** A **band** is a small number of people, like a gang of robbers or a group of musicians.

NOUN **2** A **band** can also be a strip of material such as iron, cloth or rubber.

bandage **bandages**

NOUN A **bandage** is a strip of cloth used to cover a wound.

bang **bangs, banging, banged**

NOUN **1** A **bang** is a sudden loud noise.

VERB **2** If something **bangs**, or you bang it, it makes a loud noise.

bank **banks**

NOUN **1** A **bank** is a business that looks after people's money.

NOUN **2** The **bank** of a river is the ground either side of the water.

banner **banners**

NOUN A **banner** is a long strip of cloth or paper with a message written on it.

bar **bars**

NOUN **1** A **bar** is a long piece of something hard, like metal or wood.

NOUN **2** A **bar** can also be a counter where people can buy drink.

barbecue **barbecues**

NOUN A **barbecue** is a grill on which food is cooked outdoors over hot charcoal.

barber **barbers**

NOUN A **barber** is someone who cuts men's hair.

bar chart **bar charts**

NOUN A **bar chart** is a graph where information is shown in bars.

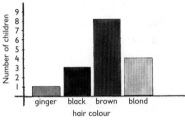

bar code **bar codes**

NOUN A **bar code** is a pattern of numbers and lines printed on something that is for sale, so that the price can be read by a machine.

bare **barer, barest**

ADJECTIVE **1** If part of your body is **bare**, it is not covered by clothes.

ADJECTIVE **2** If something is **bare**, it has nothing in it or on it. *It was winter and the trees were **bare**.*

bargain **bargains**

NOUN A **bargain** is something which is sold at a low price, and which you think is good value.

bark **barks, barking, barked**

VERB **1** When a dog **barks**, it makes a sudden rough, loud noise.

NOUN **2** **Bark** is the outside covering of a tree.

barley

NOUN **Barley** is a cereal that is grown for food and drink.

barn

barn barns
NOUN A **barn** is a large building where a farmer stores hay and other crops.

barrel barrels
NOUN A **barrel** is a large wooden, metal or plastic container for holding liquids.

barrier barriers
NOUN A **barrier** is something like a fence or wall, that stops people getting past.

base bases
NOUN **1** The **base** is the bottom of something.

NOUN **2** Number **bases** are a whole pattern of counting. A base ten counting system uses units, tens and hundreds.

basement basements
NOUN The **basement** of a building is a floor below ground level.

basic
ADJECTIVE **1** Basic is used to describe things like the food and equipment that people really need in their lives.

ADJECTIVE **2** Basic also means the simplest things you need to know about a subject. *I'm not good at this yet, but I've got the basic idea.*

basically ADVERB

basin basins
NOUN A **basin** is a wide round container which is open at the top.

basket baskets
NOUN A **basket** is used for holding or carrying things. It is usually made from strips of thin wood or cane.

bat bats, batting, batted
NOUN **1** In some games, like table tennis, you use a wooden **bat** to hit the ball.

NOUN **2** A **bat** is also a small animal like a mouse with leathery wings. Bats fly at night, and sleep hanging upside down.

VERB **3** If you are **batting**, you are having a turn at hitting the ball with a bat in cricket, baseball or rounders.

bath baths
NOUN A **bath** is a container for water. It is big enough to sit or lie in, so that you can wash yourself all over.

bathroom bathrooms
NOUN The **bathroom** is the room where the bath or shower is.

battery batteries
NOUN A **battery** is an object which stores electric power. There are tiny batteries for things like watches, and larger batteries for torches.

battle battles
NOUN A **battle** is a fight between enemy forces, on land, at sea or in the air.

bawl bawls, bawling, bawled
VERB If a child is **bawling**, it is crying very loudly and angrily.

bay bays
NOUN A **bay** is a deep curve in a coastline.

beach beaches
NOUN The **beach** is the land covered with sand or pebbles that is next to the sea.

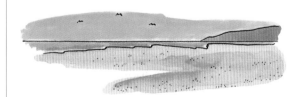

bead beads
NOUN A **bead** is a small piece of glass or plastic with a hole through it. Beads can be threaded together to make a necklace or bracelet.

beak beaks
NOUN A **beak** is the hard outside part of a bird's mouth.

beam beams, beaming, beamed

NOUN **1** A **beam** is a long thick bar of wood, metal or concrete, used to support part of a building.

NOUN **2** A **beam** is also a line of light from an object such as a torch or the sun.

VERB **3** If you **beam**, you give a big smile.

bean beans

NOUN A **bean** is a vegetable. Its outer covering is called a pod, and inside it has large seeds, also called beans. See *Vegetables* on page 256.

bear bears, bearing, bore

NOUN **1** A **bear** is a large, strong animal with thick fur and sharp claws.

VERB **2** If you **bear** something, you put up with it. *I can't bear all this homework.*

beard beards

NOUN A **beard** is the hair which grows on the lower part of a man's face.

beat beats, beating, beat, beaten

VERB **1** If you **beat** someone in a race or competition, you do better than they do.

VERB **2** If someone **beats** another person or an animal, they hit them hard.

VERB **3** If you **beat** eggs, you stir them very fast.

VERB **4** Your heart **beats** with a regular rhythm all the time.

beautiful

ADJECTIVE **1** You say something is **beautiful** if it gives you great pleasure to look at it or listen to it.

ADJECTIVE **2** You say someone is **beautiful** if they are lovely to look at.

beaver beavers

NOUN A **beaver** is a furry animal which lives in or near water.

because

CONJUNCTION You say **because** when you are going to give a reason for something. *I left the party because they were playing silly games.*

become becomes, becoming, became, become

VERB To **become** means to start being different in some way. *The smell became stronger.*

bed beds

NOUN **1** A **bed** is a piece of furniture to lie down on when you rest or sleep.

NOUN **2** The **bed** of the sea or of a river is the ground beneath it.

bedroom bedrooms

NOUN Your **bedroom** is the room where you sleep.

bedtime

NOUN Your **bedtime** is the time when you usually go to bed.

bee bees

NOUN A **bee** is a flying insect. People keep bees for the honey that they make. See **beehive**. See also *Insects* on page 259.

beech beeches

NOUN A **beech** is a large tree.

beef

NOUN **Beef** is the meat from a cow.

beehive beehives

NOUN A **beehive** is a house for bees, where a beekeeper collects the honey.

beer beers

NOUN **Beer** is a drink made from grain.

Bb

beetle **beetles**
NOUN A **beetle** is an insect with four wings. The front two act as hard covers to the body when the beetle is not flying. See *Insects* on page 259.

beetroot **beetroots**
NOUN **Beetroot** is a dark red root vegetable. See *Vegetables* on page 256.

before
PREPOSITION **1** If something happens **before** something else, it happens earlier. *Can I see you before lunch?*
ADVERB **2** If you have done something **before**, it is not the first time.

beg **begs, begging, begged**
VERB If you **beg** someone to do something, you ask them very anxiously to do it. *Tom begged his dad to take him to the football match.*

begin **begins, beginning, began, begun**
VERB When you **begin**, you start. *I began school on Thursday.*

beginner **beginners**
NOUN A **beginner** is someone who has just started to learn something.

beginning **beginnings**
NOUN The **beginning** of something is the first part of it.

begun
VERB **Begun** is the past participle of **begin**.

behave **behaves, behaving, behaved**
VERB The way you **behave** is the way you act.
behaviour NOUN

behind
PREPOSITION **1 Behind** means on the other side of something. *She was behind the counter.*
PREPOSITION **2** If you are **behind** someone, you are at the back of them.

beige
ADJECTIVE Something that is **beige** is a pale creamy-brown colour. See *Colours* on page 271.

believe **believes, believing, believed**
VERB If you **believe** something or someone, you think what is said is true.

bell **bells**
NOUN A **bell** is a piece of metal shaped like a cup, which rings when something hits it.

belong **belongs, belonging, belonged**
VERB **1** If something **belongs** to you, it is your own.
VERB **2** If you **belong** to something, like a club, you are a member of it.

below
PREPOSITION If something is **below** something else, it is underneath it.

belt **belts**
NOUN A **belt** is a strip of leather or other material that you put round your waist.

bench **benches**
NOUN A **bench** is a long seat, usually made of wood.

bend **bends, bending, bent**
VERB When something **bends**, it becomes curved or crooked.

beneath
PREPOSITION If something is **beneath** something else, it is below it.

bent

ADJECTIVE If something is **bent**, it has become curved or crooked. See **bend**.

berry **berries**

NOUN A **berry** is a small round soft fruit that grows on a bush or a tree.

beside

PREPOSITION If something is **beside** something else, it is at the side of it.

best

ADJECTIVE **Best** means the "most good", or better than anything else. *That's the **best** programme I've seen.*

better

ADJECTIVE **1** Something that is **better** than something else is of a higher standard or quality. *Your bicycle is **better** than mine.*

ADJECTIVE **2 Better** can also mean more sensible. *It would be **better** to go home.*

ADJECTIVE **3** If you are feeling **better** after an illness, you are not feeling so ill.

between

PREPOSITION If something is **between** two other things, it is in the space or time that separates them. *The toyshop is **between** the bank and the library.*

beware

VERB You tell people to **beware** if there is danger of some kind. *Beware of the bull.*

bicycle **bicycles**

NOUN A **bicycle** is a vehicle with two wheels. You sit on it and turn pedals with your feet to make it go.

big **bigger, biggest**

ADJECTIVE Something or somebody **big** is large in size or importance.

bike **bikes**

NOUN **Bike** is an abbreviation of **bicycle**.

bill **bills**

NOUN **1** A **bill** is a piece of paper saying how much money you owe. *Mum's just had the electricity **bill**.*

NOUN **2** A bird's **bill** is its beak.

bin **bins**

NOUN A **bin** is a container, usually with a lid, for putting rubbish in.

bind **binds, binding, bound**

VERB If you **bind** something, you tie something like string or cloth tightly round it so that it is held in place.

biology

NOUN **Biology** is the study of living things.

birch **birches**

NOUN A **birch** is a tall tree that has thin peeling bark.

bird **birds**

NOUN A **bird** is an animal with two legs, two wings and feathers.

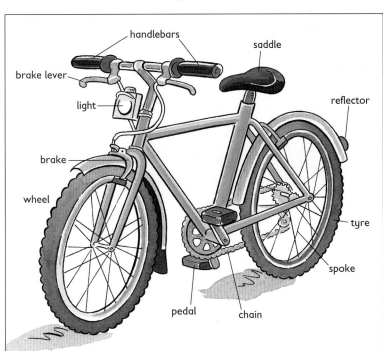

handlebars
saddle
brake lever
reflector
light
brake
wheel
tyre
spoke
pedal
chain

birth **births**

NOUN The **birth** of a baby is when it comes out of its mother's body.

birthday **birthdays**

NOUN Your **birthday** is a special date that is remembered every year, because it was the day you were born.

biscuit **biscuits**

NOUN A **biscuit** is a small, flat, crisp kind of cake.

bit **bits**

NOUN **1** A **bit** of something is a small piece of it.

NOUN **2** A **bit** is a piece of metal that goes in a horse's mouth.

VERB **3 Bit** is also the past tense of **bite**.

bite **bites, biting, bit, bitten**

VERB If you **bite** something, you use your teeth to hold, cut or tear it.

bitter

ADJECTIVE **1** If something has a **bitter** taste, it tastes sharp and unpleasant.

ADJECTIVE **2** Someone who is **bitter** feels angry and disappointed.

black **blacker, blackest**

ADJECTIVE If the colour of something is **black**, it is the colour of these letters. See *Colours* on page 271.

blackberry **blackberries**

NOUN **Blackberries** are small, soft, dark purple fruits that grow on brambles.

blackbird **blackbirds**

NOUN A **blackbird** is a European songbird.

blackboard **blackboards**

NOUN A **blackboard** is a dark board that people can write on in chalk.

blackcurrant **blackcurrants**

NOUN **Blackcurrants** are very small, dark purple fruits.

blade **blades**

NOUN **1** A **blade** is the sharp edge of a knife or sword.

NOUN **2** A single piece of grass is a **blade**.

blame **blames, blaming, blamed**

VERB If somebody **blames** a person for something bad that happened, they say that person made it happen.

blank **blanker, blankest**

ADJECTIVE If something is **blank**, it has nothing written or drawn on it.

blanket **blankets**

NOUN A **blanket** is a large warm cloth, often used to cover people in bed.

blaze **blazes**

NOUN A **blaze** is a strong bright fire.

blazer **blazers**

NOUN A **blazer** is a kind of jacket, often in the colours of a school or sports team.

bleed **bleeds, bleeding, bled**

VERB If part of your body **bleeds**, blood comes out of it.

blend **blends, blending, blended**

VERB When you **blend** two or more things together, they become a smooth mixture.

blew

VERB **Blew** is the past tense of **blow**.

blind **blinds**

NOUN **1** A **blind** is rolled material that you pull down to cover a window.

ADJECTIVE **2** Someone who is **blind** cannot see.

blindness NOUN

blindfold blindfolds

NOUN A **blindfold** is a strip of cloth tied over someone's eyes so that they cannot see.

blink blinks, blinking, blinked

VERB When you **blink**, you shut your eyes and open them again quickly.

blister blisters

NOUN A **blister** is a small bubble on your skin, containing watery liquid. Blisters are caused by a burn or rubbing.

blizzard blizzards

NOUN A **blizzard** is a bad snowstorm with strong winds.

block blocks, blocking, blocked

NOUN **1** A **block** of flats or offices is a large tall building.

NOUN **2** A **block** of something like stone or wood is a large rectangular piece of it.

VERB **3** To **block** means to get in the way.

block graph block graphs

NOUN A **block graph** is used to show information clearly, by using blocks to make columns.

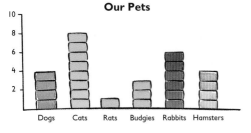

blood

NOUN **Blood** is the red liquid that your heart pumps round inside your body.

bloom blooms, blooming, bloomed

VERB When a plant **blooms**, its flowers open.

blossom

NOUN **Blossom** is the flowers that appear on a tree before the fruit.

blot blots

NOUN A **blot** is a mark made by a drop of liquid, especially ink.

blouse blouses

NOUN A **blouse** is a kind of shirt worn by a girl or a woman.

blow blows, blowing, blew, blown

VERB **1** When the wind **blows**, the air moves faster.

VERB **2** If you **blow**, you send out a stream of air from your mouth.

NOUN **3** A **blow** is a hard hit.

blue bluer, bluest

ADJECTIVE Something that is **blue** is the colour of the sky on a sunny day. See *Colours* on page 271.

bluebell bluebells

NOUN A **bluebell** is a flower that often grows wild in woods in Europe.

blunt blunter, bluntest

ADJECTIVE **1** A **blunt** knife is not sharp.

ADJECTIVE **2** Something that is **blunt** has a rounded, rather than pointed, end. *My pencil's **blunt**.*

blur blurs

NOUN A **blur** is a shape that you cannot see clearly. *The car went past so fast it was just a **blur**.*

blurred ADJECTIVE   **blurry** ADJECTIVE

blurb blurbs

NOUN A **blurb** is a short piece written to attract people's interest. There is usually a blurb on the back of a book. *The **blurb** says this book is exciting.*

blush

blush   **blushes, blushing, blushed**
VERB When you **blush** you become red in the face, usually because you are embarrassed.

boar   **boars**
NOUN A **boar** is a male pig.

board   **boards**
NOUN A **board** is a flat, thin piece of wood.

boast   **boasts, boasting, boasted**
VERB If you **boast**, you talk too proudly about something.

boat   **boats**
NOUN A **boat** is a small vessel for travelling on water. See **ship**.

body   **bodies**
NOUN **1** Your **body** is every part of you. Some animals, like elephants, have very large bodies.
See *Your body* on page 258.
NOUN **2** You can say **body** when you mean just the main part of a person, not counting head, arms and legs.
NOUN **3** A **body** is a dead person.

bog   **bogs**
NOUN A **bog** is an area of land that is always wet and spongy.

boil   **boils, boiling, boiled**
VERB **1** When liquid **boils** it gets very hot. It bubbles and steam rises from it.
VERB **2** If you **boil** food, you cook it in boiling water.
NOUN **3** A **boil** is a painful red swelling on the skin.

bold   **bolder, boldest**
ADJECTIVE **1** Someone who is **bold** is not afraid of risk or danger.
ADJECTIVE **2** Letters that are in **bold** type are thicker than ordinary printed letters.

bolt   **bolts, bolting, bolted**
NOUN **1** A **bolt** is a long round metal pin with a flat end. It screws into a nut to fasten things.

NOUN **2** A **bolt** is a metal bar that you can slide across to keep a door shut.
VERB **3** If you **bolt** a door or window, you lock it with a bolt.
VERB **4** When a person or animal **bolts**, they suddenly run very fast.

bomb   **bombs**
NOUN A **bomb** is a weapon which explodes and damages a large area.

bone   **bones**
NOUN Your **bones** are the hard parts inside your body which make up your skeleton.

bonfire   **bonfires**
NOUN A **bonfire** is a fire lit outdoors, usually to burn garden rubbish.

bonnet   **bonnets**
NOUN **1** A **bonnet** is the metal cover over a car's engine.
NOUN **2** A **bonnet** is also a baby's or woman's hat tied under the chin.

book   **books, booking, booked**
NOUN **1** A **book** is a number of pages held together inside a cover.
VERB **2** If you **book** something, you ask someone to keep it for you. *We booked seats at the cinema.*

boot   **boots**
NOUN **1** Boots are strong shoes that cover your ankle and sometimes your calf.
NOUN **2** The **boot** of a car is a space for luggage.

border   **borders**
NOUN **1** A **border** is the line dividing two countries.
NOUN **2** A **border** is a strip along the edge of something, usually as a decoration.

bore   **bores, boring, bored**
VERB **1** If somebody **bores** you, you do not find them interesting.
VERB **2** If you **bore** a hole in something, you make a hole with a drill.
VERB **3** Bore is the past tense of **bear**.

bored

ADJECTIVE When you are **bored**, you feel tired and impatient because you have nothing interesting to do.
boredom NOUN

boring

ADJECTIVE Something **boring** is so dull that you have no interest in it.

born

VERB When a baby is **born**, it comes out of its mother's body.

borrow **borrows, borrowing, borrowed**

VERB When you **borrow** something, someone lets you have it for a while but they expect you to give it back later.

boss **bosses**

NOUN Someone's **boss** is the head of the place where they work.

bossy

ADJECTIVE A **bossy** person likes to tell others what to do.

both

ADJECTIVE OR PRONOUN You use **both** when you are talking about two things or people. *She wanted **both** pairs of jeans.*

bother **bothers, bothering, bothered**

VERB 1 If something **bothers** you, it annoys you or makes you feel worried.
VERB 2 If you **bother** about something, you care about it and take trouble over it.

bottle **bottles**

NOUN A **bottle** is a container for keeping liquids in. Bottles are usually made of glass or plastic.

bottom **bottoms**

NOUN 1 The **bottom** of something is the lowest part of it.
NOUN 2 Your **bottom** is the part of your body that you sit on.

bought

VERB **Bought** is the past tense of **buy**.

boulder **boulders**

NOUN A **boulder** is a big rounded rock.

bounce **bounces, bouncing, bounced**

VERB When something **bounces**, it springs back in the opposite direction as soon as it hits something hard.

bound **bounds, bounding, bounded**

VERB 1 When animals or people **bound**, they move quickly with large leaps.
ADJECTIVE 2 If something is **bound to** happen, it is sure to happen.

boundary **boundaries**

NOUN The **boundary** of an area of land is its outer limit.

bow **bows, bowing, bowed**
(*rhymes with* **low**)

NOUN 1 A **bow** is a kind of knot with two loops used to tie laces and ribbons.
NOUN 2 A **bow** is also a weapon used for shooting arrows.
NOUN 3 The **bow** for a stringed musical instrument is a long piece of wood with horsehair stretched along it.
(*rhymes with* **now**) VERB 4 When you **bow**, you bend your body forward.

bowl **bowls**

NOUN A **bowl** is an open container used for holding liquid or serving food.

box **boxes**

NOUN A **box** is a container with straight sides, made from something stiff, like cardboard, wood or plastic.

boy **boys**

NOUN A **boy** is a male child.

bracelet **bracelets**

NOUN A **bracelet** is a band or chain which is worn round the wrist or arm as an ornament.

bracket

bracket **brackets**

NOUN **Brackets** are a pair of written marks ( ) placed round words that are not part of the main text.
See *Punctuation* on page 264.

Braille

NOUN **Braille** is a form of writing using raised dots that blind people can read by touching the dots with their fingers.

brain **brains**

NOUN Your **brain** is inside your head and controls your whole body. It lets you think, feel and remember.

brainstorm **brainstorms, brainstorming, brainstormed**

VERB When people **brainstorm**, they get together to develop ideas. *This morning we are brainstorming words about dogs.*

brake **brakes**

NOUN The **brake** is the part of a vehicle that slows it down or stops it.

bramble **brambles**

NOUN A **bramble** is a wild bush with thorns. The fruit are called blackberries.

branch **branches**

NOUN A **branch** is part of a tree that grows out from the trunk.

brass

NOUN **Brass** is a yellow metal made from copper and zinc. It is used for making things like ornaments and some musical instruments.

brave **braver, bravest**

ADJECTIVE If you are **brave**, you show you can do something even if it is frightening.

bravely ADVERB   **bravery** NOUN

bread

NOUN **Bread** is a very common food, made with flour and baked in an oven.

breadth

NOUN The **breadth** of something is the distance that it measures from one side to the other.

break **breaks, breaking, broke, broken**

VERB **1** If you **break** something, it splits into pieces or stops working.
VERB **2** If you **break** a rule or a promise, you fail to keep it.

breakdown **breakdowns**

NOUN If someone's car has a **breakdown**, it stops working during a journey.

breakfast **breakfasts**

NOUN **Breakfast** is the first meal of the day.

breast **breasts**

NOUN **Breasts** are the two round parts on the front of a woman's body, which can produce milk to feed a baby.

breath

NOUN Your **breath** is the air that you take into and let out of your lungs.

breathe **breathes, breathing, breathed**

VERB When you **breathe**, you take air into your lungs through your nose or mouth, and then let it out again.

breed **breeds**

NOUN A **breed** of an animal is a particular kind. For example, a labrador is a breed of dog.

breeze **breezes**

NOUN A **breeze** is a gentle wind.

brick **bricks**

NOUN A **brick** is a block used for building. It is made of baked clay.

bride **brides**

NOUN A **bride** is a woman on or near her wedding day.

bridegroom **bridegrooms**

NOUN A **bridegroom** is a man on or near his wedding day.

bridesmaid **bridesmaids**

NOUN A **bridesmaid** is a woman or girl who helps a bride on her wedding day.

bridge **bridges**

NOUN A **bridge** is something built over things like rivers, railways or roads, so that people or vehicles can get across.

brief **briefer, briefest**

ADJECTIVE Something that is **brief** lasts only a short time.

briefly ADVERB

briefcase **briefcases**

NOUN A **briefcase** is a flat case used for carrying papers.

bright **brighter, brightest**

ADJECTIVE **1** **Bright** colours are clear and easy to see.

ADJECTIVE **2** A light that is **bright** shines strongly.

ADJECTIVE **3** Someone who is **bright** is quick at learning or noticing things.

brilliant

ADJECTIVE **1** A **brilliant** colour or light is extremely bright.

ADJECTIVE **2** Someone who is **brilliant** is extremely clever or skilful.

brim **brims**

NOUN **1** If you fill a cup to the **brim**, you fill it right up to the top.

NOUN **2** The **brim** of a hat is the part that sticks outwards from the head.

bring **brings, bringing, brought**

VERB **1** If you **bring** someone on a visit, they come with you.

VERB **2** If you **bring** something, you have it with you when you arrive.

bristle **bristles**

NOUN The **bristles** of a brush are the thick hairs or thin pieces of plastic which are fixed to the main part of it.

brittle

ADJECTIVE If something is **brittle**, it is hard but easily broken.

broad **broader, broadest**

ADJECTIVE Something such as a road or river that is **broad** is very wide.

broadcast **broadcasts**

NOUN A **broadcast** is a programme or announcement on radio or television.

broke

VERB **Broke** is the past tense of **break**.

broken

VERB **Broken** is the past participle of **break**.

brooch **brooches**

NOUN A **brooch** is a small piece of jewellery which is worn pinned to a dress, blouse or coat.

broom **brooms**

NOUN A **broom** is a kind of brush with a long handle.

brother **brothers**

NOUN Someone's **brother** is a boy or man who has the same parents as they have.

brought

VERB **Brought** is the past tense of **bring**.

brown **browner, brownest**

ADJECTIVE Something that is **brown** is the colour of earth or of wood.

See Colours on page 271.

bruise **bruises**

NOUN A **bruise** is a purple mark on your skin where something has hit it.

brush **brushes**

NOUN A **brush** is a lot of bristles fixed to a handle. Different brushes are used for jobs like cleaning your teeth or painting.

bubble **bubbles**

NOUN A **bubble** is a ball of air or gas. You can make bubbles with soapy water. Fizzy lemonade has bubbles, too.

bucket **buckets**

NOUN A **bucket** is a container with a handle, often used for carrying water.

buckle **buckles**

NOUN A **buckle** is a fastening on the end of a belt or strap.

bud **buds**

NOUN A **bud** is a small lump on a plant which will open into a leaf or flower.

Buddhist **Buddhists**

NOUN A **Buddhist** is someone who follows the teachings of Buddha.

budgerigar **budgerigars**

NOUN **Budgerigars** are small brightly-coloured birds, often kept as pets.

buffalo **buffaloes**

NOUN A **buffalo** is an animal like a large cow with long curved horns.

bug **bugs**

NOUN 1 A **bug** is an insect.
NOUN 2 A **bug** is also an illness, such as a flu bug or a stomach bug.

build **builds, building, built**

VERB If you **build** something, you make it by joining things together.

builder **builders**

NOUN A **builder** is a person whose job is to build houses and other buildings.

building **buildings**

NOUN A **building** is a place like a house that has walls and a roof.

bulb **bulbs**

NOUN 1 A **bulb** is the glass part of a lamp that gives out light.
NOUN 2 A **bulb** is also a root shaped like an onion. Many spring flowers such as daffodils and tulips grow from bulbs.

bulge **bulges, bulging, bulged**

VERB If something **bulges**, it sticks out in a lump. *His pockets **bulged** with conkers.*

bull **bulls**

NOUN A **bull** is a male cow, elephant or whale.

bulldozer **bulldozers**

NOUN A **bulldozer** is a tractor with a steel blade on the front. It is used for moving large amounts of earth or stone.

bullet **bullets**

NOUN 1 A **bullet** is a small piece of metal fired from a gun.
NOUN 2 A **bullet point** is a heavy dot used to draw attention to a piece of text.

bully **bullies**

NOUN A **bully** is someone who hurts or frightens other people.

bump **bumps, bumping, bumped**

VERB 1 If you **bump** into something, you hit it while you are moving.
NOUN 2 If you hear a **bump**, it sounds like something falling to the ground.
NOUN 3 A **bump** is a raised uneven part on a surface such as a road.

bumper **bumpers**

NOUN **Bumpers** are bars on the front and back of a vehicle that protect it if there is an accident.

bun **buns**

NOUN A **bun** is a small round cake.

bunch **bunches**

NOUN A **bunch** is a group of things together, like flowers or grapes.
See *Collective nouns* on page 262.

a
Bb
c
d
e
f
g
h
i
j
k
l
m
n
o
p
q
r
s
t
u
v
w
x
y
z

bundle **bundles**

NOUN A **bundle** is a number of small things that have been tied together.

bungalow **bungalows**

NOUN A **bungalow** is a house with all its rooms on one floor.

bunk beds

NOUN **Bunk beds** are two single beds fixed one above the other.

burger **burgers**

NOUN A **burger** is a flat piece of minced meat. It is often eaten in a bread roll.

burglar **burglars**

NOUN A **burglar** is someone who breaks into buildings to steal things.

burn **burns, burning, burned** or **burnt**

VERB **1** If something is **burning**, it is being spoiled or destroyed by fire.
VERB **2** People often **burn** fuel, such as coal, to keep warm.
NOUN **3** A **burn** is an injury caused by heat or fire.

burrow **burrows**

NOUN A **burrow** is a hole in the ground that an animal lives in.

burst **bursts, bursting, burst**

VERB When something like a balloon or tyre **bursts**, it splits open suddenly.

bury **buries, burying, buried**

VERB If you **bury** something, you put it in a hole in the ground and cover it.

bus **buses**

NOUN A **bus** is a large motor vehicle. People pay to go on buses.

bush **bushes**

NOUN A **bush** is a large woody plant with lots of branches. It is smaller than a tree.

business **businesses**

NOUN **1** Business is the work of making, buying and selling things or services.
NOUN **2** A **business** is a group of people who make and sell things.

bus stop **bus stops**

NOUN A **bus stop** is a place where people can get on or off buses.

busy **busier, busiest**

ADJECTIVE **1** When you are **busy**, you are working hard on something.
ADJECTIVE **2** A place that is **busy** is full of people doing things or moving about.

but

CONJUNCTION You use **but** to join two parts of a sentence when the second part is unexpected. *Megan likes most green vegetables,* **but** *she won't eat broccoli.*

butcher **butchers**

NOUN A **butcher** is a shopkeeper who cuts up meat and sells it.

butter

NOUN **Butter** is a yellow fat made from cream. You spread it on bread or use it for cooking.

butterfly **butterflies**

NOUN A **butterfly** is an insect with four large wings which flies during the day. *See Insects on page 259.*

button **buttons**

NOUN **1** A **button** is a small disc used to fasten clothes.
NOUN **2** A **button** is also a part of a machine that you press to make it work.

buy **buys, buying, bought**

VERB When you **buy** something, you get it by paying money for it.

buzz **buzzes, buzzing, buzzed**

VERB If something **buzzes**, it makes a "zzz" sound like a bee.

a
b
Cc
d
e
f
g
h
i
j
k
l
m
n
o
p
q
r
s
t
u
v
w
x
y
z

Cc

cab cabs

NOUN **1** The **cab** is the place where the driver sits in a bus, truck or train.
NOUN **2** A **cab** is another word for a taxi.

cabbage cabbages

NOUN A **cabbage** is a vegetable that looks like a large ball of leaves.
See *Vegetables* on page 256.

cabin cabins

NOUN **1** A **cabin** is a room in a ship, boat or aeroplane for passengers or crew.
NOUN **2** A **cabin** is also a small house in a wild place such as a forest.

cable cables

NOUN **1** A **cable** is a thick rope or chain.
NOUN **2** A **cable** is also a bundle of wires with a rubber covering, which carries electricity.
NOUN **3 Cable television** is a system in which the signals are sent along wires.

cactus cactuses

or **cacti**
NOUN A **cactus** is a plant with spines. It can grow in hot, dry places like deserts.

café cafés

NOUN A **café** is a place with tables and chairs where you buy drinks and snacks.

cage cages

NOUN A **cage** is a box or room with bars in which birds or animals are kept.

cake cakes

NOUN A **cake** is a sweet food made with flour, sugar, fat and eggs, and baked in an oven.

calculate calculates, calculating, calculated

VERB If you **calculate** something in maths, you work it out.

calculation calculations

NOUN A **calculation** is something you work out in maths.

calculator calculators

NOUN A **calculator** is a small electronic machine which you can use to give you the answer to different calculations.

calendar calendars

NOUN A **calendar** is a list of the months, weeks and days in a year.

calf calves

NOUN **1 Calves** are young cows, elephants and whales.
See *Young animals* on page 260.
NOUN **2** Your **calf** is the part at the back of your leg between the knee and ankle.

call calls, calling, called

VERB **1** If you **call** someone, you shout for them, or telephone them.
VERB **2** If you **call** someone something, you give them a name.
VERB **3** If an animal or thing is **called** something, that is their name.

calm calmer, calmest

ADJECTIVE **1** If you are **calm**, you do not seem worried or excited.
ADJECTIVE **2** If the sea is **calm**, it is smooth and still because there is no wind.

came

VERB **Came** is the past tense of **come**.

camel camels

NOUN A **camel** is a large animal which carries people and things in the desert.

camera cameras

NOUN A **camera** is a piece of equipment you use to take pictures.

camouflage **camouflages, camouflaging, camouflaged**
VERB To **camouflage** something is to hide it by giving it the same colour or appearance as its surroundings.

camp **camps**
NOUN A **camp** is a place where people stay in tents.

can **could; cans**
VERB 1 If you **can** do something, you are able to do it. *I can swim.*
NOUN 2 A **can** is a metal container for something like food, drink or paint.

canal **canals**
NOUN A **canal** is a narrow stretch of water made for boats to travel along.

cancel **cancels, cancelling, cancelled**
VERB If you **cancel** something that has been planned, you stop it from happening.

candle **candles**
NOUN A **candle** is a wax stick with a string called a wick inside. You light the wick and it burns to give light.

cane **canes**
NOUN 1 A **cane** is the long hollow stem of a plant such as bamboo.
NOUN 2 A **cane** is a tall narrow stick used to support things.

cannot
VERB **Cannot** is the same as **can not**.

canoe **canoes**
NOUN A **canoe** is a small light boat, moved with a paddle.

can't
VERB **Can't** is a contraction of **cannot**.

canvas
NOUN **Canvas** is strong cloth, used for making things like tents and sails.

canyon **canyons**
NOUN A **canyon** is a narrow valley with very steep sides, often with a river.

cap **caps**
NOUN 1 A **cap** is a soft flat hat with a peak at the front.
NOUN 2 A **cap** is also a small flat lid on a bottle or container.

capable
ADJECTIVE If a person is **capable** of doing something, they are able to do it. *He's capable of doing better.*

capacity **capacities**
NOUN The **capacity** of something is the largest amount it can hold, produce or carry. *The capacity of this jug is one litre.*

capital **capitals**
NOUN 1 The **capital** is the main city in a country. *Paris is the capital of France.*
NOUN 2 A **capital** is a big letter of the alphabet, such as A, B and C. Capital letters are also called upper-case letters. See **lower-case**.
See *Punctuation* on page 264.

captain **captains**
NOUN 1 A **captain** is the person in charge of a ship or an aeroplane.
NOUN 2 A **captain** is the person who leads a team in sports like football.

caption **captions**
NOUN A **caption** is the words printed underneath a picture which explain what the picture is about.

capture **captures, capturing, captured**
VERB If you **capture** somebody, you take them prisoner.

car **cars**
NOUN A **car** is a road vehicle with wheels and an engine. It needs a driver and has room for passengers.

caravan **caravans**

NOUN A **caravan** is a vehicle pulled by a car in which people live or spend their holidays.

card **cards**

NOUN **1** **Card** is strong, stiff paper.

NOUN **2** A greetings **card** usually has a picture on the front and is sent to people on special days such as birthdays.

NOUN **3** Playing **cards** are small pieces of card with numbers or pictures on them. They are used for card games.

cardboard

NOUN **Cardboard** is thick, stiff paper.

cardigan **cardigans**

NOUN A **cardigan** is a knitted jacket. You fasten it at the front with buttons.

care **cares, caring, cared**

VERB **1** If you **care** about something or someone, you think they are important.

VERB **2** If you **care** for a person or animal, you look after them.

NOUN **3** If you do something with **care**, you take trouble over it.

career **careers**

NOUN Someone's **career** is the work they do, which they hope to do for a long time. *John wants a career in teaching.*

careful

ADJECTIVE If someone is **careful**, they try to do things safely and well.

careless

ADJECTIVE If you are **careless**, you do not pay attention to what you are doing.

caretaker **caretakers**

NOUN A **caretaker** is a person who looks after a large building such as a school.

cargo **cargoes**

NOUN **Cargo** is the goods carried on a ship or plane.

carnival **carnivals**

NOUN A **carnival** is a sort of party in the streets. There is usually music and dancing, and people dress up and decorate cars and trucks.

carpenter **carpenters**

NOUN A **carpenter** is a person who works with wood, usually for furniture.

carpet **carpets**

NOUN A **carpet** is a thick covering for a floor, often made of wool.

carriage **carriages**

NOUN **1** A **carriage** is one of the vehicles that make up a passenger train.

NOUN **2** A **carriage** is also a vehicle with wheels, pulled by horses.

carrot **carrots**

NOUN A **carrot** is a long thin orange vegetable that grows under the ground. *See Vegetables on page 256.*

carry **carries, carrying, carried**

VERB When you **carry** something, you pick it up and take it with you.

cart **carts**

NOUN A **cart** is a heavy wooden vehicle pulled by horses or cattle on farms.

carton **cartons**

NOUN A **carton** is a strong cardboard or plastic box for holding food or drink.

cartoon **cartoons**

NOUN **1** A **cartoon** is a film where the characters are drawn instead of being real people.

NOUN **2** A **cartoon** is also a funny drawing in a magazine, newspaper or book.

Cc

a b c d e f g h i j k l m n o p q r s t u v w x y z

cartwheel   cartwheels

NOUN A **cartwheel** is a movement. You put your hands on the floor and move your legs round in a circle until you land on your feet again.

carve   carves, carving, carved

VERB **1** If you **carve** an object, you cut it out of something like stone or wood.

VERB **2** If someone **carves** a piece of meat, they cut slices from it.

case   cases

NOUN A **case** is a box for keeping or carrying things in.

cash

NOUN **Cash** is coins and paper money.

cassette   cassettes

NOUN A **cassette** is a small flat container with magnetic tape inside, which is used for recording and playing back sounds.

cast   casts, casting, cast

NOUN **1** The **cast** of a play or film is all the people who act in it.

NOUN **2** A **cast** is an object made by pouring liquid plaster or metal into a container and leaving it to harden.

VERB **3** If something **casts** a shadow onto a place, it makes a shadow fall there.

VERB **4** If someone like a witch **casts** a spell on someone or something, they do magic that affects that person or thing.

castle   castles

NOUN A **castle** is a large building with walls or ditches round it to protect it from attack.

cat   cats

NOUN A **cat** is a small furry animal, often kept as a pet. There are also larger, wild cats, such as lions and tigers.

catalogue   catalogues

NOUN A **catalogue** is a list of things for sale or for looking at.

catch   catches, catching, caught

VERB **1** If you **catch** something, you take hold of it while it is moving.

VERB **2** If you **catch** a bus or train, you get on it to go somewhere.

VERB **3** If you **catch** something like measles, you get that illness.

catching

ADJECTIVE An illness that is **catching** can spread very quickly.

category   categories

NOUN A **category** is a set of things with a particular feature or quality in common.

caterpillar   caterpillars

NOUN A **caterpillar** is a very small animal like a worm with legs, that will change into a butterfly or moth.

cathedral   cathedrals

NOUN A **cathedral** is a large, important church.

cattle

NOUN Bulls and cows are called **cattle**.

caught

VERB **Caught** is the past tense of **catch**.

cauliflower   cauliflowers

NOUN A **cauliflower** is a round white vegetable with green leaves on the outside.

See *Vegetables* on page 256.

cause   causes, causing, caused

VERB To **cause** something means to make it happen.

cautious

ADJECTIVE Someone who is **cautious** acts carefully to avoid possible danger.

cave **caves**

NOUN A **cave** is a large hole in the side of a hill or cliff, or under the ground.

CD **CDs**

NOUN CD is an abbreviation of **compact disc**.

CD-ROM **CD-ROMs**

NOUN **CD-ROM** is an abbreviation of **compact disc read-only memory**. It is a disc which can be played on a computer to show sounds and pictures.

ceiling **ceilings**

NOUN The **ceiling** is the inside roof of a room.

celebrate **celebrates, celebrating, celebrated**

VERB If you **celebrate** something, you do something enjoyable like having a party, to show it is a special occasion.

celery

NOUN **Celery** is a vegetable with long, pale green stalks.
See *Vegetables* on page 256.

cell **cells**

NOUN **1** Animals and plants are made from tiny parts called **cells**.
NOUN **2** A **cell** is also a small room where a prisoner lives.

cellar **cellars**

NOUN A **cellar** is a room under a house where you can store things.

Celsius

ADJECTIVE You use degrees **Celsius** to measure temperature. In the Celsius scale, 0 degrees (0°C) is the freezing point of water and 100 degrees (100°C) is its boiling point.

cement

NOUN **Cement** is a grey powder which is mixed with sand and water and used to make bricks stick together.

cemetery **cemeteries**

NOUN A **cemetery** is a place where dead people are buried.

centigrade

ADJECTIVE **Centigrade** means the same as **Celsius**.

centimetre **centimetres**

NOUN A **centimetre** (cm) is a measure of length. It is the same as 10 millimetres.

centipede **centipedes**

NOUN A **centipede** is a tiny animal like a worm, but with lots of legs.

central

ADJECTIVE Something that is **central** is in the middle of an object or an area.

centre **centres**

NOUN **1** The **centre** of anything is the middle of it.
NOUN **2** A **centre** is a place where people can go for a particular purpose, for example sports.

century **centuries**

NOUN A **century** is a period of 100 years. The 21st century is the time between 2000 and 2099.

cereal **cereals**

NOUN **1** Cereal is a plant which has seeds called grain that can be used for food.
NOUN **2** Cereal is also a food made from grain that is often eaten for breakfast.

ceremony **ceremonies**

NOUN A **ceremony** is a set of formal actions performed at a special occasion such as a wedding.

certain

ADJECTIVE If you are **certain** of something, you are sure it is true.

certificate certificates

NOUN A **certificate** is a piece of paper which says that something important like a birth or marriage took place.

chain chains

NOUN A **chain** is made from rings of metal joined together in a line.

chair chairs

NOUN A **chair** is a seat with a back, for one person.

chalk

NOUN **Chalk** is a soft white rock. It can be made into sticks for writing on blackboards.

champion champions

NOUN A **champion** is a person who has beaten everyone else in a contest.

chance chances

NOUN **1** If there is a **chance** that something will happen, it might happen.
NOUN **2** If you are given a **chance** to do something, you are allowed to do it if you want to.
by chance PHRASE If something happens **by chance**, it has not been planned.

change changes, changing, changed

VERB **1** When something **changes**, it becomes different.
VERB **2** When you **change** your clothes, you put on different ones.
NOUN **3** If there is a **change** in something, it is different in some way.
NOUN **4** **Change** is the money you are given when you pay more than the right amount for something.

channel channels

NOUN **1** A **channel** is a passage for water or other liquid.
NOUN **2** Television companies use **channels** to broadcast programmes.

chaos

NOUN **Chaos** is a state of complete confusion, where nothing is organized.

chapter chapters

NOUN A **chapter** is a part of a book.

character characters

NOUN **1** The **characters** of a book, film or play are the people it is about.
NOUN **2** Someone's **character** is the sort of person they are. *She has a kind character.*

charge charges, charging, charged

VERB **1** If someone **charges** you money, they ask you to pay for something.
VERB **2** If something or someone **charges** towards you, they rush forward.
in charge PHRASE If you are **in charge** of something, you are the person looking after it.

charity charities

NOUN A **charity** is an organization which raises money for a particular cause, such as people in need.

charm charms

NOUN **1** A **charm** is a small ornament that is fixed to a bracelet or necklace.
NOUN **2** A **charm** is also a magical spell or an object that is supposed to bring good luck.

chart charts

NOUN **1** A **chart** is a sheet of paper that shows things like dates or numbers.
NOUN **2** A **chart** can also be a map of the sea or of the stars.

chase chases, chasing, chased

VERB If you **chase** someone, you run after them to try and catch them.

chat chats

NOUN A **chat** is a friendly talk about things that are not very important.

a
b
Cc
d
e
f
g
h
i
j
k
l
m
n
o
p
q
r
s
t
u
v
w
x
y
z

a

b

Cc

d

e

f

g

h

i

j

k

l

m

n

o

p

q

r

s

t

u

v

w

x

y

z

cheap **cheaper, cheapest**

ADJECTIVE Something **cheap** costs very little, or less than you might expect.

cheat **cheats, cheating, cheated**

VERB When someone **cheats**, they lie or do unfair things to get what they want.

check **checks, checking, checked**

VERB **1** If you **check** something, you make sure it is correct or safe.

NOUN **2** A **check** is a pattern of squares.

checkout **checkouts**

NOUN A **checkout** is the place in a supermarket where you pay.

cheek **cheeks**

NOUN Your **cheeks** are the sides of your face below your eyes.

cheer **cheers, cheering, cheered**

VERB When you **cheer**, you shout to show you are pleased about something or to encourage a person or team.

cheerful

ADJECTIVE Someone who is **cheerful** shows they are feeling happy.

cheese **cheeses**

NOUN **Cheese** is a food made from milk. Some cheeses have a strong flavour.

cheetah **cheetahs**

NOUN A **cheetah** is a large wild animal of the cat family, with black spots.

chemist **chemists**

NOUN **1** A **chemist** is a person who makes up medicine.

NOUN **2** The **chemist** is a shop where you can buy medicine and things like soap and toothpaste.

NOUN **3** A **chemist** can be a scientist trained in chemistry.

chemistry

NOUN **Chemistry** is the scientific study of how substances are made up and how they work together.

cheque **cheques**

NOUN A **cheque** is a piece of paper that people use to pay for things.

cherry **cherries**

NOUN A **cherry** is a small round red or black fruit with a hard seed called a stone in the middle.

See *Fruit* on page 257.

chess

NOUN **Chess** is a game for two people. It is played on a board marked in black and white squares.

chest **chests**

NOUN **1** Your **chest** is the top part of the front of your body, between your neck and your waist.

NOUN **2** A **chest** is a large heavy box, usually made of wood.

chestnut **chestnuts**

NOUN **1** A **chestnut** is a large tree.

NOUN **2** A **chestnut** is also a shiny brown nut that grows on a chestnut tree.

chew **chews, chewing, chewed**

VERB When you **chew** food, you bite it several times.

chick **chicks**

NOUN A **chick** is a baby bird.

See *Young animals* on page 260.

chicken **chickens**

NOUN A **chicken** is a bird kept on a farm for its eggs and meat.

chickenpox

NOUN **Chickenpox** is an illness that gives you itchy spots.

chief chiefs

NOUN A **chief** is a person in charge of other people.

child children

NOUN A **child** is a young boy or girl.

childhood

NOUN A person's **childhood** is the time of life when they are a child.

childish

ADJECTIVE You call a person **childish** if they are not acting in an adult way.

children

PLURAL NOUN **Children** is the plural of **child**.

chilly chillier, chilliest

ADJECTIVE If you feel **chilly**, you are not quite warm enough to be comfortable.

chime chimes

NOUN A **chime** is the musical sound made by a bell or a clock.

chimney chimneys

NOUN A **chimney** is a pipe which takes smoke from a fire up into the air.

chimpanzee chimpanzees

NOUN A **chimpanzee** is a small ape with dark fur that lives in forests in Africa.

chin chins

NOUN Your **chin** is the part of your face below your mouth.

chip chips, chipping, chipped

NOUN 1 A **chip** is a long thin fried piece of potato.
NOUN 2 A silicon **chip** is a tiny piece of special material used in computers.
VERB 3 When you **chip** something, you break a small piece off it.

chisel chisels

NOUN A **chisel** is a tool with a long thin blade and a sharp end, which is used for cutting wood or stone.

chocolate chocolates

NOUN 1 **Chocolate** is a brown sweet or drink made from cocoa.
NOUN 2 A **chocolate** is a sweet covered with a layer of chocolate.

choice choices

NOUN 1 A **choice** is the different things that you can choose from.
NOUN 2 A **choice** can also be someone or something that you choose. *If you need a captain, Jessica would be a good choice.*

choir choirs

NOUN A **choir** is a group of people who sing together.

choke chokes, choking, choked

VERB If you **choke**, you cannot breathe because not enough air can get to your lungs. *He choked on a chicken bone.*

choose chooses, choosing, chose, chosen

VERB To **choose** something is to decide which thing you want to have or do.

chop chops, chopping, chopped

VERB 1 When someone **chops** something like wood, they cut it with an axe.
NOUN 2 A **chop** is a slice of meat on a bone.

chorus choruses

NOUN A **chorus** is a part of a song which is repeated after each verse.

a
b
Cc
d
e
f
g
h
i
j
k
l
m
n
o
p
q
r
s
t
u
v
w
x
y
z

chose
VERB **Chose** is the past tense of **choose**.

chosen
VERB **Chosen** is the past participle of **choose**.

Christian **Christians**
NOUN A **Christian** is someone who follows the teachings of Jesus Christ.

Christmas **Christmases**
NOUN **Christmas** is a Christian festival held on December 25, when the birth of Jesus Christ is celebrated.

chrysalis **chrysalises**
NOUN A **chrysalis** is a butterfly or moth when it is developing from a caterpillar to a fully grown adult.

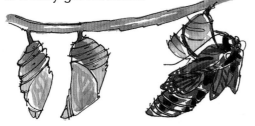

chuckle **chuckles, chuckling, chuckled**
VERB When you **chuckle**, you laugh quietly.

church **churches**
NOUN A **church** is a building where Christians worship.

cigarette **cigarettes**
NOUN A **cigarette** is a thin roll of paper with tobacco in, which people smoke.

cinema **cinemas**
NOUN A **cinema** is a place where people watch films.

circle **circles**
NOUN A **circle** is a perfect round shape.
circular ADJECTIVE
See *Colours and flat shapes* on page 271.

circuit **circuits**
NOUN A **circuit** is the complete path that an electric current flows through. You can make a simple circuit with a battery, a bulb and wires.

circumference **circumferences**
NOUN The **circumference** of a circle is the distance around its edge.

circus **circuses**
NOUN A **circus** is a travelling group of people such as clowns and acrobats.

city **cities**
NOUN A **city** is a large busy town.

claim **claims, claiming, claimed**
VERB **1** If someone **claims** something, they ask for it because it is theirs.
VERB **2** If you **claim** something is the case, you say it is the case. *Amy **claims** she was the first to finish.*

clap **claps, clapping, clapped**
VERB When you **clap**, you make a noise by hitting your hands together.

class **classes**
NOUN **1** A **class** is a group of people who are taught together.
NOUN **2** A **class** is also a group of people or things that are alike in some way.

classify **classifies, classifying, classified**
VERB To **classify** things is to arrange them in groups with similar features. *These books are **classified** as non-fiction.*

classroom **classrooms**
NOUN A **classroom** is a room in a school where children have lessons.

clause **clauses**
NOUN In grammar, a **clause** is a group of words with a subject and a verb. It may be a complete sentence or one part of a sentence. For example, "the girl laughed" is a clause because it has a subject (the girl) and a verb (laughed).

close

claw **claws**

NOUN The **claws** of a bird or animal are the hard curved nails at the end of its feet.

clay

NOUN **Clay** is a type of sticky earth that goes hard when it is dry. It is used to make bricks and pots.

clean **cleaner, cleanest**

ADJECTIVE If something is **clean**, it is free from dirt.

clear **clearer, clearest; clears, clearing, cleared**

ADJECTIVE **1** If a thing is **clear**, you can see through it.

ADJECTIVE **2** If something you say or write is **clear**, it is easy to understand.

VERB **3** If you **clear** an area, you move things that are not wanted out of the way.

clench **clenches, clenching, clenched**

VERB When you **clench** your fist or teeth, you close them tightly.

clever **cleverer, cleverest**

ADJECTIVE Someone who is **clever** is able to learn and understand things easily.

click **clicks, clicking, clicked**

VERB When you **click** something, it makes a short snapping sound.

cliff **cliffs**

NOUN A **cliff** is a steep hill by the sea.

climate **climates**

NOUN The **climate** of a place is the sort of weather it usually has.

climb **climbs, climbing, climbed**

VERB When you **climb** something, you move upwards using your hands and feet.

cling **clings, clinging, clung**

VERB If you **cling** to someone or something, you hold onto them tightly.

clinic **clinics**

NOUN A **clinic** is where people go to get help from a doctor or nurse.

clip **clips, clipping, clipped**

NOUN **1** A **clip** is something small and springy which holds things in place.

VERB **2** If you **clip** something like a hedge, you cut small pieces off it.

cloak **cloaks**

NOUN A **cloak** is a loose coat without sleeves that fastens at the neck.

cloakroom **cloakrooms**

NOUN A **cloakroom** is a room where coats can be left.

clock **clocks**

NOUN A **clock** is an instrument that measures and shows the time.

clockwise

ADVERB If something goes **clockwise**, it moves in the same direction as the hands on a clock.

clockwork

ADJECTIVE **Clockwork** toys move when they are wound up with a key.

close **closer, closest; closes, closing, closed**

(*rhymes with* **dose**) ADJECTIVE **1** If something is **close**, it is very near.

(*rhymes with* **doze**) VERB **2** When you **close** something like a door, you shut it.

closed

ADJECTIVE If something is **closed**, it is not open.

cloth **cloths**

NOUN **1** Cloth is material made from something like cotton or wool.

NOUN **2** A **cloth** is a piece of cloth used for cleaning.

clothes

PLURAL NOUN **Clothes** are the things people wear, such as shirts, trousers and dresses.

cloud **clouds**

NOUN **1** A **cloud** is a patch of white or grey mist that floats in the sky.

NOUN **2** You can use **cloud** to describe a lot of smoke, steam or dust.

cloudy ADJECTIVE

clover

NOUN **Clover** is a small wild plant. It has white or purple flowers, and leaves divided into three parts.

clown **clowns**

NOUN A **clown** is someone in a circus who wears funny clothes and does silly things to make people laugh.

club **clubs**

NOUN A **club** is an organization joined by people who are interested in the same thing, such as chess or riding.

clue **clues**

NOUN A **clue** is something that helps to solve a problem or mystery.

clump **clumps**

NOUN A **clump** is a small group of plants growing together.

clumsy **clumsier, clumsiest**

ADJECTIVE Someone who is **clumsy** moves awkwardly and carelessly.

clumsily ADVERB

clung

VERB **Clung** is the past tense of **cling**.

cluster **clusters**

NOUN A **cluster** is a number of things close together in a small group.

clutch **clutches, clutching, clutched**

VERB **1** If you **clutch** something, you hold it tightly with your hand.

NOUN **2** A **clutch** is a group of eggs laid by a bird.

See *Collective nouns* on page 262.

clutter

NOUN **Clutter** is an untidy mess.

co-

PREFIX Co- means together. For example, "coeducation" is boys and girls being taught together.

See *Prefixes* on page 264.

coach **coaches**

NOUN **1** A **coach** is a long motor vehicle used for taking passengers on long journeys.

NOUN **2** A **coach** is also a section of a train that carries passengers.

NOUN **3** A **coach** is someone who trains you for a sport or gives you extra lessons.

coal

NOUN **Coal** is a hard black rock which is dug out of the ground and burned to give heat.

coarse **coarser, coarsest**

ADJECTIVE Anything that is **coarse** looks and feels rough.

coast **coasts**

NOUN The **coast** is the place where the land meets the sea.

coat **coats**

NOUN **1** A **coat** is a piece of clothing with long sleeves, that you wear over other clothes when you go out.

NOUN **2** An animal's **coat** is its fur.

NOUN **3** A layer of paint is called a **coat**.

cobweb **cobwebs**

NOUN A **cobweb** is a net made by a spider to trap insects.

cock **cocks**

NOUN A **cock** is any male bird.

cocoa

NOUN **Cocoa** is a brown powder made from the seeds of the cacao tree, and also a hot drink made from this powder.

coconut **coconuts**

NOUN A **coconut** is a large nut with white flesh, milky juice, and a hard hairy shell.

cocoon **cocoons**

NOUN A **cocoon** is a covering of silky threads that some young insects make for themselves before they grow into adults.

cod

NOUN A **cod** is a large sea fish which is caught for food.

code **codes**

NOUN **1** A **code** is a system of changing letters in a message for other letters or symbols, so that only people who know the code can read it.

NOUN **2** A **code** is also a group of letters and numbers that identify something. *Do you know the telephone **code** for York?*

NOUN **3** A **code** is also a set of rules.

coffee

NOUN **Coffee** is a coarse powder made by grinding roasted coffee beans, and also a hot drink made from this powder.

cog **cogs**

NOUN A **cog** is a wheel with teeth which turns another part of a machine.

coil **coils**

NOUN A **coil** is a series of loops into which something has been wound.

coin **coins**

NOUN A **coin** is a small piece of metal used as money.

cold **colder, coldest; colds**

ADJECTIVE **1** If the weather is **cold**, the temperature outside is low.

NOUN **2** A **cold** is a common illness. You sneeze and your nose feels blocked.

collage **collages**

NOUN A **collage** is a picture made by sticking pieces of paper or cloth onto a surface.

collapse **collapses, collapsing, collapsed**

VERB If someone or something **collapses**, they suddenly fall down.

collar **collars**

NOUN **1** The **collar** of a shirt or jacket is the part that fits round your neck.

NOUN **2** A **collar** is also a leather band round the neck of a dog or cat.

collect **collects, collecting, collected**

VERB **1** If you **collect** a number of things, you bring them together for a special reason. *She **collected** sticks for firewood.*

VERB **2** If you **collect** someone or something from a place, you call there and take them away. *We had to **collect** her from school.*

collection **collections**

NOUN A **collection** is a group of things brought together over a period of time. *My dad's got a huge stamp **collection**.*

collective noun **collective nouns**

NOUN In grammar, a **collective noun** refers to a group of things. For example, a group of sheep is called a "flock". See *Collective nouns* on page 262.

college **colleges**

NOUN A **college** is where people go to study after they have left school.

collide

collide **collides, colliding, collided**
VERB If a moving object **collides** with something, it hits it.
collision NOUN

colon **colons**
NOUN The punctuation mark : is a **colon**. You can use it in several ways, for example in front of a list of things.
See *Punctuation* on page 264.

colour **colours**
NOUN The **colour** of something is the way it looks in daylight. *The **colour** of grass is green.*
See *Colours* on page 271.

colt **colts**
NOUN A **colt** is a young male horse.

column **columns**
NOUN **1** A **column** is a tall stone post which supports part of a building.

NOUN **2** A **column** is also a vertical strip of print in a newspaper or magazine.
NOUN **3** If numbers are arranged in vertical lists, these are called **columns**.

comb **combs**
NOUN A **comb** is a flat piece of plastic or metal with narrow teeth on one edge. You use it to tidy your hair.

come **comes, coming, came, come**
VERB **1** To **come** to a place is to move there or arrive there.
VERB **2** If you **come** from a place, you were born there, or it is your home.

comedy **comedies**
NOUN A **comedy** is a play or film that makes people laugh.

comet **comets**
NOUN A **comet** is an object which travels around the sun, leaving a long bright trail behind it.

comfort **comforts, comforting, comforted**
VERB If you **comfort** someone, you make them feel less worried or unhappy.

comfortable
ADJECTIVE If something is **comfortable**, it is easy to wear or use.

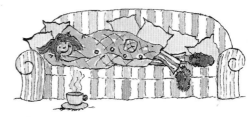

comic **comics**
NOUN A **comic** is a magazine that tells stories in pictures.

comma **commas**
NOUN A **comma** is a punctuation mark (,) which is used to separate parts of a sentence or items on a list.
See *Punctuation* on page 264.

command **commands, commanding, commanded**
VERB If you **command** someone to do something, you order them to do it.

commercial **commercials**
NOUN A **commercial** is an advertisement on television or radio.

common
ADJECTIVE If something is **common**, you often see it or it often happens.

common noun **common nouns**
NOUN **Common nouns** name things in general. For example, "boy", "dog" and "computer" are all common nouns.
See *Noun* on page 262.

common sense
NOUN If you have **common sense**, you usually act sensibly and do the right thing.

commotion
NOUN A **commotion** is a lot of noise, confusion and excitement.

communicate **communicates, communicating, communicated**
VERB If you **communicate** with someone, you give them information by talking or writing to them.

compact disc **compact discs**
NOUN A **compact disc** is a round flat silver-coloured object which can store information. It is called a **CD** for short.

company **companies**
NOUN **1 Company** is being with others so you are not lonely.
NOUN **2** A **company** is a group of people who work together to make or sell things.

comparative **comparatives**
NOUN In grammar, the **comparative** is the form of an adjective which has "more" of that adjective. For example, "happier" is the comparative of "happy".
See *Adjective* on page 263.

compare **compares, comparing, compared**
VERB When you **compare** two or more things, you look at them to see in what ways they are the same or different.

compass **compasses**
NOUN **1** A **compass** is an instrument with a needle that always points to north.
NOUN **2** A **pair of compasses** is an instrument used for drawing circles.

compass point **compass points**
NOUN The main **compass points** are north, south, east and west.

competition **competitions**
NOUN A **competition** is an event to find out who is best at doing something.

complain **complains, complaining, complained**
VERB If you **complain**, you say that you are not happy about something.

complete
ADJECTIVE **1** If something is **complete**, it has been finished.
ADJECTIVE **2** If you talk about a **complete** thing, you mean all of it. *I need a complete change of clothes.*

complicated
ADJECTIVE Something **complicated** is made up of so many parts that it is difficult to understand or deal with.

compose **composes, composing, composed**
VERB If you **compose** something, like a poem or a piece of music, you write it.

compound **compounds**
NOUN In language, a **compound** is a word that is made up of two or more words. "Playground", "armchair" and "toothache" are all compounds.

computer **computers**
NOUN A **computer** is a machine that stores information and works things out according to instructions in a program.

concave
ADJECTIVE A **concave** surface curves inwards.

conceal **conceals, concealing, concealed**
VERB If you **conceal** something, you hide it carefully.

concentrate **concentrates, concentrating, concentrated**
VERB If you **concentrate** on something, you give it all your attention.

a b **Cc** d e f g h i j k l m n o p q r s t u v w x y z

concerned

ADJECTIVE If you are **concerned** about something, it worries you.

concert concerts

NOUN A **concert** is a performance by musicians, usually in a big hall.

conclusion conclusions

NOUN **1** A **conclusion** is something you decide is true after you have thought carefully.

NOUN **2** The **conclusion** of something is its ending.

concrete

NOUN **Concrete** is a building material made of cement, sand and water, which goes hard when it is set.

condition conditions

NOUN **1** The **condition** of something is the state it is in.

NOUN **2** A **condition** is a rule you must agree to before you are allowed to do something. *You can go out on one condition – you must be home by five.*

conductor conductors

NOUN A **conductor** is someone who controls the way musicians play together.

cone cones

NOUN A **cone** is a solid curved shape with a flat circular base and a pointed top.

See *Solid shapes* on page 271.

confess confesses, confessing, confessed

VERB If you **confess**, you say that you have done something wrong.

confident

ADJECTIVE **1** If you are **confident** about something, you are sure about it.

ADJECTIVE **2** People who are **confident** know that they can do something well.

confuse confuses, confusing, confused

VERB **1** To **confuse** someone means to make them unsure what to do. *The new road layout confused everyone.*

VERB **2** If you **confuse** two things, you mix them up by mistake. *I always confuse the twins because they are so alike.*

congratulate congratulates, congratulating, congratulated

VERB If you **congratulate** someone, you say you are pleased that something special has happened to them.

conjunction conjunctions

NOUN In grammar, a **conjunction** is a word that joins two other words or parts of a sentence. "And", "but", "while" and "although" are all conjunctions.

conker conkers

NOUN **Conkers** are hard brown nuts from a horse chestnut tree.

connect connects, connecting, connected

VERB If you **connect** two things, you join them together.

connective connectives

NOUN In grammar, a **connective** is a word or phrase that joins parts of a text. For example, "and", "at last" and "because" are connectives.

conquer conquers, conquering, conquered

VERB To **conquer** people is to take control of their country by force.

conscious

ADJECTIVE If you are **conscious**, you are awake and know what is happening.

consecutive

ADJECTIVE If things are **consecutive**, they happen one after the other. *October, November and December are consecutive months.*

consider considers, considering, considered

VERB If you **consider** something, you think about it carefully.

consist consists, consisting, consisted

VERB Something that **consists** of particular things is made up of them.

consonant consonants

NOUN A **consonant** is any letter of the alphabet except a, e, i, o and u. See **vowel**.

constant

ADJECTIVE Something that is **constant** happens all the time. *She complained of a constant headache.*

construct constructs, constructing, constructed

VERB If you **construct** something, you build it or make it.

consume consumes, consuming, consumed

VERB If you **consume** something, you eat or drink it, or use it up.

contain contains, containing, contained

VERB The things that something **contains** are the things in it.

container containers

NOUN A **container** is something you put things in.

content

ADJECTIVE If you are **content**, you are happy and satisfied with your life.

contents

PLURAL NOUN The **contents** of something like a box or cake are the things in it. The **contents page** of a book tells you what is in it.

contest contests

NOUN A **contest** is a competition or game which you try to win.

continent continents

NOUN A **continent** is a very large area of land, such as Africa or Asia.

continue continues, continuing, continued

VERB If you **continue** to do something, you go on doing it.

continuous

ADJECTIVE Something that is **continuous** goes on without stopping.

contraction contractions

NOUN A **contraction** is a shortened form of word or words. For example, "I'm" is a contraction of "I am".

contradict contradicts, contradicting, contradicted

VERB If you **contradict** someone, you say the opposite of what they have just said.

control controls, controlling, controlled

VERB 1 If you **control** something, you make it behave exactly as you want it to.
NOUN 2 The **controls** on a machine are knobs or other things used to work it.

convenient

ADJECTIVE If something is **convenient**, it is easy to use or do.

conversation conversations

NOUN If you have a **conversation** with someone, you talk to each other.

convex

ADJECTIVE A **convex** surface curves outwards.

a
b
Cc
d
e
f
g
h
i
j
k
l
m
n
o
p
q
r
s
t
u
v
w
x
y
z

convince

convince convinces, convincing, convinced
VERB If someone or something **convinces** you, they make you believe that something is true.

cook cooks, cooking, cooked
VERB When you **cook** food, you prepare it for eating by heating it.

cooker cookers
NOUN A **cooker** is a piece of equipment for cooking food.

cool cooler, coolest
ADJECTIVE If something is **cool**, its temperature is low but it is not cold.

coordinates
NOUN **Coordinates** are two numbers or letters which help you find the exact position of something. They are often used on maps, graphs and charts.

cope copes, coping, coped
VERB If you **cope** with a task or problem, you deal with it successfully.

copper
NOUN **Copper** is a reddish-brown metal.

copy copies, copying, copied
NOUN **1** A **copy** is something made to look exactly like something else.
VERB **2** If you **copy** something, you make a copy of it.
VERB **3** If you **copy** what someone does, you do the same thing.

coral corals
NOUN **Coral** is a hard substance that forms in the sea from the skeletons of tiny animals called corals.

cord cords
NOUN **Cord** is thick, strong string.

core cores
NOUN The **core** of a fruit is the hard part in the middle that contains seeds.

cork corks
NOUN **1** Cork is the light bark of the cork oak tree.
NOUN **2** A **cork** is a piece of cork used to block the open end of a bottle.

corn
NOUN **Corn** is a cereal crop, such as wheat or sweet corn.

corner corners
NOUN A **corner** is the place where two edges or roads join.

correct corrects, correcting, corrected
ADJECTIVE **1** Something that is **correct** is true and has no mistakes.
VERB **2** If you **correct** your work, you put right any mistakes you made.

corridor corridors
NOUN A **corridor** is a long passage in a building or train.

cost costs, costing, cost
VERB If something **costs** an amount of money, you can buy it for that amount.

costume costumes
NOUN A **costume** is the clothes worn by an actor, or that people wear for special events.

cosy cosier, cosiest
ADJECTIVE A house or room that is **cosy** is comfortable and warm, and not too big.

cot cots
NOUN A **cot** is a bed with high sides for a baby or a young child.

cottage cottages

NOUN A **cottage** is a small house, usually in the country.

cotton

NOUN **1 Cotton** is cloth made from the soft fibres of the cotton plant.

NOUN **2 Cotton** is also a thread used for sewing.

NOUN **3 Cotton wool** is soft fluffy cotton, often used for cleaning the skin.

cough coughs

NOUN A **cough** is a noise made by someone forcing air out of their throat.

could

VERB **1 Could** is part of the verb **can**. You use **could** to say that something might happen. *It could rain tomorrow.*

VERB **2** You also say **could** when you are asking for something politely. *Could you please tell me the way to the station?*

council councils

NOUN The **council** is a group of people who look after the affairs of a town, district or county.

count counts, counting, counted

VERB **1** When you **count**, you say numbers in order. *Count up to a hundred.*

VERB **2** If you **count** a number of things, you are finding out how many there are.

counter counters

NOUN **1** A **counter** is a long narrow table in a shop, where things are sold.

NOUN **2** A **counter** is also a small round flat object, usually made of plastic, that is used in board games.

country countries

NOUN **1** A **country** is a land that has its own government and language.

NOUN **2** The **country** is land away from towns and cities.

couple couples

NOUN **1** A **couple** of things or people means two of them. *It should only take a couple of days.*

NOUN **2** Two people are sometimes called a **couple**, especially if they are married or having a relationship.

coupon coupons

NOUN A **coupon** is a piece of printed paper that allows you to pay less than usual for something.

courage

NOUN **Courage** is not showing that you are afraid of something.

course courses

NOUN **1** A **course** is a series of lessons.

NOUN **2** A **course** can also be one part of a meal.

of course PHRASE You use **of course** to make something you are saying stronger. *Of course I still want to go.*

court courts

NOUN **1** A **court** is an area marked out for a game like tennis or badminton.

NOUN **2** A **court** is also a place where things to do with the law are decided.

NOUN **3** The **court** of a king or queen is where they live with their family.

courtyard courtyards

NOUN A **courtyard** is an open flat area of ground with walls all round it.

cousin cousins

NOUN Your **cousin** is a child of your uncle or aunt.

cover covers, covering, covered

VERB **1** If you **cover** something, you put something over it to protect or hide it.

NOUN **2** The **covers** on a bed are the blankets or duvet that you have over you to keep you warm.

NOUN **3** The **cover** of a book or magazine is the outside of it.

cow **cows**

NOUN A **cow** is a large farm animal that gives milk.

coward **cowards**

NOUN A **coward** is someone who avoids anything dangerous, painful or difficult.

cowboy **cowboys**

NOUN A **cowboy** is a man whose job is to look after cattle.

crab **crabs**

NOUN A **crab** is a sea animal. It has four pairs of legs, two pincers, and a flat round body covered by a shell.

crack **cracks, cracking, cracked**

VERB **1** If you **crack** something, or it cracks, it has a small split in it but does not quite break.

NOUN **2** A **crack** is the line on something that shows it is nearly broken.

NOUN **3** A **crack** is also a sudden loud noise.

cracker **crackers**

NOUN **1** A **cracker** is a thin crisp biscuit, often slightly salty.

NOUN **2** A **cracker** can be a cardboard tube covered in coloured paper, that people have at parties. It makes a sharp sound when you pull the ends apart.

cradle **cradles**

NOUN A **cradle** is a small box-shaped bed for a baby.

crane **cranes**

NOUN **1** A **crane** is a machine that moves heavy things by lifting them.

NOUN **2** A **crane** is also a large water bird with long legs and a long neck.

crash **crashes, crashing, crashed**

NOUN **1** A **crash** is a traffic accident.

NOUN **2** A **crash** is also a sudden loud noise like something breaking.

VERB **3** If something **crashes**, it hits something else and makes a loud noise.

crate **crates**

NOUN A **crate** is a large box used for transporting or storing things.

crawl **crawls, crawling, crawled**

VERB When you **crawl**, you move forward on your hands and knees.

crayon **crayons**

NOUN A **crayon** is a coloured pencil.

craze **crazes**

NOUN A **craze** is something that is very popular for a short time.

crazy **crazier, craziest**

ADJECTIVE **1** Someone or something **crazy** is very strange or foolish.

ADJECTIVE **2** If you are **crazy** about something, you are very keen on it.

creak **creaks, creaking, creaked**

VERB If something **creaks**, it makes an odd squeaking sound.

cream

ADJECTIVE **1** Something that is **cream** in colour is yellowish-white.

NOUN **2** Cream is the pale yellow liquid taken from the top of milk.

crease **creases, creasing, creased**

NOUN **1** A **crease** is a line made by folding or wrinkling something.

VERB **2** If you **crease** something, you make lines appear on it.

create **creates, creating, created**

VERB To **create** something means to cause it to happen, or exist.

creature **creatures**

NOUN A **creature** is any animal, such as a bird, fish or insect.

creep **creeps, creeping, crept**
VERB If you **creep** somewhere, you move quietly and slowly.

crescent **crescents**
NOUN A **crescent** is a curved shape that is wider in the middle than at the ends, like a new moon.

crew **crews**
NOUN A **crew** is the people who work on a ship, aircraft or spaceship.

cricket **crickets**
NOUN **1** Cricket is an outdoor game between two teams of eleven players.
NOUN **2** A **cricket** is a small jumping insect that makes a chirping sound by rubbing its wings together.

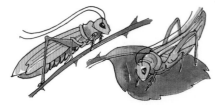

cried
VERB **Cried** is the past tense of **cry**.

cries
VERB **Cries** is a present tense form of **cry**.

crime **crimes**
NOUN A **crime** is something which is against the law.

criminal **criminals**
NOUN A **criminal** is someone who has done something that is against the law.

crimson
ADJECTIVE **Crimson** is dark red.

crinkle **crinkles, crinkling, crinkled**
VERB When something **crinkles**, it becomes slightly creased.

crisp **crisper, crispest; crisps**
ADJECTIVE **1** Things like fruit and biscuits that are **crisp** are fresh and firm.
NOUN **2** A **crisp** is a crunchy, thinly sliced piece of fried potato.

criticize **criticizes, criticizing, criticized;** also spelt **criticise**
VERB If you **criticize** someone, you say what you think is wrong with them.

crocodile **crocodiles**
NOUN A **crocodile** is a large reptile, about five metres long.
See *Reptiles* on page 259.

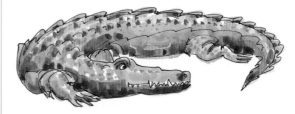

crocus **crocuses**
NOUN **Crocuses** are small yellow, purple or white spring flowers.

crooked
ADJECTIVE Something that is **crooked** is bent or twisted.

crop **crops**
NOUN A **crop** is plants grown for food.

cross **crosser, crossest; crosses, crossing, crossed**
ADJECTIVE **1** Someone who is **cross** is angry about something.
NOUN **2** A **cross** is a mark like + or ×.
VERB **3** If you **cross** something like a road, you go from one side to the other.

crossing **crossings**
NOUN A **crossing** is a place where you can cross the road safely.

crouch **crouches, crouching, crouched**
VERB If you **crouch** down, you bend your legs under you so that you are close to the ground.

crow **crows**

NOUN A **crow** is a large black bird.

crowd **crowds**

NOUN A **crowd** is a large number of people together in one place.

crowded

ADJECTIVE A place that is **crowded** is full of people.

crown **crowns**

NOUN A **crown** is an ornament that kings and queens sometimes wear on their heads.

cruel **crueller, cruellest**

ADJECTIVE Someone who is **cruel** hurts people or animals without caring.

cruise **cruises**

NOUN A **cruise** is a holiday on a ship that travels to different places.

crumb **crumbs**

NOUN A **crumb** is a very small piece of dry food such as bread or biscuit.

crumble **crumbles, crumbling, crumbled**

VERB If you **crumble** something that is soft, it breaks into lots of little pieces.

crumple **crumples, crumpling, crumpled**

VERB If you **crumple** paper or cloth, you squash it so that it is full of creases.

crunch **crunches, crunching, crunched**

VERB If you **crunch** something, you crush it noisily, for example between your teeth or under your feet.

crush **crushes, crushing, crushed**

VERB To **crush** something is to destroy its shape by squeezing it.

crust **crusts**

NOUN The **crust** is a hard layer on the outside of something such as bread.

cry **cries, crying, cried**

VERB **1** When you **cry**, tears come from your eyes.

NOUN **2** A **cry** is a sudden sound that you make when you are surprised or hurt.

crystal **crystals**

NOUN A **crystal** is a mineral that has formed into a regular shape.

cub **cubs**

NOUN A **cub** is a young wild animal such as a lion, fox or bear.
See *Young animals* on page 260.

cube **cubes**

NOUN A **cube** is a solid shape with six square faces all the same size.
See *Solid shapes* on page 271.

cuboid **cuboids**

NOUN A **cuboid** is a rectangular box shape with six faces. All the faces are rectangles.
See *Solid shapes* on page 271.

cuckoo **cuckoos**

NOUN A **cuckoo** is a grey bird. Cuckoos lay their eggs in other birds' nests.

cucumber **cucumbers**

NOUN A **cucumber** is a long, thin, dark green vegetable, eaten raw.
See *Vegetables* on page 256.

cuddle **cuddles, cuddling, cuddled**

VERB When you **cuddle** someone, you put your arms round them.

culprit **culprits**

NOUN A **culprit** is someone who has done something harmful or wrong.

cunning

ADJECTIVE Someone who is **cunning** plans to get what they want, often by tricking other people.

cup **cups**

NOUN **1** A **cup** is a small container with a handle, which you drink out of.

NOUN **2** A **cup** is also a prize for the winner of a game or competition.

cupboard **cupboards**

NOUN A **cupboard** is a piece of furniture with doors and shelves.

cure **cures, curing, cured**

NOUN **1** A **cure** is something that makes people better when they have been ill.
VERB **2** If someone or something **cures** a person, they make them well again.

curiosity

NOUN **Curiosity** is wanting to know about things.

curious

ADJECTIVE **1** Someone who is **curious** wants to know more about something.
ADJECTIVE **2** Something that is **curious** is unusual and hard to explain.

curl **curls, curling, curled**

VERB **1** If an animal **curls** up, it makes itself into a rounded shape.
NOUN **2** **Curls** are pieces of hair shaped in curves and circles.
curly ADJECTIVE

currant **currants**

NOUN **Currants** are small dried grapes.

current **currents**

NOUN **1** A **current** is a steady movement of water or air.
NOUN **2** A **current** is also the movement of electricity through a wire.

curriculum **curriculums or curricula**

NOUN A **curriculum** is the different courses taught at a school or college.

curry **curries**

NOUN **Curry** is an Indian dish made with spices.

cursor **cursors**

NOUN A **cursor** is a small sign on a computer screen that shows where the next letter or number will appear.

curtain **curtains**

NOUN A **curtain** is a large piece of material that you pull across a window to cover it.

curve **curves**

NOUN A **curve** is a smooth, gradually bending line.
curved ADJECTIVE

cushion **cushions**

NOUN A **cushion** is a soft object put on a seat to make it more comfortable.

custom **customs**

NOUN A **custom** is something that people usually do. *It's his **custom** to take the dog for a walk after supper.*

customer **customers**

NOUN A **customer** is a person who buys something, especially from a shop.

cut **cuts, cutting, cut**

VERB **1** If you **cut** yourself, you hurt yourself by accident on something sharp.
VERB **2** If you **cut** something, you use a knife or scissors to remove parts of it.

cutlery

NOUN **Cutlery** is the knives, forks and spoons that you eat your food with.

cycle **cycles, cycling, cycled**

NOUN **1** A **cycle** is a bicycle.
VERB **2** If you **cycle**, you ride a bicycle.
cyclist NOUN

cygnet **cygnets**

NOUN A **cygnet** is a young swan.
See *Young animals* on page 260.

cylinder **cylinders**

NOUN A **cylinder** is a three-dimensional shape like a tube with flat circular ends.
cylindrical ADJECTIVE
See *Solid shapes* on page 271.

a
b
Cc
d
e
f
g
h
i
j
k
l
m
n
o
p
q
r
s
t
u
v
w
x
y
z

a
b
c
Dd
e
f
g
h
i
j
k
l
m
n
o
p
q
r
s
t
u
v
w
x
y
z

Dd

dad **dads**
NOUN Your **dad** is your father.

daffodil **daffodils**
NOUN A **daffodil** is a yellow trumpet-shaped flower that blooms in the spring.

dagger **daggers**
NOUN A **dagger** is a weapon like a knife.

daily
ADJECTIVE Something that is **daily** happens every day.

dairy **dairies**
NOUN A **dairy** is a shop or company that sells milk and food made from milk, such as butter and cheese.

daisy **daisies**
NOUN A **daisy** is a small wild flower with white petals and a yellow centre.

dam **dams**
NOUN A **dam** is a wall built across a river or stream to hold back water.

damage **damages, damaging, damaged**
VERB To **damage** something means to harm or spoil it.

damp **damper, dampest**
ADJECTIVE Something that is **damp** is slightly wet.

dance **dances, dancing, danced**
VERB When you **dance**, you move your body in time to music.

dandelion **dandelions**
NOUN A **dandelion** is a wild plant with bright yellow flowers.

danger **dangers**
NOUN A **danger** is something that could harm you.

dangerous
ADJECTIVE If something is **dangerous**, it is likely to harm you.

dare **dares, daring, dared**
VERB If you **dare** to do something, you are brave enough to do it.

dark **darker, darkest**
ADJECTIVE When it is **dark**, there is not enough light to see properly.
darkness NOUN

dart **darts, darting, darted**
VERB **1** If a person or animal **darts**, they move suddenly and quickly.
NOUN **2** A **dart** is a short arrow that you throw in the game of darts.

dash **dashes, dashing, dashed**
VERB **1** If you **dash** somewhere, you run or go there quickly.
NOUN **2** A **dash** is the punctuation mark (–) which shows a change of subject, or which may be used instead of brackets.
See *Punctuation* on page 264.

data
NOUN **Data** is information, usually in the form of facts or figures.

database **databases**
NOUN A **database** is a collection of information, often stored in a computer.

date **dates**
NOUN **1** If someone asks you the **date**, you tell them the day and the month.
NOUN **2** A **date** is a small brown sticky fruit which grows on palm trees.

daughter **daughters**
NOUN A girl is the **daughter** of her parents.

dawdle **dawdles, dawdling, dawdled**
VERB If you **dawdle**, you walk slowly, taking more time than you should.

dawn

NOUN **Dawn** is the time of day when it first begins to get light.

day days

NOUN A **day** is the 24 hours between one midnight and the next.

daylight

NOUN **Daylight** is the light that there is during the day before it gets dark.

dazzle dazzles, dazzling, dazzled

VERB If a light **dazzles** you, it is so bright that you cannot really see for a while.

de-

PREFIX When **de-** is added to a noun or verb, it means to remove. For example, "deforest" means to take away the forest.

See *Prefixes* on page 264.

dead

ADJECTIVE A person, animal or plant that is **dead** is no longer living.

deaf deafer, deafest

ADJECTIVE Someone who is **deaf** cannot hear very well, or cannot hear at all.

deal deals, dealing, dealt

VERB **1** When you **deal** in a card game, you give cards to the players.

VERB **2** If you **deal** with something, you do what needs to be done with it.

dear dearer, dearest

ADJECTIVE **1** You use **Dear** at the beginning of a letter before the name of the person you are writing to.

ADJECTIVE **2** If something is **dear**, it costs a lot of money.

death

NOUN **Death** is the end of life, when an animal or person dies.

decade decades

NOUN A **decade** is a period of ten years.

decay decays, decaying, decayed

VERB When something like a plant or piece of meat **decays**, it becomes rotten.

deceive deceives, deceiving, deceived

VERB If someone **deceives** you, they make you believe something untrue.

December

NOUN **December** is the 12th month of the year. It has 31 days.

decide decides, deciding, decided

VERB If you **decide** to do something, you make up your mind to do it.

decimal decimals

ADJECTIVE **1** A **decimal** system involves counting in units of ten.

NOUN **2** A **decimal** or **decimal fraction** is written with a dot followed by numbers, such as 0·2, 8·35. The numbers after the dot represent tenths, hundredths and so on.

NOUN **3** A **decimal point** is the dot that comes between whole numbers and fractions.

NOUN **4** A **decimal place** is the position of a number after a decimal point.

decision decisions

NOUN A **decision** is a choice you make about what you think should be done.

deck decks

NOUN A **deck** is a floor on a ship or bus.

decorate decorates, decorating, decorated

VERB **1** If you **decorate** something, you add things to make it more attractive.

VERB **2** If someone **decorates** a room, they paper it or paint it.

decorations PLURAL NOUN

decrease decreases, decreasing, decreased

VERB If something **decreases**, or if you decrease it, it becomes less.

deep deeper, deepest

ADJECTIVE If something is **deep**, it goes a long way down. *The river is very **deep**.*

deer

NOUN A **deer** is a large hoofed animal. Male deer have horns called antlers.

defeat defeats, defeating, defeated

VERB If you **defeat** someone, you beat them in a game or battle.

defend defends, defending, defended

VERB If you **defend** someone or something, you do something to protect them against danger.
defence NOUN

define defines, defining, defined

VERB If you **define** something, you say what it is or what it means.

definite

ADJECTIVE **1** Something that is **definite** is unlikely to be changed. *We have a **definite** date for the outing.*

ADJECTIVE **2** **Definite** can also mean certain or true. *Lots of stories were going round, but they heard nothing **definite**.*
definitely ADVERB

definition definitions

NOUN A **definition** explains the meaning of a word.

degree degrees

NOUN **1** A **degree** is a unit of measurement of temperature, for example, 20°C.

NOUN **2** In maths, a **degree** is a unit of measurement of angles. For example, a right angle is 90°.

delay delays, delaying, delayed

VERB If something **delays** you, it causes you to slow down or be late.

delete deletes, deleting, deleted

VERB If you **delete** some writing, you cross it out or remove it.

deliberate

ADJECTIVE If you do something that is **deliberate**, you do it on purpose.
deliberately ADVERB

delicate

ADJECTIVE **1** Something that is **delicate** is small and graceful.

ADJECTIVE **2** Someone who is **delicate** becomes ill easily.

delicious

ADJECTIVE Food that is **delicious** tastes or smells very nice.

delight delights, delighting, delighted

VERB If something **delights** you, it gives you a lot of pleasure.
delighted ADJECTIVE

deliver delivers, delivering, delivered

VERB If you **deliver** something, you take it to someone and hand it to them.

demand demands, demanding, demanded

VERB If you **demand** something, you say strongly that is what you want.

demonstrate **demonstrates, demonstrating, demonstrated**
VERB **1** If someone **demonstrates** something, they show you how to do it.
VERB **2** If people **demonstrate**, they hold a public meeting or march to show they are strongly for or against something.
demonstration NOUN

den **dens**
NOUN A **den** is the home of some wild animals such as lions or foxes.

dense **denser, densest**
ADJECTIVE Something **dense** is hard to see through. *They were in a **dense** forest.*

dent **dents, denting, dented**
VERB If somebody **dents** something, they make a dip in it by hitting it.

dentist **dentists**
NOUN A **dentist** is someone who looks after people's teeth.

deny **denies, denying, denied**
VERB If you **deny** something, you say that it is untrue.

depart **departs, departing, departed**
VERB When someone or something **departs** from a place, they leave it.
departure NOUN

depend **depends, depending, depended**
VERB **1** If you **depend** on someone, you need them.
VERB **2** If you can **depend** on someone, you know you can trust them.

depth
NOUN The **depth** of something is how deep it is.

descend **descends, descending, descended**
VERB To **descend** means to go down.

descending
ADJECTIVE When things are in **descending** order, each thing is lower than the one before it. *The numbers 10, 9, 8 and 7 are in **descending** order.*

describe **describes, describing, described**
VERB If you **describe** a person or thing, you say what they are like.
description NOUN

desert **deserts**
NOUN A **desert** is very dry land with very little plant life.

deserted
ADJECTIVE If a place is **deserted**, there are no people there.

deserve **deserves, deserving, deserved**
VERB If you **deserve** something, you have earned it by what you have done.

design **designs, designing, designed**
NOUN **1** A **design** is a pattern that is used to decorate something.
VERB **2** If you **design** something, you plan it and make a drawing of it.

desk **desks**
NOUN A **desk** is a special table that you use for writing or reading.

dessert **desserts**
NOUN A **dessert** is a sweet food served after the main course of a meal.

destroy **destroys, destroying, destroyed**
VERB To **destroy** something means to damage it so much it cannot be mended.

detail **details**
NOUN A **detail** is a small part or thing that you notice when you look at something carefully.

a
b
c
Dd
e
f
g
h
i
j
k
l
m
n
o
p
q
r
s
t
u
v
w
x
y
z

detective

detective **detectives**
NOUN A **detective** is a person whose job is to find out who did a crime.

determined
ADJECTIVE If you are **determined** to do something, nothing will stop you.

develop **develops, developing, developed**
VERB When something **develops**, it grows or becomes more advanced.

dew
NOUN **Dew** is the small drops of water that form on surfaces outdoors at night.

diagonal
ADJECTIVE A **diagonal** line slants from one corner of something to the opposite corner.

diagram **diagrams**
NOUN A **diagram** is a drawing that explains something.

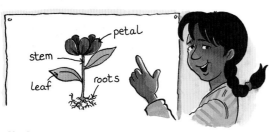

dial **dials**
NOUN A **dial** is a numbered disc on an instrument like a clock.

dialogue **dialogues**
NOUN In a story, play or film, **dialogue** is conversation.

diameter **diameters**
NOUN A **diameter** is a straight line drawn right through the centre of a circle.

diamond **diamonds**
NOUN **1** A **diamond** is a very hard, clear jewel which sparkles.
NOUN **2** A **diamond** is also a shape with four straight sides, like a square but slightly flattened.
See *Colours and flat shapes* on page 271.

diary **diaries**
NOUN A **diary** is a book in which to write about what you have done.

dice
NOUN **Dice** are small cubes with spots on each of their six sides.

dictionary **dictionaries**
NOUN A **dictionary** is a book in which words are listed alphabetically and explained.

did
VERB **Did** is the past tense of **do**.

didn't
VERB **Didn't** is a contraction of **did not**.

die **dies, dying, died**
VERB When a person, animal or plant **dies**, they stop living.

diesel **diesels**
NOUN A **diesel** is a kind of engine that burns a special oil instead of petrol.

diet **diets**
NOUN **1** A **diet** is the food that a person or animal normally eats.
NOUN **2** A **diet** is also a special range of foods that a doctor tells someone to eat if they have a health or weight problem.

difference **differences**
NOUN **1** The **difference** between two things is the way in which they are unlike each other.
NOUN **2** In maths, you can work out the **difference** between two numbers by taking the smaller number away from the larger number.

different
ADJECTIVE Something that is **different** from something else is not like it in one or more ways.

difficult
ADJECTIVE Something that is **difficult** is not easy to do or understand.
difficulty NOUN

dig **digs, digging, dug**
VERB When people **dig**, they break up soil or sand with a spade or garden fork.

digest **digests, digesting, digested**
VERB When you **digest** food, your body breaks it down so that it can be used.
digestion NOUN

digit **digits**
NOUN A **digit** is a written symbol for any of the numbers from 0 to 9. For example, 384 is a three-digit number.

digital
ADJECTIVE **1 Digital** instruments such as watches have changing numbers instead of a dial with hands. See **analogue**.
NOUN **2 Digital television** is television in which the picture is sent in digital form.

dim **dimmer, dimmest**
ADJECTIVE If the light is **dim**, it is rather dark and it is hard to see things.

din
NOUN A **din** is a loud, annoying noise.

dinghy **dinghies**
NOUN A **dinghy** is a small open boat that you sail or row.

dining room **dining rooms**
NOUN A **dining room** is the room where people have their meals.

dinner **dinners**
NOUN **Dinner** is the main meal of the day.

dinosaur **dinosaurs**
NOUN A **dinosaur** was a large reptile which lived and became extinct in prehistoric times.

Triceratops

Stegosaurus

dip **dips, dipping, dipped**
VERB If you **dip** something into a liquid, you put it in quickly.

direct **directs, directing, directed**
VERB **1** If you **direct** someone, you show them the way to go.
VERB **2** A person who **directs** something, like a film, is in charge of it.
ADJECTIVE **3 Direct** means in a straight line without stopping, for example on a journey. *Is there a direct flight to Paris?*

direction **directions**
NOUN **1** A **direction** is the way in which someone or something is moving or pointing.
NOUN **2 Directions** are instructions that tell you what to do or which way to go.

dirt
NOUN **Dirt** is dust, mud or stains on a surface or fabric.

dirty **dirtier, dirtiest**
ADJECTIVE Something that is **dirty** is marked or covered with mud or stains.

dis-
PREFIX **Dis-** is added to the beginning of words to form a word that means the opposite, for example "agree" → "disagree".
See *Prefixes* on page 264.

disabled
ADJECTIVE A **disabled** person has a condition or injury that makes it hard or impossible to do some things.
disability NOUN

disagree **disagrees, disagreeing, disagreed**
VERB If you **disagree** with someone, you think what they are saying is wrong.

disappear **disappears, disappearing, disappeared**
VERB If someone **disappears**, they go out of sight.

disappoint **disappoints, disappointing, disappointed**
VERB If something **disappoints** you, it is not as good as you thought it would be.
disappointment NOUN

a
b
c
Dd
e
f
g
h
i
j
k
l
m
n
o
p
q
r
s
t
u
v
w
x
y
z

disapprove

disapprove

VERB If you **disapprove** of something, you think it is wrong or bad.

disaster disasters

NOUN A **disaster** is something very bad that happens, such as an air crash.
disastrous ADJECTIVE

disc discs

NOUN A **disc** is a flat round object.

disco discos

NOUN A **disco** is a place where people go to dance to pop music.

discover discovers, discovering, discovered

VERB When you **discover** something, you find it or find out about it.
discovery NOUN

discuss discusses, discussing, discussed

VERB When you **discuss** something, you talk about it with someone else.
discussion NOUN

disease diseases

NOUN A **disease** is an illness in people, animals or plants.

disguise disguises

NOUN A **disguise** is something that changes the way you look, so that people do not recognize you.

disgust

NOUN **Disgust** is a feeling of strong dislike for someone or something.

dish dishes

NOUN A **dish** is a shallow container for cooking or serving meals in.

dishonest

ADJECTIVE If someone is **dishonest**, they are not to be trusted.

dishwasher dishwashers

NOUN A **dishwasher** is a machine that washes things like plates.

disk disks

NOUN A **disk** is used for storing information in a computer.

dislike dislikes, disliking, disliked

VERB If you **dislike** someone or something, you do not like them.

dismiss dismisses, dismissing, dismissed

VERB When someone in authority **dismisses** you, they tell you to leave.

display displays

NOUN A **display** is an arrangement of things which is done to show to people.

dissolve dissolves, dissolving, dissolved

VERB If something **dissolves** in a liquid, it becomes mixed in with it. See **solution**.

distance distances

NOUN The **distance** between two things is the amount of space between them.

distant

ADJECTIVE **Distant** means far away.

distinct

ADJECTIVE If something is **distinct**, you can hear or see it clearly.

distribute distributes, distributing, distributed

VERB If you **distribute** things like leaflets, you hand them out to several people.

district districts

NOUN A **district** is the area around a place. *He's the only doctor in this **district**.*

disturb disturbs, disturbing, disturbed

VERB If you **disturb** someone, you interrupt them or spoil their peace and quiet.

disturbance disturbances

NOUN A **disturbance** is something that spoils people's peace and quiet.

ditch ditches

NOUN A **ditch** is a channel dug at the side of a road or field, to drain water.

dive dives, diving, dived

VERB To **dive** is to jump head first into water with your arms above your head.

diver NOUN

divide divides, dividing, divided

VERB **1** When something is **divided**, it is separated into smaller parts.

VERB **2** When you **divide** numbers, you share them into equal groups. For example, 15 can be divided into 3 groups of 5, or 5 groups of 3.

$15 \div 3 = 5$ or $15 \div 5 = 3$

divisible

ADJECTIVE A number that is **divisible** can be divided by another number without leaving a remainder. 27 is divisible by 3.

division divisions

NOUN **1 Division** is separating something into two or more parts.

NOUN **2** In maths, **division** is the process of dividing one number by another. The sign ÷ is used for division.

divorce divorces

NOUN A **divorce** is the legal ending of a marriage.

Diwali

NOUN **Diwali** is a Hindu festival of light that is celebrated in the autumn.

dizzy dizzier, dizziest

ADJECTIVE If you feel **dizzy**, your head feels funny, as if you are going to fall over.

do does, doing, did, done

VERB **1** If you **do** something, you get on and finish it. *Have you **done** your work?*

VERB **2 Do** can be used with other verbs. *Do you want some more?*

doctor doctors

NOUN A **doctor** is a person who treats people when they are ill.

document documents

NOUN **1** A **document** is a piece of paper which is an official record of something.

NOUN **2** A **document** is also a piece of text stored as a file in a computer.

dodge dodges, dodging, dodged

VERB If you **dodge**, you move suddenly out of the way.

does

VERB **Does** is a present tense form of **do**.

doesn't

VERB **Doesn't** is a contraction of **does not**.

dog dogs

NOUN A **dog** is an animal. Dogs bark and are often kept as pets, or used to guard things.

doll dolls

NOUN A **doll** is a child's toy that looks like a baby or a small person.

dollar dollars

NOUN A **dollar** is a unit of money in countries such as the USA and Australia.

dolphin dolphins

NOUN A **dolphin** is a mammal which lives in the sea.

dome

dome **domes**
NOUN A **dome** is a round roof.

domino **dominoes**
NOUN A **domino** is a small black rectangular block, marked with spots. Dominoes are used for playing games.

done
VERB **Done** is the past participle of **do**.

donkey **donkeys**
NOUN A **donkey** is an animal like a small horse, with longer ears.

don't
VERB **Don't** is a contraction of **do not**.

door **doors**
NOUN A **door** swings or slides to open and close the entrance to something.

dose **doses**
NOUN A **dose** is the amount of a medicine that you have to take.

dot **dots**
NOUN A **dot** is a small round mark.

double
ADJECTIVE If something is **double** the size or amount of something else, it is twice as big.

doubt **doubts**
NOUN If you have a **doubt** about something, you are not sure about it.

doubtful
ADJECTIVE **1** If you are **doubtful** about something, you are not sure about it.
ADJECTIVE **2** Something that is **doubtful** seems unlikely or uncertain.

dough
NOUN **Dough** is the floury mixture used to make things like pastry or bread.

doughnut **doughnuts**
NOUN A **doughnut** is a ring of sweet dough cooked in hot fat.

dove **doves**
NOUN A **dove** is a bird like a small pigeon.

down
PREPOSITION **1** If you go **down** a hill, you go to a lower level.
ADVERB **2** If you put something **down**, you put it on a surface.
ADVERB **3** If an amount of something goes **down**, it gets less. *My pocket money's gone down.*
NOUN **4** **Down** is soft feathers.

downstairs
ADVERB If you go **downstairs**, you go towards the ground floor.

doze **dozes, dozing, dozed**
VERB When you **doze**, you sleep lightly.

dozen **dozens**
NOUN If you have a **dozen** things, you have 12 of them.

draft **drafts**
NOUN A **draft** is an early rough version of something you are writing.

drag **drags, dragging, dragged**
VERB If you **drag** a heavy object, you pull it along the ground.

dragon **dragons**
NOUN In stories, a **dragon** is a fierce animal like a big lizard. It has wings and claws and breathes fire.

dragonfly **dragonflies**
NOUN A **dragonfly** is a brightly-coloured insect, usually found near water.

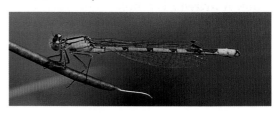

See *Insects* on page 259.

drain **drains, draining, drained**
NOUN **1** A **drain** is a pipe that carries water away.
VERB **2** If a liquid **drains** away, it flows slowly to somewhere else.

drake **drakes**

NOUN A **drake** is a male duck.

drama **dramas**

NOUN **1** A **drama** is a serious play for the theatre, television or radio.
NOUN **2** Drama is exciting and interesting things that happen.

dramatic

ADJECTIVE Something **dramatic** is very exciting and interesting.
dramatically ADVERB

drank

VERB **Drank** is the past tense of **drink**.

draught **draughts**

NOUN **1** A **draught** is a current of cold air coming into a room or vehicle.
PLURAL NOUN **2** Draughts is a game played with round pieces on a board.

draw **draws, drawing, drew, drawn**

VERB **1** When you **draw**, you use something like a pencil or crayon to make a picture or a pattern.
VERB **2** When you **draw** the curtains, you pull them across a window.
NOUN **3** A **draw** is the result in a game or competition in which nobody wins.

drawbridge **drawbridges**

NOUN A **drawbridge** is a bridge that can be pulled up to stop people getting into a castle.

drawer **drawers**

NOUN A **drawer** is a box that slides in and out of a piece of furniture.

drawing **drawings**

NOUN A **drawing** is a picture made with a pencil, pen or crayon.

dread **dreads, dreading, dreaded**

VERB If you **dread** something, you feel worried and frightened about it.

dreadful

ADJECTIVE Something that is **dreadful** is very bad or unpleasant.

dream **dreams, dreaming, dreamed** or **dreamt**

VERB **1** When you **dream**, you see events in your mind while you are asleep.

VERB **2** If you **dream** while you are awake, you think about things you would like to happen.
dream NOUN

dress **dresses, dressing, dressed**

VERB **1** When you **dress**, you put on your clothes.
NOUN **2** A **dress** is a piece of clothing for women or girls made up of a skirt and top joined together.

drew

VERB **Drew** is the past tense of **draw**.

dribble **dribbles, dribbling, dribbled**

VERB **1** When babies **dribble**, water trickles from their mouth.
VERB **2** When players **dribble** the ball in a game like football, they kick it several times quickly to keep it moving.

drift **drifts, drifting, drifted**

VERB **1** When something **drifts**, it is carried along slowly by wind or water.
NOUN **2** A **drift** is a pile of snow heaped up by the wind.

drill **drills**

NOUN A **drill** is a tool for making holes.

drink **drinks, drinking, drank, drunk**

VERB **1** When you **drink**, you take liquid into your mouth and swallow it.
NOUN **2** A **drink** is a liquid which you swallow to stop you being thirsty.

a
b
c
Dd
e
f
g
h
i
j
k
l
m
n
o
p
q
r
s
t
u
v
w
x
y
z

drip

drip drips, dripping, dripped
VERB When something **drips**, drops of liquid fall from it one after the other.

drive drives, driving, drove, driven
VERB If someone **drives** a vehicle, they make it move and control it.

drizzle
NOUN **Drizzle** is light rain.

drop drops, dropping, dropped
VERB **1** If you **drop** something, you let it fall.
NOUN **2** A **drop** is a tiny amount of liquid.

drought droughts
NOUN A **drought** is a long period of time when no rain falls.

drove
VERB **Drove** is the past tense of **drive**.

drown drowns, drowning, drowned
VERB If someone **drowns**, they die because they have gone under water and cannot breathe.

drug drugs
NOUN A **drug** is a substance that is used to treat or prevent disease, or stop pain. Some drugs can be dangerous.

drum drums
NOUN A **drum** is a musical instrument which you hit to make a noise. It has skin stretched tightly over the end.

drunk
VERB **Drunk** is the past participle of **drink**.

dry drier or dryer, driest
ADJECTIVE Something that is **dry** has no water in it at all.
dry VERB

duck ducks
NOUN A **duck** is a common water bird with short legs and webbed feet.

due
ADJECTIVE If something is **due** at a particular time, it should happen then.

dug
VERB **Dug** is the past tense of **dig**.

dull duller, dullest
ADJECTIVE **1** Something that is **dull** is not interesting.
ADJECTIVE **2** **Dull** means not bright.
ADJECTIVE **3** A **dull** pain is not sharp.

dumb
ADJECTIVE Someone who is **dumb** is unable to speak.

dungeon dungeons
NOUN A **dungeon** is a dark underground prison in a castle.

during
PREPOSITION Something that happens **during** a period of time happens in that period. *I worked during the holidays.*

dusk
NOUN **Dusk** is the part of the day when it is beginning to get dark.

dust
NOUN **Dust** is dry fine powdery material such as particles of earth, dirt or pollen.
dusty ADJECTIVE

dustbin dustbins
NOUN A **dustbin** is a large container with a lid, for rubbish.

duty duties
NOUN A **duty** is something you feel you should do. *He only went to see his aunt because he felt it was his duty.*

duvet duvets
NOUN A **duvet** is a bed cover filled with feathers or other light material.

dye dyes, dyeing, dyed
VERB If you **dye** something such as hair or cloth, you change its colour by soaking it in a special liquid.

dying
VERB See **die**.

Ee

each

ADJECTIVE **Each** means every one taken separately. *She gave **each** child a pencil.*

eager

ADJECTIVE If you are **eager**, you very much want to do or have something.

eagle eagles

NOUN An **eagle** is a large strong bird with a sharp curved beak and claws.

ear ears

NOUN Your **ears** are the parts of your body that you use for hearing.

early earlier, earliest

ADJECTIVE OR ADVERB **1 Early** means near the beginning of a period of time. *We took the **early** train to school.*

ADJECTIVE OR ADVERB **2** You also use **early** to mean sooner than expected. *I arrived at the party **early**.*

earn earns, earning, earned

VERB If you **earn** something, such as money, you get it by working for it.

earring earrings

NOUN An **earring** is a piece of jewellery that is fixed to the ear for decoration.

earth

NOUN **1** The **Earth** is the planet we live on.
NOUN **2** The soil that plants grow in is also called **earth**.

earthquake earthquakes

NOUN An **earthquake** is when the ground shakes because of movement beneath the surface.

east

NOUN **East** is one of the four main points of the compass. It is the direction in which the sun rises. See **compass point**.
eastern ADJECTIVE

Easter

NOUN **Easter** is a Christian festival that celebrates Christ's return to life.

easy easier, easiest

ADJECTIVE Something that is **easy** can be done without difficulty.
easily ADVERB

eat eats, eating, ate, eaten

VERB When you **eat**, you chew and swallow food.

echo echoes

NOUN An **echo** is a sound that bounces back from something like the walls of a cave or building.

eclipse eclipses

NOUN An **eclipse** of the Sun is when the Moon comes in front of the Sun and hides it for a short time.

edge edges

NOUN **1** An **edge** is the end or side of something.
NOUN **2** An **edge** is where two faces of a three-dimensional shape meet. For example, a cuboid has 12 edges.

edible

ADJECTIVE Something that is **edible** is safe to eat.

edit edits, editing, edited

VERB **1** If you **edit** a piece of writing, you correct it so that it is ready for printing.
VERB **2** When someone **edits** a film or television programme, they select different parts and arrange them in a particular order.

educate educates, educating, educated

VERB To **educate** someone means to teach them over a long period, so that they learn about many different things.

a
b
c
d
Ee
f
g
h
i
j
k
l
m
n
o
p
q
r
s
t
u
v
w
x
y
z

education

NOUN **Education** is the teaching you receive at school, college or university.

eel **eels**

NOUN An **eel** is a long thin fish that looks like a snake.

effect **effects**

NOUN An **effect** is a change made by something. *I'm still suffering from the effects of my cold.*

effort **efforts**

NOUN **Effort** is the physical or mental energy needed to do something.

egg **eggs**

NOUN **1** An **egg** is an oval object laid by female birds. Reptiles, fish and insects also lay eggs. A baby animal develops inside the egg until it is ready to be born.

NOUN **2** In a female mammal, an **egg** is a cell produced in its body which can develop into a baby.

elastic

ADJECTIVE **1** Something **elastic** is able to stretch easily.

NOUN **2** **Elastic** is a material, like rubber, which stretches and can then return to its original size.

elbow **elbows**

NOUN Your **elbow** is the joint in the middle of your arm where it bends.

electric

ADJECTIVE A machine or other object that is **electric** works by using electricity.

electrical ADJECTIVE

electricity

NOUN **Electricity** is a form of energy that is used for heating and lighting, and to work machines. It comes along wires.

electronic

ADJECTIVE Something **electronic** has transistors or silicon chips which control an electric current.

electronically ADVERB

elephant **elephants**

NOUN An **elephant** is a large four-legged mammal with a long trunk, large ears, and ivory tusks.

elf **elves**

NOUN In fairy stories, an **elf** is a tiny boy who can do magic things.

else

ADVERB You can use **else** to mean other than this or more than this. *Can you think of anything else?*

e-mail or **email**

NOUN **E-mail** is the sending of messages from one computer to another.

embarrass **embarrasses, embarrassing, embarrassed**

VERB To **embarrass** someone means to make them feel shy, ashamed or guilty about something.

embryo **embryos**

NOUN An **embryo** is a human being or animal which has just begun to develop inside its mother's body.

emerald **emeralds**

NOUN An **emerald** is a bright green precious stone.

emerge **emerges, emerging, emerged**

VERB If someone **emerges** from a place, they come out so that they can be seen.

emergency **emergencies**

NOUN An **emergency** is an unexpected and serious event which needs immediate action to deal with it.

emotion **emotions**

NOUN **Emotion** is a strong feeling, such a love or fear.

employ **employs, employing, employed**
VERB If someone **employs** you, they pay you to work for them.

employer **employers**
NOUN **Employers** are people who pay other people to work for them.

empty **emptier, emptiest; empties, emptying, emptied**
ADJECTIVE **1** Something that is **empty** has no people or things in it.
VERB **2** If you **empty** a container, you pour or take everything out of it.

enchanted
ADJECTIVE In stories, something that is **enchanted** is under a magic spell.

encourage **encourages, encouraging, encouraged**
VERB If you **encourage** someone, you tell them that what they are doing is good and they should go on doing it.

encyclopedia **encyclopedias**
NOUN An **encyclopedia** is a book or set of books giving information about many different subjects.

end **ends, ending, ended**
NOUN **1** The **end** of a period of time or an event is the last part.
NOUN **2** The **end** of something is the farthest point of it. *The bathroom is at the end of the passage.*
VERB **3** If something **ends**, it finishes.

ending **endings**
NOUN An **ending** is the last part of a word, story, play or film.

enemy **enemies**
NOUN Your **enemy** is someone who fights or works against you.

energetic
ADJECTIVE Someone who is **energetic** is active and lively.
energetically ADVERB

energy
NOUN **1** **Energy** is the strength you need to do things. You get energy from food.
NOUN **2** **Energy** is also the power that makes things heat up, make a sound, give light or move. Electricity is one kind of energy.

engine **engines**
NOUN **1** An **engine** is a machine that makes things move.
NOUN **2** An **engine** is also a large vehicle that pulls a railway train.

engineer **engineers**
NOUN An **engineer** is a person who designs or builds things such as machinery, instruments or bridges.

enjoy **enjoys, enjoying, enjoyed**
VERB If you **enjoy** doing something, you like doing it very much.
enjoyable ADJECTIVE   **enjoyment** NOUN

enormous
ADJECTIVE Something that is **enormous** is extremely large.

enough
ADJECTIVE **Enough** means as much as you need. *Have you had enough to eat?*

enter **enters, entering, entered**
VERB **1** If you **enter** a place, you go into it.
VERB **2** If you **enter** a competition or examination, you take part in it.

entertain **entertains, entertaining, entertained**
VERB If you **entertain** somebody, you do something that they enjoy and find amusing.

entertainment

entertainment

NOUN **Entertainment** is things that people watch for pleasure, such as shows and films.

enthusiastic

ADJECTIVE If you are **enthusiastic** about something, you are very interested in it, or excited about it.

entire

ADJECTIVE **Entire** means the whole of something. *The **entire** class came to my party.*

entrance entrances

NOUN An **entrance** is the way into a place.

envelope envelopes

NOUN An **envelope** is a folded paper cover for a letter or card.

envious

ADJECTIVE If you are **envious** of somebody, you wish you could have the same things that they have.

environment environments

NOUN The **environment** is the natural world around us.

envy envies, envying, envied

VERB If you **envy** somebody, you wish you could have the same things that they have.

episode episodes

NOUN An **episode** is one of several parts of a story or drama.

equal

ADJECTIVE If two things are **equal**, they are the same as each other in size, number or amount.

equals

VERB In maths, the symbol = stands for **equals**. The numbers on each side of it have the same value: $2 + 2 = 4$

equation equations

NOUN **Equations** are sometimes called number sentences. The numbers on the left equal the numbers on the right. For example, $3 + 3 = 2 \times 3$ is an equation.

equator

NOUN The **equator** is an imaginary line drawn round the centre of the earth, lying halfway between the North and South Poles.

equipment

NOUN **Equipment** is the things that you need to do something. *We need some new kitchen **equipment** – especially a fridge.*

erupt erupts, erupting, erupted

VERB When a volcano **erupts**, it throws out hot molten lava, ash and steam.

escape escapes, escaping, escaped

VERB If a person or animal **escapes**, they get away from somebody or something.

especially

ADVERB You say **especially** to mean most of all. *I like cats, **especially** black ones.*

essay essays

NOUN An **essay** is a short piece of writing on a particular subject.

essential

ADJECTIVE Something that is **essential** is absolutely necessary.

estate estates

NOUN **1** An **estate** is a large area of land in the country, belonging to one person or group.

NOUN **2** An **estate** is also an area of land with lots of houses on it.

estimate estimates, estimating, estimated

VERB If you **estimate** something, you guess the size or amount of it.

evaporate evaporates, evaporating, evaporated

VERB When a liquid **evaporates**, it becomes less because it is changing from a liquid into a gas.

evaporation NOUN

even

ADVERB **1** You say **even** when something is rather surprising. *I like to play outside even when it is raining.*

ADJECTIVE **2** If something like a path is **even**, it is smooth and flat.

ADJECTIVE **3** An **even** number can be divided by two, with no remainder. *2, 18 and 36 are all even numbers.*

evening evenings

NOUN The **evening** is the part of the day between late afternoon and the time you usually go to bed.

event events

NOUN An **event** is something important that happens.

eventually

ADVERB **Eventually** means in the end, after a lot of delays or problems.

ever

ADVERB **Ever** means at any time in the past or future. *Have you ever seen such a big dog?*

evergreen evergreens

NOUN An **evergreen** is a tree or other plant which keeps its leaves all year round.

every

ADJECTIVE **Every** means each one. *I spoke to every child in that class.*

every other PHRASE **Every other** means one in every two. *I see my friend every other week.*

everybody

PRONOUN **Everybody** means every person. *Everybody has to eat.*

everyone

PRONOUN You can use **everyone** instead of **everybody**.

everything

PRONOUN **Everything** means all of something.

everywhere

ADVERB **Everywhere** means in all places. *Children everywhere love stories.*

evidence

NOUN **Evidence** is anything you see, read or are told which gives you reason to believe something.

evil

ADJECTIVE An **evil** person is extremely wicked.

ewe ewes

NOUN A **ewe** is a female sheep.

ex-

PREFIX **Ex-** means former, for example "husband" → "ex-husband".
See Prefixes on page 264.

exact

ADJECTIVE Something that is **exact** is accurate in every detail.

exactly

ADVERB You say **exactly** when you mean no more and no less. *My father is exactly two metres tall.*

exaggerate exaggerates, exaggerating, exaggerated

VERB If you **exaggerate**, you say something is better or worse than it really is.

a b c d Ee f g h i j k l m n o p q r s t u v w x y z

examination examinations

NOUN **1** An **examination**, called an **exam** for short, is a test people take to find out how much they have learned.

NOUN **2** A doctor makes a medical **examination** to find out how healthy you are.

examine examines, examining, examined

VERB If you **examine** something, you look at it carefully or closely.

example examples

NOUN An **example** is one thing which shows what the rest of a set is like. *This is an example of my work.*

excellent

ADJECTIVE Something that is **excellent** is extremely good.

except

PREPOSITION **Except** means apart from. *Everyone went outside except David.*

exception exceptions

NOUN An **exception** is something that does not fit in with a general rule. *With the exception of bats, mammals cannot fly.*

exchange exchanges, exchanging, exchanged

VERB If you **exchange** something, you change it for something else.

excite excites, exciting, excited

VERB If something **excites** you, it makes you feel happy and interested.

exciting ADJECTIVE   **excitement** NOUN

excited

ADJECTIVE If you feel **excited**, you feel happy and unable to rest.

exclaim exclaims, exclaiming, exclaimed

VERB When you **exclaim**, you speak suddenly or loudly, because you are excited or angry.

exclamation NOUN

exclamation mark exclamation marks

NOUN An **exclamation mark** is a punctuation mark (!) used in writing to express a strong feeling.
See *Punctuation* on page 264.

excuse excuses

NOUN An **excuse** is a reason you give for doing something, or not doing it.

exercise exercises

NOUN **1** Exercise is regular movements you make to keep fit.

NOUN **2** An **exercise** is a piece of work that you do to help you learn something.

exhausted

ADJECTIVE When you are **exhausted**, you are so tired you have no energy left.

exhibition exhibitions

NOUN An **exhibition** is a collection of pictures or other things in a public place where people can come to see them.

exist exists, existing, existed

VERB Things that **exist** are present in the world or universe now.

existence NOUN

exit exits

NOUN An **exit** is the way out of a place.

expand expands, expanding, expanded

VERB When something **expands**, it gets bigger.

expect expects, expecting, expected

VERB If you **expect** something, you think it will happen.

expedition expeditions

NOUN An **expedition** is a journey made for a special reason.

expel **expels, expelling, expelled**
VERB If someone is **expelled** from school, they are told not to come back because their behaviour has been so bad.

expensive
ADJECTIVE Something that is **expensive** costs a lot of money.

experience **experiences**
NOUN **1** An **experience** is something that happens to you.
NOUN **2** **Experience** is knowing about something because you have been doing it for a long time.

experiment **experiments**
NOUN An **experiment** is the testing of something, either to find out its effect or to prove something.

expert **experts**
NOUN An **expert** is someone who is very skilled at doing something or who knows a lot about something.

explain **explains, explaining, explained**
VERB **1** To **explain** means to say things to help people understand.
VERB **2** When you **explain**, you give reasons for something that happened.

explanation **explanations**
NOUN **1** An **explanation** is something that helps people understand something. *She gave us a clear explanation of the way the machine works.*
NOUN **2** An **explanation** is something that tells you why something happened.

explode **explodes, exploding, exploded**
VERB If something such as a firework **explodes**, it bursts with a loud bang.
explosion NOUN

explore **explores, exploring, explored**
VERB If you **explore** a place, you travel in it to find out what it is like.
exploration NOUN   **explorer** NOUN

explosive **explosives**
NOUN An **explosive** is a substance that can explode.

express **expresses, expressing, expressed**
VERB If you **express** an idea or feeling, you put it into words or show it by the way you act. *He could only express the way he felt by bursting into tears.*

expression **expressions**
NOUN Your **expression** is the look on your face that lets people know what you are thinking or feeling.

extinct
ADJECTIVE If an animal or plant family is **extinct**, it no longer has any living members. *The dodo has been extinct for more than 300 years.*

extra
ADJECTIVE You use **extra** to mean more than usual. *You'd better take an extra jumper – it's going to be cold.*

extraordinary
ADJECTIVE Someone or something that is **extraordinary** is very special or unusual.

extreme
ADJECTIVE **Extreme** means very great. *Extreme cold can cause many problems.*
extremely ADVERB

eye **eyes**
NOUN **1** Your **eyes** are the part of your body that you use for seeing.
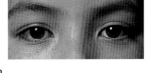
NOUN **2** The **eye** of a needle is the small hole at one end.

eyesight
NOUN **Eyesight** is the ability to see.

Ff

fable fables
NOUN A **fable** is a story that is meant to teach you something. Fables often have animals as the main characters.

fabric fabrics
NOUN **Fabric** is material made in some way such as by weaving or knitting.

face faces, facing, faced
NOUN **1** Your **face** is the front part of your head from your chin to your forehead. *See Your face on page 258.*
VERB **2** If you **face** something, you have your face towards it.
NOUN **3** The **face** of a clock or watch is the part with the numbers on it that show the time.
NOUN **4** A **face** is a surface of a three-dimensional shape.

fact facts
NOUN A **fact** is something that is true.
factual ADJECTIVE

factor factors
NOUN A **factor** is a whole number which will divide exactly into another whole number. For example, 3 is a factor of 12.

factory factories
NOUN A **factory** is a large building where a lot of things are made.

fade fades, fading, faded
VERB **1** If a colour **fades**, it gets paler.
VERB **2** If the light **fades**, it gets darker.

fail fails, failing, failed
VERB **1** If someone **fails** when they try to do something, they cannot do it.
VERB **2** If something **fails**, it stops working. *The brakes failed, and the car hit a wall.*

failure failures
NOUN If something is a **failure**, it does not work as planned. *The picnic was a failure because it rained all day.*

faint faints, fainting, fainted; fainter, faintest
VERB **1** If someone **faints**, they become unconscious for a short time.
ADJECTIVE **2** Something like a sound or mark that is **faint** is not easy to hear or see.

fair fairer, fairest; fairs
ADJECTIVE **1** Something that is **fair** seems reasonable to most people.
ADJECTIVE **2** People who are **fair** have light-coloured hair.
NOUN **3** A **fair** is a form of entertainment that takes place outside with stalls, sideshows, and machines to ride on.

fairly
ADVERB **Fairly** means quite or rather.

fairy fairies
NOUN In stories, **fairies** are tiny people with wings, who have magical powers.

fairy tale fairy tales
NOUN A **fairy tale** is a story in which magical things happen.

faithful
ADJECTIVE If you are **faithful** to someone, you can be trusted and relied on.

fake fakes
NOUN A **fake** is a copy of something made to trick people into thinking that it is genuine.

fall falls, falling, fell, fallen

VERB **1** When someone or something **falls**, they drop towards the ground.
VERB **2** If someone's face **falls**, they suddenly look upset or disappointed.

false

ADJECTIVE **1** If something is **false**, it is not the real thing. *My uncle has a false tooth.*
ADJECTIVE **2** If something you say is **false**, it is not true.

familiar

ADJECTIVE Something **familiar** is well-known or easy to recognize. *It was good to see a familiar face.*

family families

NOUN **1** A **family** is a group of people made up of parents and their children.
NOUN **2** A **family** is also a group of animals or plants of the same kind. *Lions and tigers belong to the cat family.*

famine famines

NOUN A **famine** is a shortage of food which may cause many people to die.

famous

ADJECTIVE Someone or something **famous** is very well known.

fan fans

NOUN **1** A **fan** is an object which creates a draught of cool air when it moves.

NOUN **2** If you are a **fan** of something or of someone famous, you are very interested in them.

fantastic

ADJECTIVE Something **fantastic** is wonderful and very pleasing.

fantasy fantasies

NOUN **1** A **fantasy** is a story about things that do not exist in the real world.
NOUN **2** **Fantasy** is imagining things.

far farther or further; farthest or furthest

ADVERB **1** **Far** means a long way away. *Are you going far?*
ADVERB **2** You use **far** to ask questions about distance. *How far is the town?*

fare fares

NOUN A **fare** is the money that you pay to go on something like a plane or a bus.

farm farms

NOUN A **farm** is a large area of land together with buildings, used for growing crops or keeping animals.

farmer farmers

NOUN A **farmer** is a person who owns or manages a farm.

fascinate fascinates, fascinating, fascinated

VERB If something **fascinates** you, it interests you very much.

fashion fashions

NOUN A **fashion** is the style of things like clothes that are popular for a time.
fashionable ADJECTIVE

fast faster, fastest; fasts, fasting, fasted

ADJECTIVE **1** Someone or something that is **fast** can move very quickly.
ADJECTIVE **2** If a clock is **fast**, it shows a time that is later than the real time.
VERB **3** If someone **fasts**, they eat no food for a period of time.

fasten fastens, fastening, fastened

VERB When you **fasten** something, you close it or do it up. *Remember to fasten your seat belt.*

fat fatter, fattest; fats

ADJECTIVE **1** A **fat** person or animal has a heavy body.
NOUN **2** **Fat** is a solid or liquid substance used in cooking. It comes from animals or vegetables.

father **fathers**

NOUN Your **father** is your male parent.

fault **faults**

NOUN **1** If people say something is your **fault**, they are blaming you for something bad that has happened.

NOUN **2** A **fault** is something wrong with the way something was made.

faulty ADJECTIVE

favour **favours**

NOUN A **favour** is something helpful you do for someone.

favourite **favourites**

NOUN Your **favourite** person or thing is the one you like better than all the others. *This teddy is my* **favourite** *toy.*

fax **faxes**

NOUN A **fax** is a copy of a document that can be sent along a telephone line.

fear **fears, fearing, feared**

NOUN **1** Fear is the nasty feeling you have when you think you are in danger.

VERB **2** If you **fear** someone or something, you are frightened of them.

feast **feasts**

NOUN A **feast** is a large and special meal for many people.

feat **feats**

NOUN A **feat** is a brave or impressive act.

feather **feathers**

NOUN A **feather** is one of the very light pieces that make up a bird's coat.

February

NOUN **February** is the second month of the year. It has 28 days except in a leap year, when it has 29.

fed

VERB **Fed** is the past tense of **feed**.

feed **feeds, feeding, fed**

VERB If you **feed** a person or animal, you give them food.

feel **feels, feeling, felt**

VERB **1** If you **feel** something, like happy or sad, that is how you are at that time.

VERB **2** If you **feel** an object, you touch it to find out what it is like.

feeling **feelings**

NOUN A **feeling** is something you feel, like anger or happiness.

feet

PLURAL NOUN **Feet** is the plural of **foot**.

felt

VERB **1** Felt is the past tense of **feel**.

NOUN **2** Felt is a thick cloth made by pressing short threads together.

female **females**

NOUN A **female** is a person or animal that belongs to the sex that can have babies or young.

female ADJECTIVE

feminine

ADJECTIVE Someone who is **feminine** has the qualities generally expected of a woman, such as gentleness.

fence **fences**

NOUN A **fence** is a wooden or wire barrier between two areas of land.

ferocious

ADJECTIVE A **ferocious** animal or person is violent and fierce.

ferry **ferries**

NOUN A **ferry** is a boat that takes passengers and sometimes vehicles across a short stretch of water.

festival **festivals**

NOUN **1** A **festival** is an organized series of events and performances.

NOUN **2** A **festival** can also be a special day or period of religious celebration.

fetch fetches, fetching, fetched

VERB If you **fetch** something, you go and get it and bring it back.

fete fetes

NOUN A **fete** is an outdoor event with competitions and stalls which sell things.

fever fevers

NOUN If you have a **fever** when you are ill, you have a high temperature.

few fewer, fewest

ADJECTIVE **Few** means a small number of things. *I saw him a few minutes ago.*

fibre fibres

NOUN A **fibre** is a thin thread of something such as wool or cotton.

fiction

NOUN **Fiction** is books or stories about people and events which are made up by the author. See **non-fiction**.

fidget fidgets, fidgeting, fidgeted

VERB If you **fidget**, you keep moving about because you are nervous or bored.

field fields

NOUN A **field** is a piece of land with a fence around, used to grow crops or keep animals in.

fierce fiercer, fiercest

ADJECTIVE An animal that is **fierce** is dangerous.

fight fights, fighting, fought

VERB If you **fight** someone, you try to hurt them.

figure figures

NOUN **1** A **figure** is any of the numbers from 0 to 9. See **digit**.

NOUN **2** A **figure** is also the shape of a person. *It was just getting dark when I saw a small figure coming towards me.*

file files

NOUN **1** A **file** is a box or folded piece of card that you keep papers in.

NOUN **2** A **file** is also a set of data in a computer, which is stored under a name.

NOUN **3** A **file** is also a metal tool with rough surfaces which is used to smooth things like wood or metal.

fill fills, filling, filled

VERB If you **fill** something, you put so much into it there is no room for any more.

film films

NOUN **1** A **film** is moving pictures shown on a screen.

NOUN **2** **Film** is a long narrow piece of plastic that is used in a camera to take photographs.

filthy filthier, filthiest

ADJECTIVE Something **filthy** is very dirty.

fin fins

NOUN A fish's **fins** are like small wings that stick out of its body. They help the fish to swim and to keep its balance.

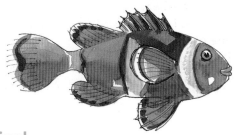

final

ADJECTIVE In a series of any kind, the **final** one is the last one.

finally ADVERB

find finds, finding, found

VERB When you **find** someone or something, you see the person or thing you have been looking for.

a
b
c
d
e
Ff
g
h
i
j
k
l
m
n
o
p
q
r
s
t
u
v
w
x
y
z

fine **finer, finest; fines**

ADJECTIVE **1** Something that is **fine** is extremely good.

ADJECTIVE **2** Something like a thread or nib that is **fine** is very thin.

ADJECTIVE **3** If you say you are **fine**, you mean you are well and happy.

ADJECTIVE **4** When the weather is **fine**, it is dry and sunny.

NOUN **5** A **fine** is money that is paid as a punishment.

finger **fingers**

NOUN Your **fingers** are the four long jointed parts at the end of your hand.

fingernail **fingernails**

NOUN Your **fingernails** are the thin hard areas that cover the ends of your fingers.

fingerprint **fingerprints**

NOUN A **fingerprint** is a mark that shows the skin pattern at the tip of a finger.

finish **finishes, finishing, finished**

VERB When you **finish** something, like a meal or a book, you reach the end of it.

fir **firs**

NOUN A **fir** is a tall pointed evergreen tree with cones, and leaves like needles.

fire **fires, firing, fired**

NOUN **1** Fire is the flames produced when something burns.

NOUN **2** A **fire** is also something powered by coal, gas or electricity that gives out heat.

VERB **3** If someone **fires** a gun, a bullet is sent from the gun they are using.

fire engine **fire engines**

NOUN A **fire engine** is a large vehicle that carries firefighters and equipment for putting out fires.

firefighter **firefighters**

NOUN A **firefighter** is a person whose job is to put out fires and rescue trapped people and animals.

fireplace **fireplaces**

NOUN A **fireplace** is the opening beneath a chimney where a fire can be lit.

firework **fireworks**

NOUN A **firework** is a thing that burns with coloured sparks when you light it. Some fireworks make a loud noise.

firm **firmer, firmest**

ADJECTIVE **1** Something that is **firm** does not move easily when you press or push it. *This pear isn't ripe – it is too **firm**!*

ADJECTIVE **2** If someone is **firm** with you about something, you know they will not change their mind.

first

ADJECTIVE OR ADVERB If something is **first** or happens first, it is number one and comes before anything else.

first aid

NOUN **First aid** is simple treatment given as soon as possible to a person who is injured or who suddenly becomes ill.

first person

NOUN The **first person** refers to yourself when you are speaking or writing. It is expressed as "I" or "we".

fish **fishes, fishing, fished**

NOUN **1** A **fish** is an animal that lives in water. It has gills, fins and a scaly skin.

VERB **2** To **fish** is to try and catch fish for food or sport.

fisherman **fishermen**

NOUN A **fisherman** is a person who catches fish as a job or for sport.

fist fists

NOUN You make a **fist** by tucking your fingers into the palm of your hand.

fit fitter, fittest; fits, fitting, fitted

ADJECTIVE **1** Someone who is **fit** is healthy.
VERB **2** If something such as clothing **fits** you, it is the right size for you.
VERB **3** If something **fits** something else, it is the right size to go with it. *This is the lid that **fits** that box.*

fix fixes, fixing, fixed

VERB **1** If you **fix** something that has broken, you make it work again.
VERB **2** If you **fix** something somewhere, you put it there firmly so that it cannot be moved. *She **fixed** a lamp to the wall.*

fizzy fizzier, fizziest

ADJECTIVE A **fizzy** drink is full of little bubbles of gas.

flag flags

NOUN A **flag** is a piece of cloth that can be fixed to a pole as a symbol of a nation, or as a signal.

flake flakes

NOUN A **flake** is a small thin piece of something.

flame flames

NOUN A **flame** is a flickering tongue or blaze of fire.

flamingo flamingos

NOUN A **flamingo** is a long-legged wading bird with pink feathers.

flannel flannels

NOUN A **flannel** is a small square of towelling, used for washing yourself.

flap flaps, flapping, flapped

NOUN **1** A **flap** is something flat that is fixed along one edge so that the rest of it can move freely.
VERB **2** When a bird **flaps** its wings, it moves them up and down quickly.

flash flashes, flashing, flashed

NOUN **1** A **flash** is a bright light which comes suddenly and only lasts a moment, like lightning in a storm.
VERB **2** If something **flashes** past, it moves so fast that you cannot see it properly.

flask flasks

NOUN A **flask** is a bottle for carrying drinks. It keeps hot drinks hot and cold drinks cold.

flat flats; flatter, flattest

NOUN **1** A **flat** is a set of rooms, usually on one level, for living in.
ADJECTIVE **2** Something that is **flat** is level and smooth.
ADJECTIVE **3** A battery that is **flat** has lost its electrical power.
ADJECTIVE **4** A **flat** shape is one like a circle, that is two-dimensional.
See *Colours and flat shapes* on page 271.

flavour flavours

NOUN The **flavour** of food is its taste.

flea fleas

NOUN A **flea** is a small jumping insect that feeds on blood.

fleece fleeces

NOUN **1** A sheep's **fleece** is its woollen coat.
NOUN **2** A **fleece** is a kind of warm jacket or pullover.

flesh

NOUN **1** Flesh is the soft part of your body.
NOUN **2** The **flesh** of a fruit or vegetable is the soft inner part that you eat.

flew

VERB Flew is the past tense of **fly**.

flick flicks, flicking, flicked

VERB If you **flick** something, you move it sharply with your finger.

flies

flies

VERB **Flies** is a present tense form of **fly**.
NOUN **Flies** is also the plural of **fly**.

flight flights

NOUN **1** A **flight** is a journey through the air by a bird or an aircraft.
NOUN **2** A **flight** of stairs is a set that leads from one level to another without changing direction.

flimsy flimsier, flimsiest

ADJECTIVE Something that is **flimsy** is made of something very thin or weak.

flip flips, flipping, flipped

VERB If you **flip** something, you turn or move it quickly. *He **flipped** a coin.*

flipper flippers

NOUN **1** A **flipper** is one of the broad flat limbs of sea animals, for example seals, that are used for swimming.
NOUN **2 Flippers** are broad flat pieces of rubber that you can wear on your feet to help you swim.

float floats, floating, floated

VERB **1** Something that **floats** is supported by water and does not sink.
VERB **2** Something that **floats** through the air moves along gently, supported by the air.

flock flocks

NOUN A **flock** is a group of birds, sheep or goats.
See *Collective nouns* on page 262.

flood floods

NOUN A **flood** is a large amount of water covering an area that is usually dry.

floor floors

NOUN **1** The **floor** of a room is the flat part that you walk on.

NOUN **2** A **floor** of a building is all the rooms on that level. *Our flat is on the third floor.*

flop flops, flopping, flopped

VERB If someone or something **flops**, they fall loosely and rather heavily.

floppy disk floppy disks

NOUN A **floppy disk** is a small magnetic disk on which computer data is stored.

flour

NOUN **Flour** is a powder made by grinding grain such as wheat. It is used to make things like bread and cakes.

flow flows, flowing, flowed

VERB If liquid **flows** in a certain direction, it moves there steadily.

flow chart flow charts

NOUN A **flow chart** is a diagram which shows how one action follows on from another. This flow chart shows how to make a cup of tea.

flower flowers

NOUN A **flower** is the part of a plant that has coloured petals. When the petals fade, fruit or seeds develop.

flown

VERB **Flown** is the past participle of **fly**.

flu

NOUN **Flu** is an illness that gives you a fever and makes you ache all over. Flu is an abbreviation of **influenza**.

fluffy fluffier, fluffiest

ADJECTIVE Something that is **fluffy** is very soft and light.

fluid **fluids**

NOUN **Fluid** is another word for liquid.

flute **flutes**

NOUN A **flute** is a musical wind instrument consisting of a long tube with holes and keys.

flutter **flutters, fluttering, fluttered**

VERB If something **flutters**, it flaps or waves with small quick movements.

fly **flies, flying, flew, flown**

NOUN **1** A **fly** is a small insect with two wings.
See *Insects on page 259.*
VERB **2** When a bird, insect or aircraft **flies**, it moves through the air.

foal **foals**

NOUN A **foal** is a young horse.
See *Young animals on page 260.*

foam

NOUN **Foam** is a mass of tiny bubbles.

focus **focuses, focusing, focused**

VERB If you **focus** something like a camera or a telescope, you adjust it so that you can see through it clearly.

fog **fogs**

NOUN **Fog** is a thick mist of water droplets in the air.
foggy ADJECTIVE

fold **folds, folding, folded**

NOUN **1** **Folds** in material are the curves in it when it does not hang flat. *The curtains hung in soft **folds**.*
VERB **2** If you **fold** something, you bend it so that one part lies over another.

folder **folders**

NOUN A **folder** is a piece of folded cardboard for keeping papers in.

folk **folks**

NOUN **Folk** or folks are people.

follow **follows, following, followed**

VERB **1** If you **follow** someone who is moving, you move along behind them.
VERB **2** If one thing **follows** another, it happens after it.
VERB **3** If you **follow** instructions or advice, you do what you are told.

fond **fonder, fondest**

ADJECTIVE If you are **fond** of someone, you like them very much.

font **fonts**

NOUN In printing, a **font** is a complete set of type of one style and size.

food

NOUN **Food** is what people and animals eat to stay alive.

food chain **food chains**

NOUN A **food chain** is a series of living things that are linked because each one feeds on the next. For example, a plant may be eaten by a rabbit that may be eaten by a fox.

grass → rabbit → fox

foolish

ADJECTIVE Something or somebody **foolish** is silly or unwise.

foot **feet**

NOUN **1** Your **feet** are the parts of your body that touch the ground when you stand or walk.
NOUN **2** A **foot** is a measure of length, equal to about 30 centimetres.

football **footballs**

NOUN **1** **Football** is a game between two teams who try to kick a ball into each other's goal.
NOUN **2** A **football** is a large ball used in games of football.

footprint footprints

NOUN A **footprint** is a mark in the shape of a foot that a person or animal leaves on a surface.

footstep footsteps

NOUN A **footstep** is the sound made by someone walking.

forbid forbids, forbidding, forbade, forbidden

VERB If someone **forbids** you to do something, they order you not to do it.

force forces, forcing, forced

VERB **1** If you **force** someone or something, you use your power or strength to make them do what you want. *Dad **forced** me to save half my pocket money.*

NOUN **2** A **force** is a push or a pull.

NOUN **3** The **force** of something is also the powerful effect it has. *The **force** of the storm damaged many trees.*

forecast forecasts, forecasting, forecast

VERB **1** If someone **forecasts** something, they say what they think is going to happen in the future.

NOUN **2** A weather **forecast** tells you what sort of weather to expect.

forehead foreheads

NOUN Your **forehead** is the front of your head, between your hair and eyebrows.

foreign

ADJECTIVE Something that is **foreign** is to do with a country that is not your own.

forest forests

NOUN A **forest** is a large area where trees grow close together.

forgave

VERB **Forgave** is the past tense of **forgive**.

forget forgets, forgetting, forgot, forgotten

VERB If you **forget** something, you do not remember or think about it.

forgive forgives, forgiving, forgave, forgiven

VERB If you **forgive** someone who has done something bad, you stop being cross with them.

fork forks

NOUN **1** A **fork** is a tool with three or four prongs on the end of a handle. You use a small fork for eating and a large fork for digging in the garden.

NOUN **2** A **fork** in a road or tree is the point where it divides into two.

form forms, forming, formed

NOUN **1** A **form** is a piece of paper with questions on it and spaces where you should write the answers.

NOUN **2** A **form** is also a class in school.

VERB **3** When something **forms**, it takes shape.

formal

ADJECTIVE Something **formal** is correct and serious.

fortnight fortnights

NOUN A **fortnight** is two weeks.

fortress fortresses

NOUN A **fortress** is a castle or other strong place that is built with defences to keep enemies out.

fortunate

ADJECTIVE **1** Someone who is **fortunate** has good luck.

ADJECTIVE **2** Something that is **fortunate** brings you success or gives you an advantage.

fortune fortunes

NOUN **1** **Fortune** is good or bad luck.

NOUN **2** A **fortune** is a lot of money.

forward

ADVERB If you move **forward** or **forwards**, you move the way you are facing.

look forward PHRASE If you **look forward** to something, you want it to happen.

fossil fossils

NOUN A **fossil** is the hardened remains of a prehistoric animal or plant that are found inside a rock.

fought

VERB **Fought** is the past tense of **fight**.

foul fouler, foulest

ADJECTIVE If something is **foul**, it is extremely unpleasant.

found

VERB **Found** is the past tense of **find**.

foundation foundations

NOUN The **foundations** of a building are the solid layers of material put below the ground to support it.

fountain fountains

NOUN A **fountain** is a jet or spray of water forced up into the air by a pump.

fox foxes

NOUN A **fox** is a wild animal like a dog, with reddish-brown fur and a thick tail.

fraction fractions

NOUN **1** In maths, a **fraction** is a part of a whole number, for example $\frac{1}{4}$.
See *Fractions on page 272*.
NOUN **2** A **fraction** is also a tiny part of something.

fracture fractures

NOUN A **fracture** is a crack or break in something, especially a bone.

fragile

ADJECTIVE Something that is **fragile** is easily broken or damaged.

fragment fragments

NOUN A **fragment** of something is a small piece or part of it.

frame frames

NOUN A **frame** is the part surrounding something like a window or picture, or the lenses of a pair of glasses.

freckle freckles

NOUN **Freckles** are small, light brown spots on someone's skin.

free

ADJECTIVE **1** If a person or animal is **free**, they can go where they want.
Tom opened the cage and set the bird free.
ADJECTIVE **2** If something is **free**, it does not cost anything.
freedom NOUN

freeze freezes, freezing, froze, frozen

VERB **1** If a liquid **freezes**, it becomes solid because the temperature is low.
VERB **2** If you **freeze** something, you store it at a very low temperature.

freezer freezers

NOUN A **freezer** is a refrigerator for freezing and storing food.

frequent

ADJECTIVE If something is **frequent**, it happens often.
frequency NOUN **frequently** ADVERB

a
b
c
d
e
Ff
g
h
i
j
k
l
m
n
o
p
q
r
s
t
u
v
w
x
y
z

fresh

fresh **fresher, freshest**
ADJECTIVE **1** If food is **fresh**, it has been picked or made recently.
ADJECTIVE **2** **Fresh** water is water that is not salty.
ADJECTIVE **3** If you feel **fresh**, you feel rested and full of energy.
ADJECTIVE **4** **Fresh** air is the air outside.

friction
NOUN **Friction** is the force which is produced when two surfaces rub against each other.

Friday **Fridays**
NOUN **Friday** is the day between Thursday and Saturday.

fridge **fridges**
NOUN A **fridge** is a large metal container. It is kept cool so that the food in it stays fresh longer. Fridge is an abbreviation of **refrigerator**.

friend **friends**
NOUN A **friend** is someone you know well and like very much.

friendly **friendlier, friendliest**
ADJECTIVE If you are **friendly** to someone, you behave in a kind and pleasant way to them.

fright
NOUN **Fright** is a sudden feeling of fear.

frighten **frightens, frightening, frightened**
VERB If something **frightens** you, it makes you afraid.

frightening
ADJECTIVE Something that is **frightening** makes you feel afraid.

frog **frogs**
NOUN A **frog** is a small amphibious animal with smooth skin, big eyes, and long back legs which it uses for jumping. See *Amphibians* on page 259.

front **fronts**
NOUN **1** The **front** of something is the part that faces forward.
ADJECTIVE **2** A **front** room or garden is on the side of a building that faces the street.
in front PHRASE **In front** means ahead or further forward.
in front of PHRASE If you do something **in front of** someone, you do it while they are there.

frost **frosts**
NOUN When there is a **frost**, the weather is very cold and the ground becomes covered with tiny ice crystals.

frown **frowns, frowning, frowned**
VERB If you **frown**, your eyebrows are drawn together. People frown when they are angry, worried, or thinking hard.

froze
VERB **Froze** is the past tense of **freeze**.

frozen
VERB **1** **Frozen** is the past participle of **freeze**.
ADJECTIVE **2** If something like a lake or river is **frozen**, its surface has turned to ice.
ADJECTIVE **3** If you say you are **frozen**, you mean you are very cold.

fruit **fruits**
NOUN A **fruit** is the part of a plant that develops from the flower and contains the seeds. Many fruits are good to eat. See *Fruit* on page 257.

fry **fries, frying, fried**
VERB When you **fry** food, you cook it in a pan that contains hot fat or oil.

fuel **fuels**
NOUN **Fuel** is something like petrol or coal, that is burned to provide heat or power.

full **fuller, fullest**
ADJECTIVE If something is **full**, there is no room for anything more.

full stop **full stops**
NOUN A **full stop** is the punctuation mark (.) which you use at the end of a sentence.
See *Punctuation* on page 264.

fun
NOUN **Fun** is something enjoyable that makes you feel happy.

funeral **funerals**
NOUN A **funeral** is a ceremony held when a person has died. The body is buried or burned.

fungus **fungi** or **funguses**
NOUN A **fungus** is a plant such as a mushroom or mould that does not have flowers or leaves.

funnel **funnels**
NOUN **1** A **funnel** is an open cone which narrows to a tube. You use a funnel to pour liquid into containers.
NOUN **2** A **funnel** is also a metal chimney on a ship or steam engine.

funny **funnier, funniest**
ADJECTIVE **1** **Funny** people or things make you laugh.
ADJECTIVE **2** Something that is **funny** is rather strange or surprising.
funnily ADVERB

fur
NOUN **Fur** is the soft thick body hair of many animals.
furry ADJECTIVE

furious
ADJECTIVE Someone who is **furious** is extremely angry.

furniture
NOUN **Furniture** is large objects such as tables, beds and chairs, that people have in rooms.

further **furthest**
ADJECTIVE **1** **Further** is a comparative form of **far**.
ADJECTIVE **2** **Further** can mean more. *Write for **further** details.*
ADVERB **3** If someone goes **further** than someone else, they travel a longer way.

fury
NOUN **Fury** is violent or extreme anger.

fuss **fusses, fussing, fussed**
NOUN **1** A **fuss** is worried or anxious behaviour that is unnecessary and often not welcome. *I don't know why you're making such a **fuss** about it.*
VERB **2** If someone **fusses**, they worry about unimportant things.

future **futures**
NOUN **1** The **future** is the time that is to come.
ADJECTIVE **2** **Future** is to do with time that is to come. *We need to look after the environment for **future** generations.*
NOUN **3** The **future tense** of a verb is the form used to talk about something that will happen in the future. For example, the sentence "Ben will be at school tomorrow" is in the future tense.

Gg

gain **gains, gaining, gained**
NOUN **1** A **gain** is an increase in the amount of something.
VERB **2** If you **gain** from something, you get something good out of it.
VERB **3** If a clock or watch **gains**, it moves too fast.

galaxy **galaxies**
NOUN **1** A **galaxy** is a large group of stars and planets in space.
NOUN **2** The **galaxy** is the group of stars and planets that the earth belongs to.
galactic ADJECTIVE

gale **gales**
NOUN A **gale** is a strong wind.

galleon **galleons**
NOUN A **galleon** is a large sailing ship used hundreds of years ago.

gallery **galleries**
NOUN **1** A **gallery** is a place that shows paintings or sculptures.
NOUN **2** In a hall or theatre, a **gallery** is a raised area at the back where people can sit and get a good view of what is happening.

gallon **gallons**
NOUN A **gallon** is a measure of volume equal to about four and a half litres.

gallop **gallops, galloping, galloped**
VERB When a horse **gallops**, it runs fast.

game **games**
NOUN A **game** is a something you play for sport or fun. Most games have rules.

gander **ganders**
NOUN A **gander** is a male goose.

gang **gangs**
NOUN A **gang** is a group of people who do things together.

gaol **gaols**
Gaol is another spelling of **jail**.

gap **gaps**
NOUN A **gap** is a space between two things, or a hole in something solid.

garage **garages**
NOUN **1** A **garage** is a building in which someone can keep a car.
NOUN **2** A **garage** is also a place that sells petrol or repairs cars.

garden **gardens**
NOUN A **garden** is land next to a house where people can grow things like trees, flowers or grass.

garlic
NOUN **Garlic** is the small white bulb of an onion-like plant which has a strong taste and smell. It is used in cooking.

garment **garments**
NOUN A **garment** is a piece of clothing.

gas **gases**
NOUN **Gas** is a substance that is not liquid or solid. Air is a mixture of gases. Another type of gas is used as a fuel for cookers and central heating.

gasp **gasps, gasping, gasped**
VERB When you **gasp**, you take a short quick breath through your mouth, especially when you are surprised or in pain.

gate **gates**

NOUN A **gate** is a type of door that is used at the entrance to a garden or field.

gather **gathers, gathering, gathered**

VERB **1** If people or animals **gather**, they come together in a group.

VERB **2** If you **gather** things, you collect them from different places. *Early people used to **gather** berries for food.*

gave

VERB **Gave** is the past tense of **give**.

gaze **gazes, gazing, gazed**

VERB If you **gaze** at something, you look steadily at it for a long time.

general **generals**

ADJECTIVE **1** You use **general** when you are talking about most of the people in a group. *There was a **general** rush for the door when the bell rang.*

NOUN **2** A **general** is an army officer of very high rank.

generally ADVERB

generous

ADJECTIVE Someone who is **generous** is kind and willing to help others by giving them money or time.

gentle **gentler, gentlest**

ADJECTIVE Someone who is **gentle** is kind, calm and sensitive.

gently ADVERB

gentleman **gentlemen**

NOUN A **gentleman** is a polite name for a man.

genuine

ADJECTIVE Something **genuine** is real and not false or pretend.

geography

NOUN **Geography** is the study of the countries of the world, and of things like their rivers, mountains and people.

geographical ADJECTIVE

gerbil **gerbils**

NOUN A **gerbil** is a small furry animal with long back legs, often kept as a pet.

germ **germs**

NOUN A **germ** is a tiny living thing that can make people ill. You cannot see germs without using a microscope.

get **gets, getting, got**

VERB **1** Get often means the same as become. *It **gets** dark earlier in winter.*

VERB **2** If you **get** into a particular situation, you put yourself in that situation. *We **got** into a muddle.*

VERB **3** If you **get** something done, you do it or you persuade someone to do it.

VERB **4** If you **get** something, you fetch it or are given it. *I'll **get** us all a cup of tea.*

VERB **5** If you **get** a train, bus or plane, you travel on it.

ghost **ghosts**

NOUN A **ghost** is a shadowy figure of someone no longer living that some people believe they see.

giant **giants**

NOUN **1** In fairy stories, a **giant** is someone who is huge and strong.

ADJECTIVE **2** Anything that is much larger than usual can be called **giant**. *A **giant** wave was coming towards us.*

giddy **giddier, giddiest**

ADJECTIVE If you feel **giddy**, you feel dizzy.

gift **gifts**

NOUN A **gift** is a present.

gigantic

ADJECTIVE Something **gigantic** is extremely large.

giggle **giggles, giggling, giggled**

VERB If you **giggle**, you make quiet little laughing noises.

gill **gills**

NOUN The **gills** of a fish are the organs on its sides which it uses for breathing.

ginger

NOUN **Ginger** is a plant root with a hot spicy flavour, used in cooking.

giraffe **giraffes**

NOUN A **giraffe** is a large African mammal with a very long neck.

girl **girls**

NOUN A **girl** is a female child.

give **gives, giving, gave, given**

VERB If you **give** someone something, you hand it to them or provide it for them. *Dad **gave** me a job cleaning the car.*

give way PHRASE If something **gives way**, it collapses.

glacier **glaciers**

NOUN A **glacier** is a huge frozen river of slow-moving ice.

glad **gladder, gladdest**

ADJECTIVE If you are **glad**, you are happy and pleased.

glance **glances, glancing, glanced**

VERB **1** If you **glance** at something, you look at it quickly.

NOUN **2** A **glance** is a quick look.

glare **glares, glaring, glared**

VERB **1** If you **glare** at someone, you look at them angrily.

VERB **2** If the sun or a light **glares**, it shines with a very bright light.

glass **glasses**

NOUN **1** Glass is a hard transparent material that is easily broken. It is used to make windows and bottles.

NOUN **2** A **glass** is a container that you can drink from, made of glass.

glasses

PLURAL NOUN **Glasses** are two lenses in a frame, which some people wear over their eyes to help them see better.

gleam **gleams, gleaming, gleamed**

VERB If something **gleams**, it shines and reflects light.

glide **glides, gliding, glided**

VERB When something **glides**, it moves silently and smoothly.

glider **gliders**

NOUN A **glider** is an aircraft that does not have an engine, but flies by floating on air currents.

glimpse **glimpses, glimpsing, glimpsed**

VERB If you **glimpse** something, you see it very briefly.

glisten **glistens, glistening, glistened**

VERB If something **glistens**, it shines or sparkles. *Her eyes **glistened** with tears.*

glitter **glitters, glittering, glittered**

VERB If something **glitters**, it shines in a sparkling way. *Her diamond necklace **glittered** under the lights.*

gloat gloats, gloating, gloated
VERB If you **gloat**, you show great pleasure in your own success or in other people's failure.

globe globes
NOUN A **globe** is a round model of the Earth with a map of the world drawn on it.

gloomy gloomier, gloomiest
ADJECTIVE **1** If a place is **gloomy**, it is dark and dull.
ADJECTIVE **2** If people are **gloomy**, they are unhappy and not at all hopeful.
gloomily ADVERB

glossary glossaries
NOUN A **glossary** is a list of explanations of special words, usually found at the back of a book.

glossy glossier, glossiest
ADJECTIVE Something that is **glossy** is smooth and shiny.

glove gloves
NOUN A **glove** is a piece of clothing which covers your hand, with separate places for each finger.

glow glows, glowing, glowed
VERB If something **glows**, it shines with a steady dull light.

glue
NOUN **Glue** is a thick sticky liquid used for joining things together.

gnarled
ADJECTIVE Something that is **gnarled** is old, twisted and rough. *The old gardener's hands were gnarled.*

gnat gnats
NOUN A **gnat** is a very small flying insect that bites people.

gnaw gnaws, gnawing, gnawed
VERB If people or animals **gnaw** something hard, they keep biting on it.

gnome gnomes
NOUN In fairy stories, a **gnome** is a tiny old man.

go goes, going, went, gone
VERB **1** If you **go** somewhere, you move or travel there.
VERB **2** If something **goes** well, it is successful.
VERB **3** If you are **going** to do something, you will do it.
VERB **4** If a clock or watch **goes**, it works.

goal goals
NOUN **1** A **goal** in games such as football or hockey is the space into which players try to get the ball so that they can score.
NOUN **2** It is also called a **goal** when a player gets the ball into the goal.
NOUN **3** If something is your **goal**, you hope to succeed in doing it one day.

goat goats
NOUN A **goat** is an animal with short coarse hair, horns, and a short tail.

goblin goblins
NOUN In fairy stories, a **goblin** is a small ugly creature who likes to make trouble.

god gods
NOUN **1** A **god** is a person or thing that people worship.
NOUN **2** The name **God** is given to the god who is worshipped by some people, such as Christians or Jews.

goddess goddesses
NOUN A **goddess** is a female god.

goggles

goggles

PLURAL NOUN **Goggles** are special glasses that fit closely round your eyes to protect them.

go-kart go-karts

A **go-kart** is a very small motor vehicle with four wheels, used for racing.

gold

NOUN **1 Gold** is a valuable, yellow-coloured metal that is used for making things like jewellery.
ADJECTIVE **2** Something that is **gold** in colour is warm yellow.

golden

ADJECTIVE Something that is **golden** is made of gold or is a gold colour.

goldfish

NOUN A **goldfish** is a gold or orange-coloured fish which is often kept as a pet.

golf

NOUN **Golf** is a game in which players use long sticks called clubs to hit a small ball into special holes.

gone

VERB **Gone** is the past participle of **go**.

good better, best

ADJECTIVE **1** Someone who is **good** is kind and caring, and can be trusted.
ADJECTIVE **2** A child or animal that is **good** is well-behaved and obedient.
ADJECTIVE **3** If something like a film or book is **good**, people like it.
ADJECTIVE **4** Someone who is **good** at something is skilful and successful at it.

goodbye

You say **goodbye** to someone when you or they are leaving.

good night

You say **good night** to someone when you or they are going to bed.

goods

PLURAL NOUN **Goods** are things that can be bought or sold.

goose geese

NOUN A **goose** is a large bird with a long neck and webbed feet. Its cry is a loud honking noise.

gorilla gorillas

NOUN The **gorilla** is the largest of the apes. It lives in African forests.

got

VERB **1 Got** is the past tense of **get**.
VERB **2** You can use **have got** instead of **have**. *We **have got** a map.*
VERB **3** You can use **have got to** instead of **have to**, when talking about something you must do. *We **have got to** win.*

government governments

NOUN A **government** is the group of people who run a country and decide about important things such as medical care and old age pensions.

grab grabs, grabbing, grabbed

VERB If you **grab** something, you take hold of it suddenly and roughly.

graceful

ADJECTIVE Someone or something that is **graceful** moves in a smooth way which is pleasant to watch.

gradual

ADJECTIVE Something that is **gradual** happens slowly.
gradually ADVERB

graffiti

NOUN **Graffiti** is words or pictures that are scribbled on walls in public places.

grain grains

NOUN **1** Grain is the seeds of plants like wheat or corn, that we use for food.

NOUN **2** A **grain** of something such as sand or salt is a tiny hard piece of it.

gram grams

NOUN A **gram** (g) is a small unit of mass and weight. One sheet of paper weighs about four grams. There are 1000 grams in a kilogram.

grammar

NOUN **Grammar** is the rules of a language.

grand grander, grandest

ADJECTIVE Buildings that are **grand** are large and look important.

grandad grandads

NOUN Your **grandad** is your grandfather.

grandchild grandchildren

NOUN Someone's **grandchild** is the child of their son or daughter.

grandfather grandfathers

NOUN Your **grandfather** is the father of one of your parents.

grandmother grandmothers

NOUN Your **grandmother** is the mother of one of your parents.

grandparent grandparents

NOUN Your **grandparents** are your parents' parents.

granny grannies

NOUN; INFORMAL Your **granny** is your grandmother.

grape grapes

NOUN A **grape** is a small green or purple fruit. Grapes grow in bunches on vines. They can be eaten raw, used for making wine, or dried to make raisins, sultanas or currants.

See *Fruit* on page 257.

grapefruit grapefruits

NOUN A **grapefruit** is a large round fruit. It is like an orange but it is larger and has a pale yellow skin.

See *Fruit* on page 257.

graph graphs

NOUN A **graph** is a diagram which shows how two sets of information are related.

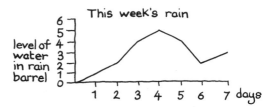

grasp grasps, grasping, grasped

VERB **1** If you **grasp** something, you hold it firmly.

VERB **2** If you **grasp** an idea, you understand it.

grass grasses

NOUN **Grass** is a common green plant with long thin leaves. It grows on lawns and in parks.

grasshopper grasshoppers

NOUN A **grasshopper** is an insect. It has long back legs and can jump well. The male makes a chirping sound by rubbing its back legs against its wings.

See *Insects* on page 259.

grate grates, grating, grated

NOUN **1** A **grate** is a framework of metal bars in a fireplace.

VERB **2** If you **grate** food, you shred it into small pieces.

grateful

ADJECTIVE If you are **grateful** for something nice that someone has done, you have warm feelings towards them and want to thank them.

grave graver, gravest; graves

ADJECTIVE **1** Something that is **grave** is important, serious and worrying.

NOUN **2** A **grave** is a place where a dead person is buried.

a
b
c
d
e
f
Gg
h
i
j
k
l
m
n
o
p
q
r
s
t
u
v
w
x
y
z

gravel

NOUN **Gravel** is small stones used for making roads and paths.

gravity

NOUN **Gravity** is the force that makes things fall when you drop them.

gravy

NOUN **Gravy** is a brown sauce made from meat juices.

graze **grazes, grazing, grazed**

VERB **1** When animals **graze**, they eat grass.

VERB **2** If you **graze** your skin, you scrape it against something and hurt yourself.

grease

NOUN **1 Grease** is a thick oil which is put on the moving parts of cars and other machines to make them work smoothly.

NOUN **2 Grease** is also an oily substance produced by your skin and found in your hair.

greasy ADJECTIVE

great **greater, greatest**

ADJECTIVE **1** You say something is **great** when it is large in size, number or amount. *The waves threw a **great** shower of pebbles onto the seafront.*

ADJECTIVE **2 Great** also means important. *I like to hear about **great** scientists.*

ADJECTIVE **3** INFORMAL **Great** can mean wonderful. *Paul had a **great** time.*

greedy **greedier, greediest**

ADJECTIVE Someone who is **greedy** wants more than they need of something.

greedily ADVERB

green **greener, greenest**

ADJECTIVE **1** Something that is **green** is the colour of grass.
See *Colours* on page 271.

ADJECTIVE **2 Green** is used to describe people who are interested in protecting the environment.

greengrocer **greengrocers**

NOUN A **greengrocer** is a shopkeeper who sells fruit and vegetables.

greenhouse **greenhouses**

NOUN A **greenhouse** is a building which has glass walls and a glass roof. It is used to grow plants in.

greet **greets, greeting, greeted**

VERB When you **greet** someone, you look pleased to see them, and say something friendly.

greeting **greetings**

NOUN A **greeting** is something friendly that you say or do when you meet someone.

grew

VERB **Grew** is the past tense of **grow**.

grey **greyer, greyest**

ADJECTIVE Something that is **grey** is the colour of clouds on a rainy day.
See *Colours* on page 271.

grid **grids**

NOUN A **grid** is a pattern of lines crossing each other to form squares.

grief

NOUN Someone who feels **grief** is very sad, often because a person or animal they love has died.

grill **grills, grilling, grilled**

VERB If you **grill** food, you cook it on metal bars under or over heat.

grim **grimmer, grimmest**

ADJECTIVE **1** If a situation or piece of news is **grim**, it is unpleasant and worrying.

ADJECTIVE **2** If someone looks **grim**, they are serious because they are worried or angry about something.

grin grins, grinning, grinned
VERB If you **grin**, you give a broad smile.

grind grinds, grinding, ground
VERB **1** If you **grind** something, such as pepper, you crush it into a fine powder.
VERB **2** If you **grind** your teeth, you rub your upper and lower teeth together.

grip grips, gripping, gripped
VERB **1** If you **grip** something, you take hold of it firmly.
VERB **2** If something **grips** you, you find it very interesting.

groan groans, groaning, groaned
VERB If you **groan**, you make a long low sound of pain or unhappiness.

groceries
PLURAL NOUN **Groceries** are foods such as flour, sugar and tinned foods.

groove grooves
NOUN A **groove** is a deep line cut into a surface.

ground grounds
NOUN **1** The **ground** is the surface of the earth or the floor of a room.
NOUN **2** A **ground** is an area of land where people play sports such as football or cricket.
PLURAL NOUN **3** The **grounds** of a large house are the land around it which belongs to it.
VERB **4** Ground is the past tense of **grind**.

group groups
NOUN **1** A **group** of things or people is a number of them that are linked together in some way.
NOUN **2** A **group** is also a number of musicians who perform music together.

grow grows, growing, grew, grown
VERB **1** When a person **grows**, they get bigger. All living things can grow.
VERB **2** If you **grow** plants, you put seeds or young plants in the ground and look after them.
VERB **3** When someone **grows up**, they gradually change from being a child into being an adult.

growl growls, growling, growled
VERB When an animal **growls**, it makes a low rumbling sound, usually because it is angry.

grown
VERB **Grown** is the past participle of **grow**.

grown-up grown-ups
NOUN; INFORMAL A **grown-up** is an adult.

growth
NOUN **Growth** means getting bigger.

grub grubs
NOUN A **grub** is a wormlike insect that has just hatched from its egg.

grumble grumbles, grumbling, grumbled
VERB If you **grumble**, you complain in a bad-tempered way.

grunt grunts, grunting, grunted
VERB When a pig **grunts**, it makes a low rough noise.

guarantee guarantees, guaranteeing, guaranteed
VERB **1** If someone or something **guarantees** something, they make certain that it will happen.
NOUN **2** A **guarantee** is a written promise that if something you have bought goes wrong it will be replaced or mended free.

a b c d e f **Gg** h i j k l m n o p q r s t u v w x y z

guard guards, guarding, guarded
VERB **1** If you **guard** a person or object, you stay near to them to keep them safe or to make sure they do not escape.
NOUN **2** A **guard** is a person who guards something or somewhere.

guess guesses, guessing, guessed
VERB If you **guess** something, you give an answer without knowing if it is right.

guest guests
NOUN A **guest** is someone who stays at your home or who goes to an event because they have been invited.

guide guides, guiding, guided
VERB **1** If you **guide** someone, you show them where to go or what to do.
NOUN **2** A **guide** is someone who shows you round places.

guidebook guidebooks
NOUN A **guidebook** is a book that gives information about a place.

guilty guiltier, guiltiest
ADJECTIVE **1** If you are **guilty** of doing something wrong, you did it.
ADJECTIVE **2** If you feel **guilty**, you are unhappy because you have done something wrong.

guinea pig guinea pigs
NOUN A **guinea pig** is a small furry animal without a tail, often kept as a pet.

guitar guitars
NOUN A **guitar** is a musical instrument with strings that you play with your fingers.

gulf gulfs
NOUN A **gulf** is a large area of sea which stretches a long way into the land.

gulp gulps, gulping, gulped
VERB **1** If you **gulp** food or drink, you swallow large amounts of it.
VERB **2** If you **gulp**, you swallow air because you are nervous.

gum gums
NOUN **1** Your **gums** are the firm flesh your teeth are set in.
NOUN **2** Gum is a soft sweet that people chew but do not swallow.
NOUN **3** Gum is also glue for sticking paper.

gumboot gumboots
NOUN **Gumboots** are long rubber boots that you wear to keep your feet dry.

gun guns
NOUN A **gun** is a weapon which fires bullets or shells.

gunpowder
NOUN **Gunpowder** is a powder that explodes when it is lit. It is used for making things such as fireworks.

gust gusts
NOUN A **gust** is a sudden rush of wind.

gutter gutters
NOUN **1** A **gutter** is the edge of a road next to the pavement, where rain collects and flows away.
NOUN **2** A **gutter** is also an open pipe at the edge of a roof, where rain collects and flows away.

gym gyms
NOUN **1** Gym is physical exercises, especially ones using equipment such as bars and ropes. Gym is an abbreviation of **gymnastics**.

NOUN **2** A **gym** is a room with special equipment for physical exercises. Gym here is an abbreviation of **gymnasium**.

Hh

habit **habits**
NOUN A **habit** is something that you do often or regularly, sometimes without thinking about it.

habitat **habitats**
NOUN The **habitat** of an animal or plant is its natural home.

had
VERB **Had** is the past tense of **have**.

haddock
NOUN A **haddock** is an edible sea fish.

haiku
NOUN **Haiku** is a Japanese poem of 17 syllables in three lines.

hail **hails, hailing, hailed**
NOUN **1 Hail** is frozen rain. It falls in small balls of ice called hailstones.
VERB **2** When it is **hailing**, frozen rain is falling.

hair **hairs**
NOUN Your **hair** is made up of a large number of fine threads that grow on your head. Hair also grows on other parts of the body and on the bodies of some other animals.

hairdresser **hairdressers**
NOUN A **hairdresser** is trained to cut and style people's hair.

hairy **hairier, hairiest**
ADJECTIVE Someone or something that is **hairy** is covered with hair.

hajj
NOUN The **hajj** is the journey to Mecca that every Muslim must make at least once in their life if they are healthy and wealthy enough to do so.

half **halves**
NOUN **1** A **half** is one of two equal parts of something.
See Fractions on page 272.

ADVERB **2** When you are talking about time, you can use **half** to mean 30 minutes after a particular hour. *She was home by **half** past three.*

halfway
ADVERB **Halfway** is the middle of the distance between two points. *He stopped **halfway** down the stairs.*

hall **halls**
NOUN **1** A **hall** is the room just inside the front door of a home which leads into other rooms.
NOUN **2** A **hall** is also a large room or building used for public events.

Halloween
NOUN **Halloween** is October 31. Children celebrate it by dressing up, often as ghosts and witches.

halve **halves, halving, halved**
VERB If you **halve** something, you divide it into two equal parts.

ham
NOUN **Ham** is meat from the back leg of a pig. It is specially treated so that it can be kept for a long time.

hamburger **hamburgers**
NOUN A **hamburger** is a piece of minced meat shaped into a flat disc. Hamburgers are often eaten in a bread roll.

a
b
c
d
e
f
g
Hh
i
j
k
l
m
n
o
p
q
r
s
t
u
v
w
x
y
z

hammer **hammers**

NOUN A **hammer** is a tool that is used for hitting things, such as nails into wood.

hammock **hammocks**

NOUN A **hammock** is a piece of strong cloth or netting which is hung between two supports and used as a bed.

hamster **hamsters**

NOUN A **hamster** is a small furry rodent which is often kept as a pet. Hamsters have very short tails, and large cheek pouches for carrying food.

hand **hands, handing, handed**

NOUN **1** Your **hand** is the part of your body which is at the end of your arm. It has four fingers and a thumb.

NOUN **2** The **hands** of a clock point to the numbers to tell you the time.

VERB **3** When you **hand** something to someone, you pass it to them.

handbag **handbags**

NOUN A **handbag** is a small bag that women use to carry things such as money and keys.

handkerchief **handkerchiefs**

NOUN A **handkerchief** is a small square of fabric that you use for wiping your nose.

handle **handles, handling, handled**

NOUN **1** The **handle** of an object is the part you hold to pick it up and carry it.

NOUN **2** The **handle** of a door or window is the knob or lever that is used for opening or closing it.

VERB **3** If you **handle** something, you touch or feel it with your hands.

handlebar **handlebars**

NOUN **Handlebars** are the bar and handles at the front of a bicycle, used for steering.

handsome

ADJECTIVE A **handsome** man has a very attractive face.

handwriting

NOUN Someone's **handwriting** is the way in which they write with a pen or pencil.

handy **handier, handiest**

ADJECTIVE **1** If something is **handy**, it is near. *I like to keep my glasses* **handy**.

ADJECTIVE **2** If an object is **handy**, it is easy to handle or use.

hang **hangs, hanging, hung**

VERB If you **hang** something up, you fix it there so that it does not touch the ground. **Hang** *your coat on the hook.*

hangar **hangars**

NOUN A **hangar** is a large building where aircraft are kept.

hanger **hangers**

NOUN A **hanger** is a curved piece of metal, wood or plastic that you hang clothes on.

hang-glider **hang-gliders**

NOUN A **hang-glider** is an aircraft without an engine. The pilot hangs in a harness from the frame.

Hanukkah or **Chanukah**

NOUN **Hanukkah** is the eight-day Jewish festival of lights.

happen **happens, happening, happened**

VERB **1** If something **happens**, it takes place. *What* **happens** *if I press this button?*

VERB **2** If you **happen** to do something, you do it by chance. *I* **happened** *to be near the phone when it rang.*

happiness

NOUN **Happiness** is a feeling of great pleasure.

happy **happier, happiest**

ADJECTIVE If you are **happy**, you feel good because something nice has happened or because most things are the way you want.

happily ADVERB

harbour **harbours**

NOUN A **harbour** is an area of deep water where boats can stay safely.

hard **harder, hardest**

ADJECTIVE **1** An object that is **hard** is very firm and stiff.

ADJECTIVE **2** If something is **hard** to do, you can only do it with a lot of effort.

hard disk **hard disks**

NOUN A **hard disk** is a permanent part of a computer. It is used to store large amounts of data.

harden **hardens, hardening, hardened**

VERB If something **hardens**, it becomes hard or gets harder.

hardly

ADVERB If you can **hardly** do something, you can only just do it. *The box was so heavy I could **hardly** lift it.*

hardware

NOUN **1** Hardware is tools and equipment made of metal.

NOUN **2** Hardware is also computer machinery.

hare **hares**

NOUN A **hare** is an animal like a large rabbit, but with longer ears and legs. It does not live in a burrow but rests in grass or in a ploughed field.

harm

NOUN **Harm** is injury to a person or animal.

harmful ADJECTIVE   **harmless** ADJECTIVE

harness **harnesses**

NOUN **1** A **harness** is a set of straps which fit round a person's body to hold the person firmly in place.

NOUN **2** A horse's **harness** is a set of straps fastened round its head or body.

harsh **harsher, harshest**

ADJECTIVE **1** A person who is **harsh** is unkind.

ADJECTIVE **2** Weather that is **harsh** is cold and unpleasant.

ADJECTIVE **3** A voice or other sound that is **harsh** sounds rough and unpleasant.

harvest **harvests**

NOUN **Harvest** is the time when farmers cut and gather their ripe crop.

has

VERB **Has** is a present tense form of **have**.

hat **hats**

NOUN A **hat** is a head covering for wearing outside.

hatch **hatches, hatching, hatched**

VERB When a baby bird, insect or other animal **hatches**, it comes out of its egg by breaking the shell.

hate **hates, hating, hated**

VERB If you **hate** something, you have a strong feeling of dislike for it.

haul **hauls, hauling, hauled**

VERB To **haul** something means to move it with a long steady pull.

haunted

ADJECTIVE A place that is **haunted** is often visited by a ghost.

have **has, having, had**

VERB **1** Have can be used with other verbs to form the past tense. *I **have** already seen that film.*

VERB **2** If you **have** something, you own or possess it. *We **have** two tickets for the football match.*

VERB **3** If you **have** to do something, you must do it.

haven't

haven't

VERB **Haven't** is a contraction of **have not**.

hawk **hawks**

NOUN A **hawk** is a large bird of prey that eats small animals.

hay

NOUN **Hay** is grass which has been cut and dried to feed animals.

head **heads, heading, headed**

NOUN **1** Your **head** is the part of your body which has your brain, eyes and mouth in it.

NOUN **2** The **head** of something is the top, start or most important end. *Our teacher sat at the **head** of the table.*

NOUN **3** The **head** of a group or organization is the person in charge.

VERB **4** If you **head** in a particular direction, you move that way.

VERB **5** To **head** a ball means to hit it with your head.

headache **headaches**

NOUN A **headache** is a pain in your head.

heading **headings**

NOUN A **heading** is a title at the top of a piece of writing.

headlight **headlights**

NOUN The **headlights** on a motor vehicle are the large powerful lights at the front.

headline **headlines**

NOUN **1** A **headline** is the title of a newspaper article printed in large type.

NOUN **2** The **headlines** are the main points of the radio or television news.

headphones

PLURAL NOUN **Headphones** are a pair of small speakers that you wear over or in your ears to listen to a recording without other people hearing.

headquarters

NOUN The **headquarters** of an organization is the place where the leaders of the organization work.

head teacher **head teachers**

NOUN The **head teacher** is the teacher who is in charge of a school.

heal **heals, healing, healed**

VERB If something **heals**, it becomes healthy or normal again.

health

NOUN A person's **health** is how their body is, and whether they are well or ill.

healthy **healthier, healthiest**

ADJECTIVE **1** Someone who is **healthy** is well and not suffering from any illness.

ADJECTIVE **2** Something that is **healthy** is good for your health.

heap **heaps**

NOUN A **heap** is a lot of things piled up, usually rather untidily.

hear **hears, hearing, heard**

VERB When you **hear** sounds, you notice them by using your ears.

hearing

NOUN **Hearing** is the sense which makes it possible for you to be aware of sounds.

heart **hearts**

NOUN **1** Your **heart** is the organ that pumps the blood round inside your body.

NOUN **2** A **heart** is a shape like a heart, used especially as a symbol of love.

heat **heats, heating, heated**

NOUN **1** Heat is warmth.

VERB **2** To **heat** something means to raise its temperature.

heather

NOUN **Heather** is a plant with small purple or white flowers that grows wild on hills and moorland.

heaven

NOUN **Heaven** is a place of happiness where God is believed to live.

heavy **heavier, heaviest**

ADJECTIVE Something that is **heavy** weighs a lot or weighs more than usual.

Hebrew

NOUN **Hebrew** is an ancient language now spoken in Israel, where it is the official language.

hedge **hedges**

NOUN A **hedge** is a row of bushes growing close together.

hedgehog **hedgehogs**

NOUN A **hedgehog** is a small animal with sharp spikes all over its back. It defends itself by rolling up into a ball.

heel **heels**

NOUN **1** Your **heel** is the back part of your foot.

NOUN **2** The **heel** of a shoe is the raised part underneath, at the back.

height **heights**

NOUN **1** The **height** of a person is how tall they are.

NOUN **2** The **height** of an object is its measurement from bottom to top.

held

VERB **Held** is the past tense of **hold**.

helicopter **helicopters**

NOUN A **helicopter** is an aircraft with large blades which turn very quickly. It can take off vertically, hover and fly.

helmet **helmets**

NOUN A **helmet** is a hard hat that you wear to protect your head.

help **helps, helping, helped**

VERB **1** To **help** someone means to make something better or easier for them.

VERB **2** If you **help yourself** to something, you take it. *Help yourself to sandwiches.*

VERB **3** If you can't **help** something, you cannot control it or change it. *I can't help feeling sorry for him.*

helpful ADJECTIVE

helping **helpings**

NOUN A **helping** of food is the amount of it that you get in a single serving.

helpless

ADJECTIVE Someone who is **helpless** cannot cope on their own.

hem **hems**

NOUN The **hem** of a piece of material is the part that is folded over and sewn.

hemisphere **hemispheres**

NOUN A **hemisphere** is one half of a sphere. It can also be half of the Earth. *See Solid shapes on page 271.*

hen **hens**

NOUN **1** A **hen** is a female chicken.

NOUN **2** A **hen** can also be any female bird.

heptagon **heptagons**

NOUN A **heptagon** is a flat shape with seven straight sides. *See Colours and flat shapes on page 271.*

her

PRONOUN **1** You use **her** to refer to a woman, girl or any female animal that has already been mentioned. *I like Katherine. I often play with her.*

ADJECTIVE **2** You also use **her** to show that something belongs to a particular female. *My dog Fluff won't eat her food.*

herd **herds**

NOUN A **herd** is a large group of animals of one kind that live together. *See Collective nouns on page 262.*

a
b
c
d
e
f
g
Hh
i
j
k
l
m
n
o
p
q
r
s
t
u
v
w
x
y
z

here

ADVERB You say **here** to mean the place where you are. *I'll stand **here** and wait.*

here and there PHRASE **Here and there** means in various places. *Bits of paper were lying **here and there** on the floor.*

hero **heroes**

NOUN **1** A **hero** is a man or boy who has done something brave and good.
NOUN **2** The **hero** of a story is the man or boy that the story is about. See **heroine**.

heroine **heroines**

NOUN **1** A **heroine** is a woman or girl who has done something brave and good.
NOUN **2** The **heroine** of a story is the woman or girl that the story is about. See **hero**.

heron **herons**

NOUN A **heron** is a bird that lives near water and eats fish.

herring **herrings**

NOUN A **herring** is a silvery fish that lives in large shoals in northern seas.

herself

PRONOUN If a girl or woman does something **herself**, no one else does it. *The baby pulled **herself** up.*

hesitate **hesitates, hesitating, hesitated**

VERB If you **hesitate**, you pause while you are doing something, or just before you do it.

hexagon **hexagons**

NOUN A **hexagon** is a flat shape with six straight sides.
hexagonal ADJECTIVE
See *Colours and flat shapes* on page 271.

hibernate **hibernates, hibernating, hibernated**

VERB When certain animals, such as bears, **hibernate**, they spend the winter in a sleep-like state.

hide **hides, hiding, hid, hidden**

VERB **1** If you **hide** somewhere, you go where you cannot be seen.
VERB **2** If you **hide** something, you put it in a place where it cannot be seen.
hidden ADJECTIVE

high **higher, highest**

ADJECTIVE **1** Something that is **high** is a long way from the bottom to the top. *The wall round the garden is quite **high**.*
ADJECTIVE OR ADVERB **2** If something is **high**, it is a long way up. *There was an aeroplane **high** above her.*

hill **hills**

NOUN A **hill** is a rounded area of land which is higher than the land surrounding it.

him

PRONOUN You use **him** to refer to a man, boy or any male animal that has already been mentioned. *James asked me to ring **him** back.*

himself

PRONOUN If a boy or man does something **himself**, no one else does it. *Ben hurt **himself** quite badly.*

Hindu **Hindus**

NOUN A **Hindu** is a person who believes in Hinduism, an Indian religion which has many gods. Hindus believe that people have another life on earth after death.

hinge **hinges**

NOUN **Hinges** are pieces of metal, wood or plastic that are used to hold a door or lid so that it can swing freely.

hint **hints, hinting, hinted**

NOUN **1** A **hint** is a suggestion, clue or helpful piece of advice.

VERB **2** If you **hint**, or **hint at** something, you suggest it in a way that is not obvious. *I **hinted** that I would like a bicycle for my birthday.*

hip **hips**

NOUN Your **hips** are the two parts at the sides of your body between your waist and your upper legs.

hippopotamus **hippopotamuses** or **hippopotami**

NOUN A **hippopotamus** is a large African animal with thick skin and short legs. It lives in herds on the banks of large rivers, and spends a lot of time in the water. It is often called a **hippo** for short.

hire **hires, hiring, hired**

VERB If you **hire** something, you pay money so that you can use it for a time.

his

ADJECTIVE OR PRONOUN You use **his** to show that something belongs to a man, boy or any male animal. *Robert combed **his** hair.*

hiss **hisses, hissing, hissed**

VERB To **hiss** means to make a long "sss" sound.

historical

ADJECTIVE **Historical** stories are stories about things that happened in the past.

history **histories**

NOUN **History** is a study or record of the past.

hit **hits, hitting, hit**

VERB If you **hit** something, you touch it quickly and hard.

hive **hives**

NOUN A **hive** is a house for bees, made so that the beekeeper can collect the honey. See **beehive**.

hoard **hoards, hoarding, hoarded**

VERB **1** If you **hoard** things, you save or store them even though they may no longer be useful.

NOUN **2** A **hoard** is a store of things that has been saved or hidden.

hoarse **hoarser, hoarsest**

ADJECTIVE A **hoarse** voice sounds rough.

hobby **hobbies**

NOUN A **hobby** is something you enjoy doing in your spare time, such as collecting stamps or bird-watching.

hockey

NOUN **Hockey** is a game in which two teams use long sticks with curved ends to try and hit a small ball into the other team's goal.

hold **holds, holding, held**

VERB **1** When you **hold** something, you keep it in your hand or arms.

VERB **2** If something **holds** a particular amount of something, it can contain that amount. *This jug **holds** one litre.*

hole **holes**

NOUN A **hole** is an opening or space in something. *The dog buried his bone in a **hole** in the garden.*

holiday **holidays**

NOUN A **holiday** is time away from school or work.

hollow

ADJECTIVE Something that is **hollow** has a space inside it. *The owl lived in a **hollow** tree trunk.*

holly

NOUN **Holly** is an evergreen tree with prickly leaves. It often has bright red berries in winter.

home **homes**

NOUN Your **home** is the place where you live and feel you belong.

homesick

ADJECTIVE If you are **homesick**, you are sad because you are away from home.

homework

NOUN **Homework** is school work that children do at home.

homograph **homographs**

NOUN **Homographs** are words which are spelt the same but have different meanings, for example "calf" (part of your leg) and "calf" (a young cow).

homonym **homonyms**

NOUN **Homonyms** are words which are pronounced or spelt in the same way but which mean different things. Homographs and homophones are homonyms.

homophone **homophones**

NOUN **Homophones** are words which sound the same but have different meanings or spellings, for example "right" and "write".

honest

ADJECTIVE Someone who is **honest** tells the truth and can be trusted.

honey

NOUN **Honey** is a sweet sticky food that is made by bees.

hood **hoods**

NOUN A **hood** is a part of a coat or jacket that you can pull over your head.

hoof **hooves** or **hoofs**

NOUN The **hoof** of an animal such as a horse is the hard bony part of its foot.

hook **hooks**

NOUN A **hook** is a curved piece of metal or plastic that is used for catching, holding or hanging things, for example a picture hook.

hoop **hoops**

NOUN A **hoop** is a large ring, often used as a toy.

hoot **hoots, hooting, hooted**

VERB 1 To **hoot** means to make a long "oo" sound like an owl.

VERB 2 If a car horn **hoots**, it makes a loud honking noise.

hop **hops, hopping, hopped**

VERB 1 If you **hop**, you jump on one foot.

VERB 2 When animals or birds **hop**, they jump with two feet together.

hope **hopes, hoping, hoped**

VERB If you **hope** that something will happen, you want it to happen.

hopeful

ADJECTIVE If you are **hopeful**, you are fairly sure that something you want to happen will happen.

hopeless

ADJECTIVE 1 You say a situation is **hopeless** when it is very bad and you do not think it will get better.

ADJECTIVE 2 If somebody is **hopeless** at doing something, they cannot do it well. *I'm **hopeless** at arithmetic.*

horizon **horizons**

NOUN The **horizon** is the line in the far distance where the sky seems to touch the land or the sea.

horizontal

ADJECTIVE Something that is **horizontal** is level, like the horizon. See **vertical**.

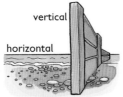

horn **horns**

NOUN **1** Horns are the hard pointed growths on the heads of animals such as goats.

NOUN **2** A **horn** is a musical instrument made of brass.

NOUN **3** On vehicles, a **horn** makes a loud noise as a warning.

horrible

ADJECTIVE Someone or something that is **horrible** is awful or very unpleasant.

horribly ADVERB

horror

NOUN **Horror** is a strong feeling of fear or disgust.

horse **horses**

NOUN A **horse** is a large animal which people can ride. Horses are also used for pulling things like carts.

horseshoe **horseshoes**

NOUN A **horseshoe** is a piece of metal shaped like a U. It is fixed under a horse's hoof, to protect it.

hose **hoses**

NOUN A **hose** is a long tube that sprays water.

hospital **hospitals**

NOUN A **hospital** is a place where sick and injured people are cared for.

hot **hotter, hottest**

ADJECTIVE **1** Something that is **hot** has a high temperature.

ADJECTIVE **2** If you feel **hot**, you feel too warm to be comfortable.

ADJECTIVE **3** You say food is **hot** if it has a strong taste caused by spices. *This curry is too **hot** for me.*

hotel **hotels**

NOUN A **hotel** is a building where people pay to stay, usually for a few nights.

hour **hours**

NOUN An **hour** is a period of 60 minutes. There are 24 hours in a day.

house **houses**

NOUN A **house** is a building where people live.

hover **hovers, hovering, hovered**

VERB When a bird or aircraft **hovers**, it stays in the same place in the air.

hovercraft **hovercraft** or **hovercrafts**

NOUN A **hovercraft** is a vehicle that travels over water or land on a cushion of air.

how

ADVERB **1** You can use **how** in questions to ask about the way something is done or known. *How did you know that?*

ADVERB **2** How can also be used to ask about a measurement or quantity. *How much is the fare to Brighton?*

ADVERB **3** How is often used in greetings. *How are you?*

a
b
c
d
e
f
g
Hh
i
j
k
l
m
n
o
p
q
r
s
t
u
v
w
x
y
z

however

ADVERB You use **however** when you are adding a comment that is surprising after what you have just said. *I was sure I was going to win the race.* **However**, *a younger girl came first.*

howl **howls, howling, howled**

VERB To **howl** means to make a long, loud cry. *The dog* **howls** *when I sing.*

hug **hugs, hugging, hugged**

VERB If you **hug** someone, you put your arms round them and hold them close.

huge

ADJECTIVE Something that is **huge** is extremely big.

hum **hums, humming, hummed**

VERB If you **hum**, you sing with your lips closed.

human **humans**

NOUN A **human** is a person.

hump **humps**

NOUN A **hump** is a large lump on the back of an animal such as a camel, which is used for storing fat and water.

hundred **hundreds**

A **hundred** is the number 100.

hung

VERB **Hung** is the past tense of **hang**.

hungry **hungrier, hungriest**

ADJECTIVE When you are **hungry**, you want to eat.

hungrily ADVERB

hunt **hunts, hunting, hunted**

VERB **1** To **hunt** means to chase wild animals to kill them for food or sport.

VERB **2** If you **hunt** for something, you look for it.

hurricane **hurricanes**

NOUN A **hurricane** is a storm with very high winds.

hurry **hurries, hurrying, hurried**

VERB If you **hurry** somewhere, you go there as quickly as you can.

hurt **hurts, hurting, hurt**

VERB **1** If part of your body **hurts**, you feel pain.

VERB **2** If you have been **hurt**, you have been injured.

ADJECTIVE **3** If someone feels **hurt**, they feel unhappy because someone has been unkind to them.

husband **husbands**

NOUN A woman's **husband** is the man she is married to.

hut **huts**

NOUN A **hut** is a small simple building with one or two rooms.

hutch **hutches**

NOUN A **hutch** is a cage made of wood and wire netting. Pets such as rabbits are kept in hutches.

hygiene

NOUN **Hygiene** is keeping yourself and your surroundings clean, especially to stop the spread of disease.

hymn **hymns**

NOUN A **hymn** is a Christian song in praise of God.

hyphen **hyphens**

NOUN A **hyphen** is a punctuation mark (-) used to join together words or parts of words, for example "left-handed". See *Punctuation* on page 264.

ice ices, icing, iced

NOUN **1** Ice is water that has frozen solid.
VERB **2** If you **ice** cakes, you cover them with icing.

iceberg icebergs

NOUN An **iceberg** is a large mass of ice floating in the sea.

ice cream ice creams

NOUN **Ice cream** is a very cold sweet-tasting creamy food.

ice skate ice skates

NOUN An **ice skate** is a boot with a metal blade fixed underneath. You wear it when you skate on ice.

icicle icicles

NOUN An **icicle** is a pointed piece of ice which hangs from roofs, or wherever water has been dripping and freezing.

icing

NOUN **Icing** is a mixture of powdered sugar and water or egg whites. It is used to cover cakes as a decoration.

icy icier, iciest

ADJECTIVE Something which is **icy** has ice on it, or is very cold. *This wind is icy.*

idea ideas

NOUN **1** If you have an **idea**, you suddenly think of a way of doing something.
NOUN **2** An **idea** is a picture in your mind.

ideal

ADJECTIVE The **ideal** person or thing is the best one possible for the situation.

identical

ADJECTIVE Things that are **identical** are exactly the same in every detail.

idle idler, idlest

ADJECTIVE An **idle** person is someone who does not do very much.

igloo igloos

NOUN An **igloo** is a dome-shaped house built out of blocks of snow.

ignore ignores, ignoring, ignored

VERB If you **ignore** someone, you deliberately take no notice of them.

ill

ADJECTIVE Someone who is **ill** has something wrong with their health.

illness illnesses

NOUN An **illness** is something like a cold or measles that people can suffer from.

illuminations

PLURAL NOUN **Illuminations** are coloured lights put up to decorate a town.

illustrate illustrates, illustrating, illustrated

VERB If you **illustrate** something, you add pictures to it.

illustration illustrations

NOUN An **illustration** is a picture or diagram in a book or magazine.

illustrator illustrators

NOUN An **illustrator** is an artist who draws pictures for books and magazines.

I'm

I'm is a contraction of **I am**.

imaginary

ADJECTIVE Something that is **imaginary** is not real. It is only in your mind. *She has imaginary talks with famous people.*

imagination

NOUN Your **imagination** is your ability to think of ideas, or to form pictures in your mind.

imagine imagines, imagining, imagined

VERB When you **imagine** something, you form a picture of it in your mind.

imitate imitates, imitating, imitated

VERB If you **imitate** someone, you copy the way they speak or behave.

imitation imitations

NOUN An **imitation** is a copy of something else.

immediately

ADVERB If something happens **immediately**, it happens right away.

impatient

ADJECTIVE Someone who is **impatient** does not like to be kept waiting.

important

ADJECTIVE **1** If someone says something is **important**, they mean it matters a lot.

ADJECTIVE **2** Someone who is **important** has a lot of power in a particular group.

impossible

ADJECTIVE Something that is **impossible** cannot be done.

impressive

ADJECTIVE If something is **impressive**, people admire it, usually because it is large or important.

imprison imprisons, imprisoning, imprisoned

VERB If someone is **imprisoned**, they are locked up, usually in a prison.

improve improves, improving, improved

VERB If something **improves**, it gets better.

improvement improvements

NOUN An **improvement** is a change in something that makes it better.

in

PREPOSITION **1** You use **in** to say where something is, or where it is going. *Put it in the box.*

PREPOSITION **2** You also use **in** to say when something should happen. *I'll be home in 20 minutes.*

ADVERB **3** You use **in** to mean at home. *Is anybody in?*

inch inches

NOUN An **inch** is a unit of length equal to about two and a half centimetres. There are 12 inches to a foot.

include includes, including, included

VERB If you **include** something in a whole thing, you make it part of the whole thing. *Batteries are included.*

increase increases, increasing, increased

VERB **1** If something **increases**, it becomes greater.

NOUN **2** An **increase** is a rise in the number, level or amount of something.

index indexes

NOUN An **index** is an alphabetical list at the back of a book that helps you find the things you want to read about.

indignant

ADJECTIVE If you are **indignant**, you feel angry about something that is unfair.

individual

ADJECTIVE **Individual** means to do with one particular person, rather than a whole group.

infant infants

NOUN An **infant** is a baby or young child.

influence influences

NOUN An **influence** is the effect that someone or something has on you, that can change the way you think or behave. *That boy is a bad influence on you.*

informal

ADJECTIVE **1 Informal** means relaxed. You usually speak or behave in this way when you are with people you know well.

ADJECTIVE **2** In a dictionary, a word shown as **informal** is more suitable for everyday talk than it is for writing.

information

NOUN If someone gives you **information** about something, they tell you about it.

infuriate **infuriates, infuriating, infuriated**

VERB If someone or something **infuriates** you, they make you extremely angry.

ingredient **ingredients**

NOUN **Ingredients** are the things that are used to make something, especially in cookery.

inhabit **inhabits, inhabiting, inhabited**

VERB If you **inhabit** a place, you live there.

inhabitant **inhabitants**

NOUN The **inhabitants** of a place are the people who live there.

initial **initials**

NOUN An **initial** is the first letter of a name. *David Hunt's* **initials** *are D.H.*

injection **injections**

NOUN If a doctor or nurse gives you an **injection**, they put medicine into your body with a special needle.

injure **injures, injuring, injured**

VERB If something **injures** a person or animal, it damages part of their body.
injury NOUN

ink **inks**

NOUN **Ink** is the coloured liquid that is used for writing and printing.

inland

ADVERB If you go **inland**, you go away from the coast towards the middle of a country.

inn **inns**

NOUN An **inn** is a small hotel.

innocent

ADJECTIVE Someone who is **innocent** has not done anything wrong.

insect **insects**

NOUN An **insect** is a small animal with six legs and usually wings. Ants, flies, butterflies and beetles are all insects.

See *Insects* on page 259.

insert **inserts, inserting, inserted**

VERB If you **insert** an object into something, you put it into it.
She **inserted** *the key in the lock.*

inside

ADVERB, PREPOSITION OR ADJECTIVE **Inside** means in something. *It was raining so they had to play* **inside**... *It was very cold* **inside** *the church... He hid his money in an* **inside** *pocket.*

insist **insists, insisting, insisted**

VERB If you **insist** on doing something, you refuse to give in.

inspect **inspects, inspecting, inspected**

VERB If you **inspect** something, you look at every part of it carefully.

inspire **inspires, inspiring, inspired**

VERB If something **inspires** you, it gives you new ideas and enthusiasm.

instant

ADJECTIVE Something **instant** happens immediately. *The new pop group were an* **instant** *success.*

a
b
c
d
e
f
g
h
Ii
j
k
l
m
n
o
p
q
r
s
t
u
v
w
x
y
z

instead

ADVERB **Instead** means in place of. *Take the stairs instead of the lift.*

instruction instructions

NOUN **1** An **instruction** is something that someone tells you to do.
PLURAL NOUN **2 Instructions** are words that tell you how to do something.

instrument instruments

NOUN **1** An **instrument** is a tool that is used to do a particular job.
NOUN **2** An **instrument** is also an object such as a piano or guitar, that you play to make music.

insult insults, insulting, insulted

VERB If you **insult** someone, you offend them by being rude to them.

integer integers

NOUN An **integer** is any of the whole numbers used for counting.

intelligent

ADJECTIVE A person who is **intelligent** can understand, learn and think things out quickly and well.

intend intends, intending, intended

VERB If you **intend** to do something, you have decided to do it or plan to do it.

interest interests

NOUN If you have an **interest** in something, you want to learn or hear more about it.

interesting

ADJECTIVE If something is **interesting**, it attracts or keeps your attention.

interfere interferes, interfering, interfered

VERB If something **interferes** with something else, it gets in the way. *Don't let TV interfere with your homework.*

interjection interjections

NOUN An **interjection** is a word you say suddenly to show surprise, pain or anger, such as "Ouch!" or "Wow!".

Internet

NOUN The **Internet** is a worldwide communication system that people use through computers.

interpret interprets, interpreting, interpreted

VERB If you **interpret** what someone says or does, you say what it means.

interrupt interrupts, interrupting, interrupted

VERB **1** If you **interrupt** someone, you start talking before they have finished what they were saying.
VERB **2** If you **interrupt** what someone is doing, you make them stop doing it for a while.

interval intervals

NOUN An **interval** is a short break during a play or concert.

interview interviews, interviewing, interviewed

VERB If you **interview** someone, you ask them questions about themselves.

introduction introductions

NOUN An **introduction** is a piece of writing at the beginning of a book, which usually tells you what it is about.

invent invents, inventing, invented

VERB **1** If you **invent** a story or an excuse, you make it up.
VERB **2** If someone **invents** something, such as a machine or an instrument, they are the first person to think of it.

invention inventions

NOUN An **invention** is something that is a completely new idea.
She is working on an invention that will help people.

inventor inventors

NOUN An **inventor** is someone who thinks of new ideas and tries them out to see if they will work.

inverse

NOUN If you turn something upside down or back to front, you have its **inverse**. *Subtraction is the **inverse** of addition.*

investigate investigates, investigating, investigated

VERB If you **investigate** something, you try to find out all the facts about it.

invisible

ADJECTIVE If something is **invisible**, it cannot be seen. For example, germs are invisible unless you use a microscope.

invitation invitations

NOUN When you get an **invitation**, someone asks you to come to something such as a party.

invite invites, inviting, invited

VERB If you **invite** someone, you ask them to come to your home, or a party.

involve involves, involving, involved

VERB If a situation **involves** someone or something, it includes or concerns them. *This project will **involve** a lot of work.*

iron irons

NOUN **1** Iron is a hard metal used to make steel, and things like gates.
NOUN **2** An **iron** is an object with a handle and a flat base. You can heat it and use it to smooth clothes.

irritable

ADJECTIVE If you are feeling **irritable**, you could easily become annoyed.

irritate irritates, irritating, irritated

VERB **1** If something **irritates** you, it annoys you.
VERB **2** If something **irritates** part of your body, it makes it sore or itchy.

Islam

NOUN **Islam** is the Muslim religion, which teaches that there is only one God, Allah. Mohammed is his prophet.
Islamic ADJECTIVE

island islands

NOUN An **island** is a piece of land completely surrounded by water.

IT

IT is an abbreviation of **information technology**.

italics

PLURAL NOUN **Italics** are letters printed in a special sloping way. *This sentence is in italics.*

itch itches, itching, itched

VERB When your skin **itches**, it makes you feel that you want to scratch it.

its

ADJECTIVE You use **its** to show that something belongs to something that has already been mentioned. *The lion lifted **its** head.*

it's

It's is a contraction of **it is**.

itself

PRONOUN If an animal does something itself, no one else does it. *The cat washed itself.*

ivory

NOUN **Ivory** is the hard smooth creamy material that comes from the tusks of some animals, such as elephants.

ivy

NOUN **Ivy** is an evergreen plant which creeps along the ground and up walls.

a
b
c
d
e
f
g
h
Ii
j
k
l
m
n
o
p
q
r
s
t
u
v
w
x
y
z

Jj

jacket jackets
NOUN A **jacket** is a short coat.

jagged
ADJECTIVE Something **jagged** has an uneven edge with sharp points on it.

jail jails
NOUN A **jail** is a building where criminals are locked up.

jam jams, jamming, jammed
NOUN **1** Jam is a food that is made by cooking fruit with a lot of sugar. You usually spread jam on bread.
NOUN **2** A **jam** is when there are so many people or vehicles in a place it is impossible for them to move.
VERB **3** If something **jams**, it becomes fixed and will not move.

January
NOUN **January** is the first month of the year. It has 31 days.

jar jars
NOUN A **jar** is a glass container with a wide top used for storing food.

jaw jaws
NOUN Your **jaw** is the bone in which your teeth are set. Some animals, like crocodiles, have very large jaws.

jealous
ADJECTIVE Someone who is **jealous** feels upset because someone else has what they want.

jeans
PLURAL NOUN **Jeans** are trousers that are usually made with a strong cotton cloth.

jelly jellies
NOUN **Jelly** is a clear sweet food that wobbles when you move it.

jellyfish jellyfishes
NOUN A **jellyfish** is a sea animal with a clear soft body and tentacles which may sting.

jerk jerks, jerking, jerked
VERB If something **jerks**, it moves suddenly and sharply.

jersey jerseys
NOUN A **jersey** is a knitted piece of clothing for the upper part of your body.

jet jets
NOUN **1** A **jet** is a stream of liquid, gas or flame forced out under pressure.
NOUN **2** A **jet** is also a plane that is able to fly very fast.

Jew Jews
NOUN A **Jew** is a person who follows the religion of Judaism.

jewel jewels
NOUN A **jewel** is a precious stone, such as a diamond or a ruby, used to make things like rings and necklaces.

jewellery
NOUN **Jewellery** is the name for ornaments that people can wear, like rings and necklaces. It is often made of valuable metal such as gold or silver and may be decorated with precious stones.

jigsaw jigsaws

NOUN A **jigsaw** is a puzzle consisting of a picture on cardboard. The picture has been cut up into small pieces that have to be put together again.

jingle jingles

NOUN A **jingle** is a short catchy phrase or rhyme set to music and used to advertise something on radio or television.

job jobs

NOUN **1** A **job** is the work that someone does to earn money.

NOUN **2** A **job** can also be anything that has to be done. *There are always plenty of jobs to do when I get home.*

joey

NOUN A **joey** is a young kangaroo. See *Young animals* on page 260.

jog jogs, jogging, jogged

VERB **1** To **jog** means to run slowly, often as a form of exercise.

VERB **2** If you **jog** something, you knock it slightly so that it shakes or moves.

VERB **3** If someone or something **jogs** your memory, they remind you of something.

join joins, joining, joined

VERB **1** When two things **join**, they come together.

VERB **2** If you **join** a club or organization, you become a member of it.

NOUN **3** A **join** is a place where two things are fastened together. *Look! You can't see the join.*

joint joints

NOUN **1** A **joint** is a part of your body, such as your elbow or knee, where two bones meet and are able to move.

NOUN **2** A **joint** can also be any place where two things are fastened together.

NOUN **3** A **joint** is also a large piece of meat for roasting.

joke jokes

NOUN A **joke** is something that you say or do to make people laugh.

jolt jolts, jolting, jolted

VERB **1** To **jolt** something means to move or shake it roughly and violently.

NOUN **2** A **jolt** is a sudden jerky movement.

NOUN **3** A **jolt** is also an unpleasant shock or surprise.

jot jots, jotting, jotted

VERB If you **jot** something down, you write it quickly in the form of a short note.

journal journals

NOUN **1** A **journal** is a diary which someone keeps regularly.

NOUN **2** A **journal** is also a magazine that deals with a particular subject, for example a medical journal.

journey journeys

NOUN If you go on a **journey**, you travel from one place to another.

joy

NOUN **Joy** is a feeling of great happiness.
joyful ADJECTIVE

joystick joysticks

NOUN **1** On a computer, a **joystick** is a lever that controls movement of the cursor on the screen.

NOUN **2** A **joystick** is a lever in an aircraft which the pilot uses to control height and direction.

Judaism

NOUN **Judaism** is the religion of the Jewish people. It is based on the Old Testament of the Bible, and the Talmud or book of laws and traditions.

a
b
c
d
e
f
g
h
i
Jj
k
l
m
n
o
p
q
r
s
t
u
v
w
x
y
z

judge

judge judges

NOUN **1** In law, a **judge** is a person who has the power to decide how the law should be used.

NOUN **2** The **judge** of a competition is a person who has been asked to choose the winner.

jug jugs

NOUN A **jug** is a container with a lip or spout used for holding or serving liquids.

juggle juggles, juggling, juggled

VERB If you **juggle** with objects, you keep throwing them into the air and catching them one at a time, so that there are several in the air at once.

juggler NOUN

juice

NOUN **Juice** is the liquid that comes from fruit such as oranges when you squeeze them.

juicy juicier, juiciest

ADJECTIVE **Juicy** food has a lot of juice in it.

July

NOUN **July** is the seventh month of the year. It has 31 days.

jumble jumbles, jumbling, jumbled

NOUN **1 Jumble** is an untidy muddle of things.

NOUN **2 Jumble** is also things like clothes and books that people no longer want.

VERB **3** If you **jumble** things, you mix them up untidily.

jumble sale NOUN

jump jumps, jumping, jumped

VERB **1** When you **jump**, you spring off the ground using your leg muscles.

VERB **2** If you **jump** something, you spring off the ground and move over or across it. *He jumped a low wall.*

VERB **3** If something or somebody makes you **jump**, you make a sudden sharp movement of surprise.

jumper jumpers

NOUN A **jumper** is a knitted piece of clothing for the top part of the body.

junction junctions

NOUN A **junction** is a place where roads or railway lines meet or cross.

June

NOUN **June** is the sixth month of the year. It has 30 days.

jungle jungles

NOUN A **jungle** is a dense tropical forest.

junior

ADJECTIVE **Junior** means younger, or less important.

junk junks

NOUN **1 Junk** is old or second-hand articles that are sold cheaply or thrown away.

NOUN **2** A **junk** is a Chinese sailing boat that has a flat bottom and square sails.

just

ADVERB **1** If you say that something has **just** happened, you mean it happened a short time ago.

ADVERB **2** If you say you are **just** going to do something, you mean you will do it very soon.

justice

NOUN **Justice** is fairness in the way that people are treated.

justify justifies, justifying, justified

VERB If you **justify** an action or idea, you explain why it is reasonable or necessary.

Kk

kangaroo **kangaroos**
NOUN A **kangaroo** is a large Australian animal which moves forward by jumping on its back legs.

keen **keener, keenest**
ADJECTIVE Someone who is **keen** to do something wants to do it very much.

keep **keeps, keeping, kept**
VERB **1** If you **keep** something for somebody, you save it for them.
VERB **2** If you **keep** doing something, you do it over and over again.
VERB **3** If something **keeps** you a certain way, you stay that way because of it.
*That dog is **keeping** me awake.*

kennel **kennels**
NOUN A **kennel** is a small house for a dog.

kept
VERB **Kept** is the past tense of **keep**.

kerb **kerbs**
NOUN The **kerb** is the edge of the pavement.

ketchup
NOUN **Ketchup** is a cold tomato sauce.

kettle **kettles**
NOUN A **kettle** is a covered container used to boil water.

key **keys**
NOUN **1** A **key** is a specially shaped piece of metal that fits into a lock.
NOUN **2** The **keys** on something like a computer keyboard or a piano are the buttons that you press to use it.
ADJECTIVE **3** **Key** words or sentences are an important part of a piece of text.

keyboard **keyboards**
NOUN A **keyboard** is a row of buttons called keys on a piano or computer.

kick **kicks, kicking, kicked**
VERB If you **kick** something, you hit it with your foot.

kid **kids**
NOUN **1** A **kid** is a young goat.
See Young animals on page 260.
NOUN **2** INFORMAL A **kid** is a child.

kidnap **kidnaps, kidnapping, kidnapped**
VERB If someone **kidnaps** another person, they take them away by force.

kill **kills, killing, killed**
VERB To **kill** someone or something means to cause them to die.

kilogram **kilograms**
NOUN A **kilogram** (kg) is a unit of mass and weight. One kilogram, or kilo, is equal to 1000 grams.

kilometre **kilometres**
NOUN A **kilometre** is a unit of distance equal to 1000 metres.

kilt **kilts**
NOUN A **kilt** is a pleated skirt worn by men as part of the national costume of Scotland.

kind **kinds; kinder, kindest**
NOUN **1** If you talk about a **kind** of object, you mean a sort of object.
ADJECTIVE **2** Someone who is **kind** behaves in a gentle, caring way.
kindness NOUN

king **kings**
NOUN A **king** is a man who rules a country. Kings are not chosen by the people, but are born into a royal family.

kingdom

kingdom **kingdoms**

NOUN **1** A **kingdom** is a country or region that is ruled by a king or queen.

NOUN **2** The animal **kingdom** is all the animals in the world. *This creature is the largest in the animal kingdom.*

kingfisher **kingfishers**

NOUN A **kingfisher** is a brightly coloured bird that lives by rivers and eats fish.

kiss **kisses, kissing, kissed**

VERB If you **kiss** someone, you touch them with your lips.

kit **kits**

NOUN A **kit** is a set of things that are used for a particular purpose. *Have you seen my first aid kit?*

kitchen **kitchens**

NOUN A **kitchen** is a room that is used for cooking and washing-up.

kite **kites**

NOUN **1** A **kite** is a frame covered with paper or cloth which you fly in the sky at the end of a piece of string.

NOUN **2** In maths, a **kite** is a flat shape with four sides, with two pairs of the same length and none of the sides parallel to each other.

See *Colours and flat shapes* on page 271.

kitten **kittens**

NOUN A **kitten** is a young cat.

See *Young animals* on page 260.

kiwi **kiwis**

NOUN A **kiwi** is a type of bird found in New Zealand. Kiwis cannot fly.

kiwi fruit **kiwi fruits**

NOUN A **kiwi fruit** is a fruit with a brown hairy skin and green flesh.

See *Fruit* on page 257.

knee **knees**

NOUN Your **knee** is the joint where your leg bends.

kneel **kneels, kneeling, kneeled or knelt**

VERB When you **kneel**, you bend your legs until your knees are touching the ground.

knew

VERB **Knew** is the past tense of **know**.

knickers

PLURAL NOUN **Knickers** are pants worn by women and girls.

knife **knives**

NOUN A **knife** is a sharp metal tool that you use to cut things.

knight **knights**

NOUN Hundreds of years ago, a **knight** was a man in armour who rode into battle for his king or queen.

knit **knits, knitting, knitted**

VERB If you **knit**, you make something from wool using two long needles.

knob **knobs**

NOUN **1** A **knob** is a round handle on a door or a drawer.

NOUN **2** A **knob** is also a round button on a piece of equipment such as a radio.

knock **knocks, knocking, knocked**

VERB If you **knock** on something, you hit it hard.

knot **knots**

NOUN A **knot** is a tie in something such as string or cloth.

know **knows, knowing, knew**

VERB **1** If you **know** a fact, you have it in your mind and do not need to learn it.

VERB **2** If you **know** somebody, you have met them before.

knowledge

NOUN **Knowledge** is all the facts and information that you know.

knuckle **knuckles**

NOUN Your **knuckles** are the bony parts where your fingers join your hands and where your fingers bend.

koala **koalas**

NOUN A **koala** is an Australian animal that looks like a small bear with grey fur.

Ll

label **labels**

NOUN A **label** is a small notice that tells you what something is or gives you information. *Read the **label** on the medicine bottle.*

laboratory **laboratories**

NOUN A **laboratory** is a place where scientists work, using special equipment.

labour

NOUN **Labour** is hard work.

lace **laces**

NOUN **1** **Lace** is a very fine decorated cloth made with a lot of holes in it.
NOUN **2** **Laces** are cords that you use to fasten your shoes.

lack **lacks, lacking, lacked**

VERB If you **lack** something, you do not have it when you need it.

ladder **ladders**

NOUN A **ladder** is a wooden or metal frame used for climbing up things like walls or trees.

ladle **ladles**

NOUN A **ladle** is a big deep spoon with a long handle, which is used to serve soup.
ladle VERB

lady **ladies**

NOUN **Lady** is a polite name for a woman. *I think this **lady** was in front of me.*

ladybird **ladybirds**

NOUN A **ladybird** is a small round flying beetle with spots on its wings.
See *Insects on page 259.*

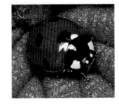

laid

VERB **Laid** is the past tense of **lay**.

lain

VERB **Lain** is the past participle of **lie**.

lake **lakes**

NOUN A **lake** is a large area of fresh water with land all round it.

lamb **lambs**

NOUN A **lamb** is a young sheep.
See *Young animals on page 260.*

lame

ADJECTIVE An animal which is **lame** cannot walk properly.

lamp **lamps**

NOUN A **lamp** is an object that gives light.

lamppost **lampposts**

NOUN A **lamppost** is a tall column in the street, with a lamp at the top.

land **lands, landing, landed**

NOUN **1** **Land** is the part of the world that is solid, dry ground.
VERB **2** When an aircraft **lands**, it comes down from the air on to land or water.

landlady **landladies**

NOUN A **landlady** is a woman who lets rooms to people.

landlord **landlords**

NOUN A **landlord** is a man who lets rooms to people.

landmark **landmarks**

NOUN A **landmark** is a building or a feature of the land that can be used to find out where you are.

landscape **landscapes**

NOUN A **landscape** is everything you can see when you look across an area of land.

lane **lanes**

NOUN **1** A **lane** is a narrow road, especially in the country.
NOUN **2** A **lane** is also part of a main road or motorway. It is marked with lines to guide drivers.

a b c d e f g h i j k **Ll** m n o p q r s t u v w x y z

language

language **languages**

NOUN A **language** is the words that are used by the people of a country when they speak or write to each other.

lantern **lanterns**

NOUN A **lantern** is a lamp in a container. It has sides which the light can shine through but which stop the wind from blowing out the light.

lap **laps, lapping, lapped**

NOUN **1** Your **lap** is the flat area formed by the tops of your legs when you are sitting down.

VERB **2** When an animal **laps** up liquid, it drinks using its tongue to get the liquid into its mouth.

large **larger, largest**

ADJECTIVE Something **large** is big.

larva **larvae**

NOUN A **larva** is an insect at an early stage of its life. It looks likes a short fat worm.

laser **lasers**

NOUN A **laser** is a machine which produces a narrow beam of light. Lasers are used for many different things, including medical operations.

last **lasts, lasting, lasted**

ADJECTIVE **1** The **last** thing or event is the most recent one. *I saw him **last** week.*

ADVERB **2** If something happens **last**, it happens after everything else. *I came **last** in the race.*

VERB **3** If something **lasts**, it continues to exist or happen. *Her speech **lasted** an hour.*

at last PHRASE If something happens **at last**, it happens after a long time.

late **later, latest**

ADJECTIVE OR ADVERB **1** If you are **late** arriving somewhere, you get there after the time you were supposed to.

ADJECTIVE OR ADVERB **2 Late** means near the end of a period of time. *We had a picnic in the **late** afternoon.*

lately

ADVERB If something has happened **lately**, it happened not long ago. *Have you seen your cousin **lately**?*

laugh **laughs, laughing, laughed**

VERB When you **laugh**, you make the sound people make when they are happy or think something is funny. **laughter** NOUN

launch **launches, launching, launched**

VERB **1** When a rocket or satellite is **launched**, it is sent into the sky.

VERB **2** To **launch** a ship means to send it into the water for the first time.

launderette **launderettes**

NOUN A **launderette** is a shop where people pay to use washing machines.

lava

NOUN **Lava** is a very hot, liquid rock which comes out of volcanoes.

lavatory **lavatories**

NOUN **1** A **lavatory** is a toilet.

NOUN **2** A **lavatory** is also the room where the lavatory is.

law **laws**

NOUN A **law** is a rule that is made by the government.

lawn **lawns**

NOUN A **lawn** is an area of short grass in a garden or park.

lawnmower **lawnmowers**

NOUN A **lawnmower** is a machine for cutting the grass on lawns.

lawyer **lawyers**

NOUN A **lawyer** is a person who understands the law and can advise people about it.

lay **lays, laying, laid**

VERB **1** If you **lay** something somewhere, you put it there carefully.

VERB **2** If you **lay** the table, you put things like knives and forks on the table ready for a meal.

VERB **3** When a bird **lays** an egg, it produces the egg out of its body.

layer **layers**

NOUN A **layer** is a single thickness of something that lies on top of or underneath something else.

layout **layouts**

NOUN The **layout** of something is the way it is arranged.

lazy **lazier, laziest**

ADJECTIVE Someone who is **lazy** does not want to work or do anything hard.

lazily ADVERB

lead **leads, leading, led**

(*rhymes with* **feed**)

VERB **1** If you **lead** someone to a particular place, you go with them to show them the way.

VERB **2** Someone who **leads** a group of people is in charge of them.

VERB **3** If you are **leading** in a race or game, you are winning at that point.

NOUN **4** A dog's **lead** is a long thin piece of leather or a chain. You fix one end to the collar and hold the other end.

(*rhymes with* **fed**) NOUN **5** **Lead** is a grey, heavy metal.

(*rhymes with* **fed**) NOUN **6** The **lead** in a pencil is the centre part of it that makes a mark on paper.

leader **leaders**

NOUN The **leader** of a group of people is the person who is in charge.

leaf **leaves**

NOUN A **leaf** is one of the flat green parts of a plant. Different sorts of plant have differently shaped leaves.

leaflet **leaflets**

NOUN A **leaflet** is a piece of paper with information or advertising printed on it.

leak **leaks, leaking, leaked**

VERB **1** If a pipe or container **leaks**, it has a hole which lets gas or liquid escape.

VERB **2** If liquid or gas **leaks**, it escapes from a pipe or container.

lean **leans, leaning, leant or leaned; leaner, leanest**

VERB **1** When you **lean** somewhere, you bend your body in that direction.

VERB **2** When you **lean** on something, you rest your body against it for support.

ADJECTIVE **3** **Lean** meat has little or no fat.

leap **leaps, leaping, leapt or leaped**

VERB If you **leap** somewhere, you jump over a long distance or high in the air.

leap year **leap years**

NOUN A **leap year** is a year with 366 days. There is a leap year every four years.

learn **learns, learning, learnt or learned**

VERB When you **learn** something, you get to know it or find out how to do it.

least

NOUN **1** The **least** is the smallest possible amount of something. *That is the **least** of my problems.*

ADJECTIVE OR ADVERB **2** **Least** is a superlative form of **little**, meaning very small in amount. *We bought the **least** expensive bike... She ate the **least** of all of them.*

a
b
c
d
e
f
g
h
i
j
k
Ll
m
n
o
p
q
r
s
t
u
v
w
x
y
z

a
b
c
d
e
f
g
h
i
j
k
Ll
m
n
o
p
q
r
s
t
u
v
w
x
y
z

leather

NOUN **Leather** is the specially treated skin of animals. It is used for making things like shoes and furniture.

leave **leaves, leaving, left**

VERB **1** When you **leave** a place, you go away from it.

VERB **2** If you **leave** someone somewhere, they stay behind after you go away.

VERB **3** In maths, when you take one number from other, it **leaves** a third number.

led

VERB **Led** is the past tense of **lead**.

ledge **ledges**

NOUN A **ledge** is a narrow shelf on the side of a cliff or rock face, or on the outside of a building.

leek **leeks**

NOUN A **leek** is a long white vegetable with green leaves. *See Vegetables on page 256.*

left

VERB **1** **Left** is the past tense of **leave**.

NOUN **2** The **left** is the side that you begin reading on in English.

ADJECTIVE OR ADVERB **3** **Left** means on or towards the left side of something. *Turn left at the end of the road.*

leg **legs**

NOUN **1** **Legs** are the parts of your body which stretch from the hips to the feet.

NOUN **2** The **legs** of an object such as a table are the parts which rest on the floor and support the object's weight.

legend **legends**

NOUN A **legend** is an old and popular story which may or may not be true.

lemon **lemons**

NOUN A **lemon** is a yellow, oval fruit. Lemons are juicy but they taste sour. *See Fruit on page 257.*

lemonade

NOUN **Lemonade** is a drink made from lemons, sugar and water.

lend **lends, lending, lent**

VERB If you **lend** something to someone, you let them have it for a while.

length **lengths**

NOUN **1** The **length** of something is the distance that it measures from one end to the other.

NOUN **2** The **length** of something like a holiday is the period of time that it lasts.

lens **lenses**

NOUN A **lens** is a curved piece of glass that makes light go in a certain way. Lenses are used in things like cameras, telescopes and glasses.

lent

VERB **Lent** is the past tense of **lend**.

leopard **leopards**

NOUN A **leopard** is a large wild cat that lives in the forests of Africa and Asia. It has yellow fur with black spots.

less

ADJECTIVE OR ADVERB **Less** is a comparative form of **little**, meaning not as much. *A shower uses less water than a bath.*

lesson **lessons**

NOUN A **lesson** is a short period of time when you are taught something.

let **lets, letting, let**

VERB **1** If you **let** someone do something, you allow them to do it.

VERB **2** If someone **lets** a house or flat that they own, they rent it out.

letter **letters**

NOUN **1** A **letter** is a written message to someone, usually sent through the post.

NOUN **2** **Letters** are written symbols which go together to make words.

letter box **letter boxes**

NOUN **1** A **letter box** is an oblong gap in the front door of a house or flat.

NOUN **2** A **letter box** is also a large metal container where you post letters.

lettuce **lettuces**

NOUN A **lettuce** is a plant with large green leaves that you eat raw in salads.

See *Vegetables* on page 256.

level **levels**

ADJECTIVE **1** A surface that is **level** is smooth, flat and parallel to the ground.

ADVERB **2** If you are **level** with someone, you are next to them.

NOUN **3** The **level** of a liquid is the height it comes up to. *After heavy rain the river rose to a dangerous level.*

lever **levers**

NOUN **1** A **lever** is a long bar that you put under a heavy object and press down on to make the object move.

NOUN **2** A **lever** is also a handle on a machine that you pull down to make the machine work.

library **libraries**

NOUN A **library** is a building where books are kept for people to come and read or borrow.

lick **licks, licking, licked**

VERB If you **lick** something, you move your tongue across it.

lid **lids**

NOUN A **lid** is a cover for a box or other container.

lie **lies, lying, lay, lain; lied**

VERB **1** To **lie** somewhere means to rest there horizontally.

VERB **2** To **lie** means to say something that is not true.

life **lives**

NOUN The **life** of a person or animal is the time between their birth and death.

lifeboat **lifeboats**

NOUN A **lifeboat** is a boat that is used to rescue people in danger at sea.

lifetime

NOUN Your **lifetime** is the period of time during which you are alive.

lift **lifts, lifting, lifted**

VERB **1** If you **lift** something, you move it to a higher position.

NOUN **2** A **lift** is a machine like a small room that carries passengers from one floor to another in a building.

light **lights; lighter, lightest; lights, lighting, lighted** or **lit**

NOUN **1** **Light** is the brightness from the sun, moon, fire or lamps, that lets you see things.

NOUN **2** A **light** is a lamp or other object that gives out brightness.

ADJECTIVE **3** A place that is **light** is bright because of the sun or the use of lamps.

ADJECTIVE **4** A **light** colour is pale.

ADJECTIVE **5** A **light** object does not weigh much.

VERB **6** To **light** something means to cause light to shine on it or in it.

VERB **7** To **light** a fire means to make it start burning.

lighthouse **lighthouses**

NOUN A **lighthouse** is a tower with a powerful flashing light at the top, which is used to guide ships or to warn them of danger.

lightning

NOUN **Lightning** is a bright flash of light in the sky produced by natural electricity during a thunderstorm.

a
b
c
d
e
f
g
h
i
j
k
Ll
m
n
o
p
q
r
s
t
u
v
w
x
y
z

like

like likes, liking, liked
PREPOSITION **1** If one thing is **like** another, it is similar to it.
VERB **2** If you **like** someone or something, you find them pleasant.

likely likelier, likeliest
ADJECTIVE Something that is **likely** will probably happen or is probably true.

limb limbs
NOUN A **limb** is an arm or leg.

limerick limericks
NOUN A **limerick** is a funny nonsense poem of five lines.

limit limits
NOUN A **limit** is a line or a point beyond which something cannot go. *There is a speed **limit** on this road.*

limp limps, limping, limped; limper, limpest
VERB **1** If you **limp**, you walk unevenly because you have hurt your leg or foot.
ADJECTIVE **2** Something that is **limp** is soft and floppy. *This lettuce is a bit **limp**.*

line lines
NOUN **1** A **line** is a long thin mark. Some writing paper has lines on it to show you where to write.
NOUN **2** A **line** of people or things is a number of them in a row.

NOUN **3** In a piece of writing, a **line** is a number of words together. *A limerick has five **lines**.*
NOUN **4** A railway **line** is one of the heavy metal rails that trains run on.

linen
NOUN **Linen** is a kind of cloth made from a plant called flax. It is used for things like sheets and tablecloths.

liner liners
NOUN A **liner** is a large passenger ship that makes long journeys.

link links
NOUN **1** A **link** is one of the rings in a chain.
NOUN **2** A **link** is also a connection between two things. *There's a high speed rail **link** between Brighton and London.*

lion lions
NOUN A **lion** is a large wild cat. Lions live in parts of Africa and Asia, in groups called prides.

lioness lionesses
NOUN A **lioness** is a female lion.

lip lips
NOUN Your **lips** are the top and bottom outer edges of your mouth.

liquid liquids
NOUN A **liquid** is anything which is not a solid or a gas, and which can be poured.

list lists
NOUN A **list** is a set of things that are written one below the other.

listen listens, listening, listened
VERB If you **listen** to a sound that you can hear, you pay attention to it.
listener NOUN

lit
VERB **Lit** is the past tense of **light**.

literacy
NOUN **Literacy** is the ability to read and write. See **numeracy**.

litre litres
NOUN A **litre** is a unit used to measure volume and capacity. A litre is equal to 1000 millilitres.

litter litters
NOUN **1** Litter is rubbish left lying untidily outside.
NOUN **2** A **litter** is a group of animals born to the same mother at the same time.
See *Collective nouns* on page 262.

little less, lesser, least
ADJECTIVE **1** Something or someone that is **little** is small in size.
ADVERB **2** Little can mean not much. *Our lazy cat does very **little**.*

live¹ lives, living, lived
(*rhymes with* **give**)
VERB **1** If you **live** in a place, that is where your home is.
VERB **2** To **live** means to be alive.

live²
(*rhymes with* **hive**)
ADJECTIVE **1** A **live** animal is living.
ADJECTIVE **2** Live television or radio is broadcast as it happens.

lively livelier, liveliest
ADJECTIVE Someone who is **lively** is cheerful and full of energy.

liver livers
NOUN Your **liver** is a large organ in your body. Its job is to clean your blood.

living
ADJECTIVE **1** Living things are plants, animals and humans that are alive. All living things need food to grow.
NOUN **2** Someone who earns a **living** earns enough money to buy all the things they need. *She earns a **living** as an artist.*

living room living rooms
NOUN The **living room** in a house is the room where the family spend most of their time.

lizard lizards
NOUN A **lizard** is a small reptile with four short legs and a long tail. It has a rough dry skin. The babies hatch from eggs.
See *Reptiles* on page 259.

llama llamas
NOUN A **llama** is a South American animal of the camel family, with long thick hair.

load loads, loading, loaded
NOUN **1** A **load** is things which are being carried somewhere.
VERB **2** When you **load** a camera, you put film into it so that it is ready to use.
VERB **3** When you **load** a computer, you put information or a program into it.

loaf loaves
NOUN A **loaf** is bread that has been baked into one shape. You cut a loaf into slices.

lobster lobsters
NOUN A **lobster** is a sea animal with a hard shell, two large claws and eight legs.

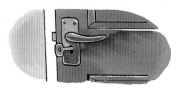

local
ADJECTIVE **Local** means belonging to the area where you live or work. *I read about it in the **local** paper.*

locate locates, locating, located
VERB To **locate** someone or something is to find out where they are.

location locations
NOUN A **location** is a place, or the position of something. *The school is being moved to a new **location**.*

loch lochs
NOUN **Loch** is a Scottish word for **lake**.

lock locks, locking, locked
VERB **1** If you **lock** something, you close it and fasten it with a key.

NOUN **2** A **lock** is used to keep something, such as a door or case, closed. You can only open a lock with the right key.

a b c d e f g h i j k **Ll** m n o p q r s t u v w x y z

locomotive **locomotives**

NOUN A **locomotive** is the engine which pulls trains along railway tracks.

loft **lofts**

NOUN A **loft** is the space under the roof of a house, often used for storing things.

log **logs**

NOUN A **log** is a piece of a thick branch from a tree.

lollipop **lollipops**

NOUN A **lollipop** is a hard sweet on a stick.

lolly **lollies**

NOUN **Lolly** is an abbreviation of **lollipop**. A **lolly** is also a piece of flavoured ice or ice cream on a stick.

lonely **lonelier, loneliest**

ADJECTIVE Someone who is **lonely** is sad because they are on their own, or do not have any friends.

long **longer, longest; longs, longing, longed**

ADJECTIVE **1** Something **long** takes up more time than usual. *It was a **long** film.*
ADJECTIVE **2** Something that is **long** is far from one end to the other. *It's a **long** way from London to New York.*
VERB **3** If you **long** for something, you want it very much.

look **looks, looking, looked**

VERB **1** If you **look** in a particular direction, you turn your eyes that way.
VERB **2** If you say how someone **looks**, you tell them how they seem to you.
VERB **3** If you **look after** someone, you care for them.
VERB **4** If you **look for** someone or something, you try to find them.
VERB **5** If you are **looking forward** to something, you want it to happen because you think you will enjoy it.

loop **loops**

NOUN A **loop** is a circular shape in something long and thin. For example, when you tie shoelaces, the bow has two loops in it.

loose **looser, loosest**

ADJECTIVE **1** Something that is **loose** is not firmly fixed. *I've got a **loose** tooth.*
ADJECTIVE **2** Things that are **loose** are not fixed together. *She had four **loose** sheets of paper in her bag.*

lord **lords**

NOUN Hundreds of years ago, a **lord** was a man who had a lot of power. Now, **Lord** is a title in front of some men's names in Britain.

lorry **lorries**

NOUN A **lorry** is a large road vehicle that is used to carry loads.

lose **loses, losing, lost**

VERB **1** If you **lose** something, you cannot find it.
VERB **2** If someone **loses** weight, they become thinner.
VERB **3** If you **lose** something like a game or a race, someone does better than you.

lost

ADJECTIVE **1** If you are **lost**, you cannot find your way or do not know where you are.

VERB **2** Lost is the past tense of **lose**.

lot **lots**

NOUN A **lot** of something, or **lots** of something, is a large amount of it.

lottery **lotteries**

NOUN A **lottery** is a way of raising money by selling tickets. The winner is chosen by chance.

loud louder, loudest

ADJECTIVE A **loud** sound is one that makes a lot of noise. *The firework went off with a loud bang.*

loudspeaker loudspeakers

NOUN A **loudspeaker** is a piece of equipment that is used so that sounds can be heard. Microphones, radios and CD players all need loudspeakers.

lounge lounges

NOUN A **lounge** in a house or hotel is a room where people sit and relax.

love loves, loving, loved

VERB **1** If you **love** someone, you have strong feelings of affection for them.
VERB **2** If you **love** something, you like it very much. *I love pizza.*

lovely lovelier, loveliest

ADJECTIVE Something that is **lovely** is very pleasing to look at or listen to.

low lower, lowest

ADJECTIVE Something that is **low** measures only a short distance from the ground to the top. *He jumped over the low wall.*

lower lowers, lowering, lowered

VERB **1** If you **lower** something, you move it slowly downwards. *As it was getting dark, she lowered the blind.*
VERB **2** If you **lower** your voice, you speak more quietly.

lower-case

ADJECTIVE **Lower-case** letters are the small letters of the alphabet, such as a, b, c and d. *The letters down the side of this page are lower-case.* See **upper-case**.

loyal

ADJECTIVE If you are **loyal** to someone, you always support them.

luck

NOUN **Luck** is something that seems to happen without any reason. Luck can be good or bad.

lucky luckier, luckiest

ADJECTIVE Someone who is **lucky** seems to have good luck.
luckily ADVERB

luggage

NOUN **Luggage** is all the suitcases, bags and things that you take with you when you are travelling.

lump lumps

NOUN **1** A **lump** is a piece of something solid. *She took a lump of modelling clay.*
NOUN **2** A **lump** on someone's body is a small swelling.

lunar

ADJECTIVE **Lunar** is used to describe something that is to do with the moon.

lunch lunches

NOUN **Lunch** is a meal that you have in the middle of the day.

lung lungs

NOUN Your **lungs** are the two parts of your body inside your chest that fill with air when you breathe.

luxury luxuries

NOUN A **luxury** is something quite expensive to buy, which you like very much but do not need.
luxurious ADJECTIVE

lying

VERB **Lying** is the present participle of **lie**.

a
b
c
d
e
f
g
h
i
j
k
Ll
m
n
o
p
q
r
s
t
u
v
w
x
y
z

Mm

machine machines
NOUN A **machine** is a piece of equipment which does a particular kind of work. It is usually powered by an engine or by electricity.

machinery
NOUN **Machinery** is machines in general.

mad madder, maddest
ADJECTIVE **1** Someone who is **mad** has an illness in their mind.

ADJECTIVE **2** If you describe someone as **mad**, you mean they are foolish or silly.

ADJECTIVE **3** INFORMAL Someone who is **mad** is angry.

ADJECTIVE **4** INFORMAL If you are **mad** about someone or something, you like them very much.

made
VERB **Made** is the past tense of **make**.

magazine magazines
NOUN A **magazine** is a thin book which comes out regularly, usually once a week or once a month. It has articles, stories and pictures.

maggot maggots
NOUN A **maggot** looks like a tiny worm. Maggots change into flies.

magic
NOUN **1** In stories, **magic** is the thing that makes impossible things happen.

ADJECTIVE **2** Magic tricks entertain and puzzle people.

magical ADJECTIVE

magician magicians
NOUN **1** In stories, a **magician** is a man who has magic powers.

NOUN **2** A **magician** is also a real person who can do magic tricks.

magnet magnets
NOUN A **magnet** is a special piece of metal. It pulls or attracts iron or steel towards it. Magnets can also push other magnets away.

magnetic ADJECTIVE

magnificent
ADJECTIVE Something that is **magnificent** is very grand.

magnifying glass magnifying glasses
NOUN A **magnifying glass** is a piece of glass that makes objects appear to be bigger than they really are.

magpie magpies
NOUN A **magpie** is a bird of the crow family. It has black and white markings and a long tail.

mail
NOUN **Mail** is things like letters and parcels that are sent through the post.

main
ADJECTIVE The **main** part of something is the most important part.

maize
NOUN **Maize** is a tall plant that produces sweet corn.

major
ADJECTIVE You use **major** to describe something important. *This is a **major** discovery.*

make makes, making, made
VERB **1** If you **make** something new, you use your skill to shape it or put it together.

VERB 2 To **make** something happen is to cause it. *My new boots **made** a loud squeak.*

VERB 3 If you **make** a mistake, you do something wrong.

VERB 4 If you **make** someone do something, you force them to do it. *My mum **makes** me eat vegetables.*

male **males**

NOUN A **male** is a person or animal that belongs to the sex that cannot have babies.

male ADJECTIVE

mammal **mammals**

NOUN A **mammal** is a warm-blooded animal. Female mammals give birth to live babies. They feed their babies with milk from their own bodies.

man **men**

NOUN A **man** is an adult male human being. See **woman**.

manage **manages, managing, managed**

VERB 1 If you **manage** to do something, you succeed in doing it. *He **managed** to get a seat on the bus.*

VERB 2 Someone who **manages** an organization is in charge of it.

mane **manes**

NOUN The **mane** of an animal such as a horse or a male lion is the long thick hair that grows from its neck.

mango **mangoes** or **mangos**

NOUN A **mango** is a sweet yellowish fruit which grows in tropical countries. See *Fruit* on page 257.

manner **manners**

NOUN 1 The **manner** in which you do something is how you do it.

NOUN 2 Your **manner** is the way in which you behave and talk. *It is good **manners** to be polite.*

mantelpiece **mantelpieces**

NOUN A **mantelpiece** is a shelf over a fireplace.

manufacture **manufactures, manufacturing, manufactured**

VERB To **manufacture** goods is to make them in a factory.

many

ADJECTIVE 1 If there are **many** people or things, there are a large number of them.

ADJECTIVE 2 You also use **many** to ask how great a quantity is or to give information about it. *How **many** tickets do you want?*

map **maps**

NOUN A **map** is a drawing of a particular area as it would look from above.

marathon **marathons**

NOUN A **marathon** is a race in which people have to run 26 miles (about 42 kilometres) along roads.

marble **marbles**

NOUN 1 Marble is a very hard stone which shines when it is polished. Statues and parts of buildings are sometimes made of marble.

NOUN 2 Marbles is a children's game played with small coloured glass balls. These balls are also called marbles.

march **marches, marching, marched**

VERB When you **march**, you walk with quick regular steps like a soldier.

March

NOUN March is the third month of the year. It has 31 days.

mare **mares**

NOUN A **mare** is an adult female horse.

margarine

NOUN **Margarine** is a food that looks like butter but is made from vegetable oil and animal fats. You can spread it on bread and use it for cooking.

margin **margins**

NOUN The **margin** is the blank space at each side on a written or printed page.

mark **marks**

NOUN **1** A **mark** is a small stain. *I can't get that mark off your shirt.*

NOUN **2** A **mark** is also something that has been written or drawn. *He made little marks on the paper with his pencil.*

NOUN **3** At school, a **mark** is a letter or number showing how well you have done in homework or in a test.

market **markets**

NOUN A **market** is a place with many small stalls selling different goods.

marmalade

NOUN **Marmalade** is a jam made from fruit like oranges or lemons. People often eat it spread on toast for breakfast.

marriage **marriages**

NOUN **Marriage** is the relationship between a husband and wife.

married

ADJECTIVE Someone who is **married** has a husband or wife.

marry **marries, marrying, married**

VERB A man and woman who **marry** become husband and wife.

marsh **marshes**

NOUN A **marsh** is an area of land which is always very wet and muddy.

marsupial **marsupials**

NOUN A **marsupial** is a mammal whose babies are carried in a pouch at the front of their mother's body. Kangaroos are marsupials.

marvellous

ADJECTIVE Something that is **marvellous** is wonderful.

masculine

ADJECTIVE **Masculine** refers to qualities and things that are typical of men.

mask **masks**

NOUN A **mask** is something you wear over your face to protect or disguise you.

mass **masses**

NOUN **1** A **mass** of things is a large number of them grouped together.

NOUN **2** The **mass** of something is the amount of matter it contains. Mass is measured in grams and kilograms. People often say "weight" when they mean "mass". Mass and weight are different. If you were on the Moon, you would weigh less than on Earth but your mass would not change. See **weight**.

NOUN **3** In the Roman Catholic church, a **Mass** is a religious service.

massive

ADJECTIVE Something **massive** is extremely large.

mast **masts**

NOUN A **mast** is the tall upright pole that supports the sail of a boat.

mat **mats**

NOUN **1** A **mat** is a small piece of carpet.

NOUN **2** A **mat** is also something used to protect a table from plates or glasses.

match matches, matching, matched

NOUN **1** A **match** is an organized game of something like tennis or football.

NOUN **2** A **match** is also a thin stick of wood that can make a flame.

VERB **3** If you **match** things, you find a connection between them. *Match the animals with the countries they come from.*

mate mates

NOUN **1** INFORMAL A **mate** is a friend.

NOUN **2** An animal's **mate** is its partner.

material materials

NOUN **1** **Material** is cloth.

NOUN **2** A **material** is anything that can be used to make something else. Wood, stone, plastic and water are all materials.

mathematics

NOUN **Mathematics** is the study of numbers, quantities and shapes.

maths

NOUN **Maths** is an abbreviation of **mathematics**.

matter matters, mattering, mattered

VERB **1** If something **matters** to you, you care about it and feel it is important.

NOUN **2** A **matter** is something that you have to deal with or think about. *This is a matter for the police.*

mattress mattresses

NOUN A **mattress** is a large flat cushion which is put on a bed to make it comfortable to lie on.

may

VERB If someone says you **may** do something, you are allowed to do it.

May

NOUN **May** is the fifth month of the year. It has 31 days.

maybe

ADVERB You say **maybe** when something is possible but you are not sure about it. *Maybe we could go tomorrow.*

mayor mayors

NOUN The **mayor** of a town or city is the man or woman who has been chosen to be its head.

maze mazes

NOUN A **maze** is a system of paths which is made like a puzzle so that it is difficult to find your way through it.

meadow meadows

NOUN A **meadow** is a field of grass and wild flowers.

meal meals

NOUN A **meal** is food that people eat, usually at set times during the day.

mean means, meaning, meant; meaner, meanest

VERB **1** If you ask what something **means**, you want it explained to you.

VERB **2** If you **mean** what you say, you are serious about it.

VERB **3** If something **means** a lot to you, it is important to you.

VERB **4** If you **mean** to do something, you intend to do it. *I meant to phone you, but I didn't have time.*

ADJECTIVE **5** Someone who is **mean** does not like spending money or sharing.

meaning meanings

NOUN The **meaning** of a word or sentence is the thing or idea that it is explaining. *Do you know the meaning of the proverb "Look before you leap"?*

meanwhile

ADVERB **Meanwhile** means while something else is happening.

measles

NOUN **Measles** is an illness caught especially by children. It gives you a fever and red spots on your skin.

measure **measures, measuring, measured**

VERB **1** If you **measure** something, you find out how large or heavy it is.

NOUN **2** A **measure** is a unit in which something such as size or speed is expressed. *Kilometres are a measure of distance.*

See *Measures* on page 270.

measurement **measurements**

NOUN A **measurement** is a result that you get by measuring something.

meat **meats**

NOUN **Meat** is the flesh of animals that is cooked and eaten.

mechanical

ADJECTIVE A **mechanical** object has moving parts and is used to do a physical task.

medal **medals**

NOUN A **medal** is a small metal disc or cross given as an award for bravery or as a prize for sport.

medical

ADJECTIVE **Medical** means to do with medicine or the care of people's health.

medicine **medicines**

NOUN **Medicine** is a tablet or liquid given to people who are ill to make them better.

medium

ADJECTIVE **Medium** means somewhere in the middle of two extremes. *He's of medium height – neither tall nor short.*

meet **meets, meeting, met**

VERB If you **meet** someone, you go to the same place at the same time as they do.

meeting **meetings**

NOUN A **meeting** is when a group of people meet to talk about particular things.

melon **melons**

NOUN A **melon** is a large fruit that is sweet and juicy inside. It has a thick, hard green or yellow skin.

See *Fruit* on page 257.

melt **melts, melting, melted**

VERB When something like ice **melts**, it changes from a solid into a liquid because it has become warmer.

member **members**

NOUN A **member** of a group is one of the people, animals or things belonging to that group.

membership NOUN

memorize **memorizes, memorizing, memorized**; also spelt **memorise**

VERB If you **memorize** something, you learn it so that you can repeat it exactly using only your memory.

memory **memories**

NOUN **1** Your **memory** is what allows you to remember things.

NOUN **2** A **memory** is something you remember from the past.

men

NOUN **Men** is the plural of **man**.

mend **mends, mending, mended**

VERB If you **mend** something that is broken or does not work, you put it right so that it can be used again.

mental

ADJECTIVE **Mental** means to do with your mind or brain. For example, mental maths is working out the answers to calculations in your head.

mention mentions, mentioning, mentioned

VERB If you **mention** something, you talk about it briefly.

menu menus

NOUN **1** A **menu** is a list of food that you can order in a restaurant.

NOUN **2** A **menu** on a computer is a list of choices.

mercury

NOUN **Mercury** is a silver-coloured metal. Liquid mercury is used in thermometers.

mercy

NOUN If you show **mercy** to someone, you do not hurt or punish them.

mermaid mermaids

NOUN In stories, a **mermaid** is a woman with a fish's tail.

merry merrier, merriest

ADJECTIVE **Merry** means happy and cheerful.

mess messes

NOUN If you say something is a **mess**, you mean it is very untidy.

messy ADJECTIVE

message messages

NOUN A **message** is words that you send or leave when you cannot speak directly to someone.

messenger messengers

NOUN A **messenger** is a person who takes a message to someone.

met

VERB **Met** is the past tense of **meet**.

metal metals

NOUN A **metal** is a hard, strong material that melts when it is heated, such as iron, gold or steel. Metals are used to make things like jewellery, tools, cars and machines.

meter meters

NOUN A **meter** is an instrument for measuring something, such as the amount of gas that you have used.

method methods

NOUN A **method** is a particular way of doing something.

metre metres

NOUN **1** A **metre** (m) is a measure of length. It is equal to 100 centimetres.

NOUN **2** In poetry, **metre** is the rhythmic arrangement of words and syllables.

metric

ADJECTIVE **Metric** relates to the system of measurement that uses metres, kilograms and litres.

miaow

NOUN A **miaow** is the short high-pitched sound that a cat makes.

mice

NOUN **Mice** is the plural of **mouse**.

micro-

PREFIX **Micro-** means small. See *Prefixes* on page 264.

microchip microchips

NOUN A **microchip** is a small piece of silicon on which electronic circuits for a computer are printed.

microphone microphones

NOUN A **microphone** is a piece of equipment that is used to make sounds louder, or to record them.

microscope microscopes

NOUN A **microscope** is a piece of equipment which makes small objects appear much larger.

microscopic ADJECTIVE

a
b
c
d
e
f
g
h
i
j
k
l
Mm
n
o
p
q
r
s
t
u
v
w
x
y
z

microwave **microwaves**

NOUN A **microwave** is a type of oven which cooks food very quickly.

mid-

PREFIX **Mid-** is used to form words that refer to the middle part of a place or period of time, for example "midday". See *Prefixes* on page 264.

midday

NOUN **Midday** is 12 o'clock (noon) in the middle of the day.

middle **middles**

NOUN **1** The **middle** of something is the part furthest from the edges.

ADJECTIVE **2** The **middle** one in a series or a row is the one that has an equal number of people or things on each side of it.

midnight

NOUN **Midnight** is 12 o'clock at night.

might

VERB **1** If you say something **might** happen, you are not sure if it will.

VERB **2** If you say something **might** be true, you are not sure about it.

migrate **migrates, migrating, migrated**

VERB When birds, fish or animals **migrate**, they move to another place at a particular time of year so that they can find food.

mild **milder, mildest**

ADJECTIVE **1** Something that is **mild** is gentle and does no harm. *You need to use a mild shampoo.*

ADJECTIVE **2 Mild** weather in the winter is warmer than usual.

mile **miles**

NOUN A **mile** is a unit of distance equal to about one and a half kilometres.

military

ADJECTIVE **Military** means to do with the armed forces of a country.

milk

NOUN **Milk** is the white liquid that female mammals make in their bodies to feed their young. People drink milk from cows and use it to make butter, cheese and yogurt.

mill **mills**

NOUN **1** A **mill** is a building in which grain is crushed to make flour. The photo shows a water mill. The water makes the mill wheel turn.

NOUN **2** A **mill** is also a factory used for making things such as cotton or paper.

millennium **millennia or millenniums**

NOUN A **millennium** is a period of 1000 years.

millilitre **millilitres**

NOUN A **millilitre** is a measure of volume and capacity. There are 1000 millilitres in a litre.

millimetre **millimetres**

NOUN A **millimetre** (mm) is a measure of length. There are 1000 millimetres in a metre. There are 10 millimetres in a centimetre.

million **millions**

NOUN A **million** is the number 1,000,000.

millionaire **millionaires**

NOUN A **millionaire** is a person who has more than a million pounds or dollars.

mince

NOUN **Mince** is meat which has been cut into very small pieces.

mincemeat

NOUN **Mincemeat** is a sticky mixture of dried fruit and other sweet things.

mind **minds, minding, minded**

NOUN **1** Your **mind** is your ability to think, together with your memory and all the thoughts you have.

NOUN **2** If you **change your mind**, you change a decision you have made.

VERB **3** If you **mind** about something, it worries you or makes you angry.

mine **mines**

PRONOUN **1** **Mine** refers to something belonging to the person who is speaking or writing. *That book is **mine**.*

NOUN **2** A **mine** is a place under the ground where people dig out things like diamonds, coal or other minerals.

NOUN **3** A **mine** can be a bomb hidden in the ground or underwater, which explodes when people or things touch it.

mineral **minerals**

NOUN **Minerals** are substances such as tin, salt or coal that are formed naturally in rocks and in the earth.

mini-

PREFIX **Mini-** is used to form nouns that refer to something smaller or less important than similar things, for example a minibus.

See *Prefixes* on page 264.

minibus **minibuses**

NOUN A **minibus** is a van with seats in the back that is used as a small bus.

minister **ministers**

NOUN **1** A **minister** is an important member of the government of a country.

NOUN **2** A **minister** is also a person in charge of a church.

minor

ADJECTIVE Something that is **minor** is not very important or serious. *She had a **minor** accident.*

mint **mints**

NOUN **1** **Mint** is a small plant. Its leaves have a strong taste and smell, and are used in cooking.

NOUN **2** A **mint** is a kind of sweet.

NOUN **3** A **mint** is also a place where coins are made.

minus

PREPOSITION **1** You use **minus** to show that one number is being subtracted from another. For example, ten minus six equals four (written $10 - 6 = 4$).

ADJECTIVE **2** Minus is used when talking about temperatures below 0° Celsius. *The temperature is **minus** two degrees.*

minute **minutes**

(*said* **min**-nit) NOUN **1** A **minute** is a unit of time equal to 60 seconds.

(*said* my-**nyoot**) ADJECTIVE **2** Something **minute** is extremely small.

miracle **miracles**

NOUN **1** A **miracle** is a wonderful event, believed to have been caused by God.

NOUN **2** A **miracle** can also be any very surprising event. *By some **miracle** he got to school early.*

mirror **mirrors**

NOUN A **mirror** is a piece of glass that reflects light. When you look in a mirror you can see yourself.

mis-

PREFIX **Mis-** is added to some words to form other words, often ones that refer to things being done wrongly, for example "misprint" or "misunderstand".

See *Prefixes* on page 264.

misbehave **misbehaves, misbehaving, misbehaved**

VERB If a child **misbehaves**, they are naughty or behave badly.

mischief

mischief

NOUN **Mischief** is silly things that some children do to annoy other people.

mischievous

ADJECTIVE **1** A **mischievous** person likes to have fun by embarrassing people or playing tricks.

ADJECTIVE **2** A **mischievous** child is often naughty but does not do any real harm.

miserable

ADJECTIVE Someone who is **miserable** is unhappy.

miserably ADVERB

misery

NOUN **Misery** is great unhappiness.

misfortune misfortunes

NOUN **Misfortune** is bad luck.

mislay mislays, mislaying, mislaid

VERB If you **mislay** something, you forget where you have put it.

mislead misleads, misleading, misled

VERB To **mislead** someone is to give them an idea that is not true.

misprint misprints

NOUN A **misprint** is a mistake in something that has been printed, for example "cow" instead of "cot".

miss misses, missing, missed

VERB **1** If you are aiming at something and **miss**, you fail to hit it.

VERB **2** If you **miss** a bus or train, you are too late to get on it.

VERB **3** If you **miss** somebody, you are lonely without them.

Miss

NOUN **Miss** is used before the name of a girl or an unmarried woman.

missile missiles

NOUN A **missile** is a weapon that goes through the air and explodes when it reaches its target.

missing

ADJECTIVE If something is **missing**, it is not in its usual place and you cannot find it.

misspell misspells, misspelling, misspelt or misspelled

VERB If you **misspell** a word, you spell it wrongly.

mist mists

NOUN A **mist** is a large number of tiny drops of water in the air. When there is a mist, you cannot see very far.

misty ADJECTIVE

mistake mistakes

NOUN A **mistake** is something that is done wrong.

misunderstand misunderstands, misunderstanding, misunderstood

VERB If you **misunderstand** someone, you do not understand them properly.

mix mixes, mixing, mixed

VERB If you **mix** things, you stir them or put them together. *The children made paste by **mixing** flour and water.*

mixture mixtures

NOUN A **mixture** is several different things mixed up.

moan moans, moaning, moaned

VERB If you **moan**, you make a low sad sound because you are in pain or trouble.

moat moats

NOUN A **moat** is a wide water-filled ditch around a building such as a castle.

mobile mobiles

ADJECTIVE **1** If you are **mobile**, you are able to travel or move to another place.

NOUN **2** A **mobile** is a decoration that you hang up so that it moves around when a breeze blows.

mobile phone **mobile phones**

NOUN A **mobile phone** is a telephone you can carry about.

model **models**

NOUN **1** A **model** is a small copy of something. It shows what it looks like or how it works.

NOUN **2** A **model** is also someone who shows clothes to people by wearing them.

modern

ADJECTIVE **Modern** is to do with new ideas and equipment. *We live in a modern house.*

modest

ADJECTIVE People who are **modest** do not boast about themselves.

moist **moister, moistest**

ADJECTIVE Something that is **moist** is slightly wet.

moisten VERB

moisture

NOUN **Moisture** is tiny drops of water in the air or on a surface.

mole **moles**

NOUN **1** A **mole** is a small burrowing animal with tiny eyes and dark silky fur.

NOUN **2** A **mole** is also a small dark lump on someone's skin.

moment **moments**

NOUN **1** A **moment** is a very short time.

NOUN **2** A **moment** is also a point in time when something happens. *At that moment, the teacher came into the room.*

Monday **Mondays**

NOUN **Monday** is the day between Sunday and Tuesday.

money

NOUN **Money** is the coins or banknotes you use to buy something.

mongrel **mongrels**

NOUN A **mongrel** is a dog with parents of different breeds.

monitor **monitors**

NOUN A **monitor** is the part of a computer that contains the screen.

monkey **monkeys**

NOUN A **monkey** is an animal that lives in hot countries. It has a long tail and climbs trees.

monster **monsters**

NOUN A **monster** is an imaginary creature that is large and terrifying.

month **months**

NOUN A **month** is a measure of time. There are 12 months in a year.

mood **moods**

NOUN Your **mood** is the way you are feeling about things at a particular time, such as how cheerful or angry you are.

moon **moons**

NOUN The **moon** is a satellite that moves round the Earth. It shines in the sky at night. You can only see it because the moon's surface reflects sunlight.

moonlight

NOUN **Moonlight** is the light that comes from the moon at night.

moor **moors**

NOUN A **moor** is an open area of land covered mainly with grass and heather.

moose

moose

NOUN A **moose** is a large North American deer. Moose have very flat, branch-shaped horns called antlers.

mop mops

NOUN A **mop** is a tool for washing floors. It has a long handle with sponge or pieces of string fixed to the end.

more

ADJECTIVE OR ADVERB **More** means a greater number or amount of something. It is the comparative of "many" or "much". *Jill thinks football is **more** fun than maths. He's got **more** chips than me.*

morning mornings

NOUN **Morning** is the part of the day before noon.

mosque mosques

NOUN A **mosque** is a building where Muslims worship.

mosquito mosquitoes or mosquitos

NOUN A **mosquito** is a small flying insect that lives in damp places. The female bites people and other animals to suck their blood.
See *Insects* on page 259.

moss mosses

NOUN **Moss** is a small green plant without roots. It grows in flat clumps on trees, rocks and damp ground.

most

ADJECTIVE, ADVERB OR NOUN **Most** means the greatest number or amount of something. It is the superlative of "many" or "much". *I saw the **most** fantastic film. **Most** children like sweets. The **most** I can give you is three pieces.*

moth moths

NOUN A **moth** is an insect like a butterfly that usually flies at night.

mother mothers

NOUN A **mother** is a woman who has a child or children of her own.

motion motions

NOUN A **motion** is a movement.

motive motives

NOUN A **motive** is a reason for doing something. *There was no **motive** for the attack.*

motor motors

NOUN A **motor** is part of a vehicle or machine. The motor uses fuel to make the vehicle or machine work.

motorbike motorbikes

NOUN A **motorbike** is a two-wheeled vehicle that is driven by an engine.

motorway motorways

NOUN A **motorway** is a wide road built for fast travel over long distances.

mould moulds

NOUN **1 Mould** is a soft grey or green substance that can form on old food.
NOUN **2** A **mould** is a container used to make something into a particular shape, for example a jelly mould.

moult moults, moulting, moulted

VERB When an animal **moults**, it loses its hair or feathers so that new ones can grow.

mount mounts, mounting, mounted

VERB If you **mount** a horse, you climb on its back.

mountain mountains

NOUN A **mountain** is a very high piece of land with steep sides.

mouse   mice

NOUN **1** A **mouse** is a small rodent with a long tail.

NOUN **2** A **mouse** is also a small object that you use to move the cursor on a computer screen.

moustache   moustaches

NOUN A man's **moustache** is hair growing on his upper lip.

mouth   mouths

NOUN **1** Your **mouth** is your lips, or the space behind them where your tongue and teeth are.

NOUN **2** The **mouth** of a cave or hole is the entrance to it.

NOUN **3** The **mouth** of a river is the place where it flows into the sea.

move   moves, moving, moved

VERB **1** To **move** means to go to a different place or position.

VERB **2** To **move** something means to change its place or position.

movement NOUN

mow   mows, mowing, mowed

VERB If a person **mows** an area of grass, they cut it with a lawnmower.

Mr   (said **miss**-ter)

Mr is used before a man's name.

Mrs   (said **miss**-iz)

Mrs is used before the name of a married woman.

Ms   (said **miz**)

Ms can be used before a woman's name. Some women choose to be called Ms because it says nothing about whether they are married or not.

much

ADVERB **1** You use **much** to show that something is true to a great extent. *I feel* ***much*** *better now.*

ADVERB **2** If something does not happen **much**, it does not happen very often.

ADJECTIVE **3** You use **much** to ask questions or give information about the size or amount of something. *How* ***much*** *money do you need?*

mud

NOUN **Mud** is wet sticky earth.

muddy ADJECTIVE

muddle   muddles

NOUN If things such as papers are in a **muddle**, they are all mixed up.

muffled

ADJECTIVE A **muffled** sound is quiet or difficult to hear.

mug   mugs

NOUN A **mug** is a large deep cup, usually with straight sides and a handle.

multiple   multiples

NOUN The **multiples** of a number are other numbers that it will divide into exactly. For example, 6, 9 and 12 are multiples of 3.

multiplication

NOUN **Multiplication** is when you multiply one number by another. The sign you use for multiplication is ×.

multiply   multiplies, multiplying, multiplied

VERB **1** When something **multiplies**, it increases greatly in number. *Fleas* ***multiply*** *very fast.*

VERB **2** When you **multiply** a number, you make it bigger by a number of times. For example, two multiplied by three (two plus two plus two) equals six. $2 \times 3 = 6$ or $2 + 2 + 2 = 6$

a
b
c
d
e
f
g
h
i
j
k
l
Mm
n
o
p
q
r
s
t
u
v
w
x
y
z

mum **mums**

NOUN Your **mum** is your mother.

mumble **mumbles, mumbling, mumbled**

VERB If you **mumble**, you speak very quietly and not clearly.

mumps

NOUN **Mumps** is an illness caught especially by children. Your neck swells and your throat hurts.

munch **munches, munching, munched**

VERB If you **munch** something, you chew it steadily and thoroughly.

murder **murders**

NOUN **Murder** is the deliberate killing of a person.

murmur **murmurs, murmuring, murmured**

VERB If you **murmur**, you say something very softly.

muscle **muscles**

NOUN **Muscles** are the parts inside your body that you use when you move.

museum **museums**

NOUN A **museum** is a building where many interesting or valuable objects are kept and displayed.

mushroom **mushrooms**

NOUN A **mushroom** is a small fungus with a short thick stem and a round top. You can eat some kinds of mushroom, but others are poisonous.

music

NOUN **1 Music** is a pattern of sounds made by people singing or playing instruments.

NOUN **2 Music** is also the written symbols that stand for musical sounds.

musical

ADJECTIVE **Musical** means relating to playing or studying music. *He wants to learn to play a **musical** instrument.*

musician **musicians**

NOUN A **musician** is a person who plays a musical instrument well.

Muslim **Muslims;** also spelt **Moslem**

NOUN A **Muslim** is a person who follows the religion of Islam.

must

VERB If something **must** happen, it is important or necessary that it happens. *You **must** be home by 5 p.m.*

mustard

NOUN **Mustard** is a hot spicy yellow paste made from mustard seeds.

my

ADJECTIVE **My** refers to something belonging or relating to the person speaking or writing. *I held **my** breath.*

myself

PRONOUN **Myself** is used when the person speaking does something and no one else does it. *I hung the picture **myself**.*

mysterious

ADJECTIVE Something that is **mysterious** is strange and puzzling.

mystery **mysteries**

NOUN **1** A **mystery** is something strange that cannot be explained.

NOUN **2** A **mystery** is also a story in which strange things happen.

myth **myths**

NOUN A **myth** is a story which was made up long ago to explain natural events and religious beliefs.

Nn

nail **nails**

NOUN **1** A **nail** is a small piece of metal with a sharp point at one end, which you hammer into objects to hold them together.

NOUN **2** Your **nails** are the thin hard areas at the ends of your fingers and toes.

naked

ADJECTIVE Someone who is **naked** is not wearing any clothes.

name **names**

NOUN A **name** is what someone or something is called.

nappy **nappies**

NOUN A **nappy** is a thick piece of soft material wrapped round a baby's bottom to help keep it dry and clean.

narrative **narratives**

NOUN A **narrative** is a story or an account of events.

narrator **narrators**

NOUN A **narrator** is a person who tells a story or explains what is happening.

narrow **narrower, narrowest**

ADJECTIVE Something **narrow** is a short distance from one side to the other. *The stream was **narrow** enough to jump across.*

nasty **nastier, nastiest**

ADJECTIVE **1** Something that is **nasty** is very unpleasant.

ADJECTIVE **2** Someone who is **nasty** is very unkind.

nastily ADVERB

nation **nations**

NOUN A **nation** is a country with its own laws.

national

ADJECTIVE Something that is **national** is to do with the whole of a country. *The Observer is a **national** newspaper.*

native

ADJECTIVE **1** Your **native** country is the country where you were born.

ADJECTIVE **2** Your **native** language is the language that you first learned to speak.

ADJECTIVE **3** Animals or plants that are **native** to a place live there naturally. They have not been brought there by people.

natural

ADJECTIVE **1** **Natural** means existing or happening in nature. For example, an earthquake is a natural disaster.

ADJECTIVE **2** Something that is **natural** is normal and to be expected.

nature **natures**

NOUN **1** **Nature** is animals, plants and all the other things in the world not made by people.

NOUN **2** The **nature** of a person or thing is their basic character.

naughty **naughtier, naughtiest**

ADJECTIVE A child who is **naughty** behaves badly.

navigate **navigates, navigating, navigated**

VERB When someone **navigates**, they work out the direction in which a ship, plane or car should go, using maps and sometimes instruments.

a
b
c
d
e
f
g
h
i
j
k
l
m
Nn
o
p
q
r
s
t
u
v
w
x
y
z

navy navies

NOUN **1** A **navy** is the part of a country's armed forces that fights at sea.

ADJECTIVE **2** Something that is **navy** is a very dark blue.

See *Colours* on page 271.

near nearer, nearest

ADJECTIVE **1** Something that is **near** is not far away. *Where is the nearest garage?*

ADVERB **2** If you are **near** something or somewhere, you are not far away from it. *We must be getting nearer.*

nearly

ADVERB **Nearly** means almost but not quite. *I nearly caught him but he ran off.*

neat neater, neatest

ADJECTIVE Something that is **neat** is very tidy and clean.

necessary

ADJECTIVE Something that is **necessary** is needed or must be done.

necessarily ADVERB

neck necks

NOUN Your **neck** is the part of your body that joins your head to the rest of your body.

necklace necklaces

NOUN A **necklace** is a piece of jewellery that you wear around your neck.

need needs, needing, needed

VERB **1** If you **need** something, you must have it in order to live and be healthy.

VERB **2** Sometimes you **need** something to help you do a particular job. *Now I need a paintbrush.*

VERB **3** If you **need** to do something, you have to do it.

needle needles

NOUN **1** A **needle** is a small thin piece of metal used for sewing. It has a hole in one end and a sharp point at the other. You put thread through the hole.

NOUN **2** A **needle** is also a thin metal tube with a sharp point, that people like doctors use to give injections.

NOUN **3** **Needles** are long thin pieces of metal or plastic used for knitting.

NOUN **4** The thin leaves on pine trees are called **needles**.

negative negatives

ADJECTIVE **1** A **negative** sentence is one that has the word "no" or "not" in it.

ADJECTIVE **2** A **negative** number is less than zero.

NOUN **3** A **negative** is a film from a camera. You can get your photographs printed from negatives.

neglect neglects, neglecting, neglected

NOUN If you **neglect** something, you do not look after it.

neighbour neighbours

NOUN Your **neighbour** is someone who lives near you.

neighbourhood neighbourhoods

NOUN A **neighbourhood** is a district where people live. *This is a friendly neighbourhood.*

nephew nephews

NOUN Someone's **nephew** is a son of their sister or brother. See **niece**.

nerve nerves

NOUN **1** Your **nerves** are the long thin threads in your body that carry messages between your brain and the other parts of your body.

NOUN **2** **Nerve** is courage. *I wanted to go on the ride but I hadn't got the nerve.*

nervous

ADJECTIVE **1** If you are **nervous**, you are worried about doing something.

ADJECTIVE **2** A **nervous** person is easily frightened.

nest nests

NOUN A **nest** is a place that a bird or other animal makes for its babies.

a b c d e f g h i j k l m **Nn** o p q r s t u v w x y z

net   **nets**

NOUN **1** Net is material made from threads woven together with small spaces in between.

NOUN **2** The **net** is the same as the Internet.

NOUN **3** In maths, the **net** of a three-dimensional shape is the flat shape that you could fold to make the three-dimensional shape.

ADJECTIVE **4** The **net** weight of something is its weight without its wrapping.

netball

NOUN **Netball** is a game played by two teams of seven players. Each team tries to score goals by throwing a ball through a net at the top of a pole.

nettle   **nettles**

NOUN A **nettle** is a wild plant covered with little hairs that sting.

never

ADVERB **Never** means at no time in the past or future. *You must **never** cross the road without looking carefully.*

new   **newer, newest**

ADJECTIVE **1** Something that is **new** has just been made or bought. *They have built some **new** houses close to us.*

ADJECTIVE **2** New can mean different. *We've got a **new** car – it's only a year old.*

news

NOUN **News** is information about something that has just happened.

newspaper   **newspapers**

NOUN A **newspaper** is sheets of paper that are printed and sold regularly. Newspapers contain news and articles.

newt   **newts**

NOUN A **newt** is a small animal that looks like a lizard. It lives near water. *See Amphibians on page 259.*

next

ADJECTIVE **1** The **next** period or thing is the one that comes immediately after this one. *The **next** programme will follow after the break.*

ADJECTIVE **2** The **next** place is the one nearest to you. *She's in the **next** room.*

nib   **nibs**

NOUN A **nib** is a small pointed piece of metal at the end of a pen. Ink comes out of the nib as you write.

nibble   **nibbles, nibbling, nibbled**

VERB If you **nibble** something, you eat it slowly by taking small bites out of it.

nice   **nicer, nicest**

ADJECTIVE **1** You say something is **nice** when you like it. *This cake is **nice**.*

ADJECTIVE **2** If you say the weather is **nice**, it is warm and pleasant.

ADJECTIVE **3** If you are **nice** to people, you are friendly and kind.

nickname   **nicknames**

NOUN A **nickname** is a name that is given to a person by friends or family. *The baby's name is Sam but his **nickname** is Dribbler.*

niece   **nieces**

NOUN Someone's **niece** is a daughter of their sister or brother. See **nephew**.

night   **nights**

NOUN The **night** is the time between evening and morning when it is dark.

nightfall

NOUN **Nightfall** is the time of day when it starts to get dark.

a b c d e f g h i j k l m **Nn** o p q r s t u v w x y z

nightingale **nightingales**

NOUN A **nightingale** is a small brown European bird. Nightingales sing after dark as well as during the day.

nightmare **nightmares**

NOUN A **nightmare** is a frightening dream.

no

1 You say **no** when you do not want something or do not agree. *"More tea?"* *"**No**, thank you."*

ADJECTIVE **2** You can use **no** to mean not any. *I had **no** help at all.*

ADVERB **3** You can use **no** to mean not. *Competition entries must be in **no** later than Friday.*

nobody

PRONOUN **Nobody** means not a single person.

nocturnal

ADJECTIVE An animal that is **nocturnal** is active mostly at night.

nod **nods, nodding, nodded**

VERB If you **nod**, you move your head quickly down and up to answer yes to a question, or to show that you agree.

noise **noises**

NOUN **1** A **noise** is a sound that someone or something makes.

NOUN **2** **Noise** is loud or unpleasant sounds.

noisy ADJECTIVE

non-

PREFIX Putting **non-** in front of a word makes it mean the opposite. *This is a **non**-smoking area.*

See *Prefixes* on page 264.

none

PRONOUN **None** means not any, or not one. ***None** of us wanted to go.*

non-fiction

NOUN **Non-fiction** is writing that is based on fact. For example, dictionaries are non-fiction. See **fiction**.

nonsense

NOUN **Nonsense** is words that do not make sense.

noon

NOUN **Noon** is 12 o'clock in the middle of the day.

no one also spelt no-one

PRONOUN **No one** means not a single person.

normal

ADJECTIVE Something that is **normal** is what you would expect.

north

NOUN **North** is one of the four main points of the compass. If you face the point where the sun rises, north is on your left. See **compass point**.

northern ADJECTIVE

north-east

NOUN **North-east** is halfway between north and east.

north-west

NOUN **North-west** is halfway between north and west.

nose **noses**

NOUN Your **nose** is the part of your face that sticks out above your mouth. It is used for smelling and breathing.

nostril **nostrils**

NOUN Your **nostrils** are the two openings at the end of your nose. You breathe through your nostrils.

a
b
c
d
e
f
g
h
i
j
k
l
m
Nn
o
p
q
r
s
t
u
v
w
x
y
z

note notes

NOUN **1** A **note** is a short written message.

NOUN **2** You take **notes** to help you remember what has been said.

NOUN **3** A **note** is also a single sound in music.

NOUN **4** A bank **note** is a printed piece of paper that is used as money.

nothing

PRONOUN **Nothing** means not anything.

notice notices, noticing, noticed

VERB **1** If you **notice** something, you pay attention to it. *She **noticed** that it was raining.*

NOUN **2** A **notice** is a sign that tells people something. *The **notice** said, "Cameras are not allowed in the museum".*

nought

NOUN **Nought** is the number 0, or zero.

noun nouns

NOUN In grammar, a **noun** is a word which names a person, a thing or an idea. "James", "newt", and "success" are all nouns.

See *Noun* on page 262.

nourishment

NOUN **Nourishment** is the food that you need in order to grow and stay healthy.

nourishing ADJECTIVE

novel novels

NOUN A **novel** is a long written story that has been made up by the author. Novels are fiction.

November

NOUN **November** is the 11th month of the year. It has 30 days.

now

ADVERB **Now** means at the present time.

nowhere

ADVERB **Nowhere** means not anywhere.

nude

ADJECTIVE Someone who is **nude** is not wearing any clothes.

nudge nudges, nudging, nudged

VERB If you **nudge** somebody, you push them gently, usually with your elbow.

nuisance nuisances

NOUN If you say that someone or something is a **nuisance**, you mean they annoy you.

numb

ADJECTIVE If something is **numb**, it does not feel anything. *My foot is so cold it is **numb**.*

number numbers

NOUN A **number** is a word or sign that tells you how many of something there are.

See *Number bank* on page 272.

numeracy

NOUN **Numeracy** is the ability to understand and work with numbers.

numerous

ADJECTIVE If there are **numerous** things or people, there are a lot of them.

nurse nurses

NOUN A **nurse** is a person whose job is to care for people who are ill or injured.

nursery nurseries

NOUN **1** A **nursery** is a place where young children can be looked after during the day.

NOUN **2** A **nursery** can also be a place where plants are grown and sold.

nut nuts

NOUN **1** A **nut** is the hard fruit of certain trees such as walnuts and chestnuts.

NOUN **2** A **nut** is also a small piece of metal with a hole in it. It screws onto a bolt to fasten things together.

nylon

NOUN **Nylon** is a strong artificial material.

a
b
c
d
e
f
g
h
i
j
k
l
m
n

Oo

p
q
r
s
t
u
v
w
x
y
z

Oo

oak oaks

NOUN An **oak** is a large tree with nuts called acorns. The wood of oak trees is often used to make furniture.

oar oars

NOUN An **oar** is a wooden pole with a wide flat end, used for rowing a boat.

oasis oases

NOUN An **oasis** is a place in a desert where water and plants are found.

oats

PLURAL NOUN **Oats** are the grains of a cereal. They are used especially for making porridge or for feeding animals.

obedient

ADJECTIVE If you are **obedient**, you do what you are told to do.

obey obeys, obeying, obeyed

VERB If you **obey** someone, you do as they say.

object objects

NOUN **1** An **object** is anything that you can touch or see, and that is not alive.
NOUN **2** In grammar, the **object** of a verb or preposition is the word or phrase which describes the person or thing affected. In the sentence "She fed the cat", "cat" is the object.

oblong oblongs

NOUN An **oblong** is a four-sided shape with two parallel short sides and two parallel long sides. See **rectangle**.
See *Colours and flat shapes* on page 271.

observe observes, observing, observed

VERB If you **observe** something or somebody, you watch them carefully.

obstinate

ADJECTIVE Someone who is **obstinate** is determined to do what they want and will not change their mind.

obvious

ADJECTIVE Something that is **obvious** is easy to see or understand.

occasion occasions

NOUN An **occasion** is an important event or celebration.

occasional

ADJECTIVE **Occasional** means happening sometimes, but not regularly or often.
occasionally ADVERB

occupant occupants

NOUN The **occupant** of a place is the person who lives or works there.

occupy occupies, occupying, occupied

VERB **1** To **occupy** a place means to live, stay or work in it.
VERB **2** If something **occupies** you, you are busy doing it or thinking about it.
ADJECTIVE **3** If something like a chair is **occupied**, someone is using it.

occur occurs, occurring, occurred

VERB **1** When something **occurs**, it happens.
VERB **2** If something **occurs** to you, you suddenly think of it or realize it.

ocean oceans

NOUN An **ocean** is one of the five large seas on the earth's surface.

o'clock

ADVERB You say **o'clock** after numbers when you say a time that is exactly on the hour.

octagon octagons

NOUN An **octagon** is a flat shape with eight straight sides.
octagonal ADJECTIVE
See *Colours and flat shapes* on page 271.

October

NOUN **October** is the 10th month of the year. It has 31 days.

octopus **octopuses**

NOUN An **octopus** is a sea animal with eight long arms called tentacles.

odd **odder, oddest**

ADJECTIVE **1** If you say something is **odd**, you mean it is strange or unusual.
ADJECTIVE **2 Odd** numbers are those which cannot be divided exactly by two. 13, 25 and 79 are odd numbers.
ADJECTIVE **3 Odd** things are those which do not belong in a pair or a set. *You can't go out wearing odd socks.*

odds and ends PHRASE **Odds and ends** are small unimportant things. *His pockets were full of odds and ends.*

odour **odours**

NOUN An **odour** is a particular smell.

off

PREPOSITION **1 Off** can show movement away from or out of a place. *They stepped off the plane.*
ADVERB **2 Off** can mean not switched on. *He turned the radio off.*
ADVERB **3 Off** can also mean time spent away from work. *He took the afternoon off.*
ADVERB **4** People use **off** to show a reduction. *All right, I'll take ten per cent off.*
ADJECTIVE **5** If food is **off**, it is going bad.

offend **offends, offending, offended**

VERB If you **offend** someone, you upset them by doing or saying something rude.
offensive ADJECTIVE

offer **offers, offering, offered**

VERB **1** If you **offer** something to someone, you ask them if they would like to have it.
VERB **2** If you **offer** to do something, you say you will do it without being asked.

office **offices**

NOUN An **office** is a room where people work at desks.

officer **officers**

NOUN **1** An **officer** is a member of the police, or of a government organization.
NOUN **2** An **officer** is also a person in the army, navy or air force who gives orders to other people.

official

ADJECTIVE Something that is **official** is written or done by the government or by someone else in charge.

often

ADVERB If something happens **often**, it happens many times.

ogre **ogres**

NOUN In fairy tales, an **ogre** is a man who is large, cruel and frightening.

oil **oils**

NOUN **1 Oil** is a smooth thick liquid that is found under the ground. It is used to keep machines running smoothly, and also for fuel.
NOUN **2 Oil** can also be made from plants or animals. This oil can sometimes be used for cooking.

ointment **ointments**

NOUN An **ointment** is an oily cream that you put on sore skin to help it get better.

old **older, oldest**

ADJECTIVE **1** Someone or something **old** has been in the world for many years.
ADJECTIVE **2** You say something is **old** if it has been used a lot, or you have had it for a long time. *These are my old shoes.*
ADJECTIVE **3** If you ask how **old** someone is, you want to know how long they have lived. *How old is your baby?*

a
b
c
d
e
f
g
h
i
j
k
l
m
n
Oo
p
q
r
s
t
u
v
w
x
y
z

old-fashioned

ADJECTIVE Something **old-fashioned** belongs to the past and has been replaced by something more modern.

olive olives

NOUN An **olive** is a small green or black fruit. Olives are eaten as a snack, or used to make oil for cooking.

omelette omelettes

NOUN An **omelette** is a food made by beating eggs and cooking them.

once

ADVERB **1** If something happens **once**, it happens one time only.

ADVERB **2** Once means at some time in the past. *Once, the Romans ruled in Britain.*

at once PHRASE If you do something **at once**, you do it straight away.

one

1 One is the number 1.

PRONOUN **2** One refers to a particular thing or person. *I think Tim's idea is the best one.*

onion onions

NOUN An **onion** is a small round vegetable with a brown papery skin and a very strong taste.

only

ADJECTIVE **1** Only means one and no more. *She was the only girl in the group.*

ADJECTIVE **2** An **only** child is someone who has no brothers or sisters.

ADVERB **3** You say **only** when you mean one person or thing and not others. *He's only interested in football.*

ADVERB **4** You can say **only** when something is not very important. *It was only a sparrow.*

ADVERB **5** Only can be used when something was less than you expected. *It only took me ten minutes.*

onomatopoeia

NOUN **Onomatopoeia** is the use of words that sound like what they mean, for example "hiss" and "buzz".

opaque

ADJECTIVE If something is **opaque**, it does not let light through and you cannot see through it.

open opens, opening, opened

VERB **1** If you **open** a door, you move it so that people can go through it.

VERB **2** If you **open** a box or a bottle, you take the lid off or unfasten it.

VERB **3** When flowers **open**, you can see their petals.

ADJECTIVE **4** When a place such as a shop or library is **open**, you can use it.

opening openings

NOUN An **opening** is a hole or space that things or people can go through.

opera operas

NOUN An **opera** is a musical play in which most of the words are sung.

operate operates, operating, operated

VERB **1** When someone **operates** a machine, they make it work.

VERB **2** When doctors **operate**, they cut open a patient's body to remove or repair a damaged part.

 Oo

operation operations

NOUN An **operation** is when doctors cut open a patient's body to remove or repair a damaged part.

opinion opinions

NOUN An **opinion** is what someone thinks about something.

opponent opponents

NOUN An **opponent** is someone who is against you in an argument or a contest.

opposite opposites

NOUN **1** The **opposite** of something is the thing that is most different from it. *Hot is the opposite of cold.*

PREPOSITION **2** If one person or thing is **opposite** another, they are on the other side of something. *In the train I sat opposite a small boy.*

optician opticians

NOUN An **optician** is someone who tests people's eyes, and sells glasses and contact lenses.

orange oranges

NOUN **1** An **orange** is a round fruit with a thick skin. Oranges are juicy and sometimes sweet.
See Fruit on page 257.

ADJECTIVE **2** Something that is **orange** has a colour between red and yellow.
See Colours on page 271.

orbit orbits, orbiting, orbited

VERB If something **orbits** a planet or the Sun, it goes round and round it.

orchard orchards

NOUN An **orchard** is an area of land where fruit trees are grown.

orchestra orchestras

NOUN An **orchestra** is a large group of musicians who play different instruments together.

order orders, ordering, ordered

NOUN **1** An **order** is something you are told to do.

VERB **2** If you **order** something, for example in a restaurant, you ask for it to be brought to you.

NOUN **3** Order is the way a set of things is organized. A dictionary is written in alphabetical order.

ordinary

ADJECTIVE Something that is **ordinary** is not special in any way.

organ organs

NOUN **1** An **organ** is a part of your body that does a special job, for example your heart, lungs or stomach.

NOUN **2** An **organ** is also a large musical instrument like a piano. It has pipes that air is forced through to make the sounds.

organic

ADJECTIVE Food that is **organic** has been produced without the use of chemicals.

organization organizations;
also spelt organisation

NOUN An **organization** is a large group of people who work together. For example, the police force is an organization.

a b c d e f g h i j k l m n **Oo** p q r s t u v w x y z

organize

organize **organizes, organizing, organized**; also spelt *organise*
VERB **1** If you **organize** an event, you plan and arrange it.
VERB **2** If you **organize** things, you arrange them in a sensible order.

origin **origins**
NOUN **1** The **origin** of something is how and why it started.
NOUN **2** You can refer to where someone comes from as their **origin**. *She was of Swedish origin.*

original
ADJECTIVE **1** Something that is **original** is new and not a copy.
ADJECTIVE **2** If you say someone's ideas are **original**, you mean they are clever at thinking of new ways of doing things.

ornament **ornaments**
NOUN An **ornament** is an object that you put somewhere because you think it is nice to look at.

orphan **orphans**
NOUN An **orphan** is a child whose parents are dead.

ostrich **ostriches**
NOUN An **ostrich** is the largest living bird. It cannot fly, but it can run very fast. Ostriches live in sandy places in Africa. Their eggs are large, weighing more than a kilo each.

other
ADJECTIVE **1** When you say **other** things or other people, you can mean more of the same kind. *He found it hard to make friends with other children.*
ADJECTIVE **2** You can also use **other** to mean different. *We got lost last time. I think we'll try some other way.*
every other PHRASE **Every other** means one in every two. *We meet every other week.*

otherwise
ADVERB You say **otherwise** to explain what will happen if you do not do something. *I'd better take an umbrella, otherwise I'll get soaked.*

otter **otters**
NOUN An **otter** is an animal with brown fur, short legs and a long tail. Otters swim well and eat fish.

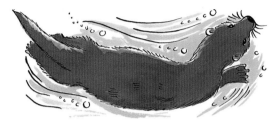

ought
VERB If you **ought** to do something, you should do it. *I ought to leave early.*

our
ADJECTIVE **Our** refers to something belonging or relating to the speaker or writer and one or more other people. *We recently sold our house.*

ourselves
PRONOUN **Ourselves** is used when the people speaking do something and no one else does it. *We made the beds ourselves.*

out
ADVERB **1** Out means towards the outside of a place. *Two dogs rushed out of the house.*
ADVERB **2** Out can also mean not at home. *She was out when I rang last night.*
ADVERB **3** Out can mean no longer shining or burning. *The lights went out.*

outer
ADJECTIVE The **outer** parts of something are the parts furthest from the centre. *The outer layer of an onion is brown and papery.*

outing **outings**
NOUN An **outing** is a short trip somewhere to enjoy yourself.

outline outlines

NOUN An **outline** is the shape of something, especially when you cannot see any details.

outside

NOUN **1** The **outside** of something is the part which surrounds the rest of it. *The **outside** of the box had a picture on it.*

ADVERB **2** You can use **outside** with a verb to mean out of a building. *Let's go **outside**.*

PREPOSITION **3** You can use **outside** before a noun to say which building you are referring to. *The bicycle was chained up **outside** the church.*

oval ovals

NOUN **1** An **oval** is a shape like an egg.

ADJECTIVE **2** Oval describes something shaped like an egg, such as an oval mirror or oval frame.

See *Colours and flat shapes* on page 271.

oven ovens

NOUN The **oven** is the part of a cooker that you use for baking or roasting food.

over

PREPOSITION **1** Over something means directly above it or covering it. *He put his hands **over** his eyes.*

PREPOSITION **2** A view **over** an area is a view across that area. *The front windows look out **over** the sea.*

PREPOSITION **3** Something that is **over** a particular amount is more than that amount.

PREPOSITION **4** If something happens **over** a period of time, it happens during that period. *I went to London **over** Christmas.*

ADVERB **5** If you lean **over**, you bend your body in a particular direction.

ADVERB **6** You can use **over** to show movement from one place to another. *She went **over** to the door.*

over-

PREFIX **Over-** is placed in front of an adjective or a verb to mean too much or to too great an extent, for example "overestimate".

See *Prefixes* on page 264.

overalls

PLURAL NOUN **Overalls** are a piece of clothing with trousers and jacket in one. You wear overalls to protect your other clothes when you are working.

overboard

ADVERB If someone falls **overboard**, they fall over the side of a ship into the water.

overcoat overcoats

NOUN An **overcoat** is a thick warm coat that people wear in winter.

overdue

ADJECTIVE If someone or something is **overdue**, they are late. *My library book is **overdue**.*

overflow overflows, overflowing, overflowed

VERB **1** If a liquid **overflows**, it spills over the edges of its container.

VERB **2** If a river **overflows**, it flows over its banks.

a
b
c
d
e
f
g
h
i
j
k
l
m
n
Oo
p
q
r
s
t
u
v
w
x
y
z

overgrown

ADJECTIVE If a place is **overgrown**, it is thickly covered with plants and weeds, usually because it has not been looked after for a long time.

overhead

ADVERB **Overhead** means above you. *Seagulls were flying overhead.*

overhear overhears, overhearing, overheard

VERB If you **overhear** someone's conversation, you hear what they are saying to someone else.

overlap overlaps, overlapping, overlapped

VERB If one thing **overlaps** another, one part of it covers part of the other thing.

overseas

ADVERB If you go **overseas**, you go to a country which is on the other side of a sea or ocean.

oversleep oversleeps, oversleeping, overslept

VERB If you **oversleep**, you sleep longer than you meant to, and wake up late.

overtake overtakes, overtaking, overtook, overtaken

VERB If you **overtake** someone, you pass them because you are moving faster than they are.

owe owes, owing, owed

VERB **1** If you **owe** someone money, they have lent it to you and you have not yet paid it back.

VERB **2** If you **owe** someone something, such as thanks, you need to give it to them.

owl owls

NOUN An **owl** is a bird with a flat face and large eyes. Usually owls hunt at night for small animals.

own owns, owning, owned

VERB **1** If you **own** something, it belongs to you.

VERB **2** If you **own up** to something wrong, you say that you did it.

on your own PHRASE If you are **on your own**, you are alone.

If you do something **on your own**, you do it without any help.

owner owners

NOUN The **owner** of something is the person it belongs to.

ox oxen

NOUN **Oxen** are cattle which are used for carrying or pulling things.

oxygen

NOUN **Oxygen** is a gas that forms part of the air we breathe. Other animals and plants also need oxygen to live, and things will not burn without it.

oyster oysters

NOUN An **oyster** is a large flat shellfish. Some oysters produce pearls. See **pearl**.

ozone

NOUN **Ozone** is a form of oxygen.

ozone layer PHRASE The **ozone layer** is the part of the Earth's atmosphere that protects living things from the dangerous rays of the Sun.

Pp

pace paces

NOUN **1** The **pace** of something is the speed at which it happens.

NOUN **2** A **pace** is a step that you take when you walk.

pack packs, packing, packed

VERB **1** When you **pack**, you put your clothes in a case or bag.

NOUN **2** A **pack** is a set of playing cards.

NOUN **3** A **pack** of wolves or other animals is a group that hunts together. See *Collective nouns* on page 262.

package packages

NOUN A **package** is a small parcel.

packaging

NOUN **Packaging** is the container that something is sold or sent in.

packet packets

NOUN A **packet** is a thin cardboard box or paper container.

pad pads

NOUN **1** A **pad** is a number of pieces of paper fixed together on one side.

NOUN **2** An animal's **pads** are the soft parts under its paws.

paddle paddles, paddling, paddled

VERB **1** If you **paddle** in the sea, you stand or walk in the shallow water.

VERB **2** If you **paddle** a small boat such as a canoe, you use a special type of oar called a paddle to move the boat along.

padlock padlocks

NOUN A **padlock** is a special kind of lock. You can use it to lock gates and bicycles.

page pages

NOUN A **page** is one side of a piece of paper in a book or newspaper.

pagoda pagodas

NOUN A **pagoda** is a tall building which is used as a temple. Pagodas can be seen in China, Japan and south-east Asia.

paid

VERB **Paid** is the past tense of **pay**.

pail pails

NOUN A **pail** is a bucket.

pain pains

NOUN A **pain** is an unpleasant feeling that you have in part of your body if you have been hurt or are ill.

painful

ADJECTIVE If you say that something is **painful**, you mean it is hurting you.

painfully ADVERB

paint paints, painting, painted

NOUN **1** **Paint** is a coloured liquid that you put onto a surface to make it look fresh.

VERB **2** When you **paint** a picture, you use paint to make a picture on paper or canvas.

painting paintings

NOUN A **painting** is a picture that has been painted.

pair pairs

NOUN **1** A **pair** is a set of two things that go together. *I need a new pair of shoes.*

NOUN **2** Some objects, such as trousers and scissors, have two main parts which are the same size and shape. This sort of object is also called a **pair**.

palace palaces

NOUN A **palace** is a large important house, especially one which is the home of a king, queen or president.

pale paler, palest

ADJECTIVE Something that is **pale** is light in colour, and not strong or bright.

a b c d e f g h i j k l m n o **Pp** q r s t u v w x y z

palm

palm palms

NOUN **1** The **palm** of your hand is the inside surface of it. Your fingers and thumb are not part of your palm.

NOUN **2** A **palm** is a tree which grows in hot countries. It has long pointed leaves that grow out of the top of a tall trunk.

pan pans

NOUN A **pan** is a container with a long handle that is used for cooking.

pancake pancakes

NOUN A **pancake** is a thin flat cake made of flour, eggs and milk, which is fried.

panda pandas

NOUN A **panda** is an animal like a black and white bear that lives in the bamboo forests of China.

pane panes

NOUN A **pane** is a sheet of glass in a window or door.

panic panics, panicking, panicked

VERB If you **panic**, you suddenly get so worried you cannot act sensibly.

pant pants, panting, panted

VERB If you **pant**, you breathe quickly with your mouth open. You usually pant when you have been running fast.

panther panthers

NOUN **Panther** is another name for a black leopard.

pantomime pantomimes

NOUN A **pantomime** is a funny musical play for children.

pants

PLURAL NOUN **Pants** are a piece of clothing that you wear under your other clothes. They have two holes for your legs and elastic round the waist.

paper papers

NOUN **1 Paper** is the material that you write on or wrap things in.

NOUN **2** A newspaper is also called a **paper**.

parable parables

NOUN A **parable** is a short story which aims to teach you something about the way you should behave.

parachute parachutes

NOUN A **parachute** is a large piece of thin cloth. It has strings fixed to it so that a person attached to it can float down to the ground from an aircraft.

parade parades

NOUN A **parade** is a lot of people marching in the road on a special day.

paraffin

NOUN **Paraffin** is a liquid used as a fuel in things like heaters and lamps.

paragraph paragraphs

NOUN A **paragraph** is a section of a piece of writing. Paragraphs begin on a new line.

parallel

ADJECTIVE Two lines or other things that are **parallel** are the same distance apart all the way along. *The road along the sea front is **parallel** with the sea.*

paralysed

ADJECTIVE Someone who is **paralysed** cannot move or feel some or all of their body.

parcel parcels

NOUN A **parcel** is one or more objects wrapped in paper. This is usually done so that it can be sent by post.

parent **parents**

NOUN Your **parents** are your mother and father.

park **parks, parking, parked**

NOUN **1** A **park** is an area of land with grass and trees, usually in a town. People go there to walk or play.

VERB **2** When someone **parks** a vehicle, they put it somewhere until they need it again.

parliament **parliaments**

NOUN The **parliament** of a country is the people who make the country's laws.

parrot **parrots**

NOUN A **parrot** is a brightly-coloured bird with a curved beak.

parsnip **parsnips**

NOUN A **parsnip** is a long, pointed, cream-coloured root vegetable. See *Vegetables* on page 256.

part **parts**

NOUN **1** A **part** of something is one of the pieces that it is made from. *We need a new part for the washing machine.*

NOUN **2** A **part** is also a particular bit of something such as an area or a body. *This part of the park is for young children only.*

NOUN **3** If you have a **part** in a play, you are one of the people in it.

participle **participles**

NOUN In grammar, a **participle** is a form of a verb. English has two participles – the past participle and the present participle. In the sentence "He has gone" the word "gone" is a past participle; in the sentence "She is winning" the word "winning" is a present participle.

particular

ADJECTIVE When you talk about a **particular** person or thing, you mean just that person or thing and not others of the same kind.

partly

ADVERB **Partly** means not completely. *The table was partly covered with a cloth.*

partner **partners**

NOUN Your **partner** is the person you are doing something with, for example when dancing or playing games.

party **parties**

NOUN A **party** is a group of people having fun together.

pass **passes, passing, passed**

VERB **1** If you **pass** someone, you go past them without stopping.

VERB **2** If you **pass** something to someone, you hand it to them.

VERB **3** If you **pass** a test or an exam, you are successful in it.

passage **passages**

NOUN **1** A **passage** is a long narrow space with walls on both sides.

NOUN **2** A **passage** is also a section in a piece of writing. *There's a wonderful passage in the book that describes their arrival at the castle.*

passenger **passengers**

NOUN A **passenger** is a person who travels in a vehicle but is not the driver.

passive

NOUN In grammar, the **passive** or **passive voice** is the form of the verb in which the person or thing to which an action is being done is the subject of the sentence. For example, the sentence "The ball was hit by the boy" is in the passive. See **voice**.

passport **passports**

NOUN A **passport** is a book with your name and photograph in it, that you need when you leave your own country.

a
b
c
d
e
f
g
h
i
j
k
l
m
n
o
Pp
q
r
s
t
u
v
w
x
y
z

password **passwords**

NOUN A **password** is a secret word or phrase that you must say to be allowed into a particular place.

past

NOUN **1** The **past** is the period of time before the present.

ADVERB **2** If you go **past** something, you move towards it and continue until you are on the other side.

PREPOSITION **3** You use **past** when you are telling the time. *It's ten **past** three.*

NOUN **4** In grammar, the **past tense** of a verb is the form used to show that something happened in the past.

pasta

NOUN **Pasta** is a type of food made from flour, eggs and water, which is formed into different shapes. Spaghetti, macaroni and noodles are types of pasta.

paste **pastes**

NOUN **Paste** is a thick wet mixture that is easy to spread.

pastime **pastimes**

NOUN A **pastime** is something you like to do in your free time.

pastry

NOUN **Pastry** is a food made of flour, fat and water, rolled flat and used for making pies.

pasture **pastures**

NOUN **Pasture** is land that is used for farm animals to graze on.

pat **pats, patting, patted**

VERB If you **pat** something, you hit it gently, usually with your open hand.

patch **patches**

NOUN A **patch** is a piece of material you put over a hole in something to mend it.

path **paths**

NOUN A **path** is a strip of ground that people walk on.

patience

NOUN **Patience** is being able to wait calmly for something, or to do something difficult without giving up.

patient **patients**

ADJECTIVE **1** If you are **patient**, you are able to wait calmly for something, or to do something difficult without giving up.

NOUN **2** A **patient** is someone who is being treated by a doctor.

patrol **patrols, patrolling, patrolled**

VERB When people like the police **patrol** a particular area, they go round it to make sure there is no trouble or danger.

pattern **patterns**

NOUN A **pattern** is a regular way something is organized. For example, lines and shapes can make patterns.

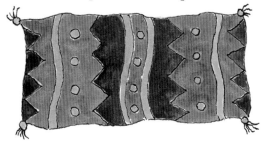

pause **pauses, pausing, paused**

VERB If you **pause** while you are doing something, you stop for a moment.

pavement **pavements**

NOUN A **pavement** is a path with a hard surface beside a road, so that people can walk in safety.

paw **paws**

NOUN A **paw** is the foot of some animals. Paws have claws at the front and soft pads underneath.

pay **pays, paying, paid**

VERB When a person **pays** someone, they give them money in exchange for work or for things that they have bought.

payment NOUN

PC PCs

NOUN **1** A **PC** is a personal computer.
NOUN **2** In Britain, a **PC** is also a police constable.

PE

NOUN **PE** is an abbreviation of **physical education**.

pea peas

NOUN **Peas** are round green seeds which are eaten as a vegetable. They grow inside a covering called a pod.
See *Vegetables* on page 256.

peace

NOUN **1** **Peace** is a feeling of quiet and calm.
NOUN **2** When a country has **peace** or is **at peace**, it is not fighting a war.

peaceful

ADJECTIVE A **peaceful** place is quiet and calm.

peach peaches

NOUN A **peach** is a round juicy fruit with a large stone in the middle. It has sweet yellow flesh and a yellow and red skin.
See *Fruit* on page 257.

peacock peacocks

NOUN A **peacock** is a large male bird with bright blue and green feathers, and long tail feathers which it spreads in a fan. The female is called a peahen.

peak peaks

NOUN **1** The **peak** of a mountain is the pointed top of it.
NOUN **2** The **peak** of a cap is the part that sticks out at the front.

peanut peanuts

NOUN **Peanuts** are small hard seeds which grow under the ground. You can buy roasted and salted peanuts to eat.

pear pears

NOUN A **pear** is a sweet juicy fruit which grows on trees. It is narrow near its stalk, and wider and rounded at the bottom.
See *Fruit* on page 257.

pearl pearls

NOUN A **pearl** is a hard round object which grows inside the shell of an oyster. It is creamy-white in colour. Pearls are used to make valuable jewellery.

pebble pebbles

NOUN A **pebble** is a small smooth stone found on seashores and river beds.

peck pecks, pecking, pecked

VERB When a bird **pecks**, it bites at something with its beak.

peculiar

ADJECTIVE Something that is **peculiar** is strange or unusual.

pedal pedals

NOUN The **pedals** on a cycle are the two parts that you push with your feet to make it move.

pedestrian pedestrians

NOUN A **pedestrian** is a person who is walking.

peek peeks, peeking, peeked

VERB If you **peek** at something, you have a quick look at it.

peel peels, peeling, peeled

VERB If you **peel** fruit or vegetables, you remove the skin.

peep peeps, peeping, peeped

VERB If you **peep** at something, you look at it very quickly, and usually secretly.

peg pegs

NOUN **1** A **peg** is a thin piece of metal or plastic that is used to hang things on.
NOUN **2** A **peg** is also a small clip that is used to hold washing on a line.

a
b
c
d
e
f
g
h
i
j
k
l
m
n
o
Pp
q
r
s
t
u
v
w
x
y
z

pelican

a
b
c
d
e
f
g
h
i
j
k
l
m
n
o
Pp
q
r
s
t
u
v
w
x
y
z

pelican **pelicans**

NOUN A **pelican** is a water bird. Its large beak has a soft lower part like a pouch.

pen **pens**

NOUN A **pen** is a long thin tool that you use to write in ink.

pence

NOUN **Pence** is the plural of **penny**.

pencil **pencils**

NOUN A **pencil** is a long thin piece of wood with a dark material called graphite in the middle. It is used for writing or drawing.

pendulum **pendulums**

NOUN A **pendulum** is a large weight which hangs from a clock. It swings from side to side to keep the clock going at the right speed.

penguin **penguins**

NOUN A **penguin** is a large black and white bird found in the Antarctic. Penguins cannot fly. They use their wings for swimming in the water.

penis **penises**

NOUN Boys and men have a **penis**. It is used to get rid of waste liquid from the body. Men can also use their penis to help make babies.

penknife **penknives**

NOUN A **penknife** is a small knife with blades that fold back into the handle.

penny **pennies** or **pence**

NOUN A **penny** is a small British coin. A hundred pence are worth one pound. The abbreviation for pence is p.

pentagon **pentagons**

NOUN A **pentagon** is a flat shape that has five straight sides.

pentagonal ADJECTIVE

See *Colours and flat shapes* on page 271.

people

PLURAL NOUN **People** are men, women and children.

pepper **peppers**

NOUN **1 Pepper** is a hot-tasting powder which is used to flavour food.

NOUN **2** A **pepper** is a red, green or yellow vegetable. It can be cooked or eaten raw in salads.

per cent

PHRASE You use **per cent** to talk about amounts as a proportion of 100. For example, ten per cent (10%) means 10 out of every 100.

perch **perches**

NOUN A **perch** is a short piece of wood for a bird to stand on.

percussion

ADJECTIVE **Percussion** instruments are instruments that you play by hitting them. Drums and cymbals are percussion instruments.

perfect

ADJECTIVE **1** Something that is **perfect** is done so well it could not be done better.

ADJECTIVE **2** If you say something is **perfect**, you mean it is wonderful.

perfectly ADVERB

perform **performs, performing, performed**

VERB If someone **performs**, they do something to entertain an audience.

performance **performances**

NOUN A **performance** is something done in front of people, like acting or dancing.

perfume **perfumes**

NOUN **1** A **perfume** is a pleasant smell.

NOUN **2** **Perfume** is a liquid that you put on your body so that you smell nice.

perhaps

ADVERB **1** If you say **perhaps** something will happen, you mean it might happen but you are not sure.

ADVERB **2** You can also say **perhaps** when you are suggesting something. *He's late – **perhaps** he missed the train.*

perimeter **perimeters**

NOUN The **perimeter** of a shape is the distance all round it.

period **periods**

NOUN A **period** is a particular length of time. *Mrs Smith will be away for a **period** of six months.*

periscope **periscopes**

NOUN A **periscope** is a tube with mirrors. When you look in one end, you can see what would otherwise be out of sight.

permanent

ADJECTIVE Something that is **permanent** lasts for ever, or for a very long time.

permission

NOUN If you have **permission** to do something, you are allowed to do it.

permit **permits, permitting, permitted**

VERB If someone **permits** you to do something, they allow you to do it.

persist **persists, persisting, persisted**

VERB If you **persist**, you go on doing something even when it is difficult or other people have told you to stop.

person **people**

NOUN A **person** is a man, woman or child.

personal

ADJECTIVE **Personal** matters relate to your feelings, relationships and health, which you may not want to talk about with other people.

persuade **persuades, persuading, persuaded**

VERB If someone **persuades** you to do something you did not want to do, you agree because they gave you a good reason.

persuasion NOUN

persuasive

ADJECTIVE **1** Someone who is **persuasive** is good at persuading others to believe or do a particular thing.

ADJECTIVE **2** **Persuasive** text aims to persuade the reader of something.

pest **pests**

NOUN A **pest** is an insect, rat or other small animal that causes damage.

pester **pesters, pestering, pestered**

VERB If you **pester** someone, you keep bothering them.

pet **pets**

NOUN A **pet** is a tame animal that you keep and look after in your home.

petal **petals**

NOUN A **petal** is part of a flower. Petals may have bright colours or scents to attract insects.

petrol

NOUN **Petrol** is a liquid used as fuel in motor vehicles.

phantom **phantoms**

NOUN A **phantom** is a ghost.

a b c d e f g h i j k l m n o **Pp** q r s t u v w x y z

phone

phone **phones**
NOUN **Phone** is an abbreviation of **telephone**.

photo **photos**
NOUN **Photo** is an abbreviation of **photograph**.

photocopier **photocopiers**
NOUN A **photocopier** is a machine that makes copies of documents.

photocopy **photocopies**
NOUN A **photocopy** is a copy of a document produced by a photocopier.

photograph **photographs**
NOUN A **photograph** is a picture that is made using a camera.

phrase **phrases**
NOUN A **phrase** is a short group of words used together.

physical
ADJECTIVE **1 Physical** means to do with things that can be touched or seen.
ADJECTIVE **2 Physical** also means to do with a person's body, rather than their mind.
physically ADVERB

piano **pianos**
NOUN A **piano** is a large musical instrument with black and white keys that you press with your fingers.

pick **picks, picking, picked**
VERB **1** To **pick** means to choose. *We need to pick three more people for our team.*
VERB **2** When you **pick** flowers or fruit, you take them off the plant.
VERB **3** If you **pick** something **up**, you lift it up from where it is.

pickle **pickles**
NOUN **Pickles** are vegetables or fruit that have been kept in vinegar or salt water.

picnic **picnics**
NOUN A **picnic** is a meal that you take with you and eat out of doors.

pictogram **pictograms**
NOUN **1** A **pictogram** is a picture or symbol used instead of a word or words.
NOUN **2** A **pictogram** is also a graph that uses pictures to show information.

picture **pictures**
NOUN A **picture** is a drawing, painting or photograph.

pie **pies**
NOUN A **pie** is fruit, vegetables, meat or fish baked in pastry.

piece **pieces**
NOUN A **piece** is a part of something.

pier **piers**
NOUN A **pier** is a long platform which sticks out over the sea. Piers often have some kind of entertainment on them.

pierce **pierces, piercing, pierced**
VERB If a sharp object **pierces** something, it goes through it and makes a hole in it.

pig **pigs**
NOUN A **pig** is a farm animal kept for its meat. It has pinkish skin and short legs.

pigeon **pigeons**
NOUN A **pigeon** is a large bird with grey feathers, often seen in towns.

piglet **piglets**
NOUN A **piglet** is a young pig.
See *Young animals* on page 260.

pile piles

NOUN A **pile** is a lot of things, such as books, which have been put one on top of the other.

pill pills

NOUN A **pill** is medicine made into a small round object that you swallow.

pillar pillars

NOUN A **pillar** is a tall post made of something such as stone or brick. It usually helps to hold up a building.

pillar box pillar boxes

NOUN A **pillar box** is an iron cylinder with a slot in it for letters.

pillow pillows

NOUN A **pillow** is a bag filled with soft material to rest your head on in bed.

pilot pilots

NOUN A **pilot** is a person who is trained to fly an aircraft.

pimple pimples

NOUN A **pimple** is a small red spot, especially on your face.

pin pins

NOUN A **pin** is a small thin piece of metal with a point at one end. Pins can be pushed through things such as pieces of paper or cloth, to hold them together.

pincers

PLURAL NOUN **1** The **pincers** of a crab or lobster are its front claws.

PLURAL NOUN **2** Pincers are also a tool used for gripping and pulling things.

pinch pinches, pinching, pinched

VERB If someone **pinches** you, they squeeze part of you quickly between their thumb and first finger.

pine pines

NOUN A **pine** is a tall evergreen tree with sharp thin leaves called needles.

pineapple pineapples

NOUN A **pineapple** is a large oval fruit with yellow flesh and a thick, lumpy skin. Pineapples grow in hot countries.

pink pinker, pinkest

ADJECTIVE Something that is **pink** has a colour between white and red. See *Colours* on page 271.

pint pints

NOUN A **pint** is a measure for liquids. A pint is equal to just over half a litre.

pipe pipes

NOUN A **pipe** is a long hollow tube, usually made of metal or plastic. Pipes are used to carry liquid or gas.

pirate pirates

NOUN In the past, a **pirate** was a robber who stole from ships.

pistol pistols

NOUN A **pistol** is a small gun.

pit pits

NOUN **1** A **pit** is a large hole that has been dug in the ground.

NOUN **2** A **pit** is also a coal mine.

pitch pitches, pitching, pitched

NOUN **1** A **pitch** is an area of ground where a game such as hockey or football is played.

NOUN **2** The **pitch** of a sound is how high or low it is.

VERB **3** When you **pitch** a tent, you put it up so that you can use it.

pity

NOUN **1** If you feel **pity** for someone, you feel sorry for them.

NOUN **2** If you say something is a **pity**, you mean it is disappointing. *What a pity Mark isn't coming.*

pizza

pizza pizzas

NOUN A **pizza** is a flat round piece of dough covered with cheese, tomato and other savoury food.

place places

NOUN 1 A **place** is any building or area.
NOUN 2 A **place** is also the position where something belongs. *Please put the tools back in their right place.*

place value

NOUN In maths, the **place value** of a digit tells you what the digit is worth in hundreds, tens or units (HTU).

plague plagues

NOUN A **plague** is a disease that spreads quickly and kills many people.

plaice

NOUN A **plaice** is a flat sea fish.

plain plainer, plainest; plains

ADJECTIVE 1 A **plain** object has no pattern on it. *She wore a plain skirt.*
ADJECTIVE 2 If something is **plain**, it is clear and easy to see.
NOUN 3 A **plain** is a large, flat area of land with very few trees on it.

plait plaits, plaiting, plaited

VERB 1 If you **plait** three lengths of hair or rope together, you twist them over each other in turn.
NOUN 2 A **plait** is a length of hair that has been plaited.

plan plans, planning, planned

NOUN 1 If you have a **plan**, you have thought of a way of doing something.
NOUN 2 A **plan** is a drawing that shows what something looks like from above.
VERB 3 If you **plan** what you are going to do, you decide exactly how to do it.

plane planes

NOUN 1 A **plane** is a flying vehicle. It has wings and one or more engines. **Plane** is an abbreviation of **aeroplane**.
NOUN 2 A **plane** is also a tool used for smoothing wood.

planet planets

NOUN A **planet** is a large round object in space that moves around a star. Earth is one of the nine planets that go round the Sun.

plank planks

NOUN A **plank** is a long flat piece of wood.

plant plants, planting, planted

NOUN 1 A **plant** is any living thing that is not an animal. Plants can make their own food.
VERB 2 When you **plant** things, such as seeds, flowers or trees, you put them in the ground so that they will grow.

plaster plasters

NOUN 1 A **plaster** is a strip of sticky material used for covering small cuts.
NOUN 2 **Plaster** is a smooth paste that dries and forms a hard layer. It is used to cover walls and ceilings inside buildings.

plastic

NOUN 1 **Plastic** is a light artificial material that does not break easily. It is used to make all sorts of things, such as buckets, bowls and plates.
ADJECTIVE 2 Something that is **plastic** is made of plastic.

Plasticine

NOUN; TRADEMARK **Plasticine** is a soft material like clay, which can be used to make models.

plate plates

NOUN A **plate** is a flat dish for food.

platform platforms

NOUN **1** A **platform** is the area in a station where you wait for the train.
NOUN **2** A **platform** is also a raised area for people to stand on so that they can be seen more easily.

play plays, playing, played

VERB **1** When you **play**, you spend time doing things you enjoy.
VERB **2** When one person or team **plays** another, they take part in a game and each side tries to win.
VERB **3** If you **play** a musical instrument, you make musical sounds with it.
NOUN **4** A **play** is a story which is acted on the stage, or on radio or television.
player NOUN

playground playgrounds

NOUN A **playground** is a piece of land for children to play on.

playscript playscripts

NOUN A **playscript** is the written version of a play.

playtime

NOUN **Playtime** is a break in the school day when you can play.

pleasant

ADJECTIVE If something is **pleasant**, you enjoy it or like it.

please pleases, pleasing, pleased

VERB If you **please** someone, you make them feel happy.

pleasure

NOUN **Pleasure** is a feeling of happiness or enjoyment.

pleat pleats

NOUN A **pleat** is a permanent fold in fabric.
pleated ADJECTIVE

plenty

NOUN If there is **plenty** of something, there is more than enough of it.

pliers

PLURAL NOUN **Pliers** are a tool used for pulling out small things like nails, or for bending or cutting wire.

plot plots, plotting, plotted

NOUN **1** A **plot** is a secret plan.
NOUN **2** The **plot** of a film, novel or play is the story and the way it develops.
NOUN **3** A **plot** of land is a small piece that has been marked out for a special purpose such as building houses or growing vegetables.
VERB **4** If people **plot** something, they plan secretly to do it.

plough ploughs

NOUN A **plough** is a farming tool that is pulled across a field to turn the soil over.

pluck plucks, plucking, plucked

VERB **1** When someone **plucks** a musical instrument, such as a guitar, they pull the strings and let them go quickly.
VERB **2** When you **pluck** a feather, flower or fruit, you pull it from where it is growing.

plug plugs, plugging, plugged

NOUN **1** A **plug** is a thick piece of rubber or plastic that fits in the drain hole of a bath or washbasin.
NOUN **2** A **plug** is also a small object that joins pieces of equipment to the electricity supply.
VERB **3** If someone **plugs** a hole, they block it with something.

plum plums

NOUN A **plum** is a small fruit with a thin, dark red or yellow skin and juicy flesh. It has a large stone in the middle.
See *Fruit* on page 257.

a b c d e f g h i j k l m n o **Pp** q r s t u v w x y z

plumber plumbers
NOUN A **plumber** is a person who fits and mends water pipes.

plump plumper, plumpest
ADJECTIVE Someone or something that is **plump** is rather fat.

plunge plunges, plunging, plunged
VERB If someone **plunges** into the water, they dive or throw themselves into it.

plural plurals
NOUN **Plural** means more than one. *The **plural** of "boy" is "boys". The **plural** of "box" is "boxes".* See **singular**.

plus
PREPOSITION **1** You use **plus** (+) to show that one number is being added to another. *Two **plus** two equals four.*
PREPOSITION **2** You can use **plus** when you mention an additional item. *You get a television **plus** a free radio.*

p.m.
ADVERB **p.m.** is the time between 12 noon and 12 midnight. See **a.m.**

poach poaches, poaching, poached
VERB If you **poach** an egg, you remove its shell and cook the egg gently in boiling water.

pocket pockets
NOUN A **pocket** is a small bag that is sewn into clothing.

pod pods
NOUN A **pod** is a seed cover. Peas and beans grow inside pods. See **pea**.

poem poems
NOUN A **poem** is a piece of writing in short lines, which sometimes rhyme. The lines usually have a particular rhythm.

poet poets
NOUN A **poet** is a person who writes poems.

poetry
NOUN **Poetry** is writing in which the lines have a rhythm and sometimes rhyme.

point points, pointing, pointed
NOUN **1** The **point** of something such as a pin is the sharp end of it.
NOUN **2** A **point** is a position or time. *I'll call you at some **point** during the day.*
NOUN **3** The **point** of doing something is the reason for doing it. *The **point** of playing is to have fun.*
NOUN **4** In a game or sport, a **point** is part of the score.
NOUN **5** The decimal **point** in a number is the dot separating the whole number from the fraction.
VERB **6** If you **point** at something, you show where it is by using your finger.
VERB **7** If something **points** in a particular direction, it faces that way.

pointed
ADJECTIVE Something that is **pointed** has a point at one end.

poison poisons
NOUN **Poison** is something that harms or kills people or animals if it gets into their body.
poisonous ADJECTIVE

poke pokes, poking, poked
VERB If you **poke** something, you push it hard with your finger.

polar bear polar bears
NOUN A **polar bear** is a large white bear that lives near the North Pole.

pole poles
NOUN **1** A **pole** is a long round post, used especially for holding things up.
NOUN **2** A **pole** is also one of the two points on the Earth that are the furthest from the equator. They are known as the North Pole and the South Pole.

police

PLURAL NOUN The **police** are an organization whose job is to protect people and their belongings, and to make sure that people obey the law.
policeman NOUN   **policewoman** NOUN

police officer   police officers

NOUN A **police officer** is a policeman or policewoman.

polish   polishes, polishing, polished

NOUN **1 Polish** is a substance that you put on an object to clean and shine it.
VERB **2** If you **polish** something, you put polish on it or rub it with a cloth to make it shine.

polite

ADJECTIVE Someone who is **polite** is well-behaved and thinks about other people's feelings.

politician   politicians

NOUN A **politician** is a person involved in the government of a country.

politics

NOUN **Politics** is the study of the way in which a country is governed.

pollen

NOUN **Pollen** is a fine, yellow powder in flowers that the wind or insects carry to other flowers to make seeds.

pollution

NOUN **Pollution** is making things like the air and water dirty and dangerous to live in or use.

poly-

PREFIX **Poly-** means many or much. For example, a polygon is a shape with many sides.
See *Prefixes* on page 264.

polyester

NOUN **Polyester** is an artificial fibre used especially to make clothes.

polygon   polygons

NOUN A **polygon** is a flat shape with three or more straight sides.

polyhedron   polyhedrons or polyhedra

NOUN A **polyhedron** is a solid shape with four or more faces.

polythene

NOUN **Polythene** is a thin plastic material that is often made into bags.

pond   ponds

NOUN A **pond** is a small lake.

pony   ponies

NOUN A **pony** is a kind of horse which is smaller than an ordinary horse.

ponytail   ponytails

NOUN A **ponytail** is long hair which is tied behind the head and hangs down like a tail.

pool   pools

NOUN A **pool** is a small area of still or slow-moving water.

poor   poorer, poorest

ADJECTIVE **1** Someone who is **poor** has very little money and few belongings.
ADJECTIVE **2** Something that is **poor** is not good. *If my work is **poor**, I have to do it again.*

pop   pops

NOUN **1 Pop** is modern music played and enjoyed especially by young people.
NOUN **2** A **pop** is a short sharp sound.

popcorn

NOUN **Popcorn** is a snack made from a type of corn that pops open when heated.

poppy   poppies

NOUN A **poppy** is a plant with a large red flower on a hairy stem.

popular

ADJECTIVE If someone or something is **popular**, they are liked by a lot of people.

a b c d e f g h i j k l m n o **Pp** q r s t u v w x y z

population

NOUN **1** The **population** of a country or area is all the people who live in it.
NOUN **2** The **population** of a place is also the number of people who live there.

porch **porches**

NOUN A **porch** is a sheltered place at the entrance to a building.

porcupine **porcupines**

NOUN A **porcupine** is an animal with lots of stiff hairs called quills on its back.

pork

NOUN **Pork** is meat from a pig.

porpoise **porpoises**

NOUN A **porpoise** is a sea mammal that looks like a dolphin or a small whale.

porridge

NOUN **Porridge** is a thick sticky food made from oats cooked in water or milk.

port **ports**

NOUN A **port** is a place where boats come to load and unload.

portable

ADJECTIVE Something that is **portable** is made to be easily carried, for example a portable television.

porter **porters**

NOUN A **porter** is a person whose job is to look after the entrance of a building, greeting and directing visitors.

portion **portions**

NOUN A **portion** of food is the amount that is given to one person at a meal.

portrait **portraits**

NOUN A **portrait** is a picture of a person.

position **positions**

NOUN **1** The **position** of someone or something is the place where they are.

NOUN **2** Someone's **position** can also be the way they are sitting or standing. *Try to stay in that **position** while I draw you.*

positive

ADJECTIVE **1** If you are **positive** about something, you are very sure about it.
ADJECTIVE **2** **Positive** numbers are those which are greater than zero.

possess **possesses, possessing, possessed**

VERB If you **possess** something, you have it or own it.
possession NOUN

possible

ADJECTIVE **1** Something that is **possible** can be done.
ADJECTIVE **2** You can also use **possible** to talk about something that may happen but is not certain. *It's **possible** we might go abroad next year.*
possibly ADVERB

possum **possums**

NOUN A **possum** is a marsupial with thick fur and a long tail.

post **posts, posting, posted**

NOUN **1** **Post** is letters or parcels that are collected and delivered.
NOUN **2** A **post** is a strong piece of wood or metal fixed upright in the ground.
VERB **3** If you **post** a letter, you send it to someone by putting it in a postbox.

postbox **postboxes**

NOUN A **postbox** is a metal box with a slot in it where you can post letters.

postcard **postcards**

NOUN A **postcard** is a piece of thin card, often with a picture on one side, that you can use to send a message to someone.

postcode **postcodes**
NOUN A **postcode** is the letters and numbers at the end of an address to help the sorting of mail.

poster **posters**
NOUN A **poster** is a large notice or picture that is put on a wall or notice board.

postman **postmen**
NOUN A **postman** is a man whose job is to deliver letters and parcels sent by post.

post office **post offices**
NOUN A **post office** is a building where you can take things to be posted.

postpone **postpones, postponing, postponed**
VERB If you **postpone** something, you put it off until later. *We had to postpone the picnic because the weather was so bad.*

pot **pots**
NOUN A **pot** is a round container for things like paint or jam, or for growing plants in.

potato **potatoes**
NOUN A **potato** is a round vegetable that grows under the ground. Potatoes can be boiled, baked or fried.
See Vegetables on page 256.

pottery
NOUN **Pottery** is objects such as dishes and ornaments that are made from clay.

pouch **pouches**
NOUN 1 A **pouch** is a small bag for keeping things in.
NOUN 2 A **pouch** can also be a pocket of skin on an animal. Female kangaroos and other marsupials have a pouch on their stomach. Their babies grow in this pouch. Hamsters have pouches in their cheeks for storing food.

pounce **pounces, pouncing, pounced**
VERB When an animal **pounces** on something, it leaps on it and grabs it.

pound **pounds**
NOUN 1 The **pound** (£) is a unit of money in Britain and in some other countries.
NOUN 2 A **pound** is also a unit of weight equal to just under half a kilogram.

pour **pours, pouring, poured**
VERB 1 If you **pour** a liquid out of a container, you make it flow out by tipping the container.
VERB 2 When it is raining heavily, you can say that it is **pouring**.

powder
NOUN **Powder** is something that has been ground into tiny pieces.

power **powers**
NOUN 1 If someone or something has **power**, they have control over other people.
NOUN 2 The **power** of something, such as the wind or the sea, is its strength.

powerful
ADJECTIVE If someone or something is **powerful**, they are very strong.

practical
ADJECTIVE 1 **Practical** people are good at working with their hands.
ADJECTIVE 2 **Practical** ideas are ones that are likely to work.

practice
NOUN **Practice** is doing something many times so that you get better at it.

practise **practises, practising, practised**
VERB If you **practise**, you do something again and again, in order to get better at it. *She has been practising this piece of music for months.*

praise **praises, praising, praised**
VERB If someone **praises** you for something you have done, they say how well you have done it.

pram

pram **prams**

NOUN A **pram** is a small carriage that a baby can be pushed around in.

prawn **prawns**

NOUN A **prawn** is a small edible shellfish with a long tail.

pray **prays, praying, prayed**

VERB When someone **prays**, they speak to the god they believe in, to give thanks or to ask for help.

prayer **prayers**

NOUN A **prayer** is the words someone says when they are praying.

pre-

PREFIX **Pre-** is used to form words that describe something as taking place before a particular time or event. *We shop early to miss the **pre-**Christmas rush.* See *Prefixes* on page 264.

precious

ADJECTIVE Something that is **precious** is worth a lot of money.

precipice **precipices**

NOUN A **precipice** is a steep side on a mountain or rock.

precise

ADJECTIVE Something that is **precise** is exact and accurate in every detail. *Take **precise** measurements of the room.* **precisely** ADVERB

predator **predators**

NOUN A **predator** is an animal that kills and eats other animals.

predict **predicts, predicting, predicted**

VERB If someone **predicts** an event, they say that it will happen in the future.

prefer **prefers, preferring, preferred**

VERB If you **prefer** someone or something, you like that person or thing better than another.

prefix **prefixes**

NOUN A **prefix** is a letter or group of letters added to the beginning of a word to make a new word, for example "dis-", "pre-" and "un-". See *Prefixes* on page 264.

pregnant

ADJECTIVE A woman who is **pregnant** is expecting a baby.

prehistoric

ADJECTIVE Something that is **prehistoric** belongs to the time before history was written down.

preparations

PLURAL NOUN **Preparations** are all the things that have to be done before an event. *The children were busy with **preparations** for the school play.*

prepare **prepares, preparing, prepared**

VERB 1 If you **prepare** for something that is going to happen, you get ready for it.
VERB 2 If you **prepare** someone or something, you get them ready.

preposition **prepositions**

NOUN In grammar, a **preposition** is a word such as "by", "for" or "with", that goes in front of a noun group. In the sentence "She fell into the pond", "into" is a preposition and "the pond" is a noun group.

present **presents, presenting, presented**

NOUN 1 A **present** is something that you give to someone for them to keep.
ADJECTIVE 2 If someone is **present** somewhere, they are there.
NOUN 3 The **present** is the time now.
VERB 4 If someone **presents** you with something, they give it to you. *The mayor **presented** her with a certificate.*
VERB 5 The person who **presents** a show introduces each part or each guest.
NOUN 6 The **present tense** of a verb is the form used to show something is happening now.

preserve preserves, preserving, preserved

VERB **1** If you **preserve** something, you do something to keep it the way it is.

VERB **2** To **preserve** food means to stop it from going bad.

president presidents

NOUN The **president** of a country or an organization is the head of it.

press presses, pressing, pressed

VERB **1** If you **press** something against something else, you hold it there firmly. *He **pressed** the phone against his ear.*

NOUN **2** Newspapers and the journalists who work for them are called the **press**.

pressure

NOUN **Pressure** is the force of one thing pressing or pushing on another.

pretend pretends, pretending, pretended

VERB If you **pretend**, you act as though something is true although it is not. *Let's **pretend** to be working.*

pretty prettier, prettiest

ADJECTIVE Someone who is **pretty** is nice to look at.

prevent prevents, preventing, prevented

VERB If you **prevent** someone from doing something, you stop them doing it.

prey

NOUN The **prey** of an animal is the creatures that it hunts for food.

bird of prey PHRASE A **bird of prey** is a bird such as an eagle or a hawk, that kills and eats smaller birds and animals.

price prices

NOUN The **price** of something is the amount of money that you must pay to buy it.

prick pricks, pricking, pricked

VERB To **prick** something means to make a tiny hole with something sharp.

prickle prickles

NOUN **Prickles** are small sharp points or thorns on plants.

pride

NOUN **1 Pride** is the good feeling you have when you have done something well.

NOUN **2** A **pride** of lions is a group of lions that live together.

See Collective nouns on page 262.

prime minister prime ministers

NOUN The **prime minister** of a country is the leader of that country's government.

prince princes

NOUN A **prince** is the son of a king or queen.

princess princesses

NOUN A **princess** is the daughter of a king or queen, or the wife of a prince.

print prints, printing, printed

VERB **1** When someone **prints** something such as a poster or a newspaper, they use a machine to make lots of copies of it.

VERB **2** If you **print** words, you write in letters that are not joined together.

printer printers

NOUN **1** A **printer** is a machine that is linked to a computer to print information on paper.

NOUN **2** A **printer** is also a person who prints things like books and magazines.

print-out print-outs

NOUN A **print-out** is a printed copy of information from a computer.

prism prisms

NOUN **1** A **prism** is an object made of clear glass with many flat sides. It separates light passing through it into the colours of the rainbow.

NOUN **2** A **prism** is also any three-dimensional shape that has the same size and shape of face at each end.

prison **prisons**

NOUN A **prison** is a building where people are kept when they have broken the law.

prisoner **prisoners**

NOUN **1** A **prisoner** is someone who is kept in prison as a punishment.

NOUN **2** A **prisoner** is also someone who has been captured by an enemy.

private

ADJECTIVE If something is **private**, it is for one person or group only. *All the rooms have a private bath.*

in private PHRASE If you do something **in private**, you do it without other people being there.

prize **prizes**

NOUN A **prize** is something that is given to someone as a reward.

probable

ADJECTIVE Something that is **probable** is likely to be true, or likely to happen.

probably ADVERB

problem **problems**

NOUN **1** A **problem** is something that is difficult.

NOUN **2** A **problem** is also something, like a puzzle, that you have to work out.

process **processes**

NOUN A **process** is a series of actions for doing or making something.

procession **processions**

NOUN A **procession** is a line of people walking or riding through the streets on a special occasion.

prod **prods, prodding, prodded**

VERB If you **prod** something, you push it with your finger.

produce **produces, producing, produced**

VERB **1** To **produce** something means to make it.

VERB **2** If you **produce** an object from somewhere such as a pocket, you bring it out so that it can be seen.

VERB **3** Someone who **produces** a play, film or television programme gets it ready to show to the public.

product **products**

NOUN **1** A **product** is something that is made to be sold.

NOUN **2** In maths, the **product** of two numbers is the answer you get when you multiply them together. For example, the product of four and two is eight.

profit **profits**

NOUN A **profit** is the money you gain when you sell something for more than it cost you to make or buy.

program **programs**

NOUN A **program** is a set of instructions that a computer uses in order to do particular things.

programme **programmes**

NOUN **1** A radio or television **programme** is the thing that is being broadcast.

NOUN **2** A **programme** is a plan of things that will take place.

progress **progresses, progressing, progressed**

NOUN **1** Progress is moving forward or getting better at something. *I'm making progress with my spelling.*

VERB **2** If you **progress**, you get better at something.

project **projects**

NOUN A **project** is work that you do to learn about something and then write about it.

promise **promises, promising, promised**

VERB If you **promise** to do something, you mean you really will do it.

prong **prongs**

NOUN The **prongs** of a fork are the long pointed parts.

pronoun **pronouns**

NOUN **1** In grammar, a **pronoun** is a word that is used to replace a noun.

NOUN **2 Personal pronouns** replace the subject or object of a sentence. In the sentence "She caught a fish", "she" is a personal pronoun.

NOUN **3 Possessive pronouns** replace the subject or object when you want to show who owns it. In the sentence "This book is mine", "mine" is a possessive pronoun.

See *Pronoun* on page 263.

pronounce **pronounces, pronouncing, pronounced**

VERB To **pronounce** a word means to say it in a particular way.

pronunciation

NOUN **Pronunciation** is the way a word is usually said.

proof

NOUN **Proof** of something is the facts that show that it is true or that it exists.

prop **props, propping, propped**

VERB If you **prop** an object somewhere, you support it against something.

propeller **propellers**

NOUN A **propeller** is the blades that turn to drive an aircraft or ship.

proper

ADJECTIVE **1 Proper** means right. *Put those things back in the proper place.*

ADJECTIVE **2** You can also use **proper** to mean real. *You need a proper screwdriver for that job.*

properly

ADVERB If something is done **properly**, it is done correctly.

proper noun **proper nouns**

NOUN A **proper noun** is the name of a particular person or place. It starts with a capital letter. "Ben" and "London" are both proper nouns.

See *Noun* on page 262.

property **properties**

NOUN **1** Someone's **property** is the things that belong to them.

NOUN **2** A **property** is a building and the land belonging to it.

prophet **prophets**

NOUN A **prophet** is a person who predicts what will happen in the future.

proportion **proportions**

NOUN The **proportion** of one amount to another is its size in comparison with the other amount. *There was a large proportion of boys in the class.*

prose

NOUN **Prose** is written language that is not poetry or a play.

protect **protects, protecting, protected**

VERB To **protect** someone or something is to prevent them from being harmed.
protection NOUN

protein **proteins**

NOUN **Protein** is a substance found in meat, eggs and milk that is needed by bodies for growth.

protest **protests**

NOUN A **protest** is something you say or do to show that you disagree with something.

proud **prouder, proudest**

ADJECTIVE If you feel **proud**, you feel glad about something you have done, or about something that belongs to you. *She was proud of her new bike.*

prove **proves, proving, proved**
VERB When you **prove** something, you show that it is definitely true.

proverb **proverbs**
NOUN A **proverb** is a short sentence that people say which gives advice about life. For example, the proverb "Look before you leap" means that you should think carefully before you do something.

provide **provides, providing, provided**
VERB If you **provide** something for someone, you give it to them so that they have it when they need it.

prune **prunes, pruning, pruned**
VERB 1 When someone **prunes** a tree, they cut off some of the branches so that it will grow better.
NOUN 2 A **prune** is a dried plum.

psalm **psalms**
NOUN A **psalm** is a poem or prayer from the Bible.

pub **pubs**
NOUN A **pub** is a building where people go to drink and talk with their friends.

public
ADJECTIVE Something that is **public** can be used by anyone. For example, anyone can pay to travel on public transport, such as trains and buses.

publish **publishes, publishing, published**
VERB When a company **publishes** a book, newspaper or magazine, they print copies of it and sell them.
publisher NOUN

pudding **puddings**
NOUN A **pudding** is a sweet food which is usually eaten after the main part of a meal.

puddle **puddles**
NOUN A **puddle** is a small shallow pool of liquid.

pull **pulls, pulling, pulled**
VERB 1 When you **pull** something, you hold it firmly and move it towards you.
VERB 2 When you **pull** a curtain, you move it across a window.
VERB 3 When a vehicle **pulls away**, **pulls out** or **pulls in**, it moves in that direction.

pulley **pulleys**
NOUN A **pulley** is for lifting heavy weights. The weight is attached to a rope or a chain which passes over a wheel.

pullover **pullovers**
NOUN A **pullover** is a jumper.

pulse
NOUN Your **pulse** is the regular beating of blood through your body. You can feel your pulse in your neck or wrist.

pump **pumps, pumping, pumped**
NOUN 1 A **pump** is a machine that is used to force gas or liquid to move the way it is wanted.
VERB 2 To **pump** is to force gas or liquid somewhere using a pump. *I must pump up these balloons.*

pumpkin **pumpkins**
NOUN A **pumpkin** is a very large, orange-coloured vegetable with a thick skin. It is soft inside, with a lot of seeds.

pun **puns**
NOUN A **pun** is a joke using a word which has two different meanings. For example, the sentence "My dog's a champion boxer" has a pun on the word "boxer".

punch **punches, punching, punched**
VERB If you **punch** someone, you hit them hard with your fist.

punctual
ADJECTIVE Someone who is **punctual** arrives somewhere or does something at exactly the right time.

punctuation

NOUN **Punctuation** is the marks such as full stops and commas that you use in writing.

punctuate VERB

See *Punctuation* on page 264.

puncture **punctures**

NOUN A **puncture** is a small hole in a tyre. When a tyre has a puncture, the air inside escapes and the tyre goes flat.

punish **punishes, punishing, punished**

VERB To **punish** someone means to make them suffer because they have done something wrong.

punishment NOUN

pupil **pupils**

NOUN **1** The **pupils** at a school are the children who go there.

NOUN **2** Your **pupils** are the small round black holes in the centre of your eyes.

puppet **puppets**

NOUN A **puppet** is a kind of doll that you can move. Some puppets have strings which you can pull. Others are made so that you can put your hand inside.

puppy **puppies**

NOUN A **puppy** is a young dog.

See *Young animals* on page 260.

purchase **purchases, purchasing, purchased**

VERB When you **purchase** something, you buy it.

pure **purer, purest**

ADJECTIVE Something that is **pure** is not mixed with anything else.

purple

ADJECTIVE Something that is **purple** is of a reddish-blue colour.

See *Colours* on page 271.

purpose **purposes**

NOUN A **purpose** is the reason for doing something.

on purpose PHRASE If you do something **on purpose**, you mean to do it. It does not happen by accident.

purr **purrs, purring, purred**

VERB When a cat **purrs**, it keeps making a low sound that shows it is happy.

purse **purses**

NOUN A **purse** is a small bag that people keep their money in.

push **pushes, pushing, pushed**

VERB When you **push** something, you press it hard.

pushchair **pushchairs**

NOUN A **pushchair** is a small folding chair on wheels in which a baby or toddler can be wheeled around.

put **puts, putting, put**

VERB **1** When you **put** something somewhere, you move it there.

VERB **2** If you **put** something **off**, you delay doing it.

VERB **3** If you **put** a light **out**, you make it stop shining.

puzzle **puzzles, puzzling, puzzled**

VERB **1** If something **puzzles** you, you do not understand it.

NOUN **2** A **puzzle** is a game or question that needs a lot of thought to solve it.

pyjamas

PLURAL NOUN **Pyjamas** are loose trousers and a top that people wear in bed.

pyramid **pyramids**

NOUN **1** A **pyramid** is a solid shape with a flat base and flat triangular faces that meet at the top in a point.

See *Solid shapes* on page 271.

PLURAL NOUN **2** The **Pyramids** are ancient stone structures built over the bodies of Egyptian kings and queens.

Qq

quack **quacks, quacking, quacked**
VERB When a duck **quacks**, it makes a loud harsh sound.

quadrilateral **quadrilaterals**
NOUN A **quadrilateral** is a flat shape with four straight sides.
See *Colours and flat shapes* on page 271.

quaint **quainter, quaintest**
ADJECTIVE Something that is **quaint** is unusual and rather pretty.

qualify **qualifies, qualifying, qualified**
VERB 1 When someone **qualifies**, they pass the examination they need to do a particular job.
VERB 2 You **qualify** if you get enough points in a competition to go on to the next stage.

quality **qualities**
NOUN The **quality** of something is how good or bad it is, compared with other things of the same kind.

quantity **quantities**
NOUN A **quantity** is an amount you can measure or count. *We shall need a huge quantity of food for the weekend.*

quarrel **quarrels**
NOUN A **quarrel** is an angry argument.

quarry **quarries**
NOUN A **quarry** is a deep hole that has been dug in a piece of land. Quarries are dug to provide materials such as stone for building and other work.

quarter **quarters**
NOUN A **quarter** is one of four equal parts of something.
See *Fractions* on page 272.

quay **quays**
(*said* **kee**)
NOUN A **quay** is a place where boats are tied up to be loaded or unloaded.

queen **queens**
NOUN 1 A **queen** is a woman who rules a country. Queens are not chosen by the people. They are born into a royal family.
NOUN 2 The wife of a king is also called a **queen**.
NOUN 3 In the insect world, a **queen** is a large female bee, ant or wasp which can lay eggs.

query **queries, querying, queried**
NOUN 1 A **query** is a question.
VERB 2 If you **query** something, you ask about it because you think it might not be right.

question **questions**
NOUN A **question** is words you say or write when you want to ask something.

question mark **question marks**
NOUN A **question mark** is the punctuation mark (?) which you use in writing at the end of a question.
See *Punctuation* on page 264.

questionnaire **questionnaires**
NOUN A **questionnaire** is a list of questions which asks for information for a survey.

queue **queues**
NOUN A **queue** is a line of people or vehicles waiting for something.

quiche **quiches**
NOUN A **quiche** is a sort of tart with a filling of eggs, and cheese or other food.

quick **quicker, quickest**

ADJECTIVE **1** Someone or something that is **quick** moves very fast.

ADJECTIVE **2** Something that is **quick** lasts only a short time. *I'll have a **quick** look at it.*

quickly

ADVERB Things that happen **quickly** happen very fast.

quiet **quieter, quietest**

ADJECTIVE **1** Someone or something that is **quiet** makes only a little noise or no noise at all.

ADJECTIVE **2** **Quiet** also means peaceful. *Let's have a **quiet** evening at home.*

quilt **quilts**

NOUN A **quilt** is a soft cover for a bed.

quit **quits, quitting, quit**

VERB **1** If you **quit** something, you stop doing it. ***Quit** teasing me!*

VERB **2** If you **quit**, you leave. *My dad has just **quit** his job.*

VERB **3** If you **quit** a file on a computer, you close it.

quite

ADVERB **1** **Quite** means rather. *I think he's **quite** nice.*

ADVERB **2** **Quite** can also mean completely. *The work is now **quite** finished.*

quiver **quivers, quivering, quivered**

VERB **1** If something **quivers**, it trembles.

NOUN **2** A **quiver** is a container for carrying arrows.

quiz **quizzes**

NOUN A **quiz** is a game or test. Someone tries to find out how much you know by asking you questions.

quotation **quotations**

NOUN A **quotation** is an extract from a book or speech that you use in your own work.

quotation marks

PLURAL NOUN **Quotation marks** are punctuation marks (" ") or (' ') used in writing to show where speech begins and ends.

quote **quotes, quoting, quoted**

VERB **1** If you **quote** something that someone has written or said, you repeat their exact words.

NOUN **2** A **quote** is a piece out of a book or speech.

quotient **quotients**

NOUN In maths, a **quotient** is a whole number you get when you divide one number into another. For example, if you divide eight by two, the quotient is four.

a
b
c
d
e
f
g
h
i
j
k
l
m
n
o
p
Qq
r
s
t
u
v
w
x
y
z

Rr

a b c d e f g h i j k l m n o p q **Rr** s t u v w x y z

rabbit **rabbits**

NOUN A **rabbit** is a small furry animal with long ears.

race **races, racing, raced**

NOUN **1** A **race** is a competition to see who is the fastest.

NOUN **2** A **race** is also a large group of people who look alike in some way. For example, different races have different skin colour, or differently shaped eyes.

VERB **3** If you **race** someone, you try to beat them in a race.

rack **racks**

NOUN A **rack** is a frame that is used for holding things or for hanging things on.

racket **rackets**

NOUN **1** A **racket** is a bat with an oval frame and strings across and down it. It is used in tennis and similar games.

NOUN **2** If someone makes a **racket**, they make a loud unpleasant noise.

radar

NOUN **Radar** is a way of showing the position and speed of ships and aircraft when they cannot be seen. Radio signals give the information on a screen.

radiator **radiators**

NOUN **1** A **radiator** is a hollow metal object that can be filled with liquid in order to heat a room.

NOUN **2** In a car, the **radiator** holds the water that is used to cool the engine.

radio **radios**

NOUN A **radio** is a piece of equipment which receives sounds through the air. You can use a radio to listen to programmes that are broadcast.

radish **radishes**

NOUN A **radish** is a small salad vegetable with a red skin and white flesh. *See Vegetables on page 256.*

radius **radii**

NOUN The **radius** of a circle is the length of a straight line drawn from its centre to any point on its edge.

raffle **raffles**

NOUN A **raffle** is a competition. You buy a numbered ticket and win a prize if your number is chosen.

raft **rafts**

NOUN A **raft** is a floating platform. Rafts are often made of large pieces of wood fixed together.

rag **rags**

NOUN **1** A **rag** is a piece of old cloth that you can use to clean or wipe things.

NOUN **2** **Rags** are old torn clothes.

rage

NOUN **Rage** is great anger. *Dad's face showed his rage.*

ragged

ADJECTIVE Clothes that are **ragged** are old and torn.

raid **raids**

NOUN A **raid** is a sudden attack against an enemy.

rail **rails**

NOUN **1** A **rail** is a horizontal bar that is firmly fixed to posts. Rails are used as fences, or for people to lean on.

NOUN **2** **Rails** are the heavy metal bars that trains run on.

railing **railings**

NOUN A **railing** is a kind of fence made from metal bars.

railway railways

NOUN A **railway** is a route along which trains travel on metal rails.

rain rains, raining, rained

NOUN **1** Rain is water that falls from the clouds in small drops.
VERB **2** When it is **raining**, rain is falling.

rainbow rainbows

NOUN A **rainbow** is an arch of different colours that sometimes appears in the sky when the sun shines through rain.

rainforest rainforests

NOUN A **rainforest** is a dense forest in a tropical area where there is a lot of rain.

raise raises, raising, raised

VERB **1** If you **raise** something, you move it so that it is higher.
VERB **2** If you **raise** your voice, you speak more loudly.
VERB **3** To **raise** money for a cause means to get people to give money towards it.

raisin raisins

NOUN A **raisin** is a dried grape.

rake rakes

NOUN A **rake** is a garden tool with a row of metal teeth fixed to a long handle.

ram rams, ramming, rammed

VERB **1** If one vehicle **rams** another, it crashes into it.
NOUN **2** A **ram** is an adult male sheep.

Ramadan

NOUN **Ramadan** is the ninth month of the Muslim year, when Muslims eat and drink nothing from sunrise to sunset.

ramp ramps

NOUN A **ramp** is a sloping surface between two places at different levels.

ran

VERB **Ran** is the past tense of **run**.

ranch ranches

NOUN In the United States, a **ranch** is a large farm for raising cattle, sheep or horses.

rang

VERB **Rang** is the past tense of **ring**.

range ranges

NOUN **1** The **range** of something is the area or distance over which it can be used.
NOUN **2** A **range** is a row of hills or mountains.

rank ranks

NOUN A **rank** is a position that a person holds in an organization. The higher the rank, the more important they are.

rap raps, rapping, rapped

VERB **1** If you **rap** something, you hit it with a series of quick blows.
NOUN **2** Rap is a style of poetry spoken to music with a strong beat.

rapid

ADJECTIVE Something that is **rapid** is very quick.

rare rarer, rarest

ADJECTIVE Something that is **rare** is not often seen, or does not happen very often.

rash rashes

NOUN A **rash** is a lot of spots that appear on your skin in certain illnesses.

raspberry raspberries

NOUN A **raspberry** is a small red fruit which is soft and juicy, with a lot of small seeds called pips.
See *Fruit* on page 257.

rat rats

NOUN A **rat** is a rodent with a long tail.

rather

ADVERB **1 Rather** means quite. *I'm **rather** angry about that.*

ADVERB **2** You can say **rather** if there is something else you want to do. *I don't want to go out. I'd **rather** watch television.*

rattle **rattles, rattling, rattled**

VERB **1** When something **rattles**, it makes short rapid knocking sounds. *Can you stop that window **rattling**?*

NOUN **2** A baby's **rattle** is a toy that makes a noise when it is shaken.

raw

ADJECTIVE Food that is **raw** is not cooked.

ray **rays**

NOUN A **ray** is a line of light.

razor **razors**

NOUN A **razor** is a tool that people use for shaving.

re-

PREFIX **Re-** is added to words to show that something is done again. For example, to "reread" means to read again. *See Prefixes on page 264.*

reach **reaches, reaching, reached**

VERB **1** When you **reach** a place, you arrive there.

VERB **2** If you **reach** somewhere, you stretch out your hand. *He **reached** across the table for the salt.*

react **reacts, reacting, reacted**

VERB When you **react** to something, you behave in a particular way because of it. *He **reacted** badly to the news.*

reaction NOUN

read **reads, reading, read**

VERB **1** When you **read**, you look at words and understand what they mean.

VERB **2** When you **read aloud**, you say the words that are written.

reading **readings**

NOUN **Reading** is the activity of reading books or other written material.

ready

ADJECTIVE If someone or something is **ready**, they are properly prepared for doing something.

real

ADJECTIVE **1** Something that is **real** is true. It is not imaginary. *I've seen a **real** princess.*

ADJECTIVE **2** You also say **real** when you mean the thing itself and not a copy. *I've got a lovely toy pony. But Jenny's got a **real** one.*

realize **realizes, realizing, realized;** also spelt **realise**

VERB If you **realize** something, you work it out or notice it. *I've just **realized** you must be Tara's sister.*

really

ADVERB You can use **really** to make something you are saying stronger. *I **really** don't like that boy.*

rear

NOUN The **rear** of something is the part that is at the back of it.

rearrange **rearranges, rearranging, rearranged**

VERB To **rearrange** something means to organize or arrange it in a different way.

reason **reasons**

NOUN The **reason** for something is why it happens. *I'm sorry I'm late, but there is a good **reason**.*

reasonable

ADJECTIVE **1** People who are **reasonable** behave in a fair and sensible way.

ADJECTIVE **2** A price that is **reasonable** seems fair and not too high.

reasonably ADVERB

rebel rebels, rebelling, rebelled
VERB To **rebel** means to fight against authority.
rebellious ADJECTIVE

receive receives, receiving, received
VERB When you **receive** something, you get it after it has been given or sent to you.

recent
ADJECTIVE Something that is **recent** happened only a short time ago.
recently ADVERB

recipe recipes
NOUN A **recipe** is a list of ingredients and instructions for cooking something.

recite recites, reciting, recited
VERB When you **recite** something like a poem, you say it aloud from memory.

reckon reckons, reckoning, reckoned
VERB If you **reckon** that something is true, you think it is true.

recognize recognizes, recognizing, recognized; also spelt recognise
VERB If you **recognize** someone, you realize that you know who they are.

recommend recommends, recommending, recommended
VERB If you **recommend** something to someone, you tell them it is good.

record records, recording, recorded
NOUN **1** If you keep a **record** of something, you keep a written account or store information in a computer.
NOUN **2** A **record** is also the best that has been done so far.
VERB **3** If someone **records** information, they write it down, put it onto tape or film, or into a computer.
VERB **4** To **record** sound means to put it on tape or compact disc.

recorder recorders
NOUN A **recorder** is a small musical instrument which you play by blowing into one end and putting your fingers over the holes.

recover recovers, recovering, recovered
VERB When you **recover** from something such as an illness, you become well again.

recreation
NOUN **Recreation** is all the things that you like doing in your spare time.
recreational ADJECTIVE

rectangle rectangles
NOUN A **rectangle** is a flat shape with four straight sides and four right angles.
rectangular ADJECTIVE
See *Colours and flat shapes* on page 271.

recycle recycles, recycling, recycled
VERB To **recycle** used products means to process them so they can be used again.

red redder, reddest
ADJECTIVE Something that is **red** is the colour of a ripe tomato.
See *Colours* on page 271.

redraft redrafts, redrafting, redrafted
VERB If you **redraft** a piece of text, you make another draft.

reduce reduces, reducing, reduced
VERB To **reduce** something means to make it smaller in size or amount.

reed reeds
NOUN A **reed** is a plant with a tall hollow stem. Reeds grow in or near water.

reef reefs
NOUN A **reef** is a long line of rocks that is just below the surface of the sea.

reel reels
NOUN A **reel** is a round object that you wrap thread, wire or film around.

refer refers, referring, referred
VERB If you **refer** to someone or something, you mention them.

referee referees
NOUN A **referee** is a person whose job is to make sure that the players in a game follow the rules properly.

reference book reference books
NOUN A **reference book** is a book that gives you information in a way that is easy to find. Dictionaries and encyclopedias are reference books.

refill refills, refilling, refilled
NOUN 1 A **refill** is a full container that replaces an empty one. *Have you got a refill for this pen?*
VERB 2 If you **refill** something, you fill it again after it has been emptied.

reflect reflects, reflecting, reflected
VERB 1 When a surface **reflects** rays of something like light or heat, the rays bounce back from the surface.
VERB 2 When a mirror **reflects** a person or thing, it shows what they look like.

reflection reflections
NOUN A **reflection** is what you see when you look in a mirror or shiny surface.

refreshing
ADJECTIVE Something that is **refreshing** makes you feel energetic or cool again after you have been tired or hot.

refreshments
PLURAL NOUN **Refreshments** are drinks and snacks.

refrigerator refrigerators
NOUN A **refrigerator** is a large cooled container in which you store food to keep it fresh. A refrigerator is often called a **fridge** for short.

refuse refuses, refusing, refused
(*said* rif-**yooz**) VERB 1 If you **refuse** to do something, you say you will not do it.
(*said* **ref**-yoos) NOUN 2 **Refuse** is rubbish or waste.

region regions
NOUN A **region** is a large area of land.

register registers, registering, registered
NOUN 1 A **register** is an official list or record of things.
VERB 2 When something is **registered**, it is recorded on an official list. *The car was registered in my mother's name.*

regret regrets, regretting, regretted
VERB If you **regret** something, you wish it had not happened.

regular
ADJECTIVE 1 Something that is **regular** does not change its pattern, for example a regular heartbeat.
ADJECTIVE 2 A **regular** polygon has all its angles and sides equal.

rehearsal rehearsals
NOUN A **rehearsal** is a practice of a play, dance or piece of music, to prepare for a public performance.

reign reigns, reigning, reigned
VERB 1 When a king or queen **reigns**, they rule a country.
NOUN 2 The **reign** of a king or queen is the period during which they reign.

rein reins

NOUN A **rein** is one of the leather straps that are used to control a horse.

reindeer

NOUN A **reindeer** is a large deer that lives in cold northern countries.

relate relates, relating, related

VERB If something **relates** to something else, it is connected or concerned with it.

related

ADJECTIVE **1** People who are **related** belong to the same family.
ADJECTIVE **2** If one thing is **related** to another, there is a connection between them. *A graph shows how two sets of numbers are related.*

relation relations

NOUN If someone is your **relation**, they belong to the same family as you.

relative relatives

NOUN If someone is your **relative**, they belong to the same family as you.

relax relaxes, relaxing, relaxed

VERB When you **relax**, you stop worrying and feel more calm.

release releases, releasing, released

VERB If someone **releases** a person or animal that has been trapped or held in some way, they set them free.

reliable

ADJECTIVE If something or someone is **reliable**, you can depend on them.

relief

NOUN **Relief** is the feeling you have if you do not need to worry about something any more.

relieved

ADJECTIVE If you are **relieved**, you are glad because you can stop worrying about something.

religion religions

NOUN A **religion** is a set of beliefs about a god, or about several gods.
religious ADJECTIVE

reluctant

ADJECTIVE If you are **reluctant** to do something, you do not want to do it.
reluctantly ADVERB

rely relies, relying, relied

VERB **1** If you **rely** on someone, you need them and depend on them.
VERB **2** If you can **rely** on someone to do something, you can trust them to do it.

remain remains, remaining, remained

VERB **1** If you **remain** in a place, you stay there and do not go away.
PLURAL NOUN **2** The **remains** of something are the parts that are left after most of it has been destroyed. *They found the remains of an ancient pyramid.*

remainder

NOUN **1** The **remainder** of something is the part that is left. *He gulped down the remainder of his coffee.*
NOUN **2** In maths, the **remainder** is the amount left over when one number cannot be exactly divided by another. For example, if nine is divided by four, the answer is two remainder one.

remark remarks, remarking, remarked

VERB If you **remark** on something, you mention it. *The teacher remarked on his strange haircut.*

remarkable

ADJECTIVE Someone or something that is **remarkable** is unusual in some way so that people notice them and feel surprised.

remember remembers, remembering, remembered

VERB If you can **remember** something, you can bring it back into your mind. *Can you remember that actor's name?*

a
b
c
d
e
f
g
h
i
j
k
l
m
n
o
p
q
Rr
s
t
u
v
w
x
y
z

remind **reminds, reminding, reminded**
VERB **1** If someone or something **reminds** you to do something, they make you remember it. *That reminds me – I must get a card for Auntie Mary.*
VERB **2** If someone **reminds** you of someone else, something about them makes you think of the other person.

remote **remoter, remotest**
ADJECTIVE **Remote** areas are far away from places where most people live.

remote control
NOUN **Remote control** is a system of controlling a machine from a distance, using radio or electronic signals.

removal **removals**
NOUN **1** The **removal** of something is the act of taking it away or getting rid of it.
NOUN **2** A **removal company** takes furniture from one building to another when people move house.

remove **removes, removing, removed**
VERB If you **remove** something from somewhere, you take it off or away.

rent **rents**
NOUN **Rent** is the amount of money you pay regularly for a house or flat.

repair **repairs, repairing, repaired**
VERB If you **repair** something that is broken or not working, you mend it.

repeat **repeats, repeating, repeated**
VERB If you **repeat** something, you say it or do it again.
repetition NOUN

replace **replaces, replacing, replaced**
VERB **1** If you **replace** something, you put it back where it was before.
VERB **2** If you **replace** something that is old, lost or broken, you get a new one.

reply **replies, replying, replied**
VERB When you **reply**, you answer someone.

report **reports, reporting, reported**
VERB **1** If you **report** that something has happened, you tell someone about it. *He reported the theft to the police.*
NOUN **2** A **report** is an account of an event or situation.

reporter **reporters**
NOUN A **reporter** is someone who works for a newspaper, radio or television. Their job is to find out what is happening in the world so that their report can be printed or broadcast.

represent **represents, representing, represented**
VERB **1** If you **represent** someone, you act for them. *The class chose Meena to represent them.*
VERB **2** If a sign or symbol **represents** something, it stands for it.

reptile **reptiles**
NOUN A **reptile** is a cold-blooded animal with a scaly skin. Female reptiles lay eggs. Snakes and crocodiles are reptiles. See *Reptiles* on page 259.

request **requests, requesting, requested**
VERB **1** If you **request** something, you ask for it politely.
NOUN **2** A **request** is a polite demand for something.

require **requires, requiring, required**
VERB If you **require** something, you need it.

rescue **rescues, rescuing, rescued**
VERB If you **rescue** someone, you save them from danger.

research **researches, researching, researched**

NOUN **1** Research is studying something and trying to find out facts about it.
VERB **2** If you **research** something, you try to discover facts about it.

resent **resents, resenting, resented**

VERB If you **resent** something, you feel angry about it.

reserve **reserves, reserving, reserved**

VERB If you **reserve** something, like a book at the library, you arrange for it to be kept for you.

reservoir **reservoirs**

NOUN A **reservoir** is a lake that is used for storing drinking water for an area.

resign **resigns, resigning, resigned**

VERB If someone **resigns** from a job, they say they want to leave it.

resist **resists, resisting, resisted**

VERB If you **resist** something, you fight against it and do not give up.

resource **resources**

NOUN The **resources** of a country, organization or person are the materials, money or skills they have.

respect **respects, respecting, respected**

VERB If you **respect** someone, you look up to them and think their opinions are important.

respectable

ADJECTIVE Someone who is **respectable** behaves in a way that other people think is right.

respond **responds, responding, responded**

VERB When you **respond** to someone, you react to them by doing or saying something.
response NOUN

responsible

ADJECTIVE **1** If you are **responsible** for something, it is your job to deal with it, and you are to blame if it goes wrong.

ADJECTIVE **2** A **responsible** person behaves properly and sensibly.

rest **rests, resting, rested**

VERB **1** When you **rest**, you sit or lie down and keep still for a while.
NOUN **2** A **rest** is a period of time when you do not work.
NOUN **3** The **rest** is all the things in a group that are left. *I've done some of the washing-up. I'll do the rest tomorrow.*

restaurant **restaurants**

NOUN A **restaurant** is a place where meals are served.

restless

ADJECTIVE If you feel **restless**, you find it hard to relax.

result **results**

NOUN **1** A **result** is something that happens because of something else. *The milk boiled over and the result was a real mess.*
NOUN **2** A **result** is also the score at the end of a game.

retire **retires, retiring, retired**

VERB When someone **retires**, they stop doing their job, usually because they are getting old.

retreat **retreats, retreating, retreated**

VERB If you **retreat** from something difficult or dangerous, you move backwards away from it. *The army retreated from the enemy.*

return **returns, returning, returned**

VERB **1** When you **return** to a place, you go back there after you have been away.
VERB **2** If you **return** something to someone, you give it back to them.
NOUN **3** A **return** is a ticket for the journey to a place and back again.

a
b
c
d
e
f
g
h
i
j
k
l
m
n
o
p
q
Rr
s
t
u
v
w
x
y
z

reveal reveals, revealing, revealed
VERB If you **reveal** something that has been secret or hidden, you tell people about it or show it to them.

revenge
NOUN **Revenge** is something a person does to hurt someone who has hurt them.

reverse reverses, reversing, reversed
VERB 1 If a car **reverses**, it goes backwards.
VERB 2 If you **reverse** the order of things, you put them in the opposite order.

revise revises, revising, revised
VERB 1 If you **revise** something, you alter it or correct it.
VERB 2 When you **revise**, you read something again so that you can learn it for a test.
revision NOUN

revolver revolvers
NOUN A **revolver** is a small gun.

reward rewards
NOUN A **reward** is something you are given for doing well.

rhinoceros rhinoceroses
NOUN A **rhinoceros** is a large African or Asian animal with a thick skin and one or two horns on its nose. Rhinoceroses are often called **rhinos** for short.

rhyme rhymes, rhyming, rhymed
VERB If two words **rhyme**, they have a similar sound. For example, "dog" rhymes with "log".

rhythm rhythms
NOUN **Rhythm** is a regular pattern of sound or movement. Music and dancing have rhythm.

rib ribs
NOUN Your **ribs** are the curved bones that go from your backbone to your chest.

ribbon ribbons
NOUN A **ribbon** is a long narrow piece of fine cloth. It is used for tying things together, or as a decoration.

rice
NOUN **Rice** is white or pale brown grains which are boiled and eaten.

rich richer, richest
ADJECTIVE Someone who is **rich** has a lot of money or valuable things.

rid
get rid of PHRASE When you **get rid of** something that you do not want, you remove it or throw it away.

riddle riddles
NOUN A **riddle** is a kind of puzzle. You ask a question which has a funny answer.

ride rides, riding, rode, ridden
NOUN 1 A **ride** is a journey using a bus, car, train, horse or bicycle.
VERB 2 When a person **rides** a horse or a bicycle, they sit on it and control it.
VERB 3 When you **ride** in a vehicle such as a car, you travel in it.

ridiculous
ADJECTIVE If you say something is **ridiculous**, you mean it is foolish.

right
ADJECTIVE 1 If something is **right**, it is correct.
ADJECTIVE OR ADVERB 2 **Right** means on or towards the right side of something. Most people write with their right hand.

right angle right angles
NOUN A **right angle** is an angle or turn of 90 degrees.

rigid
ADJECTIVE Something that is **rigid** is very stiff and does not bend or stretch.

rim rims

NOUN **1** The **rim** of a container, such as a cup, is the edge round the top.

NOUN **2** The **rim** of a round object, such as a wheel, is the outside edge of it.

rind rinds

NOUN The **rind** of a fruit such as an orange or a lemon is its thick outer skin.

ring rings, ringing, rang, rung

NOUN **1** A **ring** is an ornament that people wear on a finger.

NOUN **2** Anything in the shape of a circle can be called a **ring**.

VERB **3** If you **ring** someone, you phone them.

VERB **4** When a bell **rings**, it makes a loud clear sound.

rinse rinses, rinsing, rinsed

VERB When you **rinse** something, you wash it in clean water with no soap.

rip rips, ripping, ripped

VERB If someone **rips** something, they tear it violently.

ripe riper, ripest

ADJECTIVE When fruit or grain is **ripe**, it is ready to be eaten or harvested.

ripple ripples

NOUN A **ripple** is a little wave on the surface of water.

rise rises, rising, rose, risen

VERB **1** If something **rises**, it moves upwards.

VERB **2** When the sun or the moon **rises**, it appears above the horizon.

risk risks

NOUN A **risk** is a danger that something bad might happen.

take a risk PHRASE If someone **takes a risk**, they do something knowing that it could be dangerous.

risky ADJECTIVE

rival rivals

NOUN Your **rival** is someone who is trying to win the same things as you are.

river rivers

NOUN A **river** is a large amount of fresh water flowing towards the sea.

road roads

NOUN A **road** is a long piece of hard ground, specially treated so that people and vehicles can travel along it easily.

roam roams, roaming, roamed

VERB If you **roam**, you wander around without any particular purpose.

roar roars, roaring, roared

VERB If something **roars**, it makes a very loud noise like a lion. *The car roared off down the road.*

roast roasts, roasting, roasted

VERB When someone **roasts** meat or other food, they cook it in an oven or over a fire.

rob robs, robbing, robbed

VERB If someone **robs** you, they steal something from you.

robber NOUN   robbery NOUN

robin robins

NOUN A **robin** is a small brown bird with a red neck and chest.

robot robots

NOUN A **robot** is a machine which is programmed to move and perform tasks automatically.

rock rocks, rocking, rocked

NOUN **1** Rock is the very hard material that is in the earth. Cliffs and mountains are made of rock.

NOUN **2** A **rock** is a large piece of rock.

VERB **3** When something **rocks**, it moves slowly backwards and forwards, or from side to side.

NOUN **4** Rock or **rock music** is music with a very strong beat.

NOUN **5** Rock is also a sweet shaped into long hard sticks.

rocky ADJECTIVE

a b c d e f g h i j k l m n o p q **Rr** s t u v w x y z

rocket   rockets

NOUN **1** A **rocket** is a space vehicle, usually shaped like a long pointed tube.

NOUN **2** Rockets are fireworks that explode when they are high in the air.

rod   rods

NOUN A **rod** is a long thin pole or bar, usually made of wood or metal. *His uncle gave him a new fishing rod.*

rode

VERB **Rode** is the past tense of **ride**.

rodent   rodents

NOUN A **rodent** is a small mammal with sharp front teeth for gnawing. Rats, mice, squirrels and hamsters are rodents.

roll   rolls, rolling, rolled

VERB **1** When something **rolls**, or when you roll it, it moves along a surface, turning over and over.

NOUN **2** A **roll** of something like paper is a long piece of it that has been rolled into a tube.

NOUN **3** A **roll** is a small loaf of bread for one person.

Rollerblade   Rollerblades

NOUN; TRADEMARK **Rollerblades** are roller skates which have the wheels set in one straight line on the bottom of the boot.

roller skate   roller skates

NOUN **Roller skates** are shoes with four small wheels underneath.

roof   roofs

NOUN **1** The **roof** of a building or car is the covering on top of it.

NOUN **2** The **roof** of your mouth or of a cave is the highest part.

room   rooms

NOUN **1** A **room** is a section in a building, divided from other rooms by walls.

NOUN **2** If there is plenty of **room**, there is a lot of space.

root   roots

NOUN **1** A **root** is the part of a plant that grows underground.

NOUN **2** The **root** of a hair, tooth or nail is the part that you cannot see because it is covered with skin.

root word   root words

NOUN A **root word** is a word to which prefixes and suffixes can be added to make other words. In the word "clearly", the root word is "clear".

rope   ropes

NOUN **Rope** is thick strong string.

rose   roses

NOUN **1** A **rose** is a flower. Most roses grow on thorny stems.

VERB **2** Rose is also the past tense of **rise**.

rot   rots, rotting, rotted

VERB **1** When vegetables and other foods **rot**, they go bad.

VERB **2** When wood **rots**, it goes soft and can easily be pulled to pieces.

rotate   rotates, rotating, rotated

VERB When something **rotates**, it turns with a circular movement.

rotten

ADJECTIVE Something that is **rotten** has gone bad or soft so that it cannot be used.

rough   rougher, roughest

ADJECTIVE **1** If something is **rough**, the surface is uneven and not smooth.

ADJECTIVE **2** If someone is being **rough**, they are not being gentle.

ADJECTIVE **3** A **rough** estimate is not meant to be exact.

ADJECTIVE **4** A **rough** draft is an early version of something you are writing.

roughly

ADVERB **1** If you say **roughly**, you mean approximately. *There are **roughly** twice as many boys as girls in this club.*

ADVERB **2** If someone speaks **roughly** to you, they sound angry and aggressive.

round rounder, roundest

ADJECTIVE **1** Something **round** is shaped like a ball or a circle.

PREPOSITION **2** If something is **round** something else, it surrounds it. *There was a wall **round** the garden.*

PREPOSITION **3** If something moves **round** you, it keeps moving in a circle with you in the centre.

ADVERB **4** If you turn or look **round**, you turn so you are facing a different way.

round up or round down PHRASE
If you **round a number**, you raise it up or lower it down to the nearest 10, 100 or 1000. *If you **round** 34 to the nearest ten, it would be 30. 675 **rounded** up to the nearest hundred is 700.*

roundabout roundabouts

NOUN **1** A **roundabout** is a place where several roads meet, with a circle in the centre which vehicles have to go round.

NOUN **2** A **roundabout** is also a large machine at a fair that children can sit on and go round and round.

rounders

NOUN **Rounders** is a game in which players run between posts after hitting the ball.

route routes

NOUN A **route** is a way from one place to another. *David took his usual **route** to school.*

routine routines

ADJECTIVE **1** **Routine** things happen regularly.

NOUN **2** Your **routine** is the usual way that you do things.

row rows, rowing, rowed
(*rhymes with* **snow**)

NOUN **1** A **row** of people or things is several of them arranged in a line.

VERB **2** When you **row** a boat, you use oars to make it move through the water.

(*rhymes with* **now**) NOUN **3** A **row** is a noisy argument.

royal

ADJECTIVE **1** Someone who is **royal** belongs to the family of a king or queen.

ADJECTIVE **2** Something that is **royal** is connected with a royal family.

rub rubs, rubbing, rubbed

VERB When you **rub** something, you wipe it hard.

rubber rubbers

NOUN **1** **Rubber** is a strong stretchy material that is made from the sap of a tree. It is used to make things like tyres.

NOUN **2** A **rubber** is a small piece of rubber used to get rid of pencil marks.

rubbish

NOUN **1** **Rubbish** is waste material, such as used paper or empty tins.

NOUN **2** If you say something is **rubbish**, you think it is of very poor quality. *This new television programme is **rubbish**.*

ruby rubies

NOUN A **ruby** is a dark red jewel.

rudder rudders

NOUN A **rudder** is a piece of wood or metal on the back of a boat or plane which is moved to make the boat or plane turn.

rude **ruder, rudest**
ADJECTIVE If someone is **rude**, they behave badly and are not polite. *It's **rude** to stare at people.*

rug **rugs**
NOUN A **rug** is a piece of thick material like a small carpet.

rugby
NOUN **Rugby** is a game played with an oval ball. Two teams try to score points by carrying the ball across a line, or by kicking the ball over a bar.

ruin **ruins, ruining, ruined**
VERB 1 To **ruin** something means to spoil it completely. *Mark and Joe **ruined** my party by fighting.*
NOUN 2 The **ruins** of a building are the parts of it that are left after it has fallen down or been badly damaged.

rule **rules, ruling, ruled**
VERB 1 To **rule** a country means to be in charge of the way the country works.
NOUN 2 **Rules** tell you what you are allowed to do and what you are not allowed to do. They are used in games, and in places such as schools.

ruler **rulers**
NOUN 1 A **ruler** is a person who rules a country.
NOUN 2 A **ruler** is also a long flat piece of wood or plastic with straight edges, used for measuring or drawing straight lines.

rumour **rumours**
NOUN A **rumour** is a story or piece of information which a lot of people are talking about, but which may not be true.

run **runs, running, ran, run**
VERB 1 When you **run**, you move quickly, leaving the ground during each stride.

VERB 2 When liquid **runs**, it flows. *Don't leave the hot water **running**.*
VERB 3 Someone who **runs** something, like a school or country, is in charge of it.
VERB 4 When a vehicle such as a train or bus **runs** somewhere, it travels at set times. *The bus **runs** every 20 minutes.*
VERB 5 If you **run** out of something, you have no more of it left.

rung **rungs**
NOUN 1 A **rung** is a wooden or metal step on a ladder.
VERB 2 **Rung** is the past participle of **ring**.

running
NOUN 1 **Running** is the activity of running, especially as a sport.
ADJECTIVE 2 **Running** water is flowing rather than standing still.

runway **runways**
NOUN A **runway** is a long narrow strip of ground at an airport which planes use when they take off or land.

rush **rushes, rushing, rushed**
VERB If you **rush** somewhere, you go there quickly.

rust **rusts, rusting, rusted**
NOUN 1 **Rust** is a reddish-brown substance that forms on iron or steel which has been in contact with water.
VERB 2 When something **rusts**, rust forms on it.
rusty ADJECTIVE

rustle **rustles, rustling, rustled**
VERB When something **rustles**, it makes soft sounds as it moves. *Dry leaves **rustled** underfoot.*

rut **ruts**
NOUN A **rut** is a deep groove in the ground made by the wheels of a vehicle.

Ss

sack **sacks**

NOUN A **sack** is a large strong bag made of cloth or plastic.

sad **sadder, saddest**

ADJECTIVE If you are **sad**, you are unhappy because something has happened that you do not like.

saddle **saddles**

NOUN A **saddle** is a seat for a rider on a horse or bicycle.

safari **safaris**

NOUN A **safari** is a journey to see wild animals.

safari park **safari parks**

NOUN A **safari park** is a large protected area of land where wild animals live and move around freely.

safe **safer, safest; safes**

ADJECTIVE **1** If you are **safe**, you are not in any danger.

ADJECTIVE **2** If something is in a **safe** place, it cannot be lost or stolen.

NOUN **3** A **safe** is a strong metal cupboard with special locks. People keep money or valuable things in a safe.

safety NOUN

said

VERB **Said** is the past tense of **say**.

sail **sails, sailing, sailed**

NOUN **1** A **sail** is a large piece of material fixed to a boat. The wind blows against the sail and pushes the boat along.

NOUN **2** A **sail** is also one of the flat pieces of wood on the top of a windmill.

VERB **3** To **sail** a boat means to make it move across water using its sails.

sailor **sailors**

NOUN A **sailor** is a person who works on a ship as a member of the crew.

salad **salads**

NOUN A **salad** is a mixture of raw vegetables, for example lettuce, cucumber and tomatoes.

sale **sales**

NOUN **1** The **sale** of anything is the selling of it for money.

NOUN **2** A **sale** is a time when a shop sells things at less than their usual price.

saliva

NOUN **Saliva** is the liquid in your mouth that helps you eat food.

salmon

NOUN A **salmon** is a large silvery fish. Salmon live in the sea, but they swim up rivers to lay their eggs.

salt

NOUN **Salt** is a white powder or crystal with a bitter taste. Salt is found in the earth and in sea water. It is used to flavour or preserve food.

salute **salutes, saluting, saluted**

NOUN **1** A **salute** is a sign of respect used especially in the armed forces.

VERB **2** If you **salute** someone, you give them a salute.

same

ADJECTIVE **1** If two things are the **same**, they are exactly like each other in some way. *Look! Your dress is the **same** as mine.*

ADJECTIVE **2** **Same** means one shared thing and not two different ones. *Amy and I are in the **same** class.*

sample **samples**

NOUN A **sample** of something is a small quantity of it that you can try.

sand

NOUN **Sand** is tiny grains of rock, shells and other material. Most deserts and beaches are made of sand.

sandal **sandals**

NOUN **Sandals** are light shoes for warm weather. The soles are held on by straps which go over your foot.

sandpit **sandpits**

NOUN A **sandpit** is a shallow box in the ground with sand in it, where small children can play.

sandwich **sandwiches**

NOUN A **sandwich** is two slices of bread with a layer of food in between.

sang

VERB **Sang** is the past tense of **sing**.

sank

VERB **Sank** is the past tense of **sink**.

sap

NOUN **Sap** is the liquid that carries food through plants and trees.

sardine **sardines**

NOUN A **sardine** is a small sea fish.

sari **saris**

NOUN A **sari** is a piece of clothing worn especially by Asian women.

sat

VERB **Sat** is the past tense of **sit**.

satchel **satchels**

NOUN A **satchel** is a leather or cloth bag with a long strap.

satellite **satellites**

NOUN **1** A **satellite** is a natural object in space that moves around a larger object. The moon is a satellite of the Earth.

NOUN **2** A **satellite** is also an object sent into space to send signals back to Earth.

satellite dish **satellite dishes**

NOUN A **satellite dish** is an aerial which receives signals from an artificial satellite.

satellite television

NOUN **Satellite television** is where the programmes are sent from an artificial satellite. They can be received using a satellite dish.

satisfactory

ADJECTIVE Something that is **satisfactory** is good enough for its purpose.

satisfy **satisfies, satisfying, satisfied**

VERB To **satisfy** someone means to give them enough of something to make them pleased or contented.

Saturday **Saturdays**

NOUN **Saturday** is the day between Friday and Sunday.

sauce **sauces**

NOUN A **sauce** is a thick liquid served with other food to add to the taste.

saucepan **saucepans**

NOUN A **saucepan** is a deep metal cooking pot, usually with a long handle. Most saucepans have lids.

saucer **saucers**

NOUN A **saucer** is a small plate on which you stand a cup.

sausage **sausages**

NOUN A **sausage** is a finely minced meat mixture put into a skin.

savage

ADJECTIVE A **savage** animal is wild and fierce.

save **saves, saving, saved**

VERB **1** If you **save** someone or something, you help them to escape from harm or danger. *He fell in the river and his father dived in to save him.*

VERB **2** If you **save** money, you gradually collect it by not spending it all.

savings

PLURAL NOUN Your **savings** are the money you have saved.

saw **saws, sawing, sawed, sawn**

VERB **1 Saw** is the past tense of **see**.

NOUN **2** A **saw** is a tool for cutting wood and other materials. It has a blade with sharp teeth along one edge.

VERB **3** If you **saw** something, you cut it with a saw.

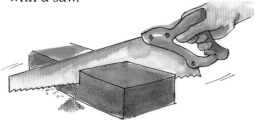

sawdust

NOUN **Sawdust** is the dust and small bits of wood made when wood is sawn.

say **says, saying, said**

VERB When you **say** something, you speak words.

scald **scalds, scalding, scalded**

VERB If you **scald** yourself, you burn yourself with very hot liquid or steam.

scale **scales**

NOUN **1** The **scale** of a map is how its size relates to the place in the real world.

NOUN **2** The **scales** of a fish or reptile are the small pieces of hard skin covering its body.

scales

PLURAL NOUN **Scales** are a piece of equipment you use for weighing things.

scamper **scampers, scampering, scampered**

VERB When people or small animals **scamper**, they move quickly and lightly.

scan **scans, scanning, scanned**

VERB **1** If you **scan** a piece of writing, you look through it quickly.

VERB **2** If a machine **scans** something, it examines it using a beam of light, X-rays or sound waves.

scar **scars**

NOUN A **scar** is a mark that is left on the skin after a wound has healed.

scarce **scarcer, scarcest**

ADJECTIVE Something that is **scarce** is not often found.

scare **scares, scaring, scared**

VERB Someone or something that **scares** you makes you feel frightened.

scarecrow **scarecrows**

NOUN A **scarecrow** is an object in the shape of a person, put in a field of crops to frighten birds away.

scared

ADJECTIVE If you are **scared**, you are frightened.

scarf **scarves**

NOUN A **scarf** is a piece of cloth that you wear round your neck to keep you warm.

scarlet

ADJECTIVE Something **scarlet** is a bright red colour.

scatter **scatters, scattering, scattered**

VERB **1** If you **scatter** things, you throw or drop a lot of them all over an area.

VERB **2** If people **scatter**, they suddenly move away in different directions.

scene **scenes**

NOUN **1** The **scene** of an event is the place where it happened. *The police went to the **scene** of the crime.*

NOUN **2** A **scene** is part of a play or film in which things happen in one place.

scenery

NOUN **1** Scenery is what you can see when you are out in the country.

NOUN **2** Scenery is also all the cloths and boards that are used as a background for the stage in a theatre.

a
b
c
d
e
f
g
h
i
j
k
l
m
n
o
p
q
r
Ss
t
u
v
w
x
y
z

scent

scent scents
NOUN A **scent** is a pleasant smell.

scheme schemes, scheming, schemed
NOUN **1** A **scheme** is a plan for doing something.
VERB **2** When people **scheme**, they make secret plans.

school schools
NOUN **1** A **school** is a place for teaching and learning.
NOUN **2** You can refer to a large group of dolphins or fish as a **school**.
See *Collective nouns* on page 262.

science
NOUN **Science** is the study of plants and animals, materials, and things like electricity, forces, light and sound.

science fiction
NOUN **Science fiction** is stories about events happening in the future or in other parts of the universe.

scientist scientists
NOUN A **scientist** is a person who finds out why things happen by doing tests and by careful study.

scissors
PLURAL NOUN **Scissors** are a cutting tool with two sharp blades.

scoop scoops, scooping, scooped
VERB **1** If you **scoop** something up, you pick it up using a spoon or the palm of your hand.
NOUN **2** A **scoop** is an object like a large spoon which is used for picking up food such as ice cream.

score scores, scoring, scored
VERB **1** If someone **scores**, they get a goal or other point in a game.
NOUN **2** The **score** in a game is the total number of points made by the two teams or players.

scowl scowls, scowling, scowled
VERB If you **scowl**, you look very cross.

scramble scrambles, scrambling, scrambled
VERB If you **scramble** over rough or difficult ground, you move over it quickly, using your hands to help you.

scrap scraps
NOUN A **scrap** of something is a small piece of it. *I need a scrap of paper.*

scrapbook scrapbooks
NOUN A **scrapbook** is a book in which you stick things such as pictures or newspaper articles.

scrape scrapes, scraping, scraped
VERB If you **scrape** something, you take off its surface by pulling a rough or sharp object over it.

scratch scratches, scratching, scratched
VERB **1** If you **scratch** your skin, you rub your fingernails against it.
VERB **2** If you **scratch** something, you damage it by making small cuts on it. *I fell into the hedge and scratched my bike.*
NOUN **3** A **scratch** is a small cut.

scream screams, screaming, screamed
VERB If you **scream**, you shout or cry in a loud high-pitched voice.

screech screeches, screeching, screeched
VERB To **screech** means to make an unpleasant high-pitched noise. *The car wheels screeched.*

screen screens
NOUN A **screen** is a flat surface on which pictures or words are shown, for example a television or computer screen.

screw **screws, screwing, screwed**

NOUN **1** A **screw** is a small sharp piece of metal used for fixing things together.

VERB **2** If you **screw** things together, you fix them together using screws.

VERB **3** If you **screw** something onto something else, you fix it there by twisting it round and round. *He screwed the top back onto the bottle of water.*

screwdriver **screwdrivers**

NOUN A **screwdriver** is a tool used for turning screws.

scribble **scribbles, scribbling, scribbled**

VERB If you **scribble**, you write quickly and roughly.

script **scripts**

NOUN The **script** of a play or film is the written version of it.

scrub **scrubs, scrubbing, scrubbed**

VERB If you **scrub** something, you rub it hard with a stiff brush and water.

sculptor **sculptors**

NOUN A **sculptor** is someone who makes sculptures.

sculpture **sculptures**

NOUN **1** A **sculpture** is a statue or model made by shaping stone, clay or other materials.

NOUN **2** Sculpture is the art of making sculptures.

sea **seas**

NOUN The **sea** is the salty water that covers about three-quarters of the earth.

seagull **seagulls**

NOUN **Seagulls** are common white, grey and black birds that live near the sea.

seahorse **seahorses**

NOUN A **seahorse** is a small fish which swims upright, with a head that looks like a horse's head.

seal **seals, sealing, sealed**

NOUN **1** A **seal** is a large mammal with flippers that lives partly on land and partly in the sea.

VERB **2** If you **seal** an envelope, you stick down the flap.

seam **seams**

NOUN A **seam** is the line where two pieces of material are sewn together.

search **searches, searching, searched**

VERB If you **search** for something, you try to find it by looking carefully.

seaside

NOUN The **seaside** is a place by the sea, especially one where people go for their holidays.

season **seasons**

NOUN A **season** is one of the four parts of a year: spring, summer, autumn and winter.

seat **seats**

NOUN A **seat** is a place where you can sit, for example a chair or a stool.

seat belt **seat belts**

NOUN A **seat belt** is a strap that you fasten across your body for safety when travelling in a car, coach or aircraft.

seaweed

NOUN **Seaweed** is a plant that grows in the sea.

a
b
c
d
e
f
g
h
i
j
k
l
m
n
o
p
q
r
Ss
t
u
v
w
x
y
z

second

second seconds
ADJECTIVE **1** The **second** item in a series is the one counted as number two.
NOUN **2** A **second** is a short period of time. There are 60 seconds in a minute.

second person
NOUN In grammar, the **second person** is the person who is addressed in speech or writing. It is expressed as "you".

secret secrets
NOUN A **secret** is something that only a few people know and that they are not to tell other people.

section sections
NOUN A **section** of something is one of the separate parts it is divided into.

secure
ADJECTIVE **1** If you feel **secure**, you feel safe and confident.
ADJECTIVE **2** If something is **secure**, it is fixed firmly in position.
security NOUN

see sees, seeing, saw, seen
VERB **1** If you **see** something, you are looking at it or you notice it.
VERB **2** To **see** something also means to understand it. *I see what you mean.*
VERB **3** If you **see** someone, you visit them or meet them. *I went to see the doctor.*

seed seeds
NOUN The **seeds** of a plant are the small hard parts from which new plants grow.

seek seeks, seeking, sought
VERB If you **seek** someone or something, you try to find them.

seem seems, seeming, seemed
VERB **1** If you say that someone **seems**, for example, to be happy or sad, you mean that is the way they look. *Tim seems to be a bit upset today.*
VERB **2** If something **seems** a certain way, that is the way it feels to you. *I only waited for ten minutes but it seemed like hours.*

seen
VERB **Seen** is the past participle of **see**.

seesaw seesaws
NOUN A **seesaw** is a long plank. A child sits on each end and they move up and down in turn.

segment segments
NOUN A **segment** of something is a small part of it.

seize seizes, seizing, seized
VERB If you **seize** something, you grab it firmly.

select selects, selecting, selected
VERB When you **select** someone or something, you choose them.

selfish
ADJECTIVE People who are **selfish** only think about themselves. They do not care about other people.

sell sells, selling, sold
VERB When someone **sells** something, they give it in exchange for money.

Sellotape
NOUN; TRADEMARK **Sellotape** is a transparent sticky tape.

semi-
PREFIX Putting **semi-** in front of a word makes it mean half or partly. For example, a "semicircle" is half of a circle.
See *Prefixes* on page 264.

semicircle semicircles
NOUN A **semicircle** is half of a circle.
See *Colours and flat shapes* on page 271.

semicolon semicolons

NOUN A **semicolon** is the punctuation mark (;) which is used in writing to separate different parts of a sentence or list, or to show a pause.
See *Punctuation on page 264.*

semifinal semifinals

NOUN The **semifinals** are the two matches in a competition played to decide who plays in the final.

send sends, sending, sent

VERB **1** When you **send** something to someone, you arrange for it to be delivered to them.
VERB **2** If someone **sends** someone somewhere, they tell them to go there. *She was **sent** home because she was ill.*
VERB **3** If someone **sends** for you, you get a message to go and see them.

senior

ADJECTIVE People who are **senior** are older or more important.

sensation sensations

NOUN A **sensation** is a physical feeling.

sense senses

NOUN **1** Your **senses** are your power to see, hear, smell, touch and taste.
NOUN **2 Sense** is knowing the right thing to do. *You should have had more sense.*
NOUN **3** If something makes **sense**, you can understand it.

sensible

ADJECTIVE People who are **sensible** know what is the right thing to do.
sensibly ADVERB

sensitive

ADJECTIVE **1** If someone or something is **sensitive**, they are easily hurt. *He is very sensitive about his big ears.*
ADJECTIVE **2** If you are **sensitive** to other people's feelings, you understand them.

sent

VERB **Sent** is the past tense of **send**.

sentence sentences

NOUN A **sentence** is a group of words that mean something.

separate separates, separating, separated

ADJECTIVE **1** If two things are **separate**, they are not connected.
VERB **2** To **separate** people or things means to part them. *Separate the yolk from the white.*

September

NOUN **September** is the ninth month of the year. It has 30 days.

sequel sequels

NOUN A **sequel** to a book or film is another book or film which continues the story.

sequence sequences

NOUN A **sequence** of events is a number of them coming one after the other.

series

NOUN **1** A **series** is a number of things of the same kind that follow each other.
NOUN **2** A radio or television **series** is a set of programmes about the same thing.

serious

ADJECTIVE **1** People who are **serious** are often quiet and do not laugh very much.
ADJECTIVE **2** Things that are **serious** are important and need careful thought.
ADJECTIVE **3** A **serious** problem or situation is very bad and worrying.

servant servants

NOUN A **servant** is someone paid to work in another person's house.

serve serves, serving, served

VERB **1** If you **serve** food or drink to people, you give it to them.

VERB **2** To **serve** customers in a shop means to help them to buy what they want.

service services

NOUN A **service** is something useful that a person or company does for people.

serviette serviettes

NOUN A **serviette** is a small piece of cloth or paper that you use to wipe your hands and mouth when you are eating.

set sets, setting, set

NOUN **1** A **set** is a number of things of the same kind that belong together, for example a set of golf clubs or a set of tools.

VERB **2** When something such as jelly or concrete **sets**, it becomes firm or hard.

VERB **3** When the sun **sets**, it goes down behind the horizon.

VERB **4** When you **set** a clock or control, you adjust it to a particular position.

settee settees

NOUN A **settee** is a long, comfortable seat for two or more people.

setting settings

NOUN The **setting** of a story or play is where it takes place. *That old castle would make a great **setting** for a creepy story.*

settle settles, settling, settled

VERB **1** If you **settle**, you sit or make yourself comfortable.

VERB **2** If something such as dust or snow **settles**, it sinks slowly and becomes still.

VERB **3** If you **settle** something, you decide it.

several

ADJECTIVE **Several** people or things means a number of them. *He was gone for **several** hours.*

severe

ADJECTIVE **Severe** is used to describe something extremely bad or unpleasant. *She woke with **severe** toothache.*

sew sews, sewing, sewed

VERB When someone **sews**, they join pieces of cloth together by using a needle and thread.

sewer sewers

NOUN A **sewer** is a large underground pipe that carries rainwater and waste away from houses and other buildings.

sex sexes

NOUN The two **sexes** are the two groups that people and other living things are divided into. One sex is male and the other is female. Only female animals can have babies.

shabby shabbier, shabbiest

ADJECTIVE Something that is **shabby** looks old and nearly worn out.

shade shades, shading, shaded

NOUN **1** **Shade** is the darkness in a place where the sun cannot reach. *She sat in the **shade** of an apple tree.*

NOUN **2** A **shade** is something that covers a light to stop it shining in your eyes.

VERB **3** If you **shade** something, you stop the sun from shining on it.

NOUN **4** **Shade** is how dark or light a colour is. *I love this **shade** of blue.*

shadow shadows

NOUN A **shadow** is a dark shape. It is formed when something opaque blocks the light coming from a lamp, a torch or the sun.

a b c d e f g h i j k l m n o p q r **Ss** t u v w x y z

shed

shake   **shakes, shaking, shook, shaken**
VERB **1** If you **shake** something, or it shakes, it moves quickly from side to side or up and down.
VERB **2** If your voice **shakes**, it trembles because you are nervous or angry.

shaky   **shakier, shakiest**
ADJECTIVE If someone or something is **shaky**, they are weak and unsteady.
shakily ADVERB

shallow   **shallower, shallowest**
ADJECTIVE Something that is **shallow**, such as a hole, a container or water, measures only a short distance from top to bottom.

shame
NOUN **1** **Shame** is an unhappy feeling that people have when they have done something wrong or foolish.
NOUN **2** If you say something is a **shame**, you mean you are sorry about it. *It's a **shame** you can't come round.*

shampoo   **shampoos**
NOUN **Shampoo** is a soapy liquid that you use for washing your hair.

shape   **shapes**
NOUN **1** The **shape** of something is the form of its outline, for example whether it is round or square.
NOUN **2** A **shape** is something that has its outside edges joining in a particular way. Shapes can be flat (two-dimensional), like a circle or a triangle, or solid (three-dimensional), like a cube or sphere.
See *Colours and flat shapes* and *Solid shapes* on page 271.

share   **shares, sharing, shared**
VERB **1** If you **share** something with another person, you both use it. *She **shared** a bedroom with her sister.*
VERB **2** If you **share** something among a group of people, you divide it so that everyone gets some.
NOUN **3** A **share** of something is a portion of it.

shark   **sharks**
NOUN **Sharks** are large powerful fish with sharp teeth.

sharp   **sharper, sharpest**
ADJECTIVE **1** A **sharp** object has a fine edge or point that is good for cutting or piercing things.
ADJECTIVE **2** A **sharp** person is quick to notice or understand things.
ADJECTIVE **3** A **sharp** pain is sudden and hurts a lot.

sharpen   **sharpens, sharpening, sharpened**
VERB If you **sharpen** something, you make its edge or point sharper.

shatter   **shatters, shattering, shattered**
VERB If something **shatters**, it breaks into a lot of small pieces.

shave   **shaves, shaving, shaved**
VERB When a man **shaves**, he removes hair from his face with a razor.

shawl   **shawls**
NOUN A **shawl** is a large piece of woollen cloth. Shawls are worn by women over their shoulders or head. They are also used to wrap babies in.

shear   **shears, shearing, sheared**
VERB To **shear** a sheep means to cut the wool off it.

shears
PLURAL NOUN **Shears** are a tool like a large pair of scissors, used especially for cutting hedges.

shed   **sheds, shedding, shed**
NOUN **1** A **shed** is a small building used for storing things.
VERB **2** When a tree **sheds** its leaves, they fall off.

sheep

NOUN A **sheep** is a farm animal with a thick woolly coat. Sheep are kept for meat or wool.

sheet **sheets**

NOUN **1** A **sheet** is a large piece of thin cloth which is put on a bed.

NOUN **2** A **sheet** of something, such as paper or glass, is a thin flat piece.

shelf **shelves**

NOUN A **shelf** is something flat which is fixed to a wall or inside a cupboard. It is for putting things on.

shell **shells**

NOUN **1** The **shell** of an egg or nut is the hard covering round it.

NOUN **2** The **shell** of an animal such as a tortoise is the hard covering on its back.

shelter **shelters, sheltering, sheltered**

NOUN **1** A **shelter** is a small building or covered place where people or animals can be safe from bad weather or danger.

VERB **2** If you **shelter** in a place, you stay there and are safe.

shepherd **shepherds**

NOUN A **shepherd** is a person who looks after sheep.

sheriff **sheriffs**

NOUN **1** In America, a **sheriff** is a person who keeps the law in a county.

NOUN **2** In Scotland, a **sheriff** is the senior judge of a county or district.

NOUN **3** In Australia, a **sheriff** is an officer of the Supreme Court.

shield **shields, shielding, shielded**

NOUN **1** A **shield** is a large piece of strong material like metal or plastic which soldiers or policemen carry to protect themselves.

VERB **2** To **shield** someone means to protect them from something.

shift **shifts, shifting, shifted**

VERB **1** If you **shift** something, you move it.

VERB **2** If something **shifts**, it moves.

NOUN **3** A **shift** is a set period during which people work in a factory or hospital. *My dad works the night **shift**.*

shimmer **shimmers, shimmering, shimmered**

VERB If something **shimmers**, it shines with a faint flickering light, for example as the moon does on water.

shin **shins**

NOUN Your **shin** is the front part of your leg, between your knee and your ankle.

shine **shines, shining, shone**

VERB **1** When something **shines**, it gives out a bright light.

VERB **2** If you make an object **shine**, you make it bright by polishing it.

shiny ADJECTIVE

ship **ships**

NOUN A **ship** is a large boat which carries passengers or cargo.

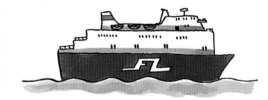

shirt **shirts**

NOUN A **shirt** is a light piece of clothing for the top part of your body, with a collar, sleeves, and buttons down the front.

shiver **shivers, shivering, shivered**

VERB When you **shiver**, your body shakes slightly, usually because you are cold or frightened.

shoal **shoals**

NOUN A **shoal** of fish is a large group of them swimming together.

See *Collective nouns* on page 262.

shock **shocks, shocking, shocked**
NOUN **1** If you have a **shock**, something happens suddenly which upsets you.
VERB **2** If you **shock** someone, you give them an unpleasant surprise.
shocking ADJECTIVE

shoe **shoes, shoeing, shod**
NOUN **1** **Shoes** are strong coverings for your feet.
VERB **2** To **shoe** a horse means to fix horseshoes onto its hooves.

shoelace **shoelaces**
NOUN A **shoelace** is a long piece of material like string that is used to fasten a shoe.

shone
VERB **Shone** is the past tense of **shine**.

shook
VERB **Shook** is the past tense of **shake**.

shoot **shoots, shooting, shot**
NOUN **1** A **shoot** is a new part growing from a plant or tree.
VERB **2** To **shoot** means to fire a bullet from a gun, or an arrow from a bow.
VERB **3** If someone **shoots** in a game such as football, they try to score a goal.
VERB **4** When a film is **shot**, it is filmed.

shop **shops, shopping, shopped**
NOUN **1** A **shop** is a place where things are sold.
VERB **2** When you **shop**, you go to the shops to buy things.
shopping NOUN

shopkeeper **shopkeepers**
NOUN A **shopkeeper** is a person who owns or looks after a small shop.

shore **shores**
NOUN The **shore** of a sea or lake is the land along the edge of it.

short **shorter, shortest**
ADJECTIVE **1** Someone who is **short** is not as tall as most other people.
ADJECTIVE **2** Something that is **short** is not very long.
PHRASE **3** If one word is **short for** another, it is a quick way of saying it. *Phone is **short for** telephone.*

shorts
PLURAL NOUN **Shorts** are trousers with short legs.

shot **shots**
VERB **1** **Shot** is the past tense of **shoot**.
NOUN **2** A **shot** is when a gun is fired.
NOUN **3** In football and tennis, a **shot** is the act of kicking or hitting the ball.

should
VERB **1** You use **should** to say that something ought to happen. *You **should** write a thank-you letter.*
VERB **2** You also use **should** to say that you expect something to happen. *We **should** have heard by now.*

shoulder **shoulders**
NOUN Your **shoulders** are the parts of your body between your neck and the tops of your arms.

shout **shouts, shouting, shouted**
VERB If you **shout** something, you say it very loudly.

shove **shoves, shoving, shoved**
VERB If you **shove** someone or something, you push them roughly.

shovel **shovels, shovelling, shovelled**
NOUN **1** A **shovel** is a tool like a spade with a rounded blade.
VERB **2** If you **shovel** earth or snow, you move it with a shovel.

show

show shows, showing, showed, shown

VERB **1** If you **show** someone something, you let them see it. *Show me your passport.*

VERB **2** If you **show** someone how to do something, you do it yourself so that they can watch you.

VERB **3** If something **shows**, people can see it. *Do you think that mark will show?*

VERB **4** If you **show** your feelings, you let people see them.

NOUN **5** A **show** is something that you watch at the theatre or on television.

shower showers

NOUN **1** A **shower** is a piece of equipment which sprays you with water so that you can wash yourself.

NOUN **2** A **shower** is also a short period of rain or snow.

shrank

VERB **Shrank** is the past tense of **shrink**.

shred shreds, shredding, shredded

NOUN **1** A **shred** of paper or material is a small narrow piece of it. *He tore the paper into shreds.*

VERB **2** If you **shred** something, you cut or tear it into small pieces.

shriek shrieks, shrieking, shrieked

VERB If you **shriek**, you give a sudden sharp scream.

shrill shriller, shrillest

ADJECTIVE A **shrill** sound is loud and high-pitched, like a whistle.

shrimp shrimps

NOUN A **shrimp** is a small edible shellfish with a long tail and many legs.

shrink shrinks, shrinking, shrank, shrunk

VERB If something **shrinks**, it becomes smaller.

shrivel shrivels, shrivelling, shrivelled

VERB When something **shrivels**, it becomes dry and curled up.

shrug shrugs, shrugging, shrugged

VERB If you **shrug** your shoulders, you raise them slightly to show that you are not interested in something.

shrunk

VERB **Shrunk** is the past participle of **shrink**.

shudder shudders, shuddering, shuddered

VERB If you **shudder**, you tremble with fear or horror.

shuffle shuffles, shuffling, shuffled

VERB **1** If you **shuffle**, you walk without lifting your feet properly off the ground.

VERB **2** If you **shuffle** a pack of cards, you mix them up before you begin a game.

shut shuts, shutting, shut

VERB **1** If you **shut** something, such as a door, you move it so that it fills a gap.

VERB **2** When a shop **shuts** you can no longer go into it.

ADJECTIVE **3** If something is **shut**, it is closed.

shy shier, shiest

ADJECTIVE A **shy** person is nervous with people they do not know well.

sick sicker, sickest

ADJECTIVE If you are **sick**, you are ill.

side sides

NOUN **1** The **side** of something is to the left or right of it. *He parted his hair on the left side.*

NOUN **2** The **side** of something can be the edge of it. *A triangle has three sides.*

NOUN **3** The **sides** of a river are its banks.

NOUN **4** The **sides** of a piece of paper are its front and back.

NOUN **5** The two **sides** in a game are the teams playing against each other.

ADJECTIVE **6** A **side** road is a small road leading off a larger one.

sideways

ADVERB **Sideways** means moving or facing towards one side. *She had to squeeze sideways through the gap.*

sigh sighs, sighing, sighed
VERB When you **sigh**, you breathe out heavily. People usually sigh when they are tired, sad or bored.

sight
NOUN **Sight** is being able to see.

sign signs, signing, signed
VERB **1** If you **sign** something, you write your name on it.
NOUN **2** A **sign** is a mark that means something, for example a plus sign (+).
NOUN **3** **Signs** can be words, pictures or symbols that tell you something.

NOUN **4** You can make a **sign** with your body that means something to other people. For example, if you shake your head it is a sign that you mean "No".

signal signals, signalling, signalled
NOUN **1** A **signal** is a message that is given by signs. For example, a flashing light is a signal that a driver is turning left or right.
VERB **2** If you **signal** to someone, you do something to give them a message.

signature signatures
NOUN Your **signature** is the way you write your own name.

sign language
NOUN **Sign language** is a way of communicating using your hands. It is often used by deaf people.

Sikh Sikhs
NOUN A **Sikh** is a person who believes in Sikhism, an Indian religion which teaches that there is only one God.

silence
NOUN **Silence** is when there is no noise.

silent
ADJECTIVE **1** If someone or something is **silent**, they are not saying anything or making any noise.
ADJECTIVE **2** A **silent** letter is one that is written but not pronounced, for example, the "g" in the word "gnat". See *Silent letters* on page 261.

silhouette silhouettes
NOUN A **silhouette** is the outline of a dark shape against a light background.

silk silks
NOUN **Silk** is a fine soft cloth. It is made from threads produced by a kind of caterpillar called a silkworm.
silky ADJECTIVE

silly sillier, silliest
ADJECTIVE If someone says you are **silly**, they mean you are behaving in a foolish or childish way.

silver
NOUN **Silver** is a greyish-white metal used for making jewellery.

similar
ADJECTIVE If things are **similar**, they are rather alike.

simile similes
NOUN A **simile** is an expression in which a person or thing is described as being similar to someone or something else. "She went as red as a beetroot" is a simile.

simple simpler, simplest
ADJECTIVE Something that is **simple** is easy to do or understand.
simply ADVERB

simplify simplifies, simplifying, simplified
VERB To **simplify** something means to make it easier to do or understand.

a b c d e f g h i j k l m n o p q r **Ss** t u v w x y z

since

PREPOSITION **1 Since** means from a particular time until now. *I've been waiting since half past three.*
CONJUNCTION **2 Since** also means because. *I had a drink, since I was feeling thirsty.*

sincere

ADJECTIVE If you are **sincere**, you say things that you really mean.
sincerely ADVERB

sing sings, singing, sang, sung

VERB **1** If you **sing** a song, you make music with your voice.
VERB **2** When birds **sing**, they make pleasant sounds.

single

ADJECTIVE **1 Single** means one of something. *We can't park here. It's a single yellow line.*
ADJECTIVE **2** People who are **single** are not married.
ADJECTIVE **3** A **single** bed or bedroom is for one person.
ADJECTIVE **4** A **single** ticket only allows you to travel one way.

singular

NOUN **Singular** means one. *The singular of "girls" is "girl". The singular of "children" is "child".* See **plural**.

sink sinks, sinking, sank, sunk

NOUN **1** A **sink** is a large basin with water taps and a drain.
VERB **2** If something **sinks**, it moves slowly down until it disappears, especially below the surface of water.
VERB **3** To **sink** something sharp into an object means to make it go deeply into it. *The tiger sank its teeth into his leg.*

sip sips, sipping, sipped

VERB If you **sip** a drink, you drink it a little at a time.

sir

NOUN **Sir** is a polite way of addressing a man. *Please sir, can I leave early?*

siren sirens

NOUN A **siren** is something that makes a loud wailing noise as a warning. Fire engines, police cars and ambulances have sirens.

sister sisters

NOUN Your **sister** is a girl or woman who has the same parents as you.

sit sits, sitting, sat

VERB **1** When you **sit**, you put your bottom on something such as a chair or the floor.
VERB **2** When a bird **sits** on its eggs, it covers them with its body to hatch them.

site sites

NOUN A **site** is a piece of ground that is used for a particular purpose. *Let's stop at the next camp site.*

situation situations

NOUN **1** A **situation** is the place where something is. *Our hotel was in a lovely situation.*
NOUN **2** A **situation** is the things that are happening to you. *You have put me in a difficult situation.*

size sizes

NOUN The **size** of something is how big or small it is.

sizzle sizzles, sizzling, sizzled

VERB If something **sizzles**, it makes a hissing sound. *The meat sizzled in the frying pan.*

skate skates

NOUN **1 Skates** are ice skates or roller skates.
NOUN **2** A **skate** is an edible flat sea fish.

skateboard skateboards

NOUN A **skateboard** is a narrow board on wheels which you stand on and ride for fun.

skeleton   skeletons

NOUN Your **skeleton** is all the bones in your body joined together. It supports your body and protects your organs.

sketch   sketches

NOUN A **sketch** is a quick drawing.

ski   skis

NOUN **Skis** are long pieces of wood, metal or plastic that you fasten to special boots so that you can move easily on snow.

skid   skids, skidding, skidded

VERB If a vehicle **skids**, it slides out of control, for example because the road is wet or icy.

skill   skills

NOUN **Skill** is the ability to do something well.

skilful ADJECTIVE

skim   skims, skimming, skimmed

VERB 1 If you **skim** something from the surface of a liquid, you remove it.

VERB 2 If you **skim** a piece of writing, you read it to get a general idea of what it is about.

skin   skins

NOUN 1 Your **skin** is the natural covering of your body.

NOUN 2 The **skin** of a fruit or vegetable is its outer covering.

skinny   skinnier, skinniest

ADJECTIVE Someone **skinny** is very thin.

skip   skips, skipping, skipped

VERB 1 When you **skip**, you move along almost as though you were dancing, with little jumps.

VERB 2 If you **skip** with a rope, you swing the rope over your head and under your feet while jumping.

VERB 3 If you **skip** something, you miss it out. *I'm going to skip lunch.*

NOUN 4 A **skip** is a large metal container for holding rubbish and rubble.

skirt   skirts

NOUN A **skirt** is a piece of clothing worn by women and girls. It hangs from the waist.

skull   skulls

NOUN Your **skull** is the bony part of your head. It protects your brain, which is inside it.

sky   skies

NOUN The **sky** is the space around the earth which you can see when you stand outside and look upwards.

skyscraper   skyscrapers

NOUN A **skyscraper** is a very tall building.

slab   slabs

NOUN A **slab** is a thick flat piece of something such as stone or concrete.

slack   slacker, slackest

ADJECTIVE Something that is **slack** is loose, and not firmly stretched.

slam   slams, slamming, slammed

VERB If you **slam** a door, you shut it hard so that it makes a loud noise.

slang

NOUN **Slang** is words that you use in everyday talk but not when you are writing or being polite.

slant   slants, slanting, slanted

VERB If something **slants**, it is not straight but lies at an angle.

a
b
c
d
e
f
g
h
i
j
k
l
m
n
o
p
q
r
Ss
t
u
v
w
x
y
z

slap slaps, slapping, slapped
VERB If you **slap** someone, you hit them with the palm of your hand.

slate slates
NOUN **Slate** is a dark grey rock that can be split into thin layers. It is often used for roofs.

sledge sledges
NOUN A **sledge** is a vehicle on runners used for travelling over snow.

sleek sleeker, sleekest
ADJECTIVE Hair or fur that is **sleek** is smooth and shiny.

sleep sleeps, sleeping, slept
VERB When you **sleep**, you close your eyes and your whole body rests.
sleepy ADJECTIVE

sleet
NOUN **Sleet** is a mixture of snow and rain.

sleeve sleeves
NOUN The **sleeves** of a coat or jumper are the parts that cover your arms.

sleigh sleighs
NOUN A **sleigh** is a sledge pulled by animals.

slept
VERB **Slept** is the past tense of **sleep**.

slice slices, slicing, sliced
NOUN **1** A **slice** is a thin piece of food that has been cut from a larger piece.
VERB **2** If you **slice** food, you cut it into thin pieces.

slide slides, sliding, slid
VERB **1** When something **slides**, it moves smoothly over a surface.
NOUN **2** A **slide** is a piece of playground equipment for sliding down.

slight slighter, slightest
ADJECTIVE Something that is **slight** is small. *She has a slight cut.*
slightly ADVERB

slim slimmer, slimmest
ADJECTIVE Someone who is **slim** has a body that is thin but not too thin.

slime
NOUN **Slime** is a thick slippery substance which covers a surface and which looks unpleasant. *The pond was covered in green slime.*
slimy ADJECTIVE

sling slings, slinging, slung
NOUN **1** A **sling** is a piece of cloth which you hang from your neck to support a broken or injured arm.
VERB **2** If you **sling** something somewhere, you throw it carelessly.

slip slips, slipping, slipped
VERB **1** If you **slip**, you accidentally slide and lose your balance.
VERB **2** If you **slip** somewhere, you go there quickly and quietly. *She slipped out of the house.*
NOUN **3** A **slip** of paper is a small piece of paper.

slipper slippers
NOUN **Slippers** are soft loose shoes that people wear in the house.

slippery
ADJECTIVE Something that is **slippery** is smooth, wet or greasy. It is difficult to keep hold of or to walk on.

slit slits, slitting, slit
VERB **1** If you **slit** something, you make a long narrow cut in it. *He slit open the envelope.*
NOUN **2** A **slit** is a long narrow opening in something.

slope slopes

NOUN A **slope** is a flat surface which has one end higher than the other.

slot slots

NOUN A **slot** is a narrow opening in something, usually for putting coins in.

slow slower, slowest

ADJECTIVE **1** Something that is **slow** moves along without much speed.
ADJECTIVE **2** If a watch or clock is **slow**, it shows a time that is earlier than the correct time.
slowly ADVERB

slug slugs

NOUN A **slug** is a small slow-moving animal with a long slimy body, like a snail but without a shell.

sly slyer, slyest

ADJECTIVE Someone who is **sly** is good at tricking people in a not very nice way.

smack smacks, smacking, smacked

VERB If a person **smacks** someone, they hit them with an open hand.

small smaller, smallest

ADJECTIVE Something that is **small** is not as large as other things of the same kind.

smart smarter, smartest

ADJECTIVE Someone who is **smart** looks neat and clean.

smash smashes, smashing, smashed

VERB **1** If something **smashes**, it falls and hits the ground. It makes a loud noise and breaks into lots of pieces. *The cup smashed when she dropped it.*
VERB **2** If someone or something **smashes** an object, they drop it or hit it so that it breaks into lots of pieces.

smell smells, smelling, smelled or smelt

VERB **1** When you **smell** something, you notice it with your nose.
VERB **2** If something **smells** nice or nasty, people's noses tell them about it.
NOUN **3** Your sense of **smell** is your ability to smell things.

smile smiles, smiling, smiled

VERB When you **smile**, the corners of your mouth move upwards and you look happy.

smoke smokes, smoking, smoked

NOUN **1** Smoke is a mixture of gas and small particles sent into the air when something burns.
VERB **2** If something is **smoking**, smoke is coming from it.

smooth smoother, smoothest

ADJECTIVE **1** Something which is **smooth** has no roughness, lumps or holes in it.
ADJECTIVE **2** A **smooth** ride is one that is comfortable because there are no bumps.

smother smothers, smothering, smothered

VERB **1** If someone **smothers** a fire, they cover it with something in order to put it out.
VERB **2** If a lot of things **smother** something, they cover it all over. *The grass was smothered in daisies.*

smudge smudges, smudging, smudged

NOUN **1** A **smudge** is a dirty mark left on something.
VERB **2** If you **smudge** something, you make it dirty by touching it.

smug smugger, smuggest

ADJECTIVE Someone who is **smug** is too pleased with how good or clever they are.

smuggle smuggles, smuggling, smuggled

VERB To **smuggle** things or people into or out of a place means to take them there secretly, or against the law.

snack snacks

NOUN A **snack** is a small amount of food that you eat quickly. *I had an apple and some crisps for a snack.*

a
b
c
d
e
f
g
h
i
j
k
l
m
n
o
p
q
r
Ss
t
u
v
w
x
y
z

snag snags
NOUN A **snag** is a small problem.

snail snails
NOUN A **snail** is a small slow-moving animal with a shell on its back.

snake snakes
NOUN A **snake** is a long thin reptile with scales on its skin and no legs.
See *Reptiles* on page 259.

snap snaps, snapping, snapped
VERB **1** If something **snaps**, it breaks suddenly with a sharp cracking noise.
VERB **2** If a dog **snaps** at you, it tries to bite you.
VERB **3** If someone **snaps** at you, they speak crossly.
NOUN **4 Snap** is a children's card game.

snarl snarls, snarling, snarled
VERB When an animal **snarls**, it makes a fierce sound in its throat while showing its teeth.

snatch snatches, snatching, snatched
VERB If you **snatch** something, you take it quickly and suddenly.

sneak sneaks, sneaking, sneaked
VERB If you **sneak** somewhere, you go there very quietly, being careful that other people do not see or hear you.

sneer sneers, sneering, sneered
VERB If a person **sneers** at something, they show that they don't like it much.

sneeze sneezes, sneezing, sneezed
VERB When you **sneeze**, you blow out suddenly through your nose, making a loud noise.

sniff sniffs, sniffing, sniffed
VERB If you **sniff**, you breathe in through your nose hard enough to make a sound.

snooze snoozes, snoozing, snoozed
VERB If you **snooze**, you sleep lightly for a short time, especially during the day.

snore snores, snoring, snored
VERB When people **snore**, they breathe very noisily while they are sleeping.

snorkel snorkels
NOUN A **snorkel** is a tube that you breathe through when your face is just under the surface of the sea.

snow snows, snowing, snowed
NOUN **1 Snow** is flakes of ice crystals which fall from the sky in cold weather.
VERB **2** When it **snows**, snow falls from the sky.

snowball snowballs
NOUN A **snowball** is a ball of snow for throwing.

snowflake snowflakes
NOUN A **snowflake** is a soft piece of falling snow.

snowman snowmen
NOUN A **snowman** is a pile of snow that is made to look like a person.

snug snugger, snuggest
ADJECTIVE If you feel **snug**, you are warm and comfortable.

snuggle snuggles, snuggling, snuggled
VERB If you **snuggle** somewhere, you cuddle up to something or someone.

soak soaks, soaking, soaked
VERB **1** When liquid **soaks** something, it makes it very wet.
VERB **2** When something **soaks** up a liquid, the liquid is drawn up into it.

soap soaps

NOUN **Soap** is a substance made of natural oils and fats, used for washing yourself.

soar soars, soaring, soared

VERB If something **soars** into the air, it goes quickly up into it.

sob sobs, sobbing, sobbed

VERB When someone **sobs**, they cry in a noisy way, breathing in short breaths.

soccer

NOUN **Soccer** is another word for the game of football.

society societies

NOUN **1 Society** is people in general.
NOUN **2** A **society** is an organization for people who have the same interests.

sock socks

NOUN A **sock** is a soft piece of clothing which covers your foot and ankle.

socket sockets

NOUN A **socket** is a place on a wall or on a piece of electrical equipment into which you can put a plug or bulb.

sofa sofas

NOUN A **sofa** is a long comfortable seat for more than one person. Sofas have a back, and usually arms.

soft softer, softest

ADJECTIVE **1** Something that is **soft** changes shape easily when you touch it.
ADJECTIVE **2** A **soft** sound or voice is quiet and gentle.
ADJECTIVE **3** A **soft** light or colour is not too bright.

software

NOUN **Software** is computer programs.

soggy soggier, soggiest

ADJECTIVE Something that is **soggy** is wet and often heavy.

soil

NOUN **Soil** is the top layer of earth, which plants can grow in.

solar

ADJECTIVE **1 Solar** is used to describe something that is to do with the sun.
ADJECTIVE **2 Solar** power uses the sun's energy to provide light and heat.

sold

VERB **Sold** is the past tense of **sell**.

soldier soldiers

NOUN A **soldier** is a person in an army.

sole soles

NOUN **1** The **sole** of your foot, shoe or sock is the underneath surface of it.

NOUN **2** A **sole** is also a flat sea fish.

solemn

ADJECTIVE Someone or something that is **solemn** is serious, rather than cheerful.

solid

ADJECTIVE **1** Something that is **solid** is firm and always keeps its shape. Metal, wood and rock are all solid.
ADJECTIVE **2** Something **solid** is not hollow.
ADJECTIVE **3** A **solid** shape is a three-dimensional shape such as a cylinder or a cone.
See *Solid shapes* on page 271.

solution solutions

NOUN **1** A **solution** is the answer to a problem.
NOUN **2** A **solution** can also be a liquid in which something, like a powder, has been dissolved.

a
b
c
d
e
f
g
h
i
j
k
l
m
n
o
p
q
r
Ss
t
u
v
w
x
y
z

solve solves, solving, solved

VERB If you **solve** a problem, you find an answer to it.

some

ADJECTIVE You use **some** to talk about an amount when you are not saying how much there is. *There's **some** money on the table.*

somebody

PRONOUN You use **somebody** to talk about a person without saying exactly who you mean.

somehow

ADVERB You use **somehow** to talk about a way of doing something when you do not know exactly how.

someone

PRONOUN You use **someone** to talk about a person without saying exactly who you mean.

somersault somersaults

NOUN A **somersault** is a forwards or backwards roll in which you place your head on the ground and bring your body over it.

something

PRONOUN You use **something** to talk about a thing without saying exactly what you mean. *We need **something** to hold the door open.*

sometimes

ADVERB **Sometimes** means occasionally, rather than always or never.

somewhere

ADVERB **1 Somewhere** is used to talk about a place without saying exactly where it is. *It must be around **somewhere**.*

ADVERB **2 Somewhere** can be used to give an approximate amount, number or time. *It was **somewhere** between 11 o'clock and midnight.*

son sons

NOUN A boy is the **son** of his parents.

song songs

NOUN A **song** is a piece of music with words.

soon sooner, soonest

ADVERB **Soon** means in the near future.

soot

NOUN **Soot** is a black powder that comes from burning coal or wood.

sore sorer, sorest

ADJECTIVE If part of your body is **sore**, it hurts. *Her throat was so **sore** she couldn't talk.*

sorrow sorrows

NOUN **Sorrow** is feeling very sad.

sorry sorrier, sorriest

ADJECTIVE **1** If you feel **sorry** about something, you feel disappointed or sad. *I was **sorry** to leave all my friends.*

ADJECTIVE **2** If you feel **sorry** for someone, you feel sad for them.

sort sorts, sorting, sorted

NOUN **1** The different **sorts** of something are the different types of it.

VERB **2** If you **sort** things, you put them into groups. *Sort your socks into pairs.*

all sorts PHRASE **All sorts** of things means lots of different things.

sought

VERB **Sought** is the past tense of **seek**.

sound sounds

NOUN A **sound** is something that you hear.

soup soups

NOUN **Soup** is liquid food made by boiling meat, fish or vegetables in water.

sour sourer, sourest

ADJECTIVE **1** Something that is **sour** tastes sharp.

ADJECTIVE **2 Sour** milk is no longer fresh.

source sources

NOUN **1** The **source** of something is the place that it has come from.

NOUN **2** The **source** of a river or stream is the place where it begins.

south

NOUN **South** is one of the four main points of the compass. If you face the point where the sun rises, south is on your right. See **compass point**.
southern ADJECTIVE

south-east

NOUN **South-east** is halfway between south and east.

south-west

NOUN **South-west** is halfway between south and west.

souvenir souvenirs

NOUN A **souvenir** is something you keep to remind you of a person or place.

sow sows, sowing, sowed

(*rhymes with* **no**) VERB **1** To **sow** seeds means to plant them in the ground. (*rhymes with* **now**) NOUN **2** A **sow** is an adult female pig.

space spaces

NOUN **1** Space is the area that is empty in a place, building or container. *There's enough space for a bigger chair in my room.*

NOUN **2** Space is also the place far above the Earth where there is no air.

spaceship spaceships

NOUN A **spaceship** is a vehicle that carries people through space.

spacesuit spacesuits

NOUN A **spacesuit** is a special suit that is worn by an astronaut, which covers the whole body.

spade spades

NOUN A **spade** is a tool for digging, with a flat metal blade and a long handle.

spaghetti

NOUN **Spaghetti** is long thin pieces of pasta.

span spans

NOUN The **span** of something is the total length of it from end to end. For example, when a bird stretches its wings, the distance from wing tip to wing tip is called its "wing span".

spanner spanners

NOUN A **spanner** is a tool with a specially shaped end that fits round a nut to turn it.

spare spares, sparing, spared

ADJECTIVE **1** Something that is **spare** is extra to what is needed. *Do you have a spare pencil you can lend me?*

VERB **2** If you **spare** something, you make it available. *Can you spare me some time?*

spark sparks

NOUN A **spark** is a tiny piece of fire. It can fly up from something burning, or it can be caused by electricity.

sparkle sparkles, sparkling, sparkled

VERB If something **sparkles**, it shines with a lot of small bright points of light.

sparrow sparrows

NOUN A **sparrow** is a small bird with brown and grey feathers.

spawn

NOUN **Spawn** is a jelly-like substance containing the eggs of fish or amphibians.

speak speaks, speaking, spoke, spoken

VERB **1** When you **speak**, you use your voice to say words.

VERB **2** If you **speak** a foreign language, you know it and can use it.

spear

spear   **spears, spearing, speared**

NOUN **1** A **spear** is a weapon consisting of a long pole with a sharp point.

VERB **2** To **spear** something means to push or throw a pointed object into it. *He **speared** a potato with his fork.*

special

ADJECTIVE **1** Something that is **special** is more important or better than other things of its kind.

ADJECTIVE **2** **Special** can also mean that something is for a particular use. *You need a **special** tool for this job.*

speck   **specks**

NOUN A **speck** is a tiny piece of something. *There wasn't a **speck** of dust anywhere.*

spectator   **spectators**

NOUN A **spectator** is a person who is watching something.

speech   **speeches**

NOUN **1** **Speech** is the ability to speak or the act of speaking.

NOUN **2** A **speech** is a formal talk given to an audience.

NOUN **3** In a play, a **speech** is a group of lines spoken by one of the characters.

speech bubble   **speech bubbles**

NOUN A **speech bubble** is drawn to show what someone is saying in a picture. There is a line round the words, with a little tail near the mouth of the speaker.

This is a speech bubble!

speechless

ADJECTIVE If you are **speechless**, you cannot speak for a short time, usually because something has amazed you.

speech marks

PLURAL NOUN **Speech marks** are punctuation marks (" ") or (' ') used in writing to show where speech begins and ends.

See Punctuation on page 264.

speed   **speeds, speeding, sped** or **speeded**

NOUN **1** The **speed** of something is how fast it moves.

VERB **2** Someone who is **speeding** is moving very fast, or too fast.

spell   **spells, spelling, spelt** or **spelled**

VERB **1** When you **spell** a word, you name or write its letters in order.

NOUN **2** A **spell** is a short time. *We're in for a **spell** of bad weather.*

NOUN **3** A **spell** is also the words used to perform magic.

spelling

NOUN The **spelling** of a word is the correct order of letters in it.

spend   **spends, spending, spent**

VERB **1** When you **spend** money, you buy things with it.

VERB **2** To **spend** time or energy means to use it.

sphere

NOUN A **sphere** is an object or shape that is like a ball.

spherical ADJECTIVE

See Solid shapes on page 271.

spice   **spices**

NOUN A **spice** is the powder or seeds from a particular plant which people put in food to give it flavour.

spicy ADJECTIVE

spider   **spiders**

NOUN A **spider** is a small animal with eight legs. Some spiders make webs that they use to catch insects for food.

spike   **spikes**

NOUN A **spike** is a long piece of metal with a sharp point at one end.

spill spills, spilling, spilled or spilt
VERB If you **spill** a liquid, you let it flow out of a container by mistake.

spin spins, spinning, spun
VERB **1** If something **spins**, it turns round and round quickly.
VERB **2** When someone **spins**, they make thread by twisting together pieces of fibre using a machine.
VERB **3** When spiders **spin**, they give out a sticky thread and make it into a web.

spinach
NOUN **Spinach** is a vegetable with large green leaves.
See *Vegetables* on page 256.

spine spines
NOUN **1** Your **spine** is your backbone.
NOUN **2** Spines are long sharp points on an animal's body or on a plant.

spiral spirals
NOUN A **spiral** is a continuous curve which winds round and round, with each curve above or outside the previous one.

spire spires
NOUN The **spire** of a church is the tall cone-shaped structure on top.

spite spites, spiting, spited
VERB If you do something to **spite** someone, you do it deliberately to hurt or annoy them.
in spite of PHRASE When you say that you are doing something **in spite of** something else, you mean that you are not going to let it stop you. *In spite of the rain, I'm still going out.*

spiteful
ADJECTIVE A **spiteful** person does or says nasty things to people to hurt them.
spitefully ADVERB

splash splashes, splashing, splashed
VERB **1** If you **splash** around in water, you disturb the water in a noisy way.

VERB **2** If liquid **splashes** something, it scatters over it in a lot of small drops.
NOUN **3** A **splash** is the sound made when something hits or falls into water.

splendid
ADJECTIVE **Splendid** means extremely good.

splinter splinters, splintering, splintered
NOUN **1** A **splinter** is a thin sharp piece of wood or glass which has broken off a larger piece.
VERB **2** If something **splinters**, it breaks into thin sharp pieces.

split splits, splitting, split
VERB **1** If something is **split**, it divides into two or more. *The village was split in two by the new road.*
VERB **2** If people **split** something between them, they share it.

spoil spoils, spoiling, spoiled or spoilt
VERB **1** If you **spoil** something, you damage it, or make it less good than it was.
VERB **2** To **spoil** children means to give them everything they want, so that they become selfish.

spoke spokes
VERB **1** Spoke is the past tense of **speak**.
NOUN **2** The **spokes** of a wheel are the bars which connect the hub to the rim.

spoken
VERB **Spoken** is the past participle of **speak**.

sponge sponges
NOUN **1** A **sponge** is a soft thing with holes in it. It soaks up water and you use it for washing things.

NOUN **2** A **sponge** or **sponge cake** is a very light cake.

a b c d e f g h i j k l m n o p q r **Ss** t u v w x y z

spoon

spoon **spoons**

NOUN A **spoon** is a tool like a small shallow bowl with a long handle. It is used for eating, mixing or serving food.

sport **sports**

NOUN **Sports** are games that you play which exercise your body.

spot **spots, spotting, spotted**

NOUN **1 Spots** are small round marks on a surface. Some fabrics have a pattern of spots.

NOUN **2** A **spot** can be a particular place. *This would be a nice spot for a picnic.*

NOUN **3** A **spot** can also be a small raised mark on a person's skin.

VERB **4** If you **spot** something, you notice it.

spotless

ADJECTIVE Something that is **spotless** is perfectly clean.

spout **spouts**

NOUN A **spout** is a tube with an end like a lip, for pouring liquid. *Teapots have a spout.*

sprang

VERB **Sprang** is the past tense of **spring**.

sprawl **sprawls, sprawling, sprawled**

VERB If you **sprawl**, you sit or lie with your legs and arms spread out.

spray **sprays, spraying, sprayed**

NOUN **1 Spray** is lots of small drops of liquid splashed or forced into the air.

VERB **2** To **spray** a liquid over something means to cover it with small drops of the liquid.

spread **spreads, spreading, spread**

VERB **1** If you **spread** something, you arrange it over a surface. *They spread their wet clothes out to dry.*

VERB **2** If you **spread** something, such as butter, you put a thin layer of it onto something.

VERB **3** If you **spread** parts of your body, such as your arms, you stretch them out until they are far apart.

spring **springs, springing, sprang, sprung**

NOUN **1 Spring** is the season between winter and summer.

NOUN **2** A **spring** is a coil of wire which returns to its shape after being pressed or pulled.

NOUN **3** A **spring** is also a place where water comes up through the ground.

VERB **4** To **spring** means to jump. *The leopard sprang on its prey.*

springbok **springboks**

NOUN A **springbok** is a small South African antelope which moves in leaps.

sprinkle **sprinkles, sprinkling, sprinkled**

VERB If you **sprinkle** a liquid or powder over something, you scatter it over it.

sprint **sprints, sprinting, sprinted**

VERB To **sprint** means to run fast over a short distance.

sprout **sprouts, sprouting, sprouted**

VERB **1** When something **sprouts**, it starts to grow.

NOUN **2 Sprouts** are small round green vegetables.

See *Vegetables* on page 256.

sprung

VERB **Sprung** is the past participle of **spring**.

spun

VERB **Spun** is the past tense of **spin**.

spurt **spurts, spurting, spurted**

VERB When a liquid or flame **spurts** out, it comes out quickly in a powerful stream. *Blood spurted from his arm.*

spy spies, spying, spied

NOUN **1** A **spy** is a person sent to find out secret information about a country or organization.

VERB **2** If you **spy** on someone, you watch them secretly.

square squares

NOUN **1** A **square** is a shape with four equal sides and four right angles. See *Colours and flat shapes* on page 271.

NOUN **2** The **square** of a number is the number multiplied by itself. For example, the square of 3, written 3^2, is 3×3.

ADJECTIVE **3 Square** is used before units of length when talking about the area of something. *The room measures 25 square metres.*

squash squashes, squashing, squashed

VERB **1** If you **squash** something, you press it so that it loses its shape.

NOUN **2** If there is a **squash** in a place, there are a lot of people pressed against each other.

NOUN **3 Squash** is a drink made from fruit juice, sugar, and water.

squat squats, squatting, squatted

VERB If you **squat**, you crouch down, balancing on your feet with your legs bent.

squawk squawks, squawking, squawked

VERB When a bird **squawks**, it makes a loud harsh noise.

squeak squeaks, squeaking, squeaked

VERB If something **squeaks**, it makes a short high-pitched sound.

squeal squeals, squealing, squealed

VERB When things or people **squeal**, they make a long high-pitched sound.

squeeze squeezes, squeezing, squeezed

VERB **1** When you **squeeze** something, you press it firmly from two sides.

VERB **2** When you **squeeze** something into a small amount of time or space, you manage to fit it in.

squirrel squirrels

NOUN A **squirrel** is a small furry animal with a long bushy tail.

squirt squirts, squirting, squirted

VERB If a liquid **squirts**, it comes out of a narrow opening in a thin fast stream.

stable stables

NOUN A **stable** is a building in which horses are kept.

stack stacks, stacking, stacked

NOUN **1** A **stack** of things is a pile of them, one on top of the other.

VERB **2** If you **stack** things, you arrange them one on top of the other in a pile.

stadium stadiums

NOUN A **stadium** is a large place where you go to watch games.

staff

NOUN The **staff** of an organization are the people who work for it.

stag stags

NOUN A **stag** is an adult male deer.

stage stages

NOUN **1** A **stage** is a part of a process that lasts for a period of time. *The final stage is really difficult.*

NOUN **2** In a theatre, the **stage** is a raised platform where the actors perform.

stagger staggers, staggering, staggered

VERB **1** If someone **staggers**, they walk unsteadily.

VERB **2** If something **staggers** you, it amazes you.

a
b
c
d
e
f
g
h
i
j
k
l
m
n
o
p
q
r
Ss
t
u
v
w
x
y
z

stain stains

NOUN A **stain** is a mark on something that is difficult to remove.

stair stairs

NOUN A **stair** is one of a set of steps in a building going from one floor to another.

staircase staircases

NOUN A **staircase** is a set of stairs.

stake stakes

NOUN A **stake** is a pointed wooden post that can be hammered into the ground and used as a support.

stale staler, stalest

ADJECTIVE **Stale** food or air is not fresh.

stalk stalks, stalking, stalked

NOUN **1** A **stalk** is the main stem of a plant.

VERB **2** To **stalk** a person or animal means to follow them slowly and quietly.

stall stalls

NOUN **1** A **stall** is a large table on which there are goods for sale.

PLURAL NOUN **2** In a theatre, the **stalls** are the seats at the lowest level, in front of the stage.

stallion stallions

NOUN A **stallion** is an adult male horse.

stammer stammers, stammering, stammered

VERB When someone **stammers**, they hesitate and repeat some sounds when they speak.

stamp stamps, stamping, stamped

NOUN **1** A **stamp** is a small piece of gummed paper which you stick on a letter or parcel before posting it.

VERB **2** If you **stamp**, you lift your foot and put it down hard on the ground.

stand stands, standing, stood

VERB **1** When you **stand**, your body is upright and you are on your feet.

VERB **2** If a letter **stands for** a particular word, it is an abbreviation of that word. *So you're J Smith. What does J **stand for**?*

VERB **3** If you cannot **stand** something, you cannot bear it. *I can't **stand** that boy.*

standard standards

NOUN **1** A **standard** is how good something is. *This is not up to your usual **standard**.*

ADJECTIVE **2** Something which is **standard** is usual, and not special or extra. *Power steering is now a **standard** feature on this car.*

stank

VERB **Stank** is the past tense of **stink**.

star stars, starring, starred

NOUN **1** A **star** is a large ball of burning gas in space that appears as a point of light in the sky at night.

NOUN **2** A **star** is also a shape with four, five or more points sticking out in a regular pattern.

See *Colours and flat shapes* on page 271.

NOUN **3** A **star** is also a famous person in entertainment or sport.

VERB **4** If an actor or actress **stars** in a film, they have one of the most important parts in it.

starch

NOUN **Starch** is a substance that gives you energy. It is found in foods such as bread and potatoes.

stare stares, staring, stared

VERB If you **stare** at something, you look at it for a long time.

starfish starfishes or starfish

NOUN A **starfish** is a flat, star-shaped sea animal with five limbs.

starling starlings

NOUN A **starling** is a common European bird with shiny dark feathers.

start starts, starting, started

VERB **1** To **start** means to begin.

VERB **2** If someone **starts** a machine or car, they use the controls to make it work.

startle startles, startling, startled

VERB If something **startles** you, it frightens you by making a sudden movement or noise.

starve starves, starving, starved

VERB When people or animals **starve**, they suffer a great deal from lack of food and sometimes die.

state states, stating, stated

NOUN **1** The **state** of someone or something is how they are. *Have you seen the state of the garden?*

NOUN **2** A **state** is a country, or a part of a country making some of its own laws.

VERB **3** If you **state** something, you say it clearly and formally.

in a state PHRASE If you are **in a state**, you are nervous or upset.

statement statements

NOUN A **statement** is something you say or write when you give facts or information in a formal way.

station stations

NOUN **1** A **station** is a building where trains or buses stop for passengers.

NOUN **2** A **station** is also a building for people such as the police or fire brigade.

stationary

ADJECTIVE If something like a vehicle is **stationary**, it is not moving.

stationery

NOUN **Stationery** is paper, pens, envelopes and other equipment used for writing.

statue statues

NOUN A **statue** is a large sculpture of a person or animal.

stay stays, staying, stayed

VERB **1** If you **stay** in a place, you do not move away from it.

VERB **2** If you **stay** with someone, you live in their house for a while.

steady steadier, steadiest

ADJECTIVE **1** If something such as a ladder is **steady**, it is firm and does not shake or move about.

ADJECTIVE **2** A **steady** look or voice is calm and controlled.

steadily ADVERB

steak steaks

NOUN A **steak** is a thick slice of meat or fish.

steal steals, stealing, stole, stolen

VERB To **steal** means to take something which does not belong to you, and keep it.

steam

NOUN **Steam** is the hot vapour formed when water boils.

steel

NOUN **Steel** is a strong metal made mostly from iron.

steep steeper, steepest

ADJECTIVE Something such as a road or hill that is **steep** slopes sharply.

steeple steeples

NOUN A **steeple** is a church tower with a high pointed top.

steer steers, steering, steered

VERB When someone **steers** something like a car or cycle, they make it go in the direction they want.

a b c d e f g h i j k l m n o p q r **Ss** t u v w x y z

stem

stem **stems**

NOUN The **stem** of a plant is the long thin centre part.

stencil **stencils**

NOUN A **stencil** is a thin sheet with a cut-out pattern. Ink or paint passes through the stencil to form a pattern on the surface below.

step **steps**

NOUN **1** A **step** is the movement you make when you lift your foot and put it down in a different place.

NOUN **2** A **step** is also a raised flat surface which you use to move from one level to another.

stereo **stereos**

NOUN A **stereo** is a machine that plays sound from tapes or CDs, with the sound coming through two speakers.

stern **sterner, sternest**

ADJECTIVE Someone who is **stern** is serious and expects to be obeyed.

stew **stews**

NOUN A **stew** is a meal which you make by cooking meat, fish or vegetables slowly for a long time.

stick **sticks, sticking, stuck**

NOUN **1** A **stick** is a long thin piece of wood.

VERB **2** If you **stick** a pointed object, such as a drawing pin, into something, you push it in.

VERB **3** If you **stick** two things together, you fix them with something like glue.

VERB **4** If something like a drawer **sticks**, it cannot be moved.

sticker **stickers**

NOUN A **sticker** is a small piece of paper that you can stick on to a surface. It has writing or a picture on one side.

sticky **stickier, stickiest**

ADJECTIVE Something that is **sticky**, like jam or glue, can stick to other things.

stiff **stiffer, stiffest**

ADJECTIVE **1** Something that is **stiff** is quite hard or firm. *Use a **stiff** broom to sweep up the leaves.*

ADJECTIVE **2** If a person is **stiff**, their muscles or joints hurt when they move.

stile **stiles**

NOUN A **stile** is a kind of fixed gate with a step on each side. It is made so that people can get into a field without letting animals out.

still **stiller, stillest**

ADVERB **1** You say **still** when something is the same as it was before. *I've **still** got a headache.*

ADVERB OR ADJECTIVE **2** **Still** means staying in the same position without moving. *He wouldn't sit **still**.*

stilt **stilts**

NOUN **Stilts** are two long pieces of wood or metal on which people walk.

sting **stings, stinging, stung**

VERB If a creature or plant **stings** you, it pricks your skin and hurts you.

stink **stinks, stinking, stank, stunk**

VERB Something that **stinks** smells bad.

stir **stirs, stirring, stirred**

VERB If you **stir** a liquid, you move it around with a spoon or a stick.

stitch **stitches, stitching, stitched**

VERB If you **stitch** fabric, you push a needle and thread in and out through it.

stocking **stockings**

NOUN **Stockings** are long pieces of thin clothing that cover a woman's legs and feet.

stole

VERB **Stole** is the past tense of **steal**.

stolen

VERB **1 Stolen** is the past participle of **steal**.

ADJECTIVE **2** If something is **stolen**, it has been taken away from its owner. *The police found the stolen bike.*

stomach **stomachs**

NOUN Your **stomach** is the part of your body that holds food when you have eaten it.

stone **stones**

NOUN **1 Stone** is a hard dry material that is dug out of the ground. It is often used for building houses and walls.

NOUN **2** A **stone** is a small piece of rock.

NOUN **3** The **stone** in a fruit such as a plum is the large seed in the centre.

NOUN **4** A **stone** is a unit of weight equal to just over six kilograms.

stony **stonier, stoniest**

ADJECTIVE **Stony** ground is rough and contains a lot of stones.

stood

VERB **Stood** is the past tense of **stand**.

stool **stools**

NOUN A **stool** is a seat with legs but no back.

stoop **stoops, stooping, stooped**

VERB If you **stoop**, you bend your body down from the waist, usually so that you can pick something up.

stop **stops, stopping, stopped**

VERB **1** If you **stop** what you are doing, you no longer do it.

VERB **2** If you **stop** somewhere, you stay there for a short while.

store **stores, storing, stored**

VERB **1** When you **store** things, you put them away and keep them until they are wanted.

NOUN **2** A **store** is a large shop.

storey **storeys**

NOUN A **storey** is all the rooms on one floor of a building.

stork **storks**

NOUN A **stork** is a large bird with a long beak and long legs.

storm **storms**

NOUN A **storm** is bad weather with heavy rain and strong winds. Often there is thunder and lightning.

stormy ADJECTIVE

story **stories**

NOUN A **story** tells you about things that have happened. It can be about something real or something made up.

stout **stouter, stoutest**

ADJECTIVE **1** Someone **stout** is rather fat.

ADJECTIVE **2** Things such as branches that are **stout** are thick and strong.

stove **stoves**

NOUN A **stove** is a piece of equipment for heating a room or for cooking.

straight **straighter, straightest**

ADJECTIVE **1** Something which is **straight** does not bend or curve. You use a ruler to draw a straight line.

ADVERB **2** **Straight** can mean immediately and directly. *We promised to go straight to school.*

straighten **straightens, straightening, straightened**

VERB If you **straighten** something, you make it straight, or neat and tidy.

strain **strains, straining, strained**

VERB **1** If you **strain** to do something, you try too hard.

VERB **2** To **strain** food means to pour away the liquid from it.

VERB **3** If you **strain** a muscle, you injure it by moving awkwardly.

strange

strange **stranger, strangest**
ADJECTIVE **1** Something that is **strange** is odd or unexpected.
ADJECTIVE **2** A **strange** place is one you have never been to before.

stranger **strangers**
NOUN A **stranger** is a person you do not know.

strap **straps**
NOUN A **strap** is a strip of something like leather which is used to carry something around, or to fasten things together.

straw **straws**
NOUN **1** Straw is dried stalks of cereal such as wheat.
NOUN **2** A **straw** is a thin tube of paper or plastic, which you drink through.

strawberry **strawberries**
NOUN A **strawberry** is a small red fruit. It is soft and juicy and has tiny yellow seeds on its skin.
See *Fruit* on page 257.

stray **strays, straying, strayed**
VERB **1** If people or animals **stray**, they wander away from where they are supposed to be.
ADJECTIVE **2** A **stray** dog or cat is one that has wandered away from home.

stream **streams**
NOUN **1** A **stream** is a small river.
NOUN **2** A **stream** is also a steady flow of something like liquid or traffic.

street **streets**
NOUN A **street** is a road in a town or village, usually with buildings along it.

strength
NOUN **Strength** is how strong something is.

stretch **stretches, stretching, stretched**
VERB **1** If you **stretch**, you hold out part of your body as far as you can.
VERB **2** If you **stretch** something, you pull it so that it becomes longer or wider.
NOUN **3** A **stretch** of land or water is an area of it.

strict **stricter, strictest**
ADJECTIVE **1** Someone who is **strict** makes you behave well.
ADJECTIVE **2** A **strict** rule or law is one that must be obeyed.

stride **strides, striding, strode**
VERB **1** To **stride** along means to walk quickly with long steps.
NOUN **2** A **stride** is a long step.

strike **strikes, striking, struck**
VERB **1** To **strike** someone or something means to hit them.
VERB **2** When a clock **strikes**, it rings a bell to show what the time is.
VERB **3** If someone **strikes** a match, they make a flame or sparks with it.
NOUN **4** A **strike** is when workers refuse to go on working.

string **strings**
NOUN **1** String is thin rope.
NOUN **2** On a musical instrument like a guitar, the **strings** are the parts that you touch to make the sounds.

strip **strips, stripping, stripped**
NOUN **1** A **strip** of paper, cloth or other material is a long narrow piece of it.
VERB **2** If you **strip**, you take off all your clothes.

stripe **stripes**
NOUN A **stripe** is a coloured line on something.

strode
VERB **Strode** is the past tense of **stride**.

stroke **strokes, stroking, stroked**
VERB If you **stroke** something, you move your hand gently over it.

stroll **strolls, strolling, strolled**
VERB To **stroll** means to walk along slowly in a relaxed way.

strong **stronger, strongest**
ADJECTIVE **1** If you are **strong**, you can work hard and carry heavy things.
ADJECTIVE **2** Objects or materials that are **strong** will not break easily.
ADJECTIVE **3** Wind or water currents that are **strong** move very fast.
ADJECTIVE **4** Smells and flavours that are **strong** are easily noticed.

struck
VERB **Struck** is the past tense of **strike**.

structure **structures**
NOUN A **structure** is something that has been built.

struggle **struggles, struggling, struggled**
VERB **1** If you **struggle** to do something, you try hard to do it but find it difficult.
VERB **2** If you **struggle** when you are being held by something or someone, you twist and kick to try and get free.

stubborn
ADJECTIVE Someone who is **stubborn** is determined to do what they want.

stuck
VERB **1** **Stuck** is the past tense of **stick**.
ADJECTIVE **2** If you are **stuck**, you cannot carry on because it is too difficult.

student **students**
NOUN A **student** is a person who is studying at a university or college.

studio **studios**
NOUN **1** A **studio** is a room where a photographer or artist works.
NOUN **2** A **studio** is also a place where films, television programmes or other recordings are made.

study **studies, studying, studied**
VERB **1** If you **study** a subject, you spend time learning about it.
VERB **2** If you **study** something, you look at it carefully.
NOUN **3** A **study** is a room for writing and studying.

stuff **stuffs, stuffing, stuffed**
NOUN **1** You can talk about a substance or group of things as **stuff**.
VERB **2** If you **stuff** something with objects, you fill it with them.

stuffy **stuffier, stuffiest**
ADJECTIVE If it is **stuffy** in a room, there is not enough fresh air in it.

stumble **stumbles, stumbling, stumbled**
VERB If you **stumble** when you are walking, you trip and almost fall.

stump **stumps**
NOUN A **stump** is the small part of something, such as a tree, that remains when most of it has been removed.

stun **stuns, stunning, stunned**
VERB **1** If you are **stunned** by something, you are very surprised by it.
VERB **2** To **stun** a person or animal means to knock them unconscious by hitting them on the head.

stung
VERB **Stung** is the past tense of **sting**.

stunk
VERB **Stunk** is the past participle of **stink**.

stupid **stupider, stupidest**
ADJECTIVE Someone who is **stupid** does things that are not at all sensible.
stupidly ADVERB

sturdy **sturdier, sturdiest**
ADJECTIVE Someone or something that is **sturdy** is strong and firm.

stutter stutters

NOUN Someone who has a **stutter** finds it difficult to speak smoothly and often repeats sounds.

sty sties

NOUN A **sty** is a hut with a yard where pigs are kept.

style styles

NOUN The **style** of something is its design. *I'd like shoes in a different style.*

sub-

PREFIX **Sub-** is used at the beginning of words that have "under" as part of their meaning, for example "submarine" (meaning underwater).
See Prefixes on page 264.

subheading subheadings

NOUN A **subheading** is a heading which is less important than the main heading. *We'll have "animals" as a main heading, and "mammals" as a subheading.*

subject subjects

NOUN **1** A **subject** is a particular thing that people study at school or college, for example science or drawing.

NOUN **2** The **subject** of a piece of writing or a conversation is the thing or person being talked about.

NOUN **3** In grammar, the **subject** is the word or words representing a person or thing doing the action. For example, in the sentence "My cat caught a bird", "my cat" is the subject.

submarine submarines

NOUN A **submarine** is a ship that can travel under water.

substance substances

NOUN Any solid, powder, liquid or paste can be called a **substance**.

subtract subtracts, subtracting, subtracted

VERB If you **subtract** one number from another, you take away the first number from the second. The symbol you use for subtract is –.

subtraction

NOUN **Subtraction** is taking one number away from another.

suburb suburbs

NOUN A **suburb** is an area of a town or city that is away from its centre.

subway subways

NOUN A **subway** is a footpath that goes underneath a road.

succeed succeeds, succeeding, succeeded

VERB If you **succeed**, you manage to do what you set out to do.

success

NOUN **Success** is managing to do something that you set out to do.

successful

ADJECTIVE If you are **successful**, you achieve what you wanted to achieve.

such

ADVERB You can use **such** to emphasize something. *She's such a nice girl.*

such as PHRASE You can use **such as** to introduce examples of something. *I like team games such as football and rounders.*

suck sucks, sucking, sucked

VERB If you **suck** something, you hold it in your mouth and pull at it with your cheeks and tongue, usually to get liquid out of it.

sudden

ADJECTIVE Something that is **sudden** happens quickly and unexpectedly.
suddenly ADVERB

suffer suffers, suffering, suffered

VERB If someone is **suffering**, they feel pain or sadness.

suffix suffixes

NOUN A **suffix** is a group of letters which is added to the end of a word to form a new word, for example "-able" or "-ful". See *Suffixes* on page 265.

sugar

NOUN **Sugar** is a sweet substance used to sweeten food and drinks.

suggest suggests, suggesting, suggested

VERB If you **suggest** something to someone, you give a plan or an idea for them to think about.
suggestion NOUN

suit suits, suiting, suited

NOUN **1** A **suit** is a matching jacket and trousers or skirt.

VERB **2** If something **suits** you, it is right for you.

suitable

ADJECTIVE Something that is **suitable** for a particular purpose is right for it. *Are these shoes suitable for running?*

suitcase suitcases

NOUN A **suitcase** is a case that you carry clothes in when you are travelling.

sulk sulks, sulking, sulked

VERB If you **sulk**, you are silent and bad-tempered for a while because you are annoyed about something.

sultana sultanas

NOUN A **sultana** is a dried white grape.

sum sums

NOUN **1** A **sum** is an amount of money.
NOUN **2** In maths, the **sum** is the answer or total that you get when you add numbers. *The sum of 2 and 3 is 5.*

summarize summarizes, summarizing, summarized; also spelt summarise

VERB To **summarize** something means to give a short account of its main points.

summary summaries

NOUN If you give a **summary** of something, you give the main points.

summer summers

NOUN **Summer** is the season between spring and autumn.

summit summits

NOUN The **summit** of a mountain is its top.

sun suns

NOUN The **sun** is the star that gives us heat and light.

sunburn

NOUN **Sunburn** is sore skin on someone's body when they have been in the sun for too long.

Sunday Sundays

NOUN **Sunday** is the day between Saturday and Monday.

sundial sundials

NOUN A **sundial** is an object that uses the sun to tell the time. It has a pointer that casts a shadow on a flat base marked with the hours.

sunflower **sunflowers**
NOUN A **sunflower** is a tall plant with large yellow flowers.

sung
VERB **Sung** is the past participle of **sing**.

sunglasses
PLURAL NOUN **Sunglasses** are glasses with dark lenses that you wear to protect your eyes from the sun.

sunk
VERB **Sunk** is the past participle of **sink**.

sunlight
NOUN **Sunlight** is the bright light produced when the sun is shining.
sunlit ADJECTIVE

sunny **sunnier, sunniest**
ADJECTIVE When the weather is **sunny**, the sun is shining brightly.

sunrise **sunrises**
NOUN **Sunrise** is the time in the morning when the sun comes up.

sunset **sunsets**
NOUN **Sunset** is the time in the evening when the sun goes down.

sunshine
NOUN **Sunshine** is the bright light produced when the sun is shining.

super
ADJECTIVE **Super** means very nice or very good. *We've just seen a **super** film.*

super-
PREFIX **Super-** is added to words to describe something that is larger or better, for example "supermarket". See Prefixes on page 264.

superlative **superlatives**
NOUN In grammar, the **superlative** is the form of an adjective which has "the most" of that adjective. For example, "fattest" is the superlative of "fat".
See Adjective on page 263.

supermarket **supermarkets**
NOUN A **supermarket** is a large shop which sells all kinds of food and things for the house.

supersonic
ADJECTIVE A **supersonic** aircraft can travel faster than the speed of sound.

superstitious
ADJECTIVE People who are **superstitious** believe in things like magic and powers that bring good or bad luck.

supper **suppers**
NOUN **Supper** is a meal or snack eaten in the evening.

supply **supplies, supplying, supplied**
VERB **1** If someone **supplies** you with something, they provide you with it.
NOUN **2** A **supply** of something is the amount of it which someone has. *The water **supply** is getting very low.*

support **supports, supporting, supported**
VERB **1** If you **support** someone, you want them to do well.
VERB **2** If something **supports** an object, it holds it up firmly.

suppose **supposes, supposing, supposed**
VERB **1** If you **suppose** that something is true, you think that it is likely to be true.
CONJUNCTION **2** You can use **suppose** or **supposing** when you are thinking about doing something. ***Supposing** we just left without saying anything, what do you think would happen?*
I suppose PHRASE You can say **I suppose** when you are not certain about something. *Yes, **I suppose** he could come.*

sure

ADJECTIVE **1** If you are **sure** something is true, you believe it is true.
ADJECTIVE **2** If something is **sure** to happen, it will definitely happen.
ADJECTIVE **3** If you are **sure** of yourself, you are very confident.
make sure PHRASE If you **make sure** of something, you check it. *Can you **make sure** we locked up properly?*

surf surfs, surfing, surfed

NOUN **1 Surf** is the white foam that forms on the top of waves when they break.
VERB **2** When you **surf**, you ride towards the shore on top of a large wave while standing on a special board.

VERB **3** When you **surf** the Internet, you go from website to website.

surface surfaces

NOUN The **surface** of something is the top or outside area of it.

surgeon surgeons

NOUN A **surgeon** is a doctor who performs operations.

surgery surgeries

NOUN **1 Surgery** is medical treatment in which part of the patient's body is cut open.
NOUN **2** A **surgery** is a room or building where a doctor or dentist works.

surname surnames

NOUN Your **surname** is the name you share with other members of your family.

surprise surprises

NOUN A **surprise** is something unexpected.

surrender surrenders, surrendering, surrendered

VERB If someone **surrenders**, they stop fighting and agree that they have lost.

surround surrounds, surrounding, surrounded

VERB If something **surrounds** something else, it is all round it.

surroundings

PLURAL NOUN Your **surroundings** are the area around you.

survey surveys

NOUN **1** A **survey** of something is a detailed examination of it, often in the form of a report.
VERB **2** A **survey** is also a set of questions to find out what people think about things.

survive survives, surviving, survived

VERB If someone **survives**, they continue to live after being close to death.

suspect suspects, suspecting, suspected

VERB If you **suspect** someone of doing something wrong, you think they have done it.

suspense

NOUN **Suspense** is excitement or worry caused by having to wait for something.

suspicious

ADJECTIVE **1** If you are **suspicious** of someone, you do not trust them.
ADJECTIVE **2** If something is **suspicious**, it makes you feel something is wrong.

swallow swallows, swallowing, swallowed

VERB **1** When you **swallow** food or drink, it goes down your throat.
NOUN **2** A **swallow** is a small bird with pointed wings and a long forked tail.

swam

swam
VERB **Swam** is the past tense of **swim**.

swamp swamps
NOUN A **swamp** is an area of extremely wet land.

swan swans
NOUN A **swan** is a large white bird with a long neck that lives on rivers and lakes.

swap swaps, swapping, swapped
VERB If you **swap** something, you give it to someone and receive something else from them in exchange.

swarm swarms
NOUN A **swarm** is a large group of bees or other insects flying together.
See *Collective nouns* on page 262.

sway sways, swaying, swayed
VERB When people or things **sway**, they lean or swing slowly from side to side.

sweat
NOUN **Sweat** is the salty liquid which comes from your skin when you are hot.

sweater sweaters
NOUN A **sweater** is a knitted piece of clothing covering your upper body and arms.

sweatshirt sweatshirts
NOUN A **sweatshirt** is a piece of clothing made of thick cotton. It covers your upper body and arms.

sweep sweeps, sweeping, swept
VERB If you **sweep** a floor or a path, you clean it by pushing a broom over it.

sweet sweeter, sweetest; sweets
ADJECTIVE **1** Food or drink that is **sweet** has a taste of sugar.

PLURAL NOUN **2 Sweets** are things such as chocolates and toffees.
NOUN **3** A **sweet** can be something that is eaten after the main part of a meal.

sweet corn
NOUN **Sweet corn** is a long stalk covered with juicy yellow seeds that can be eaten as a vegetable.
See *Vegetables* on page 256.

swell swells, swelling, swelled or swollen
VERB If something **swells**, it becomes larger and rounder than usual.

swept
VERB **Swept** is the past tense of **sweep**.

swerve swerves, swerving, swerved
VERB If something that is moving **swerves**, it suddenly changes direction.

swift swifter, swiftest
ADJECTIVE Something that is **swift** can move very quickly.

swim swims, swimming, swam, swum
VERB When you **swim**, you use your arms and legs to move through water.

swimming
NOUN **Swimming** is the activity of moving yourself through water.

swimming costume swimming costumes
NOUN A **swimming costume** is the clothing worn by a woman or girl when she goes swimming.

swimming pool swimming pools
NOUN A **swimming pool** is a place made for people to swim in.

swimming trunks

PLURAL NOUN **Swimming trunks** are shorts worn by a man or boy when they go swimming.

swing **swings, swinging, swung**

VERB **1** If something **swings**, it keeps moving backwards and forwards, or from side to side, while it is hanging.
NOUN **2** A **swing** is a seat that hangs from a frame and moves backwards and forwards when you sit on it.

switch **switches, switching, switched**

NOUN **1** A **switch** is a small control for a piece of equipment such as a light or radio.
VERB **2** To **switch** is to change one thing for another. *I switched to another school when I moved house.*

swollen

ADJECTIVE Something that is **swollen** has swelled up.

swoop **swoops, swooping, swooped**

VERB When a bird **swoops**, it suddenly flies downwards in a smooth curve.

swop

Swop is another spelling of **swap**.

sword **swords**

NOUN A **sword** is a weapon with a long blade and a short handle.

swum

VERB **Swum** is the past participle of **swim**.

swung

VERB **Swung** is the past tense of **swing**.

sycamore **sycamores**

NOUN A **sycamore** is a tree that has large five-pointed leaves.

syllable **syllables**

NOUN Each beat in a word is a **syllable**. For example, "cat" has one syllable, and "cattle" has two.

symbol **symbols**

NOUN A **symbol** is a sign or mark that stands for something else. For example, the symbol + stands for "plus".

symmetrical

ADJECTIVE If something is **symmetrical**, it has two halves that are exactly the same, except that one half is like a reflection of the other half.

symmetry

NOUN **1 Symmetry** is when one half of something is exactly like a mirror image of the other half.
NOUN **2** The **line of symmetry** is the dividing line between two symmetrical halves.

sympathy

NOUN If you feel **sympathy** for someone who is unhappy, you are sorry for them.

synagogue **synagogues**

NOUN A **synagogue** is a building where Jewish people pray.

synonym **synonyms**

NOUN **Synonyms** are words that have the same or similar meaning. The words "nice" and "pleasant" are synonyms. *See Synonyms on page 266.*

syrup

NOUN **Syrup** is a thick sweet liquid made by boiling sugar with water.

system **systems**

NOUN **1** A **system** is a way of doing something. *I've got a new system for organizing my toys.*
NOUN **2** You can refer to a set of equipment as a **system**, for example a central heating system.

Tt

table **tables**

NOUN **1** A **table** is a piece of furniture with a flat top for putting things on.

NOUN **2** A **table** is also a set of facts or figures arranged in rows or columns.

tablet **tablets**

NOUN A **tablet** is a small round pill made of powdered medicine.

table tennis

NOUN **Table tennis** is a game for two or four people. You use bats to hit a small hollow ball over a low net across a table.

tackle **tackles, tackling, tackled**

VERB **1** If you **tackle** a difficult task, you deal with it in a determined way.

VERB **2** If you **tackle** someone in a game such as football, you try to get the ball away from them.

tactful

ADJECTIVE A **tactful** person is careful not to hurt someone else's feelings.

tactfully ADVERB

tadpole **tadpoles**

NOUN **Tadpoles** are small water animals that grow into frogs or toads. They have long tails and round black heads.

tail **tails**

NOUN **1** A **tail** is the part of an animal, bird or fish that grows out of the end of its body.

NOUN **2** The back part of a plane is called the **tail**.

take **takes, taking, took, taken**

VERB **1** If you **take** something, you put your hand round it and carry it. *Let me take your coat.*

VERB **2** If someone **takes** you somewhere, you go there with them.

VERB **3** If a person **takes** something that does not belong to them, they steal it.

VERB **4** If you **take away** one number or amount from another, you find out how much is left.

talcum powder

NOUN **Talcum powder**, or **talc**, is a soft powder which you put on your skin to help dry it and make it smell nice.

tale **tales**

NOUN A **tale** is a story.

talent **talents**

NOUN **Talent** is the natural ability a person has to do something well.

talk **talks, talking, talked**

VERB When you **talk**, you say things to someone.

talkative

ADJECTIVE Someone who is **talkative** talks a lot.

tall **taller, tallest**

ADJECTIVE **1** Someone who is **tall** is higher than a lot of other people.

ADJECTIVE **2** You use **tall** to say how high somebody or something is. *My little brother is only one metre tall.*

tally **tallies**

NOUN A **tally** is a record of amounts which you add to as you go along.

tame **tamer, tamest**

ADJECTIVE A **tame** animal is not afraid of humans and will not hurt them.

tan

NOUN If someone has a **tan**, their skin has become darker than it usually is because they have been in the sun.

tangle **tangles, tangling, tangled**

NOUN **1** A **tangle** is a mass of things such as hairs or fibres that are knotted or coiled together and are hard to separate.
VERB **2** If something is **tangled**, it is twisted in knots.

tank **tanks**

NOUN **1** A **tank** is a large container for liquid or gas.
NOUN **2** A **tank** is also a vehicle for soldiers which moves on tracks. Tanks are covered with strong metal armour, and have guns or rockets.

tanker **tankers**

NOUN A **tanker** is a ship, truck or railway vehicle for carrying gas or liquid.

tap **taps, tapping, tapped**

NOUN **1** A **tap** is a handle which controls the flow of gas or liquid from a pipe.
VERB **2** If you **tap** something, you hit it lightly.

tape **tapes**

NOUN **1** Tape is a strip of sticky material which you use to stick things together.
NOUN **2** A **tape** is a long thin magnetic strip that you can record sounds or pictures on.

tape measure **tape measures**

NOUN A **tape measure** is a strip of plastic or metal that is marked in centimetres or inches. It is used to measure things.

tape recorder **tape recorders**

NOUN A **tape recorder** is a machine that records and plays sound on tape.

tar

NOUN **Tar** is a thick black substance that is used for making roads.

target **targets**

NOUN A **target** is something that people aim at and try to hit.

tart **tarts**

NOUN A **tart** is a piece of pastry filled with jam or fruit.

task **tasks**

NOUN A **task** is a piece of work which has to be done.

tassel **tassels**

NOUN A **tassel** is a tuft of loose threads tied by a knot and used for decoration.

taste **tastes, tasting, tasted**

NOUN **1** Your sense of **taste** is your ability to recognize the flavour of things in your mouth.
VERB **2** When you **taste** food, you take a little bit to see what it is like.

tasty **tastier, tastiest**

ADJECTIVE Something that is **tasty** has a pleasant flavour.

taught

VERB **Taught** is the past tense of **teach**.

tax **taxes**

NOUN **Tax** is money that people have to pay to the government.

taxi **taxis**

NOUN A **taxi** is a car that people pay to be driven somewhere in.

tea **teas**

NOUN **1** Tea is a drink made by pouring boiling water onto the dried leaves of the tea plant.
NOUN **2** Tea is also an afternoon meal.

tea bag **tea bags**

NOUN A **tea bag** is a small paper bag with tea leaves in it which is put in boiling water to make tea.

teach **teaches, teaching, taught**

VERB If someone **teaches** you something, they tell or show you how to do it.

teacher **teachers**

NOUN A **teacher** is a person whose job is to help people learn.

team

team teams
NOUN A **team** is a number of people working or playing together.

teapot teapots
NOUN A **teapot** is a container for making tea. It has a lid, a handle and a spout.

tear tears, tearing, tore, torn
(*rhymes with* **fear**) NOUN **1** Tears are the drops of liquid that come out of your eyes when you cry.
(*rhymes with* **fair**) VERB **2** If you **tear** something, such as paper or fabric, you pull it apart.

tease teases, teasing, teased
VERB If someone **teases** you, they make fun of you.

teaspoon teaspoons
NOUN A **teaspoon** is a small spoon used for stirring drinks.

technology
NOUN **Technology** is the practical use of science in areas such as industry, farming or medicine.

teddy bear teddy bears
NOUN A **teddy bear** is a child's soft toy which looks like a friendly bear.

teenager teenagers
NOUN A **teenager** is someone from 13 to 19 years of age.

teeth
NOUN **Teeth** is the plural of **tooth**.

telephone telephones
NOUN A **telephone**, or **phone**, is an instrument for talking to someone else who is in another place.

telescope telescopes
NOUN A **telescope** is an instrument for making objects that are far away look nearer and larger.

television televisions
NOUN A **television** is a machine that receives signals through the air or on cable and changes them into pictures and sounds.

tell tells, telling, told
VERB **1** If you **tell** someone something, you let them know about it.
VERB **2** If someone **tells** you to do something, they say you must do it.
VERB **3** If you **tell** the time, you find out what the time is by looking at a clock.

temper
NOUN **1** Someone's **temper** is how cheerful or how angry they are feeling.
NOUN **2** If you lose your **temper**, you become angry.

temperature temperatures
NOUN The **temperature** of something is how hot or cold it is.

temple temples
NOUN A **temple** is a building used for the worship of a god in various religions.

temporary
ADJECTIVE Something that is **temporary** only lasts for a short time.

tempt tempts, tempting, tempted
VERB If something **tempts** you, you want to do it but you think it might be wrong.
tempting ADJECTIVE

tender
ADJECTIVE **1** Someone who is **tender** shows gentle and caring feelings.
ADJECTIVE **2** Meat or other food which is **tender** is very easy to cut or chew.

tennis
NOUN **Tennis** is a game for two or four players in which a ball is hit over a net.

tense tenser, tensest; tenses
ADJECTIVE **1** If you are **tense**, you are nervous and cannot relax.
NOUN **2** The **tense** of a verb is the form which shows whether you are talking about the past, present or future.

tent **tents**

NOUN A **tent** is a shelter made of canvas or nylon, held up by poles and ropes.

tentacle **tentacles**

NOUN The **tentacles** of an animal, such as an octopus, are its long thin arms.

term **terms**

NOUN A **term** is one of the periods that each year is divided into at school.

terrace **terraces**

NOUN A **terrace** is a row of houses joined together.

terrible

ADJECTIVE Something **terrible** is serious and unpleasant.

terribly ADVERB

terrify **terrifies, terrifying, terrified**

VERB If something **terrifies** you, it makes you feel extremely frightened.

territory **territories**

NOUN **1** The **territory** of a country is the land that it controls.

NOUN **2** An animal's **territory** is an area that it considers its own and defends when other animals try to enter it.

terror

NOUN **Terror** is great fear or panic.

test **tests, testing, tested**

VERB **1** If someone **tests** something, they try to find out whether it works properly.

NOUN **2** A **test** is something you have to do to show how much you know.

tetrahedron **tetrahedrons** or **tetrahedra**

NOUN A **tetrahedron** is a solid shape with four triangular faces.

See *Solid shapes* on page 271.

text **texts**

NOUN **Text** is any written material.

textbook **textbooks**

NOUN A **textbook** is a book about a particular subject for students to use.

than

PREPOSITION OR CONJUNCTION You use **than** to link two things that you are comparing. *She's older **than** me.*

thank **thanks, thanking, thanked**

VERB You **thank** people when you are grateful for something they have done.

that **those**

ADJECTIVE **1** You use **that** or **those** to describe something which is not the nearest one. *Give me **that** book, please.*

PRONOUN **2** You can use **that** or **those** to refer to people or things which have already been mentioned. *What about going by bus? Is **that** a good idea?*

thatched

ADJECTIVE A **thatched** roof is one made of straw or reeds.

thaw **thaws, thawing, thawed**

VERB When something that is frozen **thaws**, it melts.

theatre **theatres**

NOUN A **theatre** is a building where you go to see a play or show.

their

ADJECTIVE **Their** refers to something belonging or relating to people or things that have already been mentioned. *Leave it to Sam and Joe. It's **their** problem.*

them

PRONOUN **Them** refers to people or things which have already been mentioned. *I don't want any sprouts. I don't like **them**.*

theme **themes**

NOUN A **theme** is the main idea in a piece of writing, painting, film or music.

a
b
c
d
e
f
g
h
i
j
k
l
m
n
o
p
q
r
s
Tt
u
v
w
x
y
z

themselves

PRONOUN If people do something **themselves**, no one else does it. *My parents had to educate **themselves**.*

then

ADVERB **Then** refers to a particular time in the past or future. *I left the room **then**.*

there

ADVERB **1 There** means in, at, or to that place. *He's sitting over **there**.*
PRONOUN **2 There** is used to say that something exists or does not exist. *Are **there** any more crisps?*

therefore

ADVERB **Therefore** means as a result. *It was raining, **therefore** we stayed indoors.*

thermometer   thermometers

NOUN A **thermometer** is an instrument that measures temperature.

thesaurus   thesauruses

NOUN A **thesaurus** is a book in which words with similar meanings are grouped together.

these

ADJECTIVE OR PRONOUN **These** is the plural of **this**.

thick   thicker, thickest

ADJECTIVE **1** An object that is **thick** is deeper through than other things of the same kind. *I'll have a **thick** slice, please.*
ADJECTIVE **2** Something that is **thick** is made up of a lot of things growing closely together. *She has long **thick** hair.*
ADJECTIVE **3 Thick** liquids do not flow easily.

thief   thieves

NOUN A **thief** is a person who steals something.

thigh   thighs

NOUN Your **thighs** are the top parts of your legs above your knees.

thin   thinner, thinnest

ADJECTIVE **1** Something that is **thin** is much narrower than it is long. *The witch's nose was long and **thin**.*
ADJECTIVE **2** A **thin** person weighs less than most people of the same height.
ADJECTIVE **3** Something such as paper or cloth that is **thin** has only a small distance between front and back.
ADJECTIVE **4 Thin** liquids are watery.

thing   things

NOUN **1** A **thing** is an object, rather than an animal or human being.
PLURAL NOUN **2** Your **things** are your clothes or possessions.

think   thinks, thinking, thought

VERB **1** When you **think**, you use your mind to consider ideas or problems.
VERB **2** If you say you **think** something is true, you mean you believe it is true but you are not sure.

third person

NOUN In grammar, the **third person** refers to a person, thing or group. It is expressed as "he", "she", "it", or "they".

thirsty

ADJECTIVE If you are **thirsty**, you feel that you need to drink something.
thirstily ADVERB

this   these

ADJECTIVE **1 This** is used to refer to someone or something that is nearby. *Would you like to borrow **this** book?*
PRONOUN **2** You can use **this** to introduce someone. ***This** is Ranjit.*

thistle   thistles

NOUN A **thistle** is a wild plant with prickly leaves and purple flowers.

thorn   thorns

NOUN A **thorn** is one of the sharp points on the stem of a plant such as a rose.

thorough

ADJECTIVE **1** Someone who is **thorough** is always careful in their work.

ADJECTIVE **2** A **thorough** action is one that is done carefully and completely. *The doctor gave him a thorough examination.*

thoroughly ADVERB

those

ADJECTIVE OR PRONOUN **Those** is the plural of **that**.

though

CONJUNCTION **1** You say **though** before something that makes another part of the sentence rather surprising. *She didn't take a coat, though it was raining.*

CONJUNCTION **2** You can use **though** to mean if. *It looks as though you were right.*

thought **thoughts**

VERB **1** **Thought** is the past tense of **think**.

NOUN **2** A **thought** is an idea that you have in your mind.

NOUN **3** **Thought** is the action of thinking carefully about something.

thoughtful

ADJECTIVE **1** If someone is **thoughtful**, they are thinking a lot.

ADJECTIVE **2** A **thoughtful** person remembers what other people want or need, and tries to be kind to them.

thoughtfully ADVERB

thoughtless

ADJECTIVE If you are **thoughtless**, you do not think about what other people feel.

thousand

A **thousand** is the number 1000.

thread **threads, threading, threaded**

NOUN **1** A **thread** is a long fine piece of cotton, silk, nylon or wool.

VERB **2** When you **thread** a needle, you put thread through the hole in the top.

threat **threats**

NOUN A **threat** is a warning that something unpleasant may happen.

threaten **threatens, threatening, threatened**

VERB If someone **threatens** you, they say that something unpleasant may happen if you do not do what they want.

three-dimensional

ADJECTIVE A **three-dimensional** or **3D** object or shape is not flat. It has height or depth as well as length and width.

See *Solid shapes* on page 271.

threw

VERB **Threw** is the past tense of **throw**.

thrill **thrills**

NOUN A **thrill** is a sudden feeling of great excitement or pleasure.

thrilling ADJECTIVE

throat **throats**

NOUN **1** Your **throat** is the back of your mouth and the top part of the passages inside your neck.

NOUN **2** The front part of your neck is also called your **throat**.

throb **throbs, throbbing, throbbed**

VERB **1** If a part of your body **throbs**, you feel a series of strong beats or dull pains.

VERB **2** If something **throbs**, it vibrates and makes a loud rhythmic noise.

throne **thrones**

NOUN A **throne** is a special chair used by kings and queens on important occasions.

through

PREPOSITION **Through** means moving from one side of something to the other. *We found a path through the woods.*

throw

a
b
c
d
e
f
g
h
i
j
k
l
m
n
o
p
q
r
s
Tt
u
v
w
x
y
z

throw throws, throwing, threw, thrown
VERB If you **throw** an object that you are holding, you send it through the air.

thrush thrushes
NOUN A **thrush** is a songbird with a brown back and a pale spotted chest.

thrust thrusts, thrusting, thrust
VERB If you **thrust** something somewhere, you push or move it there quickly with a lot of force.

thud thuds
NOUN A **thud** is a dull sound, such as a heavy object makes when it falls onto a carpet.

thumb thumbs
NOUN Your **thumb** is the short thick finger on the side of your hand.

thump thumps, thumping, thumped
VERB If you **thump** something, you hit it hard, usually with your fist. *He shouted and **thumped** the table.*

thunder
NOUN **Thunder** is the loud noise that you hear after a flash of lightning in a storm.

thunderstorm thunderstorms
NOUN A **thunderstorm** is a storm with thunder, lightning and heavy rain.

Thursday Thursdays
NOUN **Thursday** is the day between Wednesday and Friday.

tick ticks
NOUN A **tick** is a sign to show that something is correct.

2+2=4 ✓

ticket tickets
NOUN A **ticket** is a small piece of card or paper that shows that you have paid for something such as a train ride.

tickle tickles, tickling, tickled
VERB When you **tickle** someone, you move your fingers lightly over their body to make them laugh.

tide tides
NOUN The **tide** is the regular change in the level of the sea on the shore.

tidy tidier, tidiest; tidies, tidying, tidied
ADJECTIVE **1** Something that is **tidy** is neat and well arranged.
VERB **2** When you **tidy** a room, you put things away in their proper place.
tidily ADVERB

tie ties, tying, tied
NOUN **1** A **tie** is a long narrow piece of cloth that is worn round the neck.
NOUN **2** A **tie** in a race or competition is when two people have the same result.
VERB **3** If you **tie** an object to something, you fasten it with something such as string.

tiger tigers
NOUN A **tiger** is a large wild cat that lives in Asia. Its fur is usually orange with black stripes.

tight tighter, tightest
ADJECTIVE **1** Clothes that are **tight** fit too closely to your body.
ADJECTIVE **2** Something that is **tight** is firmly fastened and difficult to move.

tights
PLURAL NOUN **Tights** are a piece of clothing made of thin material that fit closely over your hips, legs and feet.

tile tiles
NOUN A **tile** is a small thin piece of something such as slate or carpet, that is used to cover surfaces.

till tills
PREPOSITION OR CONJUNCTION **1 Till** means the same as until. *Wait **till** morning... Wait **till** I get back.*
NOUN **2** A **till** is a drawer or box in a shop or bank where money is kept.

tilt tilts, tilting, tilted

VERB If you **tilt** something, you make it slope.

timber

NOUN **Timber** is wood used for building, and making furniture.

time

NOUN **1 Time** is what is measured in seconds, minutes, hours, days and years. See *Time* on page 268.

NOUN **2** If it is **time** to do something, that thing ought to be done now.

times

NOUN **1 Times** is used after numbers to say how often something happens.

NOUN **2** In maths, **times** is used to link numbers that are multiplied together. *Four **times** three is twelve.*

timetable timetables

NOUN A **timetable** is a list of the times when things happen, or when trains and buses go.

timid

ADJECTIVE A **timid** person is not brave.

tin tins

NOUN **1 Tin** is a soft silvery-white metal.

NOUN **2** A **tin** is a metal container with a lid, for storing food.

tingle tingles, tingling, tingled

VERB When part of your body **tingles**, you feel a slight prickling or stinging.

tinkle tinkles, tinkling, tinkled

VERB If something **tinkles**, it makes a sound like a small bell ringing.

tinned

ADJECTIVE **Tinned** food has been preserved by being sealed in a tin.

tin opener tin openers

NOUN A **tin opener** is something you use for opening tins of food.

tiny tinier, tiniest

ADJECTIVE Something that is **tiny** is very small.

tip tips, tipping, tipped

VERB **1** If you **tip** an object, you move it so that it is no longer straight. *She **tipped** her chair back and almost fell over.*

NOUN **2** The **tip** of something long and narrow is the end of it.

tiptoe tiptoes, tiptoeing, tiptoed

VERB If you **tiptoe** somewhere, you walk there very quietly on your toes.

tired

ADJECTIVE If you are **tired**, you feel that you want to rest or sleep.

tissue tissues

NOUN A **tissue** is a piece of soft paper that you can use as a handkerchief.

title titles

NOUN **1** A **title** is the name of something such as a book or film.

NOUN **2** Someone's **title** is a name such as Mr, Mrs or Sir, that goes in front of their own name.

toad toads

NOUN A **toad** is an amphibian. It looks like a frog but it has a drier skin and lives mostly on land.
See *Amphibians* on page 259.

toadstool toadstools

NOUN A **toadstool** is a type of poisonous fungus.

toast

NOUN **Toast** is a slice of bread made brown and crisp by heating.

toboggan toboggans

NOUN A **toboggan** is a vehicle for travelling on snow. It has a flat seat, with two metal or wooden runners.

today

ADVERB **Today** is the day that is happening now.

toddler toddlers

NOUN A **toddler** is a small child who has only just learned to walk.

toe toes

NOUN Your **toes** are the five parts at the end of your foot which you can move.

toffee toffees

NOUN A **toffee** is a sticky, chewy sweet made from butter and sugar.

together

ADVERB **1** If two people do something **together**, they both do it.
ADVERB **2** If two things happen **together**, they happen at the same time.

toilet toilets

NOUN **1** A **toilet** is a bowl connected to a drain and fitted with a seat. You use it to get rid of waste matter from your body.
NOUN **2** A **toilet** is also a small room containing a toilet.

told

VERB **Told** is the past tense of **tell**.

tomato tomatoes

NOUN A **tomato** is a soft, small red fruit. It can be cooked or eaten raw in salads. See *Fruit* on page 257.

tomorrow

ADVERB **Tomorrow** is the day after today.

ton tons

NOUN A **ton** is a unit of weight equal to about 1000 kilograms.

tongue tongues

NOUN Your **tongue** is the soft, moving part inside your mouth. You use your tongue for tasting, eating and speaking.

tongue twister tongue twisters

NOUN A **tongue twister** is a sentence or expression which is difficult to say properly. For example, "She sells seashells on the seashore" is a tongue twister.

tonight

ADVERB **Tonight** is the evening of today or the night that follows today.

tonne tonnes

NOUN A **tonne** is a metric measure of weight. It is equal to 1000 kilograms.

too

ADVERB **1 Too** means also, or as well. *I was there **too**.*
ADVERB **2 Too** also means more than is needed. *I've had **too** much to eat.*

took

VERB **Took** is the past tense of **take**.

tool tools

NOUN A **tool** is anything that you use to help you do something, such as a hammer.

tooth teeth

NOUN **1** A **tooth** is one of the hard white objects in your mouth. You use your teeth for biting and chewing food.
NOUN **2** The **teeth** of a comb, saw or zip are the parts that stick out in a row.

toothbrush toothbrushes

NOUN A **toothbrush** is a small brush that you use for cleaning your teeth.

toothpaste

NOUN **Toothpaste** is a substance which you use to clean your teeth.

top tops

NOUN **1** The **top** of something is its highest point, part or surface.
NOUN **2** The **top** of a bottle, jar or tube is its cap or lid.

topic topics

NOUN A **topic** is a particular subject that you write or talk about.

a b c d e f g h i j k l m n o p q r s **Tt** u v w x y z

torch torches

NOUN A **torch** is a small electric lamp which you can carry in your hand.

tore

VERB **Tore** is the past tense of **tear**.

torn

VERB **Torn** is the past participle of **tear**.

tornado tornadoes or tornados

NOUN A **tornado** is a very strong wind that moves round in a circle and can cause a lot of damage.

tortoise tortoises

NOUN A **tortoise** is a slow-moving reptile with a hard thick shell.
See Reptiles on page 259.

toss tosses, tossing, tossed

VERB **1** If you **toss** something, you throw it lightly and carelessly.
VERB **2** If something **tosses**, it keeps moving from side to side.

total totals

NOUN **1** A **total** is the number you get when you add several numbers together.
ADJECTIVE **2** **Total** means complete.
*The party was a **total** success.*

touch touches, touching, touched

VERB **1** If you **touch** something, you feel it with your hand.
VERB **2** If two things are **touching**, there is no space between them.

tough tougher, toughest

ADJECTIVE Something that is **tough** is strong and difficult to cut, tear or break.

tour tours

NOUN A **tour** is a journey to visit interesting places.

tourist tourists

NOUN A **tourist** is a person who visits places for pleasure and interest.

tournament tournaments

NOUN A **tournament** is a competition in which lots of matches are played, until just one person or team is left.

tow tows, towing, towed

VERB If a vehicle **tows** another vehicle, it pulls it along behind.

towards

PREPOSITION **1** If you move **towards** something, you go in that direction.
PREPOSITION **2** If you give money **towards** something, you help pay for it.

towel towels

NOUN A **towel** is a piece of soft thick cloth that you use to dry yourself with.

tower towers

NOUN A **tower** is a tall narrow building or a tall part of a building.

town towns

NOUN A **town** is a place with a lot of streets and buildings where people live and work.

toy toys

NOUN A **toy** is something you play with, such as a doll or a model car.

trace traces, tracing, traced

VERB **1** If you **trace** something such as a map, you copy it by covering it with a piece of thin paper and drawing over the lines underneath.
VERB **2** If you **trace** something, you find it after looking for it.

track tracks

NOUN **1** A **track** is a rough narrow road or path.
NOUN **2** A **track** is also a special road or path that is used for racing.
NOUN **3** A railway **track** is a strip of ground with rails that trains travel on.

tracksuit tracksuits

NOUN A **tracksuit** is a loose warm suit of trousers and a top, worn for outdoor sports.

tractor **tractors**

NOUN A **tractor** is a vehicle with large rear wheels. Tractors are used on farms for pulling or lifting things.

trade **trades**

NOUN **Trade** is the buying and selling of goods or services. Trade can be between people, companies or countries.

trademark **trademarks**

NOUN A **trademark** is a name or symbol that a manufacturer always uses on its products. It is usually protected by law so that nobody else can use it.

tradition **traditions**

NOUN A **tradition** is something that people have done or believed in for a long time.
traditional ADJECTIVE
traditionally ADVERB

traffic

NOUN **Traffic** is the movement of vehicles on the road, in the air or on water.

traffic light **traffic lights**

NOUN **Traffic lights** are special signals to control the flow of traffic. Red lights mean stop and green lights mean go.

traffic warden **traffic wardens**

NOUN A **traffic warden** is a person who makes sure that cars are parked correctly.

tragedy **tragedies**

NOUN **1** A **tragedy** is an event or situation that is very sad.
NOUN **2** A **tragedy** is also a serious play, that usually ends with the death of the main character.
tragic ADJECTIVE

trail **trails, trailing, trailed**

NOUN **1** A **trail** is a rough path across open country or through forests.
NOUN **2** A **trail** is also the scent, footprints and other signs that people and animals leave behind them.
VERB **3** If you **trail** something or it **trails**, it drags along behind you.

trailer **trailers**

NOUN **1** A **trailer** is a vehicle pulled by a car, used for carrying things.
NOUN **2** A **trailer** can also be a series of short pieces from a film or television programme in order to advertise it.

train **trains, training, trained**

NOUN **1** A **train** is a number of carriages or trucks which are joined together and pulled by an engine along a railway.
VERB **2** If someone **trains** you to do a job, they teach you the skills you need.
VERB **3** If you **train** a dog, you teach it to behave properly.

trainer **trainers**

NOUN **1** A **trainer** is a person who coaches people in sports such as boxing.
NOUN **2** **Trainers** are special shoes people wear for running or jogging.

tram **trams**

NOUN A **tram** is a vehicle which runs on rails along the street.

trampoline **trampolines**

NOUN A **trampoline** is something that is used for jumping on. It is made of strong cloth held into a frame by springs.

transfer **transfers, transferring, transferred**

VERB If you **transfer** something, you move it to a different place or position.

translate **translates, translating, translated**

VERB If you **translate** something, you put the words into a different language.
translation NOUN

translucent

ADJECTIVE If something is **translucent**, light passes through it so that it glows.

transparent

ADJECTIVE If something is **transparent**, it lets light through and you can see through it.

transplant **transplants**

NOUN A **transplant** is an operation to put part of one person's body into another person.

transport

NOUN **Transport** is using vehicles to move people and things from one place to another.

trap **traps, trapping, trapped**

NOUN **1** A **trap** is something that is specially made to catch animals.
VERB **2** If a person is **trapped**, they cannot escape.

trap door **trap doors**

NOUN A **trap door** is a small door in a floor or ceiling.

trapeze **trapezes**

NOUN A **trapeze** is a bar hung from a high place by ropes. People swing from trapezes in circuses.

travel **travels, travelling, travelled**

VERB If you **travel**, you go from one place to another.
traveller NOUN

tray **trays**

NOUN A **tray** is a flat object with raised edges, used for carrying food or drinks.

treacherous

ADJECTIVE **1** A person who is **treacherous** cannot be trusted.
ADJECTIVE **2** If something like the sea is **treacherous**, it is dangerous.

treacle

NOUN **Treacle** is a thick sweet sticky liquid made from sugar.

tread **treads, treading, trod, trodden**

VERB If you **tread** on something, you walk on it or step on it.

treasure **treasures**

NOUN **Treasure** is valuable things such as jewels or paintings.

treat **treats, treating, treated**

VERB **1** If you **treat** someone in a certain way, you behave that way towards them. *My uncle **treats** me as if I'm five.*
VERB **2** If someone **treats** a person who is ill, they help them get well again.
NOUN **3** A **treat** is something enjoyable.

tree **trees**

NOUN A **tree** is a large plant with a hard woody trunk, branches and leaves.

tremble **trembles, trembling, trembled**

VERB If you **tremble**, you shake slightly, because you are frightened or cold.

trespass **trespasses, trespassing, trespassed**

VERB To **trespass** means to go on someone else's land without asking.

trial **trials**

NOUN **1** A **trial** is when you try something out to see if it works.
NOUN **2** In law, a **trial** is a time in court. People decide whether a person is guilty of a crime.

triangle **triangles**

NOUN A **triangle** is a flat shape with three straight sides and three angles.
triangular ADJECTIVE
See Colours and flat shapes on page 271.

a b c d e f g h i j k l m n o p q r s **Tt** u v w x y z

tribe

tribe tribes

NOUN A **tribe** is a group of people of the same race, customs and language, who are ruled by one chief.

trick tricks, tricking, tricked

NOUN **1** A **trick** is a clever or skilful act that someone does to entertain people.
VERB **2** If a person **tricks** someone, they deceive them.

trickle trickles, trickling, trickled

VERB When a liquid **trickles**, it flows slowly in small amounts.

tricycle tricycles

NOUN A **tricycle** is a vehicle similar to a bicycle, but with three wheels.

tried

VERB **Tried** is the past tense of **try**.

tries

VERB **Tries** is a present tense form of **try**.

trifle trifles

NOUN **Trifle** is a cold pudding made of layers of sponge, fruit, jelly and custard.

trigger triggers

NOUN A **trigger** is a small lever on a gun, which is pulled to fire the gun.

trim trims, trimming, trimmed

VERB If a person **trims** something, such as a hedge or your hair, they cut off small amounts of it to make it neat.

trip trips, tripping, tripped

NOUN **1** A **trip** is a journey to a place and back again.
VERB **2** If you **trip**, you catch your foot on something and fall over.

triumph triumphs

NOUN A **triumph** is a great success.

triumphant

ADJECTIVE Someone who is **triumphant** feels extremely happy because they have been very successful.

trod

VERB **Trod** is the past tense of **tread**.

trolley trolleys

NOUN A **trolley** is a small cart on wheels used for carrying heavy objects.

troops

PLURAL NOUN **Troops** are soldiers.

trophy trophies

NOUN A **trophy** is a cup or shield given to the winner of a competition.

tropical

ADJECTIVE **Tropical** means to do with the tropics, which are the hottest part of the world, near the equator.

trot trots, trotting, trotted

VERB When a horse **trots**, it moves at a speed a little faster than a walk.

trouble troubles

NOUN **Trouble** is something that worries or bothers you.

trough troughs

NOUN A **trough** is a long narrow container which holds food or drink for farm animals.

trousers

PLURAL NOUN **Trousers** are a piece of clothing for the body from the waist down, with a separate part for each leg.

trout

NOUN A **trout** is a fish that lives in lakes and rivers.

trowel trowels

NOUN A **trowel** is a small garden tool with a curved and pointed blade used for planting or weeding.

truant truants

NOUN A **truant** is a child who stays away from school without permission.

truce truces

NOUN A **truce** is an agreement between two people or groups to stop fighting or quarrelling for a time.

truck trucks

NOUN **1** A **truck** is a large motor vehicle which is open at the back. Trucks are used for carrying heavy loads.

NOUN **2** A **truck** is also an open vehicle used for carrying things on a railway.

trudge trudges, trudging, trudged

VERB If you **trudge**, you walk with slow heavy steps.

true truer, truest

ADJECTIVE **1** A **true** story or statement is based on facts and is not made up.

ADJECTIVE **2** **True** feelings are sincere.

truly ADVERB

trumpet trumpets

NOUN A **trumpet** is a brass musical instrument that you blow into.

trunk trunks

NOUN **1** The **trunk** of a tree is its main stem, from which the branches grow.

NOUN **2** An elephant's **trunk** is its long flexible nose.

NOUN **3** A **trunk** is also a large box with a lid used for storing things.

trust trusts, trusting, trusted

VERB If you **trust** someone, you believe that they are honest and will not do anything to hurt you.

truth

NOUN The **truth** is the facts about something or someone, rather than things that are imagined or made up.

truthful

ADJECTIVE A **truthful** person is honest and tells the truth.

truthfully ADVERB

try tries, trying, tried

VERB **1** If you **try** to do something, you do your best to do it.

VERB **2** If you **try** something, you test it to see what it is like.

T-shirt T-shirts

NOUN A **T-shirt** is a simple short-sleeved cotton shirt with no collar.

tub tubs

NOUN A **tub** is a round container for food.

tube tubes

NOUN **1** A **tube** is a round hollow pipe.

NOUN **2** A **tube** is also a container with a cap at one end that you squeeze to get the contents out.

tuck tucks, tucking, tucked

VERB If you **tuck** something, you put the end of it under or into something else. *He **tucked** his shirt into his trousers.*

Tuesday Tuesdays

NOUN **Tuesday** is the day after Monday and before Wednesday.

tuft tufts

NOUN A **tuft** of something, such as hair, is a bunch of it growing closely together.

tug tugs, tugging, tugged

VERB If you **tug** something, you give it a quick strong pull.

tug-of-war

NOUN A **tug-of-war** is a sport in which two teams pull against each other on opposite ends of a rope.

tulip tulips

NOUN A **tulip** is a spring flower shaped like an upside-down bell.

tumble tumbles, tumbling, tumbled

VERB If you **tumble**, you fall over and over.

tuna

NOUN **Tuna** are large edible fish that live in warm seas.

tune tunes

NOUN A **tune** is a series of musical notes that are nice to listen to.

a
b
c
d
e
f
g
h
i
j
k
l
m
n
o
p
q
r
s
Tt
u
v
w
x
y
z

tunnel **tunnels**
NOUN A **tunnel** is a long passage under the ground or through a hill.

turkey **turkeys**
NOUN A **turkey** is a large bird that is kept on a farm for its meat.

turn **turns, turning, turned**
VERB **1** When you **turn**, you move so that you are facing a different way.
VERB **2** When you **turn** something, you move it round.
VERB **3** When something **turns into** something else, it becomes that thing. *When water freezes, it **turns into** ice.*
NOUN **4** If people take **turns** to do something, they do it one after the other.

turnip **turnips**
NOUN A **turnip** is a round root vegetable with a white or yellow skin.
See *Vegetables* on page 256.

turquoise
ADJECTIVE Something **turquoise** is a blue-green colour.
See *Colours* on page 271.

turtle **turtles**
NOUN A **turtle** is a large reptile with a thick shell. It lives mostly in the sea.
See *Reptiles* on page 259.

tusk **tusks**
NOUN **Tusks** are long pointed teeth that some animals have. For example, elephants and walruses have tusks.

TV **TVs**
NOUN TV is an abbreviation of **television**.

twice
ADVERB **Twice** means two times.

twig **twigs**
NOUN A **twig** is a small thin branch of a tree or bush.

twilight
NOUN **Twilight** is the time after sunset when it is just getting dark.

twin **twins**
NOUN If two people are **twins**, they have the same mother and were born on the same day.

twinkle **twinkles, twinkling, twinkled**
VERB If something **twinkles**, it shines with little flashes.

twirl **twirls, twirling, twirled**
VERB If something **twirls**, or if you twirl it, it spins round and round.

twist **twists, twisting, twisted**
VERB **1** When you **twist** something, you turn one end in the opposite direction to the other.
VERB **2** When something **twists**, it moves or bends into a strange shape.

two-dimensional
ADJECTIVE Something that is **two-dimensional**, or **2D**, is a flat shape. For example, a circle is two-dimensional.
See *Colours and flat shapes* on page 271.

tying
VERB **Tying** is a present tense form of **tie**.

type **types, typing, typed**
NOUN **1** **Type** means kind or sort. *What type of plant is it?*
VERB **2** If you **type** words, you use a computer or typewriter.

typhoon **typhoons**
NOUN A **typhoon** is a storm with extremely strong winds.

typical
ADJECTIVE Something that is **typical** is what you would expect.

tyre **tyres**
NOUN A **tyre** is a thick ring of rubber fitted round each wheel of a vehicle.

Uu

ugly **uglier, ugliest**
ADJECTIVE Someone or something that is **ugly** is not pleasant to look at.

umbrella **umbrellas**
NOUN An **umbrella** is a shelter from the rain. It consists of a folding frame covered in thin cloth, attached to a long stick.

un-
PREFIX **Un-** is added to the beginning of a word to make it mean the opposite, for example "happy" → "unhappy". *See Prefixes on page 264.*

unable
ADJECTIVE If you are **unable** to do something, you cannot do it.

unaware
ADJECTIVE If you are **unaware** of something, you do not know about it.

unbearable
ADJECTIVE Something **unbearable** is so unpleasant, painful or upsetting you feel you cannot stand it.

unbelievable
ADJECTIVE **1** Something **unbelievable** is extremely great or surprising. *She showed unbelievable courage.*
ADJECTIVE **2** Unbelievable can also be used to describe something that is so unlikely you cannot believe it.

unbreakable
ADJECTIVE Something that is **unbreakable** cannot be broken.

uncertain
ADJECTIVE If you are **uncertain**, you are not sure what to do.

uncle **uncles**
NOUN Your **uncle** is the brother of one of your parents, or your aunt's husband.

uncomfortable
ADJECTIVE If you are **uncomfortable**, you do not feel easy.

uncommon
ADJECTIVE Something **uncommon** does not often happen, or is not often seen.

unconscious
ADJECTIVE Someone who is **unconscious** is unable to see, hear or feel anything that is going on. This is usually because they have fainted or have been badly injured.

under
PREPOSITION **1** Under means below or beneath.

PREPOSITION **2** Under can also mean less than. *Children under five can go in free.*

under-
PREFIX **1** Under- is added to the beginning of a word to form a new word meaning under the thing mentioned, for example "ground" → "underground".
PREFIX **2** Under- can also be used as a prefix to mean not enough. *The hungry rabbit was underfed.*
See Prefixes on page 264.

underground

ADJECTIVE **1** Something **underground** is below the surface of the ground.

NOUN **2** The **underground** is a railway that runs in tunnels under some cities.

undergrowth

NOUN **Undergrowth** is bushes or plants growing together under the trees in a forest or jungle.

underline underlines, underlining, underlined

VERB If you **underline** a word or sentence, you draw a line under it.

underneath

PREPOSITION OR ADVERB **Underneath** means below or beneath. *They found the missing card **underneath** the table... They couldn't move the car because their cat was **underneath**.*

understand understands, understanding, understood

VERB If you **understand** something, you know what it means.

underwear

NOUN Your **underwear** is the clothing that you wear next to your skin under your other clothes.

undo undoes, undoing, undid, undone

VERB If you **undo** something that is tied up, you untie it.

undress undresses, undressing, undressed

VERB When you **undress**, you take off your clothes.

uneasy

ADJECTIVE If you are **uneasy**, you are worried that something is wrong.

unemployed

ADJECTIVE Someone who is **unemployed** does not have a job.

uneven

ADJECTIVE Something that is **uneven** does not have a flat, smooth surface.

unexpected

ADJECTIVE Something that is **unexpected** surprises you.

unexpectedly ADVERB

unfair

ADJECTIVE If you think that something is **unfair**, it does not seem right or reasonable to you.

unfairly ADVERB

unfortunate

ADJECTIVE **1** Someone who is **unfortunate** is unlucky.

ADJECTIVE **2** If you say something is **unfortunate**, you mean you wish it had not happened.

unfortunately ADVERB

unfriendly

ADJECTIVE Someone who is **unfriendly** is not kind to you.

ungrateful

ADJECTIVE If someone is **ungrateful**, they are not thankful for something that has been given to them or done for them.

unhappy unhappier, unhappiest

ADJECTIVE Someone who is **unhappy** is sad or miserable.

unhappily ADVERB

unhealthy unhealthier, unhealthiest

ADJECTIVE **1** Someone who is **unhealthy** is often ill.

ADJECTIVE **2** Something that is **unhealthy** is likely to cause illness.

unicorn unicorns

NOUN A **unicorn** is an imaginary animal like a white horse with a horn in the middle of its forehead.

uniform uniforms

NOUN A **uniform** is a special set of clothes that is worn by people to show that they belong to the same group.

unique

ADJECTIVE If something is **unique**, it is the only one of its kind.

unit units

NOUN **1** A **unit** is an amount that is used for measuring things. For example, a second is a unit of time.

NOUN **2** In maths, the number of ones is the number of **units**. *The number 37 has 3 tens and 7 units.*

unite unites, uniting, united

VERB If people **unite**, they work as a group.

united ADJECTIVE

universe

NOUN The **universe** is the whole of space including all the stars and planets.

university universities

NOUN A **university** is a place where people can carry on their education when they have left school.

unkind

ADJECTIVE Someone who is **unkind** is rather cruel and unpleasant.

unleaded

ADJECTIVE **Unleaded** petrol has a smaller amount of lead in it, in order to reduce the pollution from vehicles.

unless

CONJUNCTION You use **unless** to introduce a condition which is necessary for something else to happen. *I won't come unless you invite me.*

unlike

PREPOSITION If one thing is **unlike** another, the two things are different.

unlikely

ADJECTIVE If something is **unlikely**, it is probably not true or probably will not happen.

unload unloads, unloading, unloaded

VERB If people **unload** something, such as a lorry, they take the load off it.

unlock unlocks, unlocking, unlocked

VERB If you **unlock** something, such as a door, you open it with a key.

unlucky

ADJECTIVE Someone who is **unlucky** has bad luck.

unluckily ADVERB

unnatural

ADJECTIVE Something **unnatural** is strange because it is not usual. *There was an unnatural stillness.*

unnaturally ADVERB

unnecessary

ADJECTIVE Something that is **unnecessary** is not needed.

unpack unpacks, unpacking, unpacked

VERB When you **unpack**, you take everything out of a suitcase, bag or box.

unpleasant

ADJECTIVE Something that is **unpleasant** is rather nasty and not enjoyable.

unpopular

ADJECTIVE Someone or something that is **unpopular** is disliked by most people.

unsafe

ADJECTIVE If something like a building or a machine is **unsafe**, it is dangerous.

unselfish

ADJECTIVE People who are **unselfish** care more about other people than they do about themselves.

a b c d e f g h i j k l m n o p q r s t **Uu** v w x y z

untidy **untidier, untidiest**

ADJECTIVE **1** Someone who is **untidy** does not care whether things are neat and well arranged.

ADJECTIVE **2** An **untidy** place is not neat or well arranged.

untie **unties, untying, untied**

VERB If you **untie** something, you undo the knots in the string around it.

until

PREPOSITION OR CONJUNCTION **Until** means up to a certain time. *The shop was open* **until** *midnight... He waited* **until** *the dog was asleep.*

untrue

ADJECTIVE Something that is **untrue** is false and not based on facts.

unusual

ADJECTIVE Someone or something that is **unusual** is different from the ordinary.

up

PREPOSITION OR ADVERB **1** Up means towards or in a higher place. *She ran* **up** *the stairs... It was high* **up** *in the mountains.*

ADVERB **2** If an amount of something goes **up**, it increases. *The price of butter has gone* **up***.*

upper-case

ADJECTIVE **Upper-case** letters are capital letters. See **lower-case**.

upright

ADJECTIVE If you are **upright**, you are standing up straight.

uproar **uproars**

NOUN An **uproar** is a lot of noise and shouting.

upset **upsets, upsetting, upset**

VERB **1** If someone **upsets** something, they turn it over by accident. *He* **upset** *a tin of paint on the carpet.*

ADJECTIVE **2** If you are **upset**, you are unhappy or disappointed.

upside down

ADJECTIVE Something that is **upside down** has been turned so that the part that should be at the top is at the bottom.

upstairs

ADVERB **1** If you go **upstairs** in a building, you go up to a higher floor.

ADVERB **2** Someone or something that is **upstairs** is on a higher floor than you.

up-to-date

ADJECTIVE Something that is **up-to-date** is new or modern.

urgent

ADJECTIVE Something that is **urgent** needs to be done at once.

use **uses, using, used**

VERB If you **use** something, you do something with it that helps you.

used

VERB Something that **used** to be done was done in the past.

used to PHRASE If you are **used to** something, you are familiar with it and have often experienced it.

useful

ADJECTIVE If something is **useful**, it helps you in some way.

useless

ADJECTIVE If something is **useless**, you cannot use it.

usual

ADJECTIVE Something that is **usual** happens, or is done or used, most often.

usually

ADVERB If something **usually** happens, it happens most often.

Vv

vacant

ADJECTIVE Somewhere that is **vacant** has nobody in it.

vaccination **vaccinations**

NOUN A **vaccination** is an injection that stops you getting an illness.

vacuum cleaner **vacuum cleaners**

NOUN A **vacuum cleaner** is an electric machine which cleans by sucking up dirt.

vagina **vaginas**

NOUN The **vagina** is an opening in a woman's body through which babies pass when they are being born.

vague **vaguer, vaguest**

ADJECTIVE Things that are **vague** are not definite or clear. *He had a **vague** feeling he should be doing something.*

vain

ADJECTIVE A **vain** person is too proud of how they look or what they can do.

valley **valleys**

NOUN A **valley** is a low piece of land between hills. Valleys often have rivers flowing through them.

valuable

ADJECTIVE **1** Things that are **valuable** are worth a lot of money.

ADJECTIVE **2** Help or advice that is **valuable** is very useful.

value

NOUN **1** The **value** of something is its importance or usefulness.

NOUN **2** The **value** of something such as jewellery is the amount of money that it is worth.

vampire **vampires**

NOUN In horror stories, **vampires** are creatures that suck the blood of living people.

van **vans**

NOUN A **van** is a vehicle larger than a car but smaller than a lorry. Vans are used for carrying goods.

vandal **vandals**

NOUN A **vandal** is someone who damages something useful or beautiful on purpose and for no good reason.

vanilla

NOUN **Vanilla** is a flavouring for food. It comes from the pods of a tropical plant.

vanish **vanishes, vanishing, vanished**

VERB If something **vanishes**, it disappears suddenly.

vapour **vapours**

NOUN **Vapour** is a mass of tiny drops of water or other liquids in the air, which appear as clouds, mist or fumes.

variety **variety**

NOUN A **variety** of things is lots of different types.

various

ADJECTIVE You say **various** to mean several different things of one kind. *There were **various** questions she wanted to ask.*

vase **vases**

NOUN A **vase** is a kind of jar used as an ornament, or to hold cut flowers.

vast

ADJECTIVE Something that is **vast** is extremely large.

a
b
c
d
e
f
g
h
i
j
k
l
m
n
o
p
q
r
s
t
u
Vv
w
x
y
z

vegetable vegetables

NOUN **Vegetables** are plants, or parts of plants such as leaves, that can be eaten.

See *Vegetables* on page 256.

vegetarian vegetarians

NOUN A **vegetarian** is a person who does not eat meat or fish.

vehicle vehicles

NOUN A **vehicle** is a machine such as a car or bus that carries people or things from place to place.

veil veils

NOUN A **veil** is a piece of thin soft cloth that some women wear over their face or head.

vein veins

NOUN A **vein** is a tube inside the body which carries blood to the heart.

velvet

NOUN **Velvet** is a material which has soft short threads on one side.

verb verbs

NOUN In grammar, a **verb** is a word that expresses actions and states, for example "take" and "run".

See *Verb* on page 263.

verdict verdicts

NOUN In a law court, a **verdict** is whether a prisoner is guilty or not guilty.

verse verses

NOUN **1** Verse is another word for poetry.

NOUN **2** A **verse** is one of the parts that a poem or song is divided into.

version versions

NOUN A **version** of something is a form of it in which some details are different from earlier or later forms. *This is a different version of my story.*

vertex vertexes or vertices

NOUN **1** The **vertex** of something is its highest point.

NOUN **2** The **vertex** can also be the corner point of a polygon or polyhedron. For example, a triangle has three vertices and a cuboid has eight.

vertical

ADJECTIVE Something that is **vertical** stands straight up from a flat surface. See **horizontal**.

very

ADVERB **Very** is used before words to make them stronger. *He had very bad dreams.*

vessel vessels

NOUN A **vessel** is a ship or boat.

vest vests

NOUN A **vest** is a piece of underwear for the top half of the body.

vet vets

NOUN A **vet** is a person whose job is to look after sick and injured animals. Vet is an abbreviation of **veterinary surgeon**.

via

PREPOSITION If you go **via** a particular place, you go through it to get to somewhere else. *We go to Cambridge via the Dartford Tunnel.*

viaduct viaducts

NOUN A **viaduct** is a long high bridge that carries a road or railway across a valley.

vibrate vibrates, vibrating, vibrated

VERB If something **vibrates**, it shakes with a very slight, very quick movement.

vicious

ADJECTIVE Someone or something that is **vicious** is cruel and violent.

victim victims

NOUN A **victim** is someone who has been harmed or injured by someone or something.

victory victories

NOUN A **victory** is a success in a battle or competition.

video videos, videoing, videoed

NOUN **1** A **video** is a machine that records television programmes so that you can watch them later.

NOUN **2** A **video** is also a tape that you use to record television programmes.

NOUN **3** A **video** is also a taped recording of a film that you can watch on your television set.

VERB **4** If you **video** something, you record it on tape so that you can watch it later.

view views

NOUN The **view** from a window or a high place is everything that can be seen from there.

village villages

NOUN A **village** is a small group of houses and other buildings in a country area.

vine vines

NOUN A **vine** is a climbing plant that produces grapes.

vinegar

NOUN **Vinegar** is a sharp-tasting liquid that is used to add taste to some foods, and is also used for pickling.

violence

NOUN **Violence** is behaviour that is meant to hurt or kill people.

violent

ADJECTIVE **1** Someone who is **violent** uses force to hurt or kill people.

ADJECTIVE **2** Something that is **violent** happens suddenly and with great force. *A **violent** earthquake shook the city.*

violently ADVERB

violet violets

NOUN A **violet** is a small plant with purple or white flowers.

violin violins

NOUN A **violin** is a musical instrument with four strings. It is held under the chin and played with a bow.

virtual

ADJECTIVE **Virtual** means something that is very like a real thing but is not actually the same. *What he said was a **virtual** lie.*

virtual reality

NOUN **Virtual reality** is an image created by a computer that looks real to the person using it.

virus viruses

NOUN **1** A **virus** is a tiny germ which you cannot see without a microscope. Viruses can cause diseases.

NOUN **2** A disease caused by a virus can also be called a **virus**.

visible

ADJECTIVE Something that is **visible** can be seen.

visibly ADVERB

vision visions

NOUN **1** Vision is the ability to see clearly. *Your **vision** will be better if you wear glasses.*

NOUN **2** A **vision** is a picture in your mind.

visit visits, visiting, visited

VERB If you **visit** a person or a place, you go to see them.

visitor visitors

NOUN A **visitor** is someone who is visiting a person or place.

a
b
c
d
e
f
g
h
i
j
k
l
m
n
o
p
q
r
s
t
u
Vv
w
x
y
z

vital

ADJECTIVE If something is **vital** when you are doing something, you will not succeed without it. *It is **vital** to get the measurements exactly right.*

vitamin **vitamins**

NOUN A **vitamin** is one of the substances which you need to stay healthy. There are vitamins in many kinds of food.

vivid

ADJECTIVE **1** A **vivid** colour is very bright.
ADJECTIVE **2** Memories or descriptions that are **vivid** are clear and remain firmly fixed in your mind.
vividly ADVERB

vixen **vixens**

NOUN A **vixen** is a female fox.

vocabulary

NOUN Someone's **vocabulary** is the total number of words in a language that they know.

voice **voices**

NOUN **1** Someone's **voice** is the sound they make when they speak or sing.
NOUN **2** In grammar, the active **voice** and the passive voice refer to the relation between a verb and its subject. For example, the sentence "Tom hit the ball" is in the active voice, and "The ball was hit by Tom" is in the passive voice. See **active** and **passive**.

volcano **volcanoes**

NOUN A **volcano** is a mountain with a hole called a crater in the top. Sometimes hot melted rock, gas, steam and ash burst from the crater.

volume **volumes**

NOUN **1** A **volume** is a book.
NOUN **2** The **volume** of something is the amount of space that it takes up.

NOUN **3** The **volume** of something, such as a radio or television, is how loud or quiet its sound is. *He played his radio at full **volume**.*

voluntary

ADJECTIVE **1 Voluntary** actions are ones that you offer to do, rather than being asked to or made to.
ADJECTIVE **2 Voluntary** work is done by people who are not paid for what they do.
voluntarily ADVERB

volunteer **volunteers, volunteering, volunteered**

VERB **1** If you **volunteer** to do something, you offer to do it without expecting any reward.
NOUN **2** A **volunteer** is someone who does work for which they are not paid.

vote **votes, voting, voted**

VERB **1** If you **vote**, you make a choice, usually by raising your hand or writing on a piece of paper. *We **voted** for Tim as group leader.*
VERB **2** If you **vote** that a particular thing should happen, that is what you suggest. *I **vote** we all go swimming.*

voucher **vouchers**

NOUN A **voucher** is a ticket or piece of paper that can be used instead of money.

vowel **vowels**

NOUN In the English language, the letters a, e, i, o and u are **vowels**. See **consonant**.

voyage **voyages**

NOUN A **voyage** is a long journey on a ship or in a spacecraft.

vulture **vultures**

NOUN A **vulture** is a large bird which feeds on dead animals. Vultures live in hot countries.

wade wades, wading, waded
VERB To **wade** means to walk through fairly shallow water.

wafer wafers
NOUN A **wafer** is a thin crisp biscuit.

wag wags, wagging, wagged
VERB When a dog **wags** its tail, it waves it from side to side because it is happy.

wagon wagons
NOUN **1** A **wagon** is a strong cart for carrying heavy loads. Wagons are usually pulled by a horse or tractor.
VERB **2** A **wagon** is also a railway truck.

wail wails, wailing, wailed
VERB If someone **wails**, they make a long crying noise.

waist waists
NOUN Your **waist** is the narrow middle part of your body, just below your chest.

wait waits, waiting, waited
VERB If you **wait**, you spend time before something happens.

wake wakes, waking, woke, woken
VERB When you **wake**, you stop sleeping.

walk walks, walking, walked
VERB When you **walk**, you move along by putting one foot in front of the other.

wall walls
NOUN **1** A **wall** is one of the vertical sides of a building or a room.
NOUN **2** A **wall** can also be used to divide or go round an area of land.

wallet wallets
NOUN A **wallet** is a small flat case that fits in a pocket. It is used to hold things such as paper money and credit cards.

wallpaper wallpapers
NOUN **Wallpaper** is thick coloured or patterned paper that is used for covering and decorating the walls of a room.

walnut walnuts
NOUN A **walnut** is a nut with a wrinkled shape and a light brown shell.

walrus walruses
NOUN A **walrus** is a mammal that lives in the sea and looks like a large seal. It has coarse whiskers and two long tusks.

wand wands
NOUN A **wand** is a long thin rod that magicians wave when they are performing tricks and magic.

wander wanders, wandering, wandered
VERB If you **wander**, you walk around without going in any particular direction.

want wants, wanting, wanted
VERB If you **want** something, you wish for it or need it.

war wars
NOUN A **war** is a period of fighting between countries.

wardrobe wardrobes
NOUN A **wardrobe** is a tall cupboard where you can hang your clothes.

warehouse warehouses
NOUN A **warehouse** is a large building which is used to store things.

warm warmer, warmest
ADJECTIVE **1** Something that is **warm** has some heat but not enough to be hot.
ADJECTIVE **2** Clothes and blankets that are **warm** are made of a material that stops you feeling cold.

a
b
c
d
e
f
g
h
i
j
k
l
m
n
o
p
q
r
s
t
u
v
Ww
x
y
z

warmth

NOUN **Warmth** is a comfortable amount of heat.

warn warns, warning, warned

VERB If you **warn** someone, you tell them about a danger or problem that they might meet.

warning warnings

NOUN A **warning** is something that tells you about a possible problem or danger.

warren warrens

NOUN A **warren** is a group of holes in the ground which rabbits live in. The holes are connected by tunnels.

wary warier, wariest

ADJECTIVE If you are **wary** about something, you are careful because you are not sure about it.

warily ADVERB

wash washes, washing, washed

VERB If you **wash** something, you clean it with soap and water.

washable

ADJECTIVE Clothes or materials that are **washable** can be washed in water without being damaged.

washing

NOUN **Washing** is clothes, towels and bedding that need to be washed.

washing machine washing machines

NOUN A **washing machine** is a machine for washing clothes in.

washing-up

NOUN If you do the **washing-up**, you wash things such as plates, pans and knives after a meal.

wasp wasps

NOUN A **wasp** is a flying insect with yellow and black stripes across its body. Wasps can sting.

waste wastes, wasting, wasted

VERB **1** If you **waste** something, such as time or money, you use too much of it on something that is not important.
NOUN **2 Waste** is material that is no longer wanted. This is often because the useful part of it has been taken out.

watch watches, watching, watched

NOUN **1** A **watch** is a small clock that you can wear on your wrist.
VERB **2** If you **watch** something, you look at it carefully to see what happens.

water waters, watering, watered

NOUN **1 Water** is a clear liquid that all living things need in order to live.
VERB **2** If you **water** a plant or animal, you give it water to drink.

waterfall waterfalls

NOUN A **waterfall** is water that flows over the edge of a cliff to the ground below.

waterlogged

ADJECTIVE Land that is **waterlogged** is so wet the soil cannot contain any more water.

waterproof

ADJECTIVE A material that is **waterproof** does not let water pass through it.

watertight

ADJECTIVE Something that is **watertight** is closed so tightly that it does not allow water to pass through.

wave waves, waving, waved

VERB **1** If you **wave**, you move your hand in the air, to say hello or goodbye.

VERB **2** If something **waves**, it moves gently up and down or from side to side. *The flags waved in the wind.*

NOUN **3** A **wave** is a raised line of water on the surface of the sea caused by wind or tides.

NOUN **4** A **wave** is also a gentle curving shape in someone's hair.

wax

NOUN **Wax** is a solid, slightly shiny substance, made of fat or oil. It is used to make candles and polish.

way ways

NOUN **1** A **way** of doing something is how it can be done.

NOUN **2** The **way** to a particular place is the direction you have to go to get there.

weak weaker, weakest

ADJECTIVE **1** People or animals that are **weak** do not have much strength or energy.

ADJECTIVE **2** If an object or part of an object is **weak**, it could break easily.

ADJECTIVE **3** Drinks, such as tea or coffee, that are **weak** do not have a strong taste.

wealthy wealthier, wealthiest

ADJECTIVE Someone who is **wealthy** has a lot of money.

weapon weapons

NOUN A **weapon** is an object such as a gun or missile which is used to hurt or kill people in a fight or war.

wear wears, wearing, wore, worn

VERB **1** When you **wear** things, such as clothes, you have them on your body.

VERB **2** When something **wears out**, it has been used so much that it cannot be used any more.

weary wearier, weariest

ADJECTIVE If you are **weary**, you are tired.

wearily ADVERB

weather

NOUN The **weather** is what it is like outside, for example raining, sunny or windy.

See Weather words on page 269.

weave weaves, weaving, wove, woven

VERB When someone **weaves** cloth, they make it by crossing threads over and under each other, using a machine called a loom.

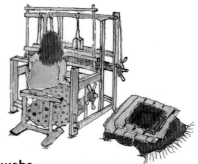

web webs

NOUN **1** A **web** is a fine net made by a spider to catch flies.

NOUN **2** The **web** is short for the World Wide Web, which is where information can be stored on the Internet.

webbed

ADJECTIVE **Webbed** feet have the toes connected by a piece of skin.

website websites

NOUN A **website** is a group of pages on the Internet which contain information about a particular subject.

wedding weddings

NOUN A **wedding** is when a man and woman become husband and wife.

Wednesday Wednesdays

NOUN **Wednesday** is the day between Tuesday and Thursday.

weed weeds

NOUN A **weed** is any wild plant that grows where it is not wanted. Weeds grow strongly and stop other plants growing properly.

week weeks

NOUN A **week** is a period of seven days.

a
b
c
d
e
f
g
h
i
j
k
l
m
n
o
p
q
r
s
t
u
v
Ww
x
y
z

weekend

weekend **weekends**

NOUN A **weekend** is Saturday and Sunday.

weep **weeps, weeping, wept**

VERB If someone **weeps**, they cry.

weigh **weighs, weighing, weighed**

VERB **1** If something **weighs** a particular amount, that is how heavy it is.

VERB **2** If you **weigh** something, you use scales to measure how heavy it is.

weight

NOUN The **weight** of something is its heaviness. Weight and mass are connected. Weight is usually measured in grams and kilograms. See **mass**.

weird **weirder, weirdest**

ADJECTIVE Something that is **weird** seems strange and peculiar.

welcome **welcomes, welcoming, welcomed**

VERB If you **welcome** someone, you speak to them in a friendly way when they arrive.

well **better, best; wells**

ADJECTIVE **1** If you are **well**, you are healthy.

ADVERB **2** If you do something **well**, you do it to a high standard.

NOUN **3** A **well** is a deep hole in the ground that has been dug to reach water or oil.

wellington **wellingtons**

NOUN **Wellingtons** are long waterproof rubber boots.

went

VERB **Went** is the past tense of **go**.

wept

VERB **Wept** is the past tense of **weep**.

west

NOUN The **west** is one of the four main points of the compass. It is the direction in which you look to see the sun set. See **compass point**.

western ADJECTIVE

wet **wetter, wettest**

ADJECTIVE **1** If something is **wet**, it is covered in water or some other liquid.

ADJECTIVE **2** If the weather is **wet**, it is raining.

ADJECTIVE **3** If something such as ink or cement is **wet**, it has not yet dried.

whale **whales**

NOUN A **whale** is a huge mammal that lives in the sea. Whales breathe through an opening in the top of their head.

what

ADJECTIVE OR PRONOUN **1** **What** is used in questions. *What time is it? What is your name?*

PRONOUN **2** You can use **what** to refer to information about something. *I don't know **what** you mean.*

what about PHRASE You say **what about** at the beginning of a question when you are making a suggestion or offer. *What about a sandwich?*

wheat

NOUN **Wheat** is a cereal plant grown for its grain, which is used to make flour.

wheel **wheels**

NOUN A **wheel** is a circular object which turns round on a rod fixed to its centre. Wheels are fitted under things such as cars, bicycles and prams so that they can move along.

wheelbarrow **wheelbarrows**

NOUN A **wheelbarrow** is a small cart with a single wheel at the front.

wheelchair **wheelchairs**

NOUN A **wheelchair** is a chair with large wheels for use by people who find walking difficult or impossible.

Ww

when

ADVERB **1** You use **when** to ask what time something happened or will happen. *When are you leaving?*

CONJUNCTION **2** You use **when** to refer to a certain time. *I met him when we were at school together.*

where

ADVERB **1** You use **where** to ask questions about place. *Where is my book?*

CONJUNCTION **2** You use **where** to talk about the place in which something is situated or happening. *I don't know where we are.*

whether

CONJUNCTION You can use **whether** instead of **if**. *I don't know whether I can go.*

which

ADJECTIVE **1** You use **which** to ask for information about something when there are two or more possibilities. *Which room are you in?*

PRONOUN **2** You also use **which** when you are going to say more about something you have already mentioned. *We have a car which is dropping to bits.*

while

CONJUNCTION **1** If something happens **while** something else is happening, the two things happen at the same time.

NOUN **2** A **while** is a period of time. *She had to wait a little while.*

whimper   whimpers, whimpering, whimpered

VERB When children or animals **whimper**, they make soft unhappy sounds, as if they are about to cry.

whine   whines, whining, whined

VERB To **whine** is to make a long high-pitched noise because you are unhappy about something.

whip   whips, whipping, whipped

VERB If you **whip** cream or eggs, you beat them until they are thick and frothy or stiff.

whirl   whirls, whirling, whirled

VERB When something **whirls**, it turns round very fast.

whirlpool   whirlpools

NOUN A **whirlpool** is a small place in a river or the sea where the water is moving quickly round and round, so that anything floating near it is pulled into its centre.

whirlwind   whirlwinds

NOUN A **whirlwind** is a tall column of air which spins round and round very quickly.

whirr   whirrs, whirring, whirred

VERB When something like a machine **whirrs**, it makes a series of low sounds so fast that it seems like one sound.

whisk   whisks, whisking, whisked

VERB If you **whisk** something like cream, you stir it very fast.

whisker   whiskers

NOUN The **whiskers** of an animal such as a cat or mouse are the long stiff hairs near its mouth.

whisper   whispers, whispering, whispered

VERB When you **whisper**, you talk very quietly, using your breath and not your voice.

whistle   whistles, whistling, whistled

NOUN **1** A **whistle** is a small metal tube which makes a loud sound when you blow it.

VERB **2** When you **whistle**, you make a loud high noise by using a whistle or by forcing your breath out between your lips.

white

white whiter, whitest; whites

ADJECTIVE **1** Something that is **white** is the colour of milk.
See *Colours* on page 271.
ADJECTIVE **2** If someone goes **white**, their face becomes very pale because they are afraid, shocked or ill.
NOUN **3** The **white** of an egg is the transparent liquid surrounding the yolk.

who

PRONOUN **1** You use **who** when you are asking about someone. *Who told you?*
PRONOUN **2** You use **who** at the beginning of a clause when you want to say more about someone you have just mentioned. *I've got a brother who wants to be a vet.*

whole wholes

NOUN **1** The **whole** of something is all of it. *It was the only pair in the whole of Brighton.*
ADJECTIVE **2** You use **whole** to describe all of something. *Take the whole cake.*
ADJECTIVE **3** **Whole** means in one piece.

whose

PRONOUN **1** You use **whose** to ask who something belongs to. *Whose book is this?*
PRONOUN **2** You use **whose** in front of information relating to a person or thing you have just mentioned. *That's the girl whose mother is a lawyer.*

why

ADVERB **1** You use **why** in questions when you ask about the reason for something. *Why did you do that?*
ADVERB **2** You also use **why** to talk about the reasons for something. *She wondered why he was there.*

wicked

ADJECTIVE Someone or something **wicked** is very bad.

wide wider, widest

ADJECTIVE **1** Something that is **wide** measures a lot from one side to the other.
ADVERB **2** If you open something **wide**, you open it a long way.

widow widows

NOUN A **widow** is a woman whose husband has died. See **widower**.

widower widowers

NOUN A **widower** is a man whose wife has died. See **widow**.

width widths

NOUN The **width** of something is the distance from one side to the other.

wife wives

NOUN A man's **wife** is the woman he is married to.

wig wigs

NOUN A **wig** is a false head of hair. People wear wigs because they are bald, or to cover their own hair.

wigwam wigwams

NOUN A **wigwam** is a kind of tent used by some North American Indians.

wild wilder, wildest

ADJECTIVE **1** **Wild** animals, birds and plants live in natural surroundings and are not looked after by people.
ADJECTIVE **2** **Wild** behaviour is excited and not controlled.

wildlife

NOUN **Wildlife** means wild animals and plants.

will

VERB **1** You use **will** to form the future tense. *Robin will be quite annoyed.*
VERB **2** You use **will** when asking or telling someone to do something. *Will you do me a favour?*

willing

ADJECTIVE **1** If you are **willing** to do something, you are ready and happy to do it if someone wants you to.

ADJECTIVE **2** A **willing** person is someone who does things cheerfully.

willow willows

NOUN A **willow** is a tree with long thin branches and narrow leaves that likes to grow near water.

win wins, winning, won

VERB **1** If you **win** a race or game, you do better than the others taking part.
VERB **2** If you **win** a prize, you get it as a reward for doing something well.

wind winds, winding, wound

(*rhymes with* **tinned**) NOUN **1** A **wind** is a current of air that moves across the earth's surface.
(*rhymes with* **mind**) VERB **2** If a road or river **winds**, it has lots of bends in it.
(*rhymes with* **mind**) VERB **3** When you **wind** something round something else, you wrap it round several times.

windmill windmills

NOUN A **windmill** is a building with large sails on the outside, which turn as the wind blows. This works a machine that grinds corn to make flour.

window windows

NOUN A **window** is a space in a wall or vehicle. It has glass in it so that light can come in and you can see through.

windscreen windscreens

NOUN The **windscreen** of a vehicle is the glass window at the front.

windy windier, windiest

ADJECTIVE If it is **windy**, the wind is blowing hard.

wine wines

NOUN **Wine** is a strong drink usually made from the juice of grapes.

wing wings

NOUN **1** The **wings** of a bird or insect are the two limbs on its body that it uses for flying.
NOUN **2** The **wings** of an aeroplane are the long flat parts sticking out of its sides, which support it in the air.

wink winks, winking, winked

VERB When you **wink**, you close one eye for a moment. *She **winked** to show that she was joking.*

winner winners

NOUN If someone or something wins a prize, race or competition, they are the **winner**.

winter winters

NOUN **Winter** is the season between autumn and spring.

wipe wipes, wiping, wiped

VERB If you **wipe** something, you rub its surface lightly to remove dirt or liquid.

wire wires

NOUN **Wire** is a long, thin, flexible piece of metal which can be used to make or fasten things or to carry an electric current.

wise wiser, wisest

ADJECTIVE Someone who is **wise** can use their experience and knowledge to make sensible decisions.
wisdom NOUN

wish wishes, wishing, wished

VERB **1** If you **wish** that something would happen, you would like it to happen.
NOUN **2** A **wish** is the act of wishing for something you would like to happen.

witch witches

NOUN In fairy stories, a witch is a woman who has magic powers. See **wizard**.

a b c d e f g h i j k l m n o p q r s t u v **Ww** x y z

with

with

PREPOSITION **1** If you are **with** someone, you are in their company. *I was there* **with** *Mum and Dad.*

PREPOSITION **2 With** can mean using or having. *She worked* **with** *a big brush.*

wither **withers, withering, withered**

VERB If a plant **withers**, it shrivels up and dies.

within

PREPOSITION **1 Within** means not going outside certain limits. *Stay* **within** *the school grounds.*

PREPOSITION **2 Within** can also mean before a period of time has passed. *You must write back* **within** *ten days.*

without

PREPOSITION **1 Without** means not having or using. *You can't get in* **without** *a key.*

PREPOSITION **2 Without** can mean not in someone's company. *He went* **without** *me.*

PREPOSITION **3 Without** can also mean that something does not happen. *She rang three times* **without** *an answer.*

witness **witnesses, witnessing, witnessed**

NOUN **1** A **witness** is someone who has seen an event such as an accident and can describe what happened.

VERB **2** If you **witness** an event, you see it happen.

wizard **wizards**

NOUN In fairy stories, a **wizard** is a man who has magic powers. See **witch**.

wobble **wobbles, wobbling, wobbled**

VERB If something **wobbles**, it makes small movements from side to side.

woke

VERB **Woke** is the past tense of **wake**.

woken

VERB **Woken** is the past participle of **wake**.

wolf **wolves**

NOUN A **wolf** is a wild animal that looks like a large dog. Wolves live in a group called a pack.

woman **women**

NOUN A **woman** is an adult female human being. See **man**.

won

VERB **Won** is the past tense of **win**.

wonder **wonders, wondering, wondered**

VERB **1** If you **wonder** about something, you wish you knew more about it.

VERB **2** If you **wonder** what to do about something, you are not sure what to do about it.

NOUN **3 Wonder** is a feeling of great and pleasant surprise.

wonderful

ADJECTIVE If something is **wonderful**, it makes you feel very happy.

won't

VERB **Won't** is a contraction of **will not**.

wood **woods**

NOUN **1 Wood** is the substance which forms the trunks and branches of trees.

NOUN **2** A **wood** is a large area of trees growing near each other.

wooden

ADJECTIVE Something that is **wooden** is made of wood.

woodpecker **woodpeckers**

NOUN A **woodpecker** is a bird with a long sharp beak. It drills holes in trees to find insects.

woodwork

NOUN **1** The **woodwork** in a house is all the parts that are made of wood, such as the doors and window frames.

NOUN **2 Woodwork** is making things out of wood.

woof woofs

NOUN **Woof** is the noise that a dog makes when it barks.

wool

NOUN **1 Wool** is the hair that grows on sheep and on some other animals.

NOUN **2 Wool** is also the yarn spun from the wool of animals which is used to knit, weave, and make things like clothes, blankets and carpets.

woollen

ADJECTIVE Something that is **woollen** is made from wool.

woolly woollier, woolliest

ADJECTIVE Something that is **woolly** is made of wool, or looks like wool.

word words

NOUN A **word** is a set of sounds or letters that has a meaning. A word can be written or spoken. When it is written, there are no spaces between the letters.

word processor word processors

NOUN A **word processor** is a computer which is used to store and print words that are typed into it.

wore

VERB **Wore** is the past tense of **wear**.

work works, working, worked

VERB **1** When you **work**, you spend time and energy doing something useful.

VERB **2** People who **work** have a job that they are paid to do.

VERB **3** If something **works**, it does what it is supposed to do.

work out works out, working out, worked out

VERB **1** If you **work out** the answer to a problem, you find the answer.

VERB **2** If you **work out**, you do exercises to make your body fit and strong.

world worlds

NOUN The **world** is the planet we live on.

worm worms

NOUN A **worm** is a small animal with a long thin body. Worms have no bones and no legs. They live in the soil.

worn

VERB **1 Worn** is the past participle of **wear**.

ADJECTIVE **2** Something that is **worn** is damaged or thin because it is old and has been used a lot.

worry worries, worrying, worried

VERB If you **worry**, you keep thinking about problems or about unpleasant things that might happen.

worse

ADJECTIVE **1 Worse** is the comparative form of **bad**.

ADJECTIVE **2** If someone who is ill gets **worse**, they are more ill than before.

worship worships, worshipping, worshipped

VERB If you **worship** a god, you show your respect by praying and singing hymns.

worst

ADJECTIVE **Worst** is the superlative form of **bad**.

worth

ADJECTIVE **1** If something is **worth** a particular amount of money, it could be sold for that amount.

ADJECTIVE **2** If something is **worth** doing, it is enjoyable or useful. *That film is worth seeing.*

would

VERB **1** You use **would** to say what someone thought was going to happen. *We were sure it would rain.*

VERB **2** You also use **would** to say you want something to happen. *I would like to know how they do that.*

a
b
c
d
e
f
g
h
i
j
k
l
m
n
o
p
q
r
s
t
u
v
Ww
x
y
z

wound

wound **wounds**
(*rhymes with* **round**) VERB **1** Wound is the past tense of **wind**.
(*said* **woond**) NOUN **2** A **wound** is an injury to your body, especially a cut in your skin.

wove
VERB **Wove** is the past tense of **weave**.

woven
VERB **Woven** is the past participle of **weave**.

wrap **wraps, wrapping, wrapped**
VERB When you **wrap** something, you cover it tightly with something like paper.

wrapping **wrappings**
NOUN **Wrapping** is the material used to cover and protect something.

wreath **wreaths**
NOUN A **wreath** is an arrangement of flowers and leaves, often in the shape of a circle.

wreck **wrecks, wrecking, wrecked**
VERB **1** If someone or something **wrecks** something, they destroy it completely.
VERB **2** If a ship is **wrecked**, it is so badly damaged that it can no longer sail.
NOUN **3** A **wreck** is a vehicle that has been badly damaged in an accident.

wren **wrens**
NOUN A **wren** is a tiny brown bird.

wrestle **wrestles, wrestling, wrestled**
VERB If you **wrestle** with someone, you fight them by holding or throwing them, but not hitting them.

wriggle **wriggles, wriggling, wriggled**
VERB When you **wriggle**, you twist and turn your body with quick movements.

wring **wrings, wringing, wrung**
VERB If you **wring** a wet piece of cloth, you squeeze the water out of it by twisting it.

wrinkle **wrinkles**
NOUN **1** A **wrinkle** is a line in someone's skin, especially on their face, that forms as they grow old.
NOUN **2** A **wrinkle** is also a raised fold in something like cloth or thin paper.

wrinkled
ADJECTIVE If something is **wrinkled**, it has folds or lines in it.

wrist **wrists**
NOUN Your **wrist** is the part of your body between your hand and your arm, which bends when you move your hand.

write **writes, writing, wrote, written**
VERB **1** When you **write**, you use a pen or pencil to make words, letters or numbers.
VERB **2** If you **write** something such as a poem or a story, you create it.
VERB **3** When you **write** to someone, you tell them about something in a letter.

writing
NOUN **1** **Writing** is something that has been written or printed.
NOUN **2** Your **writing** is the way you write with a pen or pencil.

written
VERB **Written** is the past participle of **write**.

wrong
ADJECTIVE **1** Something that is **wrong** is not correct.
ADJECTIVE **2** If there is something **wrong** with a machine, vehicle, or piece of equipment, it is not working properly.
ADJECTIVE **3** If a person does something **wrong**, they do something bad.

wrote
VERB **Wrote** is the past tense of **write**.

wrung
VERB **Wrung** is the past tense of **wring**.

X-ray **X-rays**

NOUN An **X-ray** is a ray that can pass through some solid materials. X-rays are used by doctors to examine bones or organs inside people's bodies.

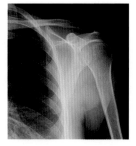

xylophone **xylophones**

NOUN A **xylophone** is a musical instrument made of wooden bars of different lengths which are arranged in a row. You play a xylophone by hitting the bars with special hammers.

Yy

yacht **yachts**

NOUN A **yacht** is a large boat with sails or a motor. Yachts are used for racing or for pleasure trips.

yam **yams**

NOUN A **yam** is a root vegetable which grows in tropical regions.

yard **yards**

NOUN **1** A **yard** is a unit of length equal to just under one metre.

NOUN **2** A **yard** is also an enclosed area that is usually next to a building.

yarn **yarns**

NOUN **Yarn** is thread made from something such as wool or cotton. It is used for knitting or making cloth.

yawn **yawns, yawning, yawned**

VERB When you **yawn**, you open your mouth wide and take in more air than usual. You often yawn when you are tired or bored.

a b c d e f g h i j k l m n o p q r s t u v w

X x
Y y

z

year **years**

NOUN A **year** is a period of time. It is equal to 12 months, or 52 weeks, or 365 days.

yeast

NOUN **Yeast** is a kind of fungus that is used to make bread rise. It is also used in making drinks such as beer.

yell **yells, yelling, yelled**

VERB If you **yell**, you shout loudly. People sometimes yell if they are excited, angry, or in pain.

yellow

ADJECTIVE Something that is **yellow** is the colour of lemons or egg yolks. *See Colours on page 271.*

yelp **yelps, yelping, yelped**

VERB If people or animals **yelp**, they give a sudden short cry. This is often because they are frightened or in pain.

yes

You say **yes** to agree with someone, to say that something is true, or to accept something.

yesterday

ADVERB **Yesterday** is the day before today.

yet

ADVERB **1** You say **yet** when you mean up till now. *She hasn't come yet.*

ADVERB **2** If something should not be done **yet**, it should be done later. *Don't switch it off yet.*

CONJUNCTION **3** You can use **yet** to introduce something which is rather surprising. *He doesn't like maths, yet he always does well.*

yew **yews**

NOUN A **yew** is an evergreen tree with thin, dark green leaves. Some yew trees have red berries.

yogurt **yogurts; also spelt yoghurt**

NOUN **Yogurt** is a slightly sour, thick liquid food made from milk.

yolk **yolks**

NOUN A **yolk** is the yellow part in the middle of an egg.

young **younger, youngest**

ADJECTIVE **1** A **young** person, animal or plant has not been alive for very long.

NOUN **2** The **young** of an animal are its babies.

your

ADJECTIVE **Your** means belonging or relating to the person or group of people that someone is speaking to. *Your teacher seems nice.*

yourself **yourselves**

PRONOUN If you do something **yourself**, no one else does it. *If you do that, you'll hurt yourself.*

by yourself PHRASE If you are **by yourself**, you are on your own. *What are you doing here all by yourself?*

youth **youths**

NOUN **1** A **youth** is a boy or young man.

NOUN **2** Your **youth** is the time in your life when you are young.

yo-yo **yo-yos**

NOUN A **yo-yo** is a round wooden or plastic toy attached to a piece of string. You play by making the yo-yo rise and fall on the string.

Zz

zap **zaps, zapping, zapped**

VERB **1** If you **zap** something or somebody in a computer game, you get rid of them.

VERB **2** To **zap** also means to keep changing channels on the television.

zebra **zebras**

NOUN A **zebra** is a type of African wild horse with black and white stripes over its body.

zebra crossing **zebra crossings**

NOUN A **zebra crossing** is a place where you can cross the road safely. The road is marked with black and white stripes.

zero **zeros**

1 Zero is the number 0.

NOUN **2** Zero is also the freezing point of water, 0°C.

zigzag **zigzags**

NOUN A **zigzag** is a line which keeps changing direction sharply.

zinc

NOUN **Zinc** is a bluish-white metal which is used to make other metals, or to cover other metals such as iron to stop them rusting.

zip **zips**

NOUN A **zip** is a long narrow fastener with two rows of teeth that are closed or opened by a small clip pulled between them.

zone **zones**

NOUN A **zone** is an area of land or sea that is considered to be different from the areas around it. *My dad wants to turn the garden into a cat-free **zone**.*

zoo **zoos**

NOUN A **zoo** is a park where wild animals are kept so that people can look at them or study them.

zoom **zooms, zooming, zoomed**

VERB **1** To **zoom** somewhere means to go there very quickly.

VERB **2** If a camera **zooms** in on a person or thing being photographed, it gives a close-up picture of them.

a
b
c
d
e
f
g
h
i
j
k
l
m
n
o
p
q
r
s
t
u
v
w
x
y

Zz

Vegetables

celery

aubergine

garlic

cabbage

broccoli

radish

cucumber

cauliflower

lettuce

onion

courgette

asparagus

beetroot

pea

potato

mangetout

pepper

turnip

bean

sprout

parsnip

sweet potato

spinach

sweet corn

carrot

leek

apple

avocado

tomato

cherry

kiwi fruit

grape

grapefruit

lime

pear

plum

passion fruit

orange

lemon

mango

peach

strawberry

raspberry

melon

banana

pineapple

Your body

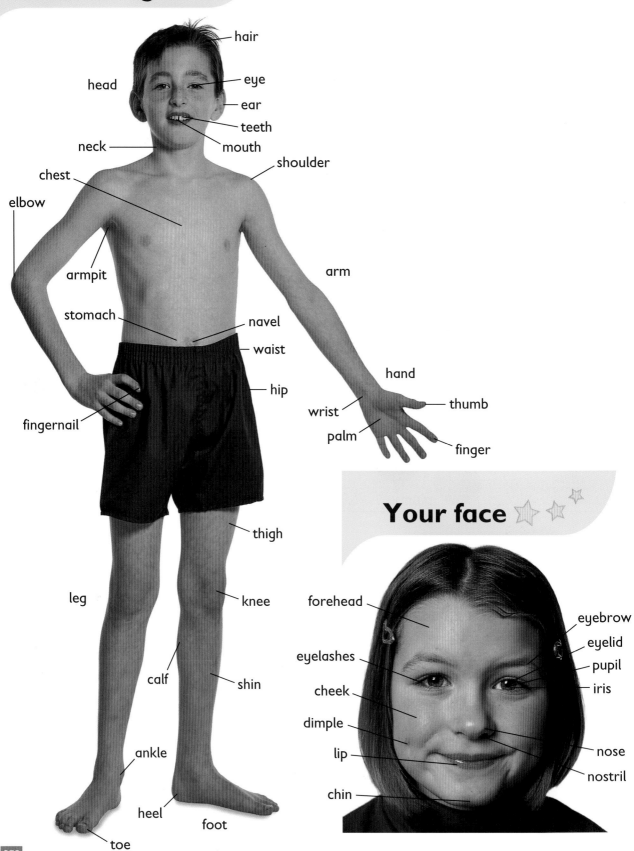

hair

head

eye

ear

teeth

mouth

neck

chest

shoulder

elbow

armpit

arm

stomach

navel

waist

hip

hand

fingernail

wrist

thumb

palm

finger

thigh

leg

knee

calf

shin

ankle

heel

foot

toe

Your face

forehead

eyebrow

eyelid

pupil

iris

eyelashes

cheek

dimple

lip

nose

nostril

chin

258

Insects

ant

bee

beetle

fly

butterfly

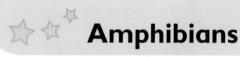

grasshopper

ladybird

mosquito

dragonfly

Amphibians

frog

newt

toad

Reptiles

alligator

crocodile

lizard

snake

tortoise

turtle

Young animals

bear and **cub**

cat and **kitten**

deer and **fawn**

goat and **kid**

goose and **gosling**

hare and **leveret**

horse and **foal**

kangaroo and **joey**

pig and **piglet**

rabbit and **kitten**

seal and **calf** or **pup**

sheep and **lamb**

tiger and **cub**

swan and **cygnet**

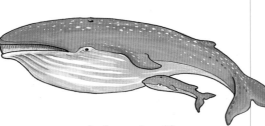

whale and **calf**

More young animals

bird and **chick**

chicken and **chick**

cow and **calf**

dog and **puppy**

duck and **duckling**

elephant and **calf**

fox and **cub**

lion and **cub**

wolf and **cub**

Words we use a lot

a	began	for	home	must	said	this	when
about	being	from	how	my	saw	three	where
after	but	get	I	name	say	to	which
again	by	go	if	next	seen	too	who
all	came	goes	in	no	she	took	why
along	can	going	is	not	should	two	will
am	can't	got	it	now	so	up	with
an	come	had	its	of	some	upon	woman
and	coming	hadn't	it's	off	suddenly	us	would
another	could	has	just	okay	take	very	wouldn't
are	couldn't	hasn't	last	on	than	want	yes
aren't	did	have	made	once	that	was	you
as	didn't	haven't	make	one	the	wasn't	your
at	do	he	man	or	their	way	
away	does	heard	many	our	them	we	
back	doesn't	her	may	out	then	went	
be	don't	here	me	over	there	were	
because	every	him	more	people	these	weren't	
been	first	his	much	put	they	what	

Silent letters

Each of these words has a silent letter. Can you think of any other words like these?

clim**b**	**k**nit
colum**n**	**k**nock
com**b**	**k**not
dou**b**t	**k**now
ghost	lam**b**
gnat	s**c**issors
gnaw	s**w**ord
gnome	**w**rap
hour	**w**riggle
knee	**w**rite
knife	

Confusable words

These words have different meanings but are easy to mix up.

its (belongs to it)   *The dog wagged <u>its</u> tail.*
it's (it is)   *<u>It's</u> not funny.*

loose   *My tooth's <u>loose</u>.*
lose   *Don't <u>lose</u> your pen.*

passed   *I <u>passed</u> my test.*
past   *It's ten <u>past</u> three.*

their (belongs to them)   *The girls counted <u>their</u> money.*
they're (they are)   *<u>They're</u> going to the shop.*
there   *<u>There</u> are 26 chairs in this room.*
    Put your bag down <u>there</u>.

than   *I am shorter <u>than</u> you.*
then (at that time)   *<u>Then</u> I heard footsteps.*

too   *Can I come <u>too</u>? This is <u>too</u> hard.*
two   *I'd like <u>two</u> cakes.*
to   *I want <u>to</u> swim. Let's go <u>to</u> the beach.*

whose (belongs to whom)   *<u>Whose</u> bag is this?*
who's (who is   *<u>Who's</u> that?*
    or who has)   *I know <u>who's</u> been sending you notes.*

261

Parts of speech

Noun

A **noun** is a person, place, thing or idea.
There are different types of noun.

cat

cats

A noun can be **singular**, which means one ...

... or **plural**, which means more than one.

Common nouns name people, places, things, or ideas in general. For example, "boy", "dog", "school", "computer" and "happiness" are common nouns.

Proper nouns are the names of particular people, places or things. They start with a capital letter. For example, "Ben", "France" and "Buckingham Palace" are proper nouns.

Collective nouns

A **collective noun** names a group of things.

a **bunch** of grapes

a **clutch** of eggs

a **pack** of wolves

a **flock** of sheep

a **litter** of puppies

a **herd** of cows

a **pride** of lions

a **school** of dolphins

a **shoal** of fish

a **swarm** of bees

Pronoun

A **pronoun** is used to replace a noun.

I	me	my	mine	myself
you	you	your	yours	yourself, yourselves
he, she, it	him, her, it	his, her, its	his, hers, its	himself, herself, itself
we	us	our	ours	ourselves
they	them	their	theirs	themselves

Personal pronouns are used for a person or thing that has already been named, for example "me", "her", "you", "it". *John jumped for the ball. He caught it!*

Possessive pronouns show that a noun belongs to a person or thing that has already been named, for example, "my", "their", "his", "our". *The bird flapped its wings.*

Adjective

An **adjective** describes a noun. For example, "tall", "happy" and "lucky" are all adjectives.

Some adjectives have a **comparative** and a **superlative** form. In most cases, these forms are made by adding "-er" or "-est" to the adjective.

adjective	comparative (more)	superlative (most)
tall	taller	tallest
hot	hotter	hottest
good	better	best
lucky	luckier	luckiest

Verb

A **verb** is an action word. It tells you what people and things do. For example, "sleep", "think" and "play" are all verbs.

Verbs have different forms called **tenses**. A tense shows whether you are talking about the past, present or future.

past	present	future
I *played*	I *play* I *am playing*	I *will play*

Adverb

An **adverb** tells you more about a verb. For example, "shyly", "brightly" and "happily" are all adverbs. Many adverbs end in the suffix "-ly".

How did Mary and Brian talk?
*They talked **loudly**.*

Other adverbs tell you "where", "when", or "how often" something happens.

where: outside, inside, here, there
when: today, soon, immediately
how often: never, frequently, often, always

Punctuation

A B C	A **capital letter** is used at the beginning of a sentence and for proper nouns.	*My brother Jim lives in New Zealand.*
.	You put a **full stop** at the end of a sentence.	*This is a sentence.*
?	You put a **question mark** at the end of a question.	*Can you come to my party?*
,	You use a **comma** to separate parts of a sentence or items on a list.	*She brought sandwiches, crisps, apples and juice to the picnic.*
!	You use an **exclamation mark** at the end of a sentence to show a strong feeling.	*Wow!*
'	An **apostrophe** is used in contractions and to show belonging.	*I didn't mean to break my brother's toy.*
" " ' '	**Speech marks** show where speech begins and ends.	*"I like your hair," she said.*
-	You use a **hyphen** to join together words or parts of words.	*I'm left-handed.*
( )	**Brackets** are used to show that something is not part of the main text.	*My cousin (the one from America) is coming to stay.*
—	A **dash** can be used instead of brackets, or to show a change of subject.	*My best friend – besides you – is George.*
:	You can use a **colon** for several things, for example in front of a list.	*You will need the following: strong walking boots, a map and a compass.*
;	A **semicolon** is used to separate different parts of a sentence or list, or to show a pause.	*The pizza choices are: cheese; onions, peppers and mushrooms; ham and pineapple; pepperoni; or sausage.*

Prefixes

A **prefix** is a group of letters added to the beginning of a word to make a new word.

prefix	meaning	example	prefix	meaning	example
anti-	opposite of, against	anticlockwise	**over-**	too much	oversleep
			poly-	many	polygon
co-	together	copilot	**pre-**	before	prehistoric
de-	take away	decode	**re-**	again	rearrange
dis-	opposite of	disappear	**semi-**	half	semicircle
ex-	former	ex-husband	**sub-**	under, part of	subheading
micro-	very small	microscope	**super-**	larger, more than	supersonic
mid-	middle	midnight			
mini-	smaller	minibus	**un-**	not	unlucky
mis-	wrong	misspell	**under-**	under or not enough	underground
non-	not	non-fiction			

A **suffix** is a letter or group of letters added to the end of a word to make a new word.

Some suffixes can change nouns into other nouns:

-hood   child → child**hood**
-ist   art → art**ist**   science → scient**ist**
-ship   friend → friend**ship**

Some suffixes can make nouns feminine:

-ess   lion → lion**ess**   prince → princ**ess**

Some suffixes can form a diminutive (a small word):

-ette   disk → disk**ette**

Some suffixes can change nouns or verbs into adjectives:

-able   comfort → comfort**able**   enjoy → enjoy**able**
-al   music → music**al**
-ary   imagine → imagin**ary**
-ful   help → help**ful**
-ible   sense → sens**ible**
-ic   angel → angel**ic**   drama → dram**atic**
-ish   child → child**ish**
-ive   act → act**ive**   persuade → persuas**ive**
-less   care → care**less**
-like   life → life**like**
-ous   poison → poison**ous**
-worthy   trust → trust**worthy**
-y   thirst → thirst**y**

Some suffixes can change adjectives into adverbs:

-ally   automatic → automatic**ally**
-ly   slow → slow**ly**   happy → happi**ly**

Some suffixes can change verbs or adjectives into nouns:

-ment   advertise → advertise**ment**   enjoy → enjoy**ment**
-ness   ill → ill**ness**   happy → happi**ness**
-sion   divide → divi**sion**
-tion   add → addi**tion**   invite → invita**tion**

Some suffixes can change nouns into verbs:

-ate   illustration → illustr**ate**

Synonyms ⭐⭐

Synonyms are words that have the same, or almost the same, meaning.
Here are some useful synonyms for everyday words.

angry
furious, mad, annoyed, outraged, indignant

bad
a bad person – wicked, nasty
a bad child – naughty, spiteful, defiant
bad food – rotten, decayed
a bad pain – severe
bad news – distressing, grave, terrible

big
huge, large, enormous, gigantic, vast, colossal

good
a good dog – well-behaved
a good painting – fine
a good film – enjoyable
a good worker – able, clever

happy
cheerful, content, delighted, glad, pleased, thrilled

kind
kind of person or thing – type, class, group

level
grade, position, stage

lots or **a lot**
plenty, a great deal, heaps, loads, many, a large amount, masses, piles

lovely
a lovely day – pleasant, glorious, sunny, splendid
a lovely meal – tasty, scrumptious, delicious
a lovely person – warm, kind, helpful, friendly
a lovely time – enjoyable, great, fantastic, wonderful, fabulous

nasty
a nasty person – unkind, rude, unpleasant
a nasty taste – horrible, foul, disgusting, awful

nice
nice food – delicious
a nice person – kind, helpful, pleasant
a nice view – lovely

rough
a rough road – bumpy, stony
a rough sea – choppy, stormy

small
a small problem – unimportant, trivial
a small child – little, tiny, young
a small room – cramped, cosy, modest

What else can you say?

The word "said" is useful, but here are some more interesting words that you can use to describe speech.

answer
reply, respond, retort, admit, agree

ask
enquire, demand, beg, query, wonder

said
announced, whispered, shouted, stammered, mumbled, yelled, shrieked, screamed, cried, murmured, remarked, declared, groaned, snarled, whimpered, admitted

Antonyms are words that have the opposite meaning.

for   against

exact   approximate

on   off

left   right

old   new

old   young

digital   analogue

wide   narrow

right   wrong

up   down

cold   hot

before   after

exciting   boring

to   from

gentle   rough

formal   informal

above   below

empty   full

under   over

deep   shallow

fiction   non-fiction

rough   smooth

with   without

in   out

sink   float

thin   fat

short   long

thin   thick

concave   convex

closed   open

short   tall

beginning   end

happy   sad

ascend   descend

hollow   solid

Time

9:50 a.m.

10 minutes to 10

7:25 p.m.

25 minutes past 7

Telling time

a.m.

p.m.

o'clock

half past

quarter past

quarter to

analogue

digital

clock

watch

timer

More time words

yesterday
today
tomorrow

calendar
date
weekend
holiday
birthday

second
minute
hour
day
week
fortnight
month
year
leap year
decade
century
millennium

dawn
morning
midday
noon
afternoon
dusk
evening
night
midnight

bedtime
daytime
dinnertime
playtime

Months
January
February
March
April
May
June
July
August
September
October
November
December

How often?
never
once
twice
sometimes
often
usually
always

Days
Monday
Tuesday
Wednesday
Thursday
Friday
Saturday
Sunday

Seasons
spring
summer
autumn
winter

bright   sunny   dry   breeze   clear   hot

freezing   cold   icy   snow   frost

dry   hot   drought   sun

cloudy   chilly   foggy   drizzle   misty

rain   windy   wet   sleet   cool

hail lightning gale storm thunder

showers rainbow sunshine warm breeze

Measures

Length
millimetre (mm)
centimetre (cm)
metre (m)
kilometre (km)
mile

Mass or weight
gram (g)
half-kilogram
kilogram (kg)

Capacity
millilitre (ml)
half-litre
litre (l)
pint (pt)

Abbreviations

a.m.	in the morning
°C	degrees Celsius
CD	compact disc (such as a music CD)
CD-ROM	a CD that is played on a computer (an abbreviation of "compact disc read-only memory")
cm	centimetre
cm²	square centimetre
DIY	do-it-yourself
Dr	Doctor
DVD	digital video disc *or* digital versatile disc
etc.	"et cetera", which means "and so on" in Latin
EU	European Union
g	gram
GP	general practitioner (a doctor)
ICT	information and communications technology
IT	information technology
kg	kilogram
km	kilometre
l	litre
m	metre
ml	millilitre
MP	Member of Parliament

Mr	a title used before a man's name
Mrs	a title used before the name of a married woman
Ms	a title used before a woman's name
OAP	old age pensioner
p	pence
p.	page
PC	personal computer *or* police constable
PE	physical education
p.m.	in the afternoon or evening
pp.	pages
PS	PS is written at the end of a letter, before an extra message (an abbreviation of "postscript")
PTO	please turn over
RSVP	please reply (an abbreviation of the French phrase "répondez s'il vous plaît")
SOS	a Morse code signal for help, especially used by ships or planes (sometimes said to be an abbreviation of "save our souls")
TV	television
UFO	unidentified flying object
VIP	very important person
www	World Wide Web

Colours and flat shapes (2D)

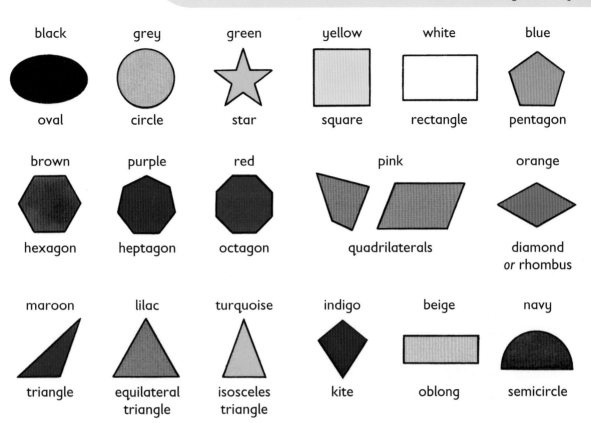

black — oval
grey — circle
green — star
yellow — square
white — rectangle
blue — pentagon

brown — hexagon
purple — heptagon
red — octagon
pink — quadrilaterals
orange — diamond *or* rhombus

maroon — triangle
lilac — equilateral triangle
turquoise — isosceles triangle
indigo — kite
beige — oblong
navy — semicircle

Solid shapes (3D)

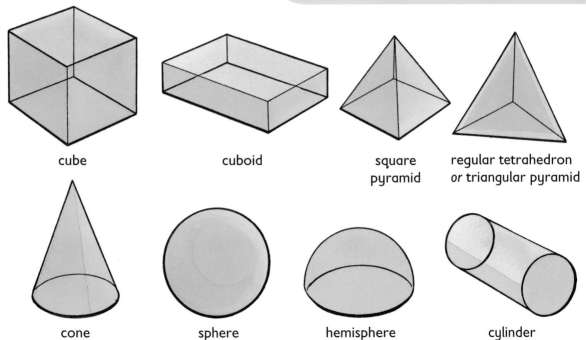

cube

cuboid

square pyramid

regular tetrahedron *or* triangular pyramid

cone

sphere

hemisphere

cylinder

Number bank

0	zero	30	thirty	1st	first
1	one	31	thirty-one	2nd	second
2	two	40	forty	3rd	third
3	three	41	forty-one	4th	fourth
4	four	50	fifty	5th	fifth
5	five	51	fifty-one	6th	sixth
6	six	60	sixty	7th	seventh
7	seven	61	sixty-one	8th	eighth
8	eight	70	seventy	9th	ninth
9	nine	71	seventy-one	10th	tenth
10	ten	80	eighty	11th	eleventh
11	eleven	81	eighty-one	12th	twelfth
12	twelve	90	ninety	13th	thirteenth
13	thirteen	91	ninety-one	14th	fourteenth
14	fourteen	100	one hundred	15th	fifteenth
15	fifteen	101	one hundred and one	16th	sixteenth
16	sixteen	150	one hundred and fifty	17th	seventeenth
17	seventeen	200	two hundred	18th	eighteenth
18	eighteen	1000	one thousand	19th	nineteenth
19	nineteen	10 000	ten thousand	20th	twentieth
20	twenty	100 000	one hundred thousand	21st	twenty-first
21	twenty-one	1 000 000	one million		

Fractions

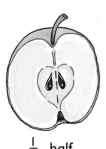

$\frac{1}{2}$ half

$\frac{1}{4}$ quarter

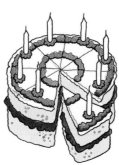

$\frac{1}{8}$ eighth

$\frac{1}{3}$ third

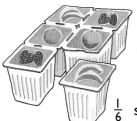

$\frac{1}{6}$ sixth

$\frac{1}{5}$ fifth

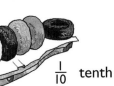

$\frac{1}{10}$ tenth

Days of the week

Most of the days of the week were named by the Saxons. The Saxons came from Denmark and Germany to live in Britain over 1500 years ago.

Sunday is named after the sun.

Monday is named after the moon.

Tuesday is named after Tiu, the Saxon god of war and of the sky.

Wednesday is named after Woden, leader of the Viking gods.

Thursday is named after Thor, the Saxon god of thunder and lightning.

Friday was named after Frigga. She was goddess of love, and sat on a throne beside her husband, Woden.

Saturday is named after Saturn, the Roman god of farmers and farming.

Months of the year

The months of the year were given their names by the Romans.

January is named after **Janus**, the Roman god of doorways and beginnings.

February is named after **Februa**, a Roman festival when people were purified.

March is named after **Mars**, the Roman god of war.

April's name comes from the Latin word **aperire**, meaning "to open". Spring is when the year "opens".

May is named after **Maiesta**, Roman goddess of honour and reverence.

June is named after the Roman goddess **Juno**, queen of heaven.

July was named after **Julius Caesar**, army general and ruler of Ancient Rome.

August was named after the Roman emperor **Augustus**.

September comes from the Latin word **septem**, meaning "seven". The Roman year used to begin in March, so September was their seventh month.

October comes from the Latin word **octo**, meaning "eight". October was once the eighth month.

November comes from the Latin word **novem**, meaning "nine". November was once the ninth month.

December comes from the Latin word **decem**, meaning "ten". December was once the tenth month.

Where words come from

Words from the world

Lots of the words we use in the English language today come from other parts of the world. Here are some examples.

alphabet

This word comes from Greece. **Alpha** was the first letter of the Greek alphabet, and **beta** was the second. The two words together give us alphabet.

amphibian

This is another word from Greece. It comes from the Greek word **amphibious**, which means "living a double life". Amphibians are animals that can live on land or in water – so they live a double life!

bungalow

This word, which means a low house, comes from India. The Hindi word for house is **bangla**.

bus

This word comes from Italy. It is short for **omnibus**, the Latin word for "everybody". Buses carry lots of people.

dandelion

This word comes from the French words **dent de lion**, meaning a lion's tooth. This is because people thought the petals of the dandelion looked like a lion's teeth!

fete

This is another French word. It means "feast" in French. In English it means an outdoor event with competitions and stalls which sell things.

jungle

Jungle is a word from India. The Hindi word for jungle is **jangal**.

muscle

This word comes from the Latin word **musculus**, meaning "little mouse", because people thought muscles looked like mice beneath the skin!

porcupine

This comes from the Old French words **porc-espin**, meaning "pig with spines".

pyjamas

This word comes from Iran (which used to be called Persia). In Persia, **pay jama** meant "leg clothes".

We write letters for all sorts of reasons, such as asking for information and exchanging news. Each kind of letter has its own style. Here are some examples.

Asking for information

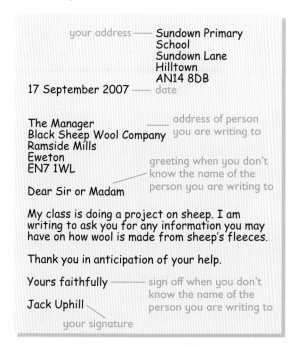

your address —— Sundown Primary School
Sundown Lane
Hilltown
AN14 8DB

17 September 2007 —— date

The Manager —— address of person you are writing to
Black Sheep Wool Company
Ramside Mills
Eweton
EN7 1WL

—— greeting when you don't know the name of the person you are writing to

Dear Sir or Madam

My class is doing a project on sheep. I am writing to ask you for any information you may have on how wool is made from sheep's fleeces.

Thank you in anticipation of your help.

Yours faithfully —— sign off when you don't know the name of the person you are writing to

Jack Uphill —— your signature

An invitation

your address —— 32 Forge Street
Hilltown
AN12 9TC

30 November 2007 —— date

Jack Uphill
16 Smith Road —— address of person you are writing to
Hilltown
AN13 8TZ

—— greeting when you know the person you are writing to

Dear Jack

I am having a birthday party at my house on Saturday 5 December at 3 o'clock. I should be very pleased if you could come.

Best wishes —— sign off when you know the person you are writing to

Jill —— your signature

Saying thank you

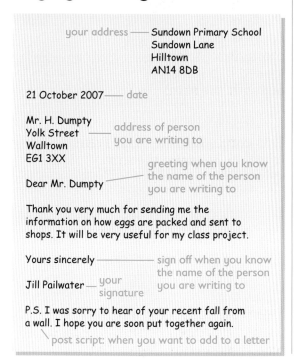

your address —— Sundown Primary School
Sundown Lane
Hilltown
AN14 8DB

21 October 2007 —— date

Mr. H. Dumpty
Yolk Street —— address of person you are writing to
Walltown
EG1 3XX

—— greeting when you know the name of the person you are writing to

Dear Mr. Dumpty

Thank you very much for sending me the information on how eggs are packed and sent to shops. It will be very useful for my class project.

Yours sincerely —— sign off when you know the name of the person you are writing to

Jill Pailwater —— your signature

P.S. I was sorry to hear of your recent fall from a wall. I hope you are soon put together again.

—— post script: when you want to add to a letter

A reply

your address —— 16 Smith Road
Hilltown
AN13 8TZ

1 December 2007 —— date

Jill Pailwater
32 Forge Street —— address of person you are writing to
Hilltown
AN12 9TC

—— greeting when you know the person you are writing to

Dear Jill

Thank you very much for inviting me to your party on Saturday 5 December at 3 o'clock. I shall be very pleased to come.

Best wishes —— sign off when you know the person you are writing to

Jack —— your signature

Word families

A **word family** is a set of words containing the same groups of letters.

These words are members of the **oa** word family.

toad	goat	coast

? Using the dictionary, find some more **oa** words beginning with these letters.

t a heated slice of bread.

b to talk too proudly about something.

r to wander around.

These words are members of the **oi** family.

oil	soil	point

? Using the dictionary, find some more **oi** words beginning with these letters.

m slightly wet.

n a sound that someone or something makes.

c a series of loops into which something has been wound.

These words are members of the **ar** word family.

dart	market	star

? Using the dictionary, find some more **ar** words beginning with these letters.

p the person you are doing something with.

s a small sea fish

b something which is sold at a low price.

These words are members of the **air** word family.

stairs	fairy	aircraft

? Using the dictionary, find some more **air** words beginning with these letters.

f quite or rather.

p a set of two things that go together.

d a shop or company that sells milk and food made from milk.

Answers

oa words	**ar words**	**oi words**	**air words**
toast	partner	moist	fairly
boast	sardine	noise	pair
roam	bargain	coil	dairy

Top tips for tricky words

Sometimes thinking of a silly phrase or sentence can help you remember how to spell tricky words. Here are some examples.

beautiful

Big elephants are useful.

qu words (q is always followed by u)

The Queen always carries an umbrella.

See how many of these you can remember. Then see if you can think up some of your own!

all right
It's either all right or all wrong.

believe
Believe has a lie in it.

hear
You hear with your ear.

February
You say "br" in February because it's cold.

different
One thing differs from another.

piece
Have a piece of pie.

friend
I'm seeing my friend on Friday, which comes at the end of the week.

library
Look into books. Reach and read yours.

because
Ben eats cake and uses six eggs.

necessary
Necessary has one collar and two socks (one c and two s's!).

receive
R-e-c-e is very easy.

separate
Separate has a rat in it.

there
There is a place like here.

weather
We eat in all kinds of weather.

whose
Whose hose is that?

Sound it out!

Another good way to remember the spelling of some words is to sound out their different parts. Try these!

answer	cupboard	**Wednesday**	**together**
ans-wer	cup-board	Wed-nes-day	to-get-her

Top tips for tricky words

Top tips for learning to spell a tricky word

- **Look** at the word in the dictionary and point to it.
- **Say** the word out loud, then spell it out.
- **Cover** the word up, remembering what it looks like.
- **Write** the word down on a piece of paper and say it out loud again.
- **Check** your spelling against the dictionary.
- If you got it wrong, cover the page again and **try again**!

Tricky words to learn

The words on this list are tricky, so learn all of them to be a top speller!

address	definite	remember
among	does	rhyme
autumn	everybody	scissors
awful	exciting	sentence
beginning	exercise	straight
breakfast	guess	through
build	interest	trouble
careful	necessary	until
certain	people	usually
course	really	whole

Plurals

A plural word is what we use when there is more than one of something. It is often made by adding **s** to a word, like this.

> singular **day**
> plural **days**

Sometimes plurals are made by taking away the **y** at the end of the word and adding **ies**, like this.

> singular **pony**
> plural **ponies**

❓ Now use the dictionary to find the plural of these words. See how many ways you can find to make a word plural.

1. **horse**
2. **thief**
3. **party**
4. **class**
5. **torch**
6. **volcano**
7. **child**
8. **fly**
9. **monkey**
10. **woman**

Word jumble

 Here are some words with their meanings. The letters in the words are all jumbled up. Can you put them in the right order? (Clue! They all begin with **d**.) Use the dictionary to help you.

1. **streed**   A very dry land with very little plant life.
2. **ogunned**   A dark underground prison in a castle.
3. **caddee**   A period of ten years.
4. **mode**   A round roof.
5. **loadinned** A wild plant with bright yellow flowers.
6. **rotcod**   A person who treats people when they are ill.
7. **cilisudoe** Food that tastes or smells very nice.
8. **reapsapid** What happens when someone goes out of sight.
9. **zoed**   A light sleep.
10. **flagondry** A brightly coloured insect, usually found near water.

Getting the most from guide words

The guide words in this dictionary are at the top of the page. They can help you find the word you want quickly.

> **frequent**
>
> ...ve forward or ...ove the way you are
>
> ...ASE If you **look** ...ing, you want it to
>
> **fracture** **fractures**   a
> NOUN A **fracture** is a crack or break in something, especially a bone.   b
> **fragile**   c
> ADJECTIVE Something that is **fragile** is easily broken or damaged.   d

True or false?

Use the guide words in the dictionary to work out if these statements are true or false.

1. **pointed** comes between **plumber** and **popular**
2. **steep** comes between **stem** and **strain**
3. **colour** comes between **closed** and **college**
4. **fungus** comes between **fresh** and **future**
5. **awful** comes between **assembly** and **axis**
6. **somebody** comes between **solve** and **speak**

Where is the word?

Which of these words would you find between **pizza** and **plum**?

pasta	plastic
pram	play
plug	poor
pitch	plump

Internet know-how

Surfing the net!

Can a dictionary really teach me to surf?

Well, it can tell you a bit about surfing – but don't worry. The only kind of board you'll need is a computer keyboard, plus access to the Internet.

What is the Internet?

Good question! The Internet is a collection of computer networks that are all linked together. The Internet can let you look at lots of different sites in just a few seconds to help you find what you're looking for.

Do I look at all of the sites myself?

No, you don't need to. The Internet does all the work for you! All you have to do is type a word or phrase into something called a search engine and click on "go". The search engine looks like a little box on the screen. Fill in the subject you want to find out about and you're all set to go "surfing" on the Internet.

What sort of things can I find out about?

You can find out about all kinds of things! Are you potty about pyramids? Dotty about dinosaurs? Batty about ballet? Serious about sport? You can

look for information on whatever you want. You can even find out more about your favourite books or authors. Just enter the word you want into the search engine.

But where do I start?

There are thousands and thousands of sites out there. The search engine will take you to all of them that contain the word or words you have typed into it. It helps if you make your key word (the word or words that you type into the search engine) as clear as possible. For example, you might want to find out about parrots. Parrots are birds. If you type in "birds", you'll be taken to all websites containing that word. If you type in "parrots", you'll only be shown sites about parrots. This can save a lot of time!

Is there anything else I need to know before I start?

Just as you need to take care when you're playing out of doors, you need to take care when you're playing or working on the Internet. There are a few things you need to remember:

Never go to meet someone you have met online without a parent or carer accompanying you.

Never give out your personal details online.

If you find something online that makes you feel uncomfortable or you aren't sure about, tell a parent, carer or teacher.

Safe surfing! To find out more information about websites that will be fun to use, go to **www.collins.co.uk/word_wizard**